THE OUTRAGEOUS MARK TWAIN

Books by Charles Neider

FICTION

Overflight
Naked Eye
The Authentic Death of Hendry Jones
The White Citadel

NONFICTION

Beyond Cape Horn: Travels in the Antarctic
Edge of the World: Ross Island, Antarctica
Susy: A Childhood
Mark Twain
The Frozen Sea: A Study of Franz Kafka

EDITED BY CHARLES NEIDER

Mark Twain at His Best
Papa, by Susy Clemens
The Comic Mark Twain Reader
The Complete Short Stories of Mark Twain

THE
OUTRAGEOUS
MARK TWAIN

Some Lesser-known
But Extraordinary Works

With "Reflections on Religion"
Now in Book Form for the First Time

Selected and Edited
With an Introduction by
CHARLES NEIDER

Doubleday
NEW YORK   LONDON   TORONTO   SYDNEY   AUCKLAND

Published by Doubleday, a division of
Bantam Doubleday Dell Publishing Group, Inc.,
666 Fifth Avenue, New York, New York 10103.

Doubleday and the portrayal of an anchor with a dolphin
are trademarks of Doubleday, a division of
Bantam Doubleday Dell Publishing Group, Inc.

Library of Congress Cataloging-in-Publication Data
Twain, Mark, 1835–1910.
The outrageous Mark Twain.
I. Neider, Charles, 1915–   . II. Title.
PS1303.N37   1987   818'.409   86-32912
ISBN 0-385-23522-4

2 4 6 8 9 7 5 3

BG

CONTENTS

THE OUTRAGEOUS MARK TWAIN

INTRODUCTION

by Charles Neider

Many readers of Mark Twain are unaware, or not much aware, of his extreme side. They take him to be an extraordinarily pleasing "funny" man, a marvelously genial spirit, a remarkable American humorist, and little more. Others still believe him to be primarily the creator of two classic "children's" books with a Mississippi River and Mississippi Valley setting.

The purpose of the present collection is to disturb such notions by showing an altogether different side of him—the unsettling, far-out side, the side that acts like a bracing tonic, that can be apparently sacrilegious ("Reflections on Religion"), bawdy ("1601"), openly shocking ("Science of Onanism": masturbation), irreverent ("Extract from Captain Stormfield's Visit to Heaven"), outraged ("Goldsmith's Friend Abroad Again" and "The Indignity Put Upon the Remains . . ."), obstreperous ("Is Shakespeare Dead?"), infuriating (to some readers: *Christian Science),* and finally, the side that is uproariously gifted in the uses of invective ("Open Letter to Commodore Vanderbilt," "John Camden Hotten," and "Mr. Duncan of the *Quaker City").*

If some of these pieces, such as "1601," seem mild by today's standards, consider what they must have seemed at the time of composition. Above all, compare them with the rest of Mark Twain's works and you will understand why I have titled the volume *The Outrageous Mark Twain.*

Mark Twain wrote "Reflections on Religion" (my title for five chapters on religion meant for his autobiography) in June 1906, some four years before his death. They were published for the first and only time in October 1963 in *The Hudson Review,* a literary quarterly issued in New York, after being suppressed for fifty-seven years, first by Clemens himself, then by Albert Bigelow Paine, his friend, official biographer, and literary executor, and finally by Clemens's daughter Clara.

They make their first appearance in book form in the present volume eighty-one years after their composition. The remarkable story of their censorship is probably unique in American literature and deserves to be recorded in some detail. But before I present it, let me briefly describe them, as well as the circumstances in which they were composed.

If read superficially they may seem savagely irreverent, yet they are the work of a profoundly religious man. They are attacks on orthodoxy, cant, and sham in religion, and are an indication of the boldness and strength of Clemens's mind. He discusses, among other things, the character of God, the defects of bibles, the Immaculate Conception, the evil influence of the Bible, his belief that the present God and religion won't endure, and his conviction that Christ didn't prove he was God. He complains that man's concept of God is a shoddy one, stemming from man's own shortcomings, and that man is presumptuous in thinking he has an inside track with God. He waxes hot, as though the Bible were written yesterday, blaming man for his anthropocentric views. He makes full use of the effects of anachronism, using nineteenth-century knowledge as a sword against Biblical man's ignorance and fatuousness in assuming he is God's darling, nub and navel of the universe.

At times he seems to suggest a double God: the God of the Bible, man's creation in his attempts to rationalize history; and the God of modern man, who identifies God with the irrationalism of nature and with nature's unconcern with man's welfare. Clemens combines these two concepts for his own dramatic purposes. He can be furious not so much with man as with the God-Nature that torments man. His famous inclination to help the underdog causes him to view God as the prime bully and man as the prime victim. For his own purposes he reads the Bible as a literalist, then accuses man of stupidity for being a fundamentalist.

As we shall presently see, certain churchmen, reacting to the publication of "Reflections on Religion," said he was ignorant of nineteenth-century Biblical studies, which, they declared, had largely outmoded or at least modified fundamentalism, and that therefore his attacks were anachronistic, misguided, and motivated by personal bitterness. In his defense it may be said the world didn't lack for fundamentalists in 1906; that there had been long ages when fundamentalism was unmodified by Biblical studies; and that he was addressing those times as firmly as his own. He was not limiting his criticisms to Hebrew-Christian man. He was concerning himself with the follies of man the superstitious animal in all ages. He was using the Hebrew-Christian Bible as his text because he was more familiar with it than with other bibles but he was by no means limiting his remarks to it, he wasn't singling out for his invective any special sect of the human race. The *whole* human race, from beginning to end, was his subject, something the churchmen failed to understand when they reacted to the publication of "Reflections on Religion."

Clemens may have made a tactical error in sticking too close to the text and by involving himself too specifically (and too sarcastically) in details of theory and practice. Perhaps the churchmen were right to misread him. His view was cosmic but his application of it wasn't. As if to correct this deficiency, he wrote, months before his death, *Letters from the Earth* (not published until 1962), in which sarcasm gave way in many instances to irony and in which the cosmic view was embodied in the figure of Satan, with his incomparably greater perspective, in time and space, than man's.

"Reflections on Religion" is straightforward opinion. *Letters from the Earth* is opinion in the disguise of fiction. "Reflections on Religion" is bolder in statement and more detailed and extreme in the views espoused. It deals specifically with religion and its harmful effects. *Letters from the Earth* is also concerned with religion but in a more general way, and devotes more energy to the question of the foolishness of mankind. "Reflections on Religion" contains withering remarks about Christian Science and its founder, Mary Baker Eddy. *Letters from the Earth* ignores both.

Clemens composed *Letters from the Earth* at Stormfield, his house in Redding, Connecticut, in October and possibly also in November 1909. Clara Clemens had married early in October and was not living at Stormfield now. Clemens's daughter Jean was there, and Paine was an almost constant visitor, sometimes spending the nights at Stormfield as well as the days, his room separated from Clemens's only by a bathroom. In a letter of that time to his friend Elizabeth Wallace, Clemens wrote: "This book *[Letters from the Earth]* will never be published—in fact it couldn't be, because it would be felony.

. . . Paine enjoys it, but Paine is going to be damned one of these days, I suppose."

Letters from the Earth consists of eleven letters from Satan to the archangels Michael and Gabriel. Satan, banished from heaven for a thousand Earth-years, visits Earth to see how the new human-race experiment is coming along. From Satan's outlander point of view man is a microscopic, insane tissue of life. Satan writes about man's concept of heaven, and about the concept's curiousness, and about sexual intercourse, which Clemens rarely explicitly and candidly discusses elsewhere in his work.

The attack on the Christian ideal of heaven is in some respects like those of Nietzsche and D. H. Lawrence. Letter 2 is a rip-roaring onslaught on man's hubris in his religious thinking, on his imaginative shortcomings, and on his being a sheep to follow the teachings of the priesthood against his own instincts. Clemens cannot easily forgive man for what he, Clemens, views as man's religious asininities. He regarded religion not as the opiate of the masses but rather as extremely willful self-delusion and self-harm. Early in his career as an author, when he first went to Europe, he already showed signs of being anti-clerical. In *The Innocents Abroad* he was sarcastic about the well-fed, comfortable priests of Rome.

If in real life Clemens was at times the devil's advocate, in *Letters from the Earth,* a piece of fiction, Satan was *his* advocate for the reason that any of the other angels wouldn't have been shrewd and biting enough in his observations. Clemens, in pain with increasing frequency because of the angina condition that was soon to give him the ultimate peace he longed for, was now making statements on religion from an Olympian height but at the price of having to mute them with the guises of fiction.

Common to both "Reflections on Religion" and *Letters from the Earth* is his insistence on injecting his deterministic views, which he seems to have deduced from the omnipotence and omniscience of God. But he is not doctrinaire in his determinism; he is often more poetic than logical; and he implies contradictory things. He implies that God is more sinful than man, while at the same time implying that man is free of sin because God is responsible for sin. But he also implies that man is not free of sin because the God who is responsible for sin is only man's creation. He sometimes seems to say there are no elect among mankind, that all are equally doomed to unhappiness, that the nature of the human condition is reprobation, that we are all reprobates, yet not true reprobates because essentially we're innocent (our nature having been foreordained, we can't be blamed for being unable to act counter to it), we are only reprobates in the judgment of a vengeful, small-minded God.

In his view God is far from dead where man is concerned. Although God may not presently be interested in man's condition, he long ago foreordained the circumstances guaranteed to make man suffer. Clemens believes that man's suffering ends with death; he is too indignant about the unfairness of hell to believe it exists. At times he seems to believe that man's sole escape from God is through death, at others that there is no God, or at least no God in the way that man has been able to imagine him, that there are only the vast reaches of the inorganic world, blazing endlessly with a purpose far beyond man's comprehension, interspersed on rare occasions with a bit of heartrending, quenchable life.

As for the public reception of *Letters from the Earth*, far from being found unacceptable to the community at large, as Clara Clemens had feared, it was excerpted by *Life*, it received many favorable reviews, and it became a best-seller. The book was published at a time when the question of whether God is dead was already being discussed publicly and when increasing numbers of believers felt that God had deserted man or that it was no longer possible to have a personal, direct experience of God or a proof of his existence.

Clemens's reading was encyclopedic in certain areas but not intense and not sophisticated, as may be seen in the fact that he regarded religion as something sacrosanct and criticism of it as not fit for public consumption. He was his own censor in the cold war which he thought he was conducting with the religious thought of his time. He was conservative in matters of religion and sex and had an outmoded understanding about the shockability of the American public, traits which he seemed able to inject successfully into Paine and Clara Clemens.

He dictated the chapters on religion in a rented house a couple of miles from Dublin, New Hampshire. This was the Upton House, located on a slope of Mount Monadnock. With him during the summer of 1906 were his daughter Jean, a stenographer (Miss Josephine Hobby), and Paine. Clemens's wife had died two years previously in

Florence, Italy. Clara Clemens lived at this time in a retreat in Norfolk, Connecticut, under her doctor's care.

It was a pleasant summer environment, although Paine found it somewhat spectral, perhaps because of a west wind that never seemed to relent. Clemens's mornings were chiefly devoted to dictating his autobiography. Paine, who lodged in the village for the summer, would drive up to the house each morning to be present for the session, sometimes returning in the afternoon to interview Clemens. Whenever the weather permitted, Clemens dictated while pacing a long colonnaded veranda open to the country views, or while sitting in a rocker. These are the veranda and rocker pictured in the famous series of seven photographs of Clemens which Paine, a former photographer, took that August and which Clemens inserted in his autobiography. On rainy days Clemens worked indoors, pacing constantly. After work there would be relaxation with music, usually Beethoven, Chopin, or Schubert.

On Sunday, June 17, 1906, Clemens wrote to his friend William Dean Howells, who was at Kittery Point, Maine: "Tomorrow I mean to dictate a chapter which will get my heirs and assigns burnt alive if they venture to print it this side of 2006 A.D.—which I judge they won't. There'll be lots of such chapters if I live three or four years longer. The edition of A.D. 2006 will make a stir when it comes out. I shall be hovering around taking notice, along with other dead pals. You are invited."

The next day Clemens began a dictation on a religious subject but almost immediately strayed to other topics. On the 19th he composed the first of the chapters, on the 20th the second, on the 22nd and 23rd the third and fourth, and on the 25th he dictated the final chapter. The next day he went to New York for business reasons and wrote to Howells in the evening.

"I have been dictating some fearful things, for four successive mornings—for no eye but yours to see until I have been dead a century—if then. But I got them out of my system, where they had been festering for years—and that was the main thing. I feel better now."

Writing to Howells, Clemens dared his heirs and assigns to print the chapters a century thence. But on his own manuscripts he specifically prohibited his heirs and assigns from publishing the chapters until five centuries thence. His injunction is penned in his own hand

on the title pages of the first two of the chapters: "Not to be exposed
to any eye until the edition of A.D. 2406. SLC."

And so we see that the tale of censorship begins with a bold act of
self-censorship. Bold, defiant—and possibly facetious, for what can
"not to be exposed to any eye" seriously mean? *Any* eye? Even the
stenographer's? Even Paine's? Even Clemens's own? "Exposed to
any eye until the *edition* of A.D. 2406"? But the making of an "edition" requires that the manuscript be exposed to many eyes. I am by
no means quibbling. Clemens is one of the great wordsmiths in the
language, he's supremely conscious of what he writes, and there was
absolutely no evidence of linguistic or mental lapses in the summer
of 1906, if indeed in any summer of his life.

In his official biography of Clemens, issued in 1912, Paine quoted
from the chapters but didn't identify them. He offered a few fragments as musings or table talk and scattered them about, abridging,
rewriting, and rearranging. His edition of Clemens's autobiography
(Mark Twain's Autobiography, 1924) omitted the chapters, although
he could have printed them if he had wished, for he was Clemens's
literary executor and editor of the Mark Twain Papers.

Bernard DeVoto tried to publish them in 1940 in *Mark Twain in
Eruption,* which culled material from the unpublished sections of the
autobiography, but was prevented from doing so by Clemens's sole
surviving daughter, then Mrs. Clara Clemens Gabrilowitsch.
DeVoto had succeeded Paine as editor of the Mark Twain Papers. In
the original typescript of the Papers at Berkeley, three of the chapters have penciled on their title pages: "Edited, for publication in
Mark Twain in Eruption, by BDV, but omitted at the request of
Mme. Gabrilowitsch." In his introduction to *Mark Twain in Eruption,* DeVoto made the surprising mistake of assuming responsibility
not only for what he had included in the volume but also for everything he had omitted, a sweeping gesture that necessarily included
the chapters which had been denied him. "I have left out nothing
that seemed to me important, and I assume responsibility for the
omissions as well as for what is printed."

In May 1958, under contract to Harper & Brothers to gather,
arrange, and edit *The Autobiography of Mark Twain* (1959), I went
to Berkeley to work in the Mark Twain Papers in the Bancroft Library of the University of California. While there I studied the five
chapters on religion in the autobiographical typescript and encoun-

tered the notation that they had been omitted from *Mark Twain in Eruption* at the request of Clara Clemens Gabrilowitsch. Neither Harper's nor the Mark Twain estate had placed any restrictions on my use of materials for my edition, nor had they or Clara Clemens (then married to Jacques Samossoud) indicated to me that certain portions of the autobiographical typescript had been suppressed. I believed that technically the restrictions placed by Clara Clemens on DeVoto did not apply to me, but I felt obliged nevertheless to remind her she had denied DeVoto the right to publish the chapters almost two decades earlier. At the same time I asked her for permission to include them in my edition of the autobiography.

Mrs. Samossoud, who was eighty-four, replied on June 6:

"I presume you refer to that portion of the M.S. which was called 'Letters from the Earth.' My purpose in refusing its publication was prompted solely by my desire to protect my father's wishes as far as I was able to estimate them. When he wished to publish any of his writings there was nothing in the way of his doing so. Certainly his withholding anything from the public eye was not his fear of 'shocking people.' If anyone can be shocked into a state of truth or wisdom, let him be thoroughly shocked. It would take a long letter to describe my father's ready condemnation of his own extravagant expressions of convictions which through imbalance could give false impressions. In my small book about my experience with Christian Science, written two years ago, I made a point of quoting Father's approving remarks about Mrs. Eddy and her great work for mankind's comfort; remarks that flatly contradicted his diatribes previously launched against Mrs. Eddy in his book on Ch. Science.

"I know that Father agreed with the attitude that the size of an individual's genius and intellect was only important in a large way as it affected mankind for *good* or *evil*. Why otherwise did he spend so much effort on studying the wrongs of accepted conventions or the sins inflicted on the people of conquered countries? The most steadfast occupation of his thoughts displayed the urge to help victims of injustice and misfortune.

"That I personally *agree* with his attacks on most of the Bible and the humanized concept of God has no bearing on this situation which must be divested of all personal considerations. I am very sorry that I cannot write what you would wish me to, but my feelings towards my father have not weakened since 1940."

She added a postscript: "Of course Father *was* innately *religious.*"

I replied that the manuscript to which I had referred was not "Letters from the Earth" but part of the autobiographical dictations and soon thereafter sent her four of the five chapters on religion: the dictations of June 19, 20, 23 and 25, 1906. The fifth chapter, dictated June 22, by some error hadn't been sent to me by the Mark Twain Papers. I promised I would send it to her as soon as I received it.

She replied on July 6, 1958:

"I find the first selection (God of the Testaments) utterly delightful and completely true for anyone who thinks at all. Though powerful in expression this chapter includes such charming humour. The second section also is fascinating and the portion about the immaculate conception is profoundly convincing, in case the reader needs convincing along that line. I heartily agree with everything 'Mark' says about the Christianity of the Bible and find nothing harmful in that kind of fact-revealing. The thing I have always wondered about is mankind's acceptance of Biblical assertions, as though voiced by *God Himself,* and therefore undeniably true. This weakness I don't remember Father calling attention to. But my memory may be inexact (?).

"In Christian Science so much stress is laid on the *statement* that God made the world and called it 'good,' thus precluding the possibility of evil anywhere. Now my letter is growing too long.

"The parting of your and my ways comes partially when Mark offers his feeling about the 'real God' derived from a broader personal attitude and then switches into tirades against the very man-made God that Biblical 'cusses' have shaped Him into. Of course there is so much wonderful writing and truth in these pages following, that I wish they might be used somewhere else—not just where Mark has started to let some cheer into the depressing darkness. How I wish you and I could talk! I feel incapable of setting on paper the things I feel about the heavy weight of tragedy in these many pages with *no relief.* And my thoughts are too many to go into a letter. At the same time I believe Father is in sympathy with them! At present the two last sections shrink the portrait of Mark Twain both as artist and man. He would not choose to deluge thousands, maybe millions of souls, in massive sadness when they are struggling away from the agonies of human finitude into a wider, *enlightening* realm of charm created by the God-comforting gift of Imagination and extensive Intuition. Quite falsely Mark appears as an almost malignant searcher for evil instead of for good. In these chapters he does not present any balance between the perfection of *Beauty* in God's creative genius and the evidence of ugliness—which latter may be the invention of Beelzebub completely unrelated to the wonders of *spiritual* power.

"In the last sections there is too much great writing to admit of cancellation, but I do think Father would himself transfer or scatter it into other portions. Father actually relished *joy* as a sublime treasure definitely incompatible with evil in any form. He said: 'Don't part with your illusions. When they are gone you may still exist but you have ceased to live.' And these very illusions may eventually be revealed as a higher *Reality*.

"Father enlarges on the 'punishments' inflicted on man without knowing whether they *are* punishments. What goes on in the invisible source of existence is an *unyielding Mystery*. In 'The Mysterious Stranger' and other of his writings, Mark has gone so explicitly into the superiority of the beast over man that I doubt whether the public needs any more of that viewpoint, which was never anything but a *mood* easily proved by his outpouring of admiration for man's phenomenal intellect at other times.

"I am going to ask the Citadel Press to send you my 'Awake to a Perfect Day.' It is not long, besides you need only read the parts referring to Mark's *genuine* religious nature. I don't want Father to ever appear as a dark Angel. But danger lies where condemnation is feverish without the accompaniment of constructive ideas.

"I am keeping the M.S. a day longer so that my husband can read it.

"With many friendly wishes,

"Cordially yours
"Clara C. Samossoud

"Later

"My husband is even stronger than I in his feeling *against* publication of those two sections! Among many other things he points out that the communists would make *generous* use of such a weapon as Mark Twain's attack on God. They would advertise it all over the world. Jacques [Samossoud] also emphasizes the fact that this land is definitely *religious;* that the signs of it are so universal that tremendous resentment of Father's sacrilege would sweep through all circles

—political, religious, and social. A lamentable attack on Father would ensue. My husband also wisely remarks that this material was not to be used until Father, through death, was 'safe from public opinion.' But Mark Twain has *not* died. His words and thoughts live as a potent influence. Therefore those sections must be deleted much as I hate to disappoint you."

Before I could reply to this letter I received another one, dated July 8.

"Dear, oh dear! What confusion and confounding disorder! I sent you the M.S. today with a letter that is completely *bla.* In driving towards the effort to *save* parts of the M.S. I lost the main point of it all! The 'later' portion of my letter applies to every line of the material you sent me. *None* of it can see the printing press; we certainly are not going to place my blessed father and superior character on the side of the *all-good-destroying Communists.* What a kind of Hades that would be—Mark Twain an *upholder* of the Soviet regime. My dear husband alone has protected the American nation from that revolutionizing disaster. What a narrow escape! No, dear Mr. Neider, in these disorderly times none of my dear Father's assaults on the Citadel of Spirit (however faultily presented to mankind) can be published.

"If the remaining selection from Berkeley is in the same vein don't trouble to send it."

I wrote: "Naturally, from my point of view it is regrettable that such fine and important writing by your father must remain unknown except to scholars. Intellectually it seems to me a pity that the community at large is not permitted to judge how deleterious the chapters are by being exposed to them. . . . The other day, by a coincidence, I found samples of the chapters printed in Paine's biography (Vol. III, pages 1354–57)."

On July 24 Mrs. Samossoud wrote:

"Doubtless you felt that I adopted an almost Mark Twainious extreme of expression in prophesying what the communists would stage in the way of triumphant shows if they actually got my father on their bandwagon, yet certain it is that they would make drastic use of such an advantage; and I would be bombarded with questions and demands for explanations from countless newspapers, magazines, not to mention a deluge of letters. The passages you refer to in Paine's biography were written at a vastly different period of mankind's history. The horrors today of Russian communism are a hideous threat to man's higher progress along spiritual lines. Is any other viewpoint valid?"

The Autobiography of Mark Twain was published in February 1959. When I met Clara Samossoud at the Bahia Hotel in Mission Beach, California (a suburb of San Diego), on March 28, 1959, I was impressed by her physical and mental vigor. She was bent with age and had pathetically thin small hands but her dark eyes were lively, although she was in pain from an old neuritis, which caused her occasionally to press a hand against the left side of her breastbone.

During our hour or so of conversation (part of the time her husband and her physician were also present) I expressed as diplomatically as I could the hope that she would not consider the matter of the religious chapters closed just because the *Autobiography* had recently been issued, but would reconsider the advantages of allowing them to be made public, perhaps in a second edition of the *Autobiography*.

In the introduction to the *Autobiography* I specifically divorced myself from responsibility for the omission of the chapters on religion.

"I do not assume responsibility for all of the omissions. Had the authority been mine I would have included in this edition the dictations of five days—June 19, June 20, June 22, June 23 and June 25 of 1906. But I would not have put them into the body of the Autobiography, for they are more essayistic than autobiographical; I would have made an appendix of them. Mark Twain's surviving daughter, Mrs. Jacques Samossoud, who has the authority and the responsibility, has decided that it would serve no good purpose to publish the chapters at this time."

Although the disclaimer was written in plain English it did not prevent the *Literary Gazette* of Moscow, in its issue of August 18, 1959, from accusing me of willful censorship, as well as crying out that Mark Twain was being censored "officially" (by me) in his own country. The *Gazette*, known in the Soviet Union as *Literaturnaya Gazeta*, attacked me specifically for suppressing the chapters and thereby "censoring" Mark Twain. The *Gazette* was no small paper. It had, and may still have, strong official standing as the official newspaper of the Union of Writers of the U.S.S.R.

Its criticism of the *Autobiography* came to my attention in the fourth week of September. The gist of it was that America had an official line on Mark Twain, that the nation tried to suppress or forget him, that his editors had followed the line carefully, and that I was the worst offender in this respect. Since I had been dealing with materials in my own language and had had access to the original manuscripts and typescripts, and since my volume had enjoyed a critical success in my own country (all these facts were available to the Soviet critic), it seemed to me that the writer's self-confidence was presumptuous and foolhardy. Still, I was encountering the official Soviet literary line regarding America and so I was not entirely surprised by the content of the criticism or by its harsh and self-righteous tone.

Normally I did not reply to criticisms of my books. This particular one, however, offered a special and complex challenge. It was obviously "protected." It struck through me at the society of which I was a part. And it seemed to discount the possibility of free literary endeavor in my country. Consequently I decided to take some action to bring my views to the attention of those readers who had been exposed to the article defaming me.

It seemed a quixotic enough hope in view of the fact that no rebuttal by an American in the *Literary Gazette* was on record. I didn't think I stood much chance of receiving favorable treatment from the editors of the *Gazette*. But Soviet Premier Nikita Khrushchev had recently visited President Eisenhower at Camp David and was in an expansive mood, so I applied directly to him. On October 13 I sent him a two-sentence letter in which I said in part: "In the interest of cultural relations between our two nations, will you please ask the *Literary Gazette* to open its pages to me for a reply?"

Being uncertain what it cost to send an airmail letter to Moscow, I had to experience the embarrassment of taking my letter to a post office substation in Manhattan, where I hoped the clerk, who knew me by sight, wouldn't notice the name and address on the envelope. He did notice them, however.

"What? Khrushchev? The Kremlin? Are you *crazy?*" he exclaimed.

I couldn't blame him.

Anyway, in November 1959, through Khrushchev's intervention I was allowed to defend myself in the pages of the *Gazette* itself. This extraordinary development made front-page news. It is unnecessary for me to repeat the story here or my exchange of views with the *Gazette*'s critic, for both were published as a brochure, as an appendix to two paperback editions of the *Autobiography*, and as a chapter in my book *Mark Twain*. I mention the matter now because the Soviet attack played a significant role in Clara Clemens's decision to lift the ban on her father's work.

From time to time in my correspondence with her I urged that the chapters be released, pointing out, among other things, that their suppression was giving the very aid and comfort to the Russians she had feared their publication would afford them. When the brochure appeared in May 1960 I sent her a copy, stressing that publication of the chapters would be the best refutation of the Soviet charge that America was censoring Mark Twain. But, as far as I could judge, she was politely adamant in the matter. There was perhaps another reason for her suppressing the chapters, one which she never mentioned to me: the offense she must have taken because of her father's comments on Mary Baker Eddy. As we know, she was a Christian Scientist.

On October 28, 1960, I once more raised the subject of the chapters on religion with her, asking if she and her husband would let them be published in an appendix of a contemplated second edition of *The Autobiography of Mark Twain*.

Her reply of November 2 startled me.

"My husband's objection to publishing Father's unsympathetic attacks on God, was that if I were still living, I would have to face the many types of resentment hurled at me by those who disagree with these splenetic outbursts of Father's. My objection was merely that I think the word of a famous man should be to *uphold* rather than destroy the vision of something so spiritual and needed as God.

"I should hurry up and die and thus the coast would be entirely clear. I personally advise their (his writings on this subject) appearance in print, simply because I don't wish to be an intruder in this matter and because if Father were living he probably would say 'go ahead.'

"This is a non-committal letter, dear Mr. Neider, which you and Harpers better interpret as you think wisest."

Despite her characterization of her letter as "non-committal" it was clear to me she had finally permitted publication of the long-suppressed chapters. The year 1960 saw many Mark Twain celebrations, for it was the 125th anniversary of his birth. I suspected that its spirit had influenced her thinking. I phoned my editor at Harper & Brothers and gave her the news.

Mrs. Samossoud wrote to me again on November 21. (November 30 would be Clemens's 125th birthday.)

"Jacques or I will write Harpers and give them the permission they want. Possibly we have already written them. I am a bit vague. Someone wrote me the other day that I was regretfully preventing the publication of Father's most important opinions, which I had forgotten all about. Then Jacques explained that he had objected to their publishing a controversial subject from which the painful results would naturally come to my door. It's already in the past now so we can act oblivious to the whole incident."

I replied on November 24:

"Dear Mrs. Samossoud:

"I am delighted to learn of your decision, after reconsidering the matter, to grant permission to publish the 'religious' chapters of your father's Autobiography.

"In truth, the chapters are not 'shocking' by modern standards, and will cause hardly a ripple of comment. All that they assert regarding Mark Twain's views has long been known; the only loss has been that his inimitable language has been missing. Your father himself overrated the 'shocking' qualities of the opinions expressed in the chapters. He was behind his time when it came to 'shocking.' After all, Freud's books were already beginning to be well known when your father dictated the chapters.

"It has always seemed to me that Mark Twain was most shocking in his first important book *(The Innocents Abroad)* when he made some pretty strong statements regarding the churches and priests of Italy. In the *Connecticut Yankee* he also made a few potent remarks about the Roman Catholic Church. In later years the intensity of his attacks lessened, giving way to more general statements, which included Protestantism as well. His objections were to sectarianism, pride, bureaucracy and empty forms in religion."

On November 26 she wrote:

"I have tonight finished your copy [of *The Autobiography of Mark Twain]* with a sense of having become acquainted with Mark Twain, in certain respects, for *the first* time.

"A terrific sadness fills my heart, for his whole life seems much darker than I ever guessed, though living in the house with him all through most of his trials and disappointments. There is so much to say, that I better not start. . . . The closing pages would draw floods of tears from the eyes of the most *hardened* of men. Beautifully tragic they are!"

During the two years that followed I made many unsuccessful attempts to arrange for the publication of "Reflections on Religion" in a more permanent form—in a new edition of *The Autobiography of Mark Twain;* or as an appendix of a new edition; or as a brochure or pamphlet. When Mrs. Samossoud died on November 19, 1962, I suspected, ironically, that I had lost an important ally in my efforts. Twenty-three years would elapse before I would finally obtain permission to publish the "Reflections," with their cogency, courage, noble utterance, and anthropological view of religion and man, in book form.

In January 1961 I was in communication with my editor at Harper's about the chapters. She said: she had read them and was worried; she didn't like them, they were so different in tone from the rest of the *Autobiography of Mark Twain,* which was "a family book"; they lacked his sense of humor; it was too bad about the timing, they would have shocked people if they had been published when he wrote them, but now they weren't shocking, yet they would offend just as many people; she couldn't make up her mind about them; maybe it would be best if all the censored material appeared in a separate book; she just didn't know.

I wrote to her:

"I have read the religious chapters once again and have thought about them for a few days. It's my opinion that they belong in the *Autobiography* and not in another volume, and I hope that you and Harpers will decide to include them in a second edition.

"The fact that they are humorless and severe does not make them untypical. Mark Twain had two sides—the jolly, funny one, and the serious one which was often colored by his gift of invective. My edition of the *Autobiography* amply exemplifies the second side—in the attacks on Bret Harte, on Webster, on Mrs. Aldrich, and in the several biting comments on man.

"It is easy to see my edition as 'a family book' but that is after the fact, for if I had been allowed to include the religious chapters originally I would certainly have done so, and the book would then have obtained a tone different from the one it has now. The important thing is that Mark Twain is a giant of American letters, and all effort ought to be made to publish everything he wrote, regardless of how we may feel about a particular piece. I think it would be a mistake to make an exception of these chapters by publishing them in a volume other than the one for which they were intended.

"Obviously the chapters are going to offend people, but that is what Mark Twain intended them to do. He wanted to shake up people's thinking in an area where he thought they desperately needed it. We have waited so long to bring these chapters to the public. Now that Clara Samossoud has finally consented to their release it would be a shame to stand in the way of their proper presentation. To publish them elsewhere than in the *Autobiography* would be to invite speculation and comment on why we side-stepped doing what is clear and forthright and expected of us. In an age in which Bertrand Russell is a best seller these chapters may find fewer people who are shocked than some of us may think.

"I think it is worth keeping in mind that Clara Samossoud released the chapters specifically for the *Autobiography* and even *that* she did with reluctance. To publish them elsewhere would, I believe, require her approval, and it is possible that she would withhold it and even change her mind altogether. In the latter event all of us interested in contributing to American letters would be the losers."

In November 1961 I learned from my editor that Harper's had no plans to publish the chapters but would publish *Letters from the Earth* the following September. On August 24, 1962, the *New York Times* printed an article about the book's forthcoming publication.

"Anti-Religious Work by Twain, / Long Withheld, To Be Published / Author's Daughter, Who Barred Release / of Venomous 'Letters from the Earth' / in Thirties, Now Agrees to Printing" said the headlines.

"A series of highly inflammatory anti-religious essays written by Mark Twain in his later years will be made public for the first time on Sept. 21.

"Withheld by the humorist's daughter since 1939, when they were edited by the late Bernard DeVoto, the essays will be published by Harper & Row. The pieces, humorous in style but venomous in viewpoint, have been collected in a volume entitled 'Letters from the Earth.'

"It was learned yesterday that Mark Twain's 88-year-old daughter, Mrs. Clara Clemens Samossoud, who is an invalid and lives in Mission Beach, Calif., recently agreed to publication on the grounds that 'Mark Twain belonged to the world' and that public opinion had become more tolerant.

"It was understood that another factor leading to Mrs. Samossoud's change of mind was her annoyance by Soviet charges that some of her father's ideas were being suppressed in the United States.

"Mrs. Samossoud, who is bed-ridden, was unable to be interviewed by phone yesterday. Her husband, Jacques, said that both he and his wife hoped that the controversial tone of the essays would not lead to letters of protest from persons who have identified the author mainly with 'Tom Sawyer' and 'Huckleberry Finn.' He added that his wife, now writing her memoirs, is a Christian Scientist.

"In the opening section of 'Letters from the Earth,' Mark Twain, in the guise of Satan, writes detailed reports to the Archangels Gabriel and Michael. He describes the inhabitants of earth as long-suffering victims of their own ludicrous religious beliefs.

"The essays were written during a period of personal tragedy in the author's life, after he had lost his wife and a daughter and was plunged into debt. He died in 1910.

"Mr. DeVoto assumed the editing job after the death in 1937 of Twain's biographer, Albert Bigelow Paine. Harper & Brothers recommended to the estate's trustees that Mr. DeVoto, who was the author of 'Mark Twain's America,' be asked to prepare for publication material from Twain's unpublished writings.

"In March, 1939, when the edited manuscript was ready for the printer, Mrs. Samossoud objected to parts of it on the ground that they presented a 'distorted view' of her father's ideas and attitudes. The project was dropped.

"Mrs. Samossoud's recent change of heart was partly influenced by Charles Neider, who edited 'The Autobiography of Mark Twain' for Harper & Brothers in 1959.

"In selecting material for the work, Mr. Neider excluded five chapters on the advice of Mrs. Samossoud. The chapters, according to Mr. Neider, contain 'the most violent attacks on religion by Mark Twain.'

" 'The chapters are among his best writing,' Mr. Neider said yesterday, 'but they are extremely vituperative. I noted in the published autobiography in 1959 that the chapters had been excluded and this was seized upon by the Soviet literary critics as American censorship.'

"Mark Twain is a literary hero in the Soviet Union.

" 'I wrote Mrs. Samossoud on several occasions,' Mr. Neider continued, 'to point out that by not publishing all her father's writings we were giving aid and comfort to the Russians. I explained that the public was mature enough to make up its own mind what was in its interest. I felt, too, that Mark Twain should be taken in the round, as it were, and that we should not exclude parts of his work because they may not be fashionable.'

"It was about that time—Nov. 30, 1960—that the 125th anniversary of Twain's birth was being widely celebrated. Mr. Neider said that Mrs. Samossoud informed him that she had searched her conscience and decided to step aside.

" 'It was a great change and I was rather startled,' Mr. Neider recalled.

"He immediately got in touch with Harper, who decided to go ahead with the manuscript edited by Mr. DeVoto. Mr. Neider is now planning to have the five chapters previously deleted from 'The Autobiography of Mark Twain' published in a magazine. Two magazines have already rejected the chapters as being 'too inflammatory.' "

The editor of *The Hudson Review*, Frederick Morgan, read the story while on vacation in Maine, phoned me and asked to see the chapters in order to consider them for publication. On August 28, 1962, he wrote me: "We are pleased and honored to have the opportunity of publishing these powerful and moving reflections, never before in print, by one of America's greatest writers." At the request of Harper & Brothers, he agreed not to publish them until a year after the appearance of *Letters from the Earth*. Harper's feared their publication might adversely affect the sales of the forthcoming book.

The publication of the "Reflections" in *The Hudson Review* elicited from United Press International a long, two-part story dated New York, October 5, 1963, which was carried with startling headlines by newspapers across the country.

"Twain's Attack / On God Bared" *(Houston Chronicle*, page 1).

"Twain's Attack on God, Written / As Sick, Bitter Old Man, Re-called" *(Houston Chronicle,* page 19). "Mark Twain Assailed / God and Christianity" (Louisville *Courier-Journal,* page 1, section 4). "Mark Twain's Bitter Attack on Religion / He Wrote It 4 Years Before Death, / Hoped It Would Be Secret 'til 2406" (Philadelphia *Sunday Bulletin).*

Among other papers that featured the story were the *Oakland Tribune,* the *Denver Post,* the *Indianapolis Star,* the *Sacramento Bee,* the *Dallas Times Herald,* the *New Haven Register,* the *Los Angeles Times,* the *Chicago Tribune,* the *Seattle Post-Intelligencer,* the Pasadena *Independent Star-News,* the *Chicago Sun-Times,* the *San Francisco Examiner,* the *Minneapolis Sunday Tribune,* the *Detroit News,* the Little Rock *Arkansas Gazette,* and the *Detroit Free Press.*

I quote from the Philadelphia *Sunday Bulletin,* October 6, page 37, section 1. Most of the page was devoted to the story. The headlines of the second part of the story read: "Churchmen Deplore Twain's Views, / Call Him Bitter and Confused."

"Church leaders said today that they doubted that Mark Twain's views on religion will have much effect on shaking the religious faith of his readers.

"One said that Twain's attack, published today, might even do some good by stirring up new loyalty in Christians who have become sluggish in their faith.

"Church leaders noted that at the time Twain wrote these reflections he was a sick, bitter, disillusioned man who apparently did not understand the teachings of the Bible.

"Dr. Eugene Carson Blake, State Clerk, General Assembly of the United Presbyterian Church in the U.S.A.:

" 'I would prefer to hold him in honor and remember him as the American humorist who gave us "The Celebrated Jumping Frog of Calaveras County," or as the author whose *Tom Sawyer* and *Huckleberry Finn* have enthralled several generations of American youth.

" 'Twain reflects on religion out of the depths of his own despair. He writes about a God whose goodness and mercy he could not make a part of his own experience in life.

" 'At the time of this writing (1906), his life was a combination of public success and private misfortune. Two of his children had died, one a favorite daughter. His wife had died, only two years earlier. These harsh events he seemingly could not understand, and in his reflections on religion he "takes it out" on God for his loneliness, his sadness, and his despair.

" 'It would be little more than an intellectual exercise to take Twain's anti-religious statements and refute them.

[Really? Apply logic to faith? In what court of opinion? But on the whole, Blake's reaction was temperate.]

" 'His error in confusing the doctrine of the Virgin Birth with that of the Immaculate Conception is not nearly as serious as his failure to acknowledge the wonder of the mystery of the Incarnation itself.' . . .

"Dr. Norman Vincent Peale, minister, Reformed Church in America, author and lecturer, said:

" 'Mark Twain's "Reflections on Religion" is hardly reflective. It is a highly emotional outburst by a man sick with hate and anger and the disappointing thing is his spinelessness; his pathetic lack of guts to publish this diatribe in his lifetime. He talks tough, but hides behind the cover of time.

["Sick with hate and anger"? How did Peale know Clemens was "sick"? He called Clemens a coward, and by doing so exposed his own ignorance of everything Clemens stood for and which the civilized world (Peale excluded) was well informed about. Peale's opinions are anachronistic, applying, as they do, social codes of 1963 to 1906.]

" 'The article, I feel, is much too jaundiced to have any real effect except perhaps to stimulate a little latent loyalty to the faith which he attacks. It has been a long time since Christianity has been so bitterly attacked and as a result it has grown soft. Millions of Christians have become indifferent. Perhaps this onslaught will stir new loyalty in the sluggish.

" 'This article reveals not a little ignorance, which would seem to bear out the less than high opinion of Twain held by men of letters in his day.

["Less than high opinion"? "Held by men of letters"? Clemens was admired by "men of letters" of many countries in his day and was honored with a doctorate by Oxford University.]

" 'This delayed article will do Mark Twain's reputation no good among those to whom he brought much pleasure in childhood days. It is all rather pathetic.' "

[More than half a century after Clemens's death Peale ignorantly believed Clemens's works were meant primarily for children. What kind of education in American history and literature did he have? And in logic? In his response to the "Reflections" he substituted mindless judgments and name-calling for thought.]

"Rabbi Theodore Friedman, President of the Rabbinical Assembly:

" '. . . Why cavil on this or that point in Mark Twain's broadside when his reflections reveal a radical failure to understand the Old Testament? . . . As for the evils committed under the guise of religion, had Mark Twain read his Old Testament with less of a jaundiced eye, he would have found that he had been anticipated by at least 2,500 years by the Hebrew prophets. The corruption of the best leads to the worst, says the old Latin proverb. But then, are the rivers of blood that were spilt in the name of social progress and democracy, from the French Revolution to the Red Terror, less wide and less deep than those of the wars of religion?

" 'Virtually all that Mark Twain has to say on the Bible and religion indicates that he read Robert Ingersoll more carefully than he read the Bible.'

[Ingersoll, known as the "Great Agnostic," was a lawyer, 1833–1899, who polemicized against the Bible.]

"Rt. Rev. Horace W. B. Donegan, Bishop of the Episcopal Diocese of New York:

" 'Mark Twain's "Reflections on Religion" are, in common with most things one has to get out of one's system, an astonishing collection of undigested material.

" 'His attack on the doctrine of the Virgin Birth (which he mistakenly calls the Immaculate Conception) is based entirely on the simple fact that he personally finds it incredible, an approach which would, were it generally applied, make subjective acceptance the only criterion of objective fact.

[Are the Virgin Birth, the Immaculate Conception, and the existence and nature of God "objective facts"? "This rather pathetic meandering"(two paragraphs later)—as with Peale, emotive name-calling.]

" 'There are serious objections to the doctrine of the Virgin Birth, profound theological ones, and they have to be faced before one can intelligently and loyally accept the Church's creeds. Mark Twain, strangely enough, never mentions one of them. . . .

" 'It is easy to see why anyone attached to him would not want this rather pathetic meandering published, but it is difficult to believe that the "anti-religious" will receive any aid or comfort from it.'

"Dr. Ralph W. Sockman, retired Methodist radio minister:

" 'Mark Twain's "Reflections on Religion" sadden our hearts but need not shake our faith. We are grieved that one who gave so much cheer to others should end his years in such gloom of spirit. The loss of loved ones and the ills that flesh is heir to dropped him into a mental depression which distorted his views of religious verities. . . .

" 'Twain took the language of the Bible literally without understanding its spirit and symbolism. Furthermore, the faulty interpretations of the Scripture which he heard preached insulted his intelligence and aroused his anger.

" 'In censuring him for his bitter denunciations of God and the Church, we must put part of the blame on the narrow and rigid presentations of religion current in his day. It is not much wonder Twain's temper became overheated by so much hell-fire kindled by the pulpits.' "

But not all the reported comments on the "Reflections" were critical, by any means. For example, the *Lexington* (Kentucky) *Leader* of October 12 headlined a long article: "Twain's 'Reflections on Religion' / Provocative, Incisive, Important." And the former theater critic of the *New York Times,* Brooks Atkinson, wrote an article in the *Times* titled "Critic at Large," which was headlined: "Mark Twain's Religious Views Reflect / Compassion for Human Suffering."

"1601. Conversation As It Was by the Social Fireside in the Time of the Tudors" is Clemens's famous exercise in Elizabethan ribaldry, written in the summer of 1876 under the spell of Pepys's *Diary* and out of curiosity to see if he could emulate the language of Shakespeare's time, a language much freer than that of his own. Although it was never officially published, it had an underground life in a number of privately printed editions of limited circulation.

Paine says, "It was written as a letter to that robust divine, Rev. Joseph Twichell [a Hartford neighbor and close friend of Clemens's], who had no special scruples concerning Shakespearian parlance and customs. Before it was mailed it was shown to David Gray, who was spending a Sunday at Elmira [New York]. Gray said: 'Print it and put your name to it, Mark. You have never done a greater piece of work than that.' " Gray, a native of Scotland, was a journalist and minor poet from Buffalo, New York. It is said that on occasion, during long walks together, Clemens and Twichell would stop to read the piece aloud with gusto and laughter.

In a letter to William Dean Howells, August 23, 1876, Clemens remarked, "When we exchange visits I'll show you an unfinished sketch of Elizabeth's time which shook David Gray's system up pretty exhaustively." Some three years later, as a joke, he submitted "1601" to Howells for publication in the *Atlantic*, of which Howells was editor.

John Hay, a friend of Clemens's and a lawyer and a writer who was later to become Ambassador to Great Britain and Secretary of State, in July 1880 wrote to Clemens to express his thanks for a copy of "that most exquisite bit of English morality, 1601. . . . I don't wonder Howells declined it. It would have set so high a standard in the *Atlantic* that subsequent numbers would have shown a ruinous decline." In August of the same year Hay wrote: "Here is the Meisterstück. It got into such appreciative hands among the Vampire Club [of Cleveland] that it was read into rags . . . and then the noble-minded Vampires, being pricked in the conscience, did have it copied, as you see . . . Do not think it has been vulgarized—only a half-dozen proofs were pulled and the type was faithfully distributed."

In his book *My Mark Twain*, published soon after Clemens's death, Howells recalled: "Throughout my long acquaintance with him his graphic touch was always allowing itself a freedom which I cannot bring my fainter pencil to illustrate. He had the Southwestern, the Lincolnian, the Elizabeth breadth of parlance, which I suppose one ought not to call coarse without calling one's self prudish; and I was often hiding away in discreet holes and corners the letters in which he had loosed his bold fancy to stoop on rank suggestion; I could not bear to burn them, and I could not, after the first reading, quite bear to look at them."

Clemens noted in a notebook entry written at a later period than the one in which "1601" was composed: "It depends on who writes a thing whether it is coarse or not. I once wrote a conversation between Elizabeth, Shakespeare, Ben Jonson, Beaumont, Sir W. Raleigh, Lord Bacon, Sir Nicholas Throckmorton, and a stupid old nobleman—this latter being cup-bearer to the queen and ostensible reporter of the talk. There were four maids of honor present and a sweet young girl two years younger than the boy Beaumont. I built a conversation which *could* have happened—I used words such as *were* used at that time—1601. I sent it anonymously to a magazine, and how the editor abused it and the sender! But that man was a praiser of Rabelais, and had been saying, 'O that we had a Rabelais!' I judged that I could furnish him one."

During a Paris sojourn sometime in the spring of 1879, Clemens attended a dinner given by the Stomach Club, a sub rosa organization that enjoyed earthy humor. A typescript of the speech he gave there, "Science of Onanism," survives in the Mark Twain Papers in Berkeley. It it not known whether the original manuscript is still extant. Presumably it was this manuscript that was the basis of the first (and private) publication of the speech in January 1952. The speech was again privately printed in 1964, in which year it also appeared in *Fact* magazine. It was later republished in *Playboy*.

"Extract from Captain Stormfield's Visit to Heaven" was first published in *Harper's Magazine* in December 1907 and January 1908, and was issued as a book in 1909. But it was written many years earlier and was suppressed by Clemens because he believed that, far in advance of its time, if published it would be perceived as blasphemous. On October 15, 1881, he wrote to Howells: "I am hard at work on Capt. Ned Wakeman's adventures in heaven—merely for the love of it; for laws bless you, it can't ever be published. At least not unless I trim it like everything and then father it on some good man . . . This is my purpose at present."

Ned Wakeman was an actual skipper: Edgar Wakeman of the steamer *America*, in which Clemens sailed in 1866 from San Francisco to Nicaragua en route to New York. Clemens later said his narrative was based on a personal dream Wakeman related to him. The narrative is one of his most inspired creations, and is brilliantly executed.

"Open Letter to Commodore Vanderbilt" was published in *Packard's Monthly*, March 1869. "Goldsmith's Friend Abroad Again" appeared in *The Galaxy*, October and November 1870 and January 1871. "The Indignity Put Upon the Remains . . ." was published in *The Galaxy*, February 1871. And "Mr. Duncan of the *Quaker City*"

was published in the *New York World* of February 18 and 25, 1877.
These are all brilliant examples of Clemens's extraordinary invective,
sarcasm, and irony. Duncan was the captain on the *Quaker City*
Holy Land Excursion, the voyage which was to result in the publica-
tion of many travel letters by Clemens as well as of *The Innocents
Abroad,* his first, and extraordinarily successful, travel book.

"Is Shakespeare Dead?," a lengthy essay, was first published in
April 1909, as a book. Clemens originally intended it to be part of his
Autobiography. The latter in its raw stage was a monstrously sprawl-
ing affair, a resplendent grab bag brought to its highest degree of
superfluity, a repository for anything and everything.

He wrote: "[Howells] . . . asked me if I meant to make a library
of it. I said that was my design but that if I should live long enough
the set of volumes could not be contained merely in a city, it would
require a state, and that there would not be any multibillionaire
alive, perhaps, at any time during its existence who would be able to
buy a full set, except on the installment plan. Howells applauded,
and was full of praises and indorsement, which was wise in him and
judicious. If he had manifested a different spirit I would have thrown
him out of the window. I like criticism, but it must be my way."

A broad joke, but not without a modicum of truth.

He wrote: "In this Autobiography I shall keep in mind the fact
that I am speaking from the grave. I am literally speaking from the
grave, because I shall be dead when the book issues from the press."

Throw a whole book in, what does it matter? Leave it to future
editors to figure out, if they can, what to do with the results of such a
remarkable method of composition. The Autobiography is "only"
for posthumous publication, so why trouble overmuch about it? Yet
in 1906 and 1907 he published "Chapters from My Autobiography"
in the *North American Review,* and "Is Shakespeare Dead?" almost
exactly a year before his death. So much for consistency where the
Autobiography was concerned.

Paine in his biography of Clemens reported that Clemens "had the
fullest conviction as to the Bacon authorship of the Shakespeare
plays. One evening, with Mr. Edward Loomis, we attended a fine
performance of *Romeo and Juliet* given by Sothern and Marlowe. At
the close of one splendid scene he said, quite earnestly, 'That is about
the best play that Lord Bacon ever wrote.' " But the question is: just
how earnest *was* Clemens? In "Is Shakespeare Dead?" he cautiously

avoids fully embracing the Bacon-authorship theory. Still, he argues strongly, even stridently, against the notion that Shakespeare was capable of creating the works generally believed to be his.

Clemens is naïve textually. On the one hand he makes a case based on the fact that not a single page of Shakespeare's manuscripts is known to have survived. Yet he believes as gospel that Shakespeare was responsible for every literary work or part of a work ascribed to him, even the doggerel inscribed on his supposed grave. He accepts without a shred of skepticism the pronouncements of so-called authorities regarding Shakespeare's legal knowledge—without stopping to consider that additions to the works may have been made with or without Shakespeare's consent, during or after his lifetime, by colleagues, by editors, by printers.

As for Bacon's supposed authorship of the works: If Shakespeare's manuscripts have failed to survive because he was relatively anonymous in his day (Clemens's argument), why haven't they survived (in the form of at least one single page) as the works of the famous-in-his-day Bacon? And beyond the textual point: Bacon was an extremely busy man, heavily involved in positions of public service and as an author. How could he have also found the time and energy to compose the Shakespeare plays? But Clemens is too much of a born-again enthusiast to be skeptical.

Nevertheless the essay is fascinating because it reveals the play of his mind, because it is written in his inimitable manner, and because it contains significant autobiographical details.

Clemens was a believer in mind cure (mental science) before he became interested in Mary Baker Eddy and Christian Science. That he was experimenting with mind cure as early as 1886, in his fifty-first year, we know from the March 14th entry of that year in his favorite daughter Susy's biography of him, written when she was fourteen.

"Papa has been very much interested of late, in the 'Mind Cure' theory. And in fact so have we all. A young lady in town has worked wonders, by using the 'Mind Cure' upon people; she is constantly busy now curing peoples deseases in this way. And curing her own even, which to me seems the most remarkable of all.

"A little while past, papa was delighted, with the knowledge of what he thought the best way of curing a cold, which was by starving it. This starving did work beautifully, and freed him from a great many severe colds. Now he says it wasn't the starving that helped his colds, but the trust in the starving, the mind cure connected with the starving.

"I shouldn't wonder if we finally became firm believers in Mind Cure. The next time papa has a cold, I haven't a doubt he will send for 'Miss Holden' the young lady who is doctoring in the 'Mind Cure' theory, to cure him of it.

"Mamma was over at Mrs. George Warners to lunch the other day, and Miss Holden was there too. Mamma asked if any thing as natural as near sightedness could be cured she said oh yes just as well as other deseases.

"When mama came home, she took me into her room, and told me that perhaps my near-sightedness could be cured by the 'Mind Cure'; and that she was going to have me try the treatment any way, there could be no harm in it, and there might be great good. If her plan succeeds there certainly will be a great deal in 'Mind Cure' to my oppinion, for I am *very* near sighted and so is mamma, and I never expected there could be any more cure for it, than for blindness, but now I dont know but what theres a cure for *that*. . . .

"April 19. Yes the Mind Cure *does* seem to be working wonderfully. papa who has been using glasses now, for more than a year, has laid them off entirely. And my nearsightedness is realy getting better. It seems marvelous! When Jean has stomack ache, Clara and I have tried to divert her, by telling her to lie on her side and try Mind Cure. The novelty of it, has made her willing to try it, and then Clara and I would exclaim about how wonderful it was it was getting better! and she would think it realy was finally, and stop crying, to our delight.

"The other day mamma went into the library, and found her lying on the sofa with her back toward the door. She said 'Why Jean what's the matter? dont you feel well? Jean said that she had a little stomack ache, and so thought she would lie down. Mamma said 'why dont you try Mind Cure? 'I am' Jean answered."

In later years Clemens occasionally sought out mental scientists for minor ailments, and at times urged Susy to seek their help to make her happier and more robust. When she died of cerebral meningitis in Hartford on August 18, 1896, at the age of twenty-four, he was devastated. Her sister Clara said she had been "murdered" by mental science and spiritualism, with both of which she had experimented. To what extent his attack on Christian Science, a form of mental science, was due to Susy's death is not clear, but the dates seem suggestive. His first published criticism of Christian Science, "Christian Science and the Book of Mrs. Eddy," appeared in *Cosmopolitan Magazine* in October 1899, a little more than three years after Susy's death. It was followed by articles on Christian Science in the *North American Review* in December 1902 and January and February 1903. His book *Christian Science* was published in February 1907.

Although Clemens analyzes and criticizes Christian Science and Mary Baker Eddy's writings and character persistently and unfalteringly, it would be a mistake to assume his book is without humor. It contains broad, hilarious humor, at least in the beginning, before he settles down to his formidable task. His intellectual energy is unflagging and his linguistic zest is boundless. Being in his company is always a bracing experience, and often a surprising one.

While working in the Mark Twain Papers in Berkeley I came upon the typescript of Book II of *Christian Science*. On a subtitle page marked "Mrs. Eddy. Book II," Clemens had written in ink: "Please send me no first proofs nor second proofs—I do not wish to see the wig till the very finest fine-tooth comb has been through it. Through it for *Sunday*. SLC."

Santa Cruz, California
February 1, 1987

REFLECTIONS ON RELIGION

One

Tuesday, June 19, 1906

Our Bible reveals to us the character of our God with minute and remorseless exactness. The portrait is substantially that of a man—if one can imagine a man charged and overcharged with evil impulses far beyond the human limit; a personage whom no one, perhaps, would desire to associate with now that Nero and Caligula are dead. In the Old Testament His acts expose His vindictive, unjust, ungenerous, pitiless and vengeful nature constantly. He is always punishing —punishing trifling misdeeds with thousandfold severity; punishing innocent children for the misdeeds of their parents; punishing unoffending populations for the misdeeds of their rulers; even descending to wreak bloody vengeance upon harmless calves and lambs and sheep and bullocks as punishment for inconsequential trespasses committed by their proprietors. It is perhaps the most damnatory biography that exists in print anywhere. It makes Nero an angel of light and leading by contrast.

It begins with an inexcusable treachery, and that is the keynote of the entire biography. That beginning must have been invented in a pirate's nursery, it is so malign and so childish. To Adam is forbidden the fruit of a certain tree—and he is gravely informed that if he disobeys he shall die. How could that be expected to impress Adam? Adam was merely a man in stature; in knowledge and experience he was in no way the superior of a baby of two years of age; he could have no idea of what the word death meant. He had never seen a dead thing; he had never heard of a dead thing before. The word meant nothing to him. If the Adam child had been warned that if he ate of the apples he would be transformed into a meridian of longitude, that threat would have been the equivalent of the other, since neither of them could mean anything to him.

The watery intellect that invented the memorable threat could be depended on to supplement it with other banalities and low grade notions of justice and fairness, and that is what happened. It was decreed that all of Adam's descendants, to the latest day, should be punished for the baby's trespass against a law of his nursery fulminated against him before he was out of his diapers. For thousands and thousands of years his posterity, individual by individual, has been unceasingly hunted and harried with afflictions in punishment of the juvenile misdemeanor which is grandiloquently called Adam's Sin. And during all that vast lapse of time there has been no lack of rabbins and popes and bishops and priests and parsons and lay slaves eager to applaud this infamy, maintain the unassailable justice and righteousness of it, and praise its Author in terms of flattery so gross and extravagant that none but a God could listen to it and not hide His face in disgust and embarrassment. Hardened to flattery as our Oriental potentates are through long experience, not even they would be able to endure the rank quality of it which our God endures with complacency and satisfaction from our pulpits every Sunday.

We brazenly call our God the source of mercy, while we are aware all the time that there is not an authentic instance in history of His ever having exercised that virtue. We call Him the source of morals, while we know by His history and by His daily conduct as perceived with our own senses that He is totally destitute of anything resembling morals. We call Him Father, and not in derision, although we would detest and denounce any earthly father who should inflict upon his child a thousandth part of the pains and miseries and cruelties which our God deals out to His children every day, and has dealt out to them daily during all the centuries since the crime of creating Adam was committed.

We deal in a curious and laughable confusion of notions concerning God. We divide Him in two, bring half of Him down to an obscure and infinitesimal corner of the world to confer salvation upon a little colony of Jews—and only Jews, no one else—and leave the other half of Him throned in Heaven and looking down and eagerly and anxiously watching for results. We reverently study the history of the earthly half and deduce from it the conviction that the earthly half has reformed, is equipped with morals and virtues, and in no way resembles the abandoned, malignant half that abides upon the throne. We conceive that the earthly half is just, merciful, charitable, benevolent, forgiving and full of sympathy for the sufferings of mankind and anxious to remove them. Apparently we deduce this character not by examining facts but by diligently declining to search them, measure them and weigh them. The earthly half requires us to be merciful and sets us an example by inventing a lake of fire and brimstone in which all of us who fail to recognize and worship Him as God are to be burned through all eternity. And not only *we*, who are offered these terms, are to be thus burned if we neglect them, but also the earlier billions of human beings are to suffer this awful fate, although they all lived and died without ever having heard of Him or the terms at all. This exhibition of mercifulness may be called gorgeous. We have nothing approaching it among human savages, nor among the wild beasts of the jungle. We are required to forgive our brother seventy times seven times and be satisfied and content if on our death-bed, after a pious life, our soul escape from our body before the hurrying priest can get to us and furnish it a pass with his mumblings and candles and incantations. This example of the forgiving spirit may also be pronounced gorgeous.

We are told that the two halves of our God are only seemingly disconnected by their separation; that in very fact the two halves remain one, and equally powerful, notwithstanding the separation. This being the case, the earthly half—who mourns over the sufferings of mankind and would like to remove them, and is quite competent to remove them at any moment He may choose—satisfies Himself with restoring sight to a blind person here and there instead of restoring it to all the blind; cures a cripple here and there instead of curing all the cripples; furnishes to five thousand famishing persons a meal and lets the rest of the millions that are hungry remain hungry —and all the time He admonishes inefficient man to cure these ills which God Himself inflicted upon him, and which He could extinguish with a word if He chose to do it, and thus do a plain duty which He had neglected from the beginning and always will neglect while time shall last. He raised several dead persons to life. He manifestly regarded this as a kindness. If it was a kindness it was not just to confine it to half-a-dozen persons. He should have raised the rest of the dead. I would not do it myself, for I think the dead are the only human beings who are really well off—but I merely mention it in passing as one of those curious incongruities with which our Bible history is heavily overcharged.

Whereas the God of the Old Testament is a fearful and repulsive character He is at least consistent. He is frank and outspoken. He makes no pretense to the possession of a moral or a virtue of any kind—except with His mouth. No such thing is anywhere discoverable in His conduct. I think He comes infinitely nearer to being respectworthy than does His reformed self as guilelessly exposed in the New Testament. Nothing in all history—nor even His massed history combined—remotely approaches in atrocity the invention of Hell.

His heavenly self, His Old Testament self, is sweetness and gentleness and respectability, compared with His reformed earthly self. In Heaven he claims not a single merit and hasn't one—outside of those claimed by His mouth—whereas in the earth He claims every merit in the entire catalogue of merits, yet practised them only now and then, penuriously, and finished by conferring Hell upon us, which abolished all His fictitious merits in a body.

Two

Wednesday, June 20, 1906

There are one or two curious defects about Bibles. An almost pathetic poverty of invention characterizes them all. That is one striking defect. Another is that each pretends to originality without possessing any. Each borrows from the others and gives no credit, which is a distinctly immoral act. Each in turn confiscates decayed old stage-properties from the others and with naïve confidence puts them forth as fresh new inspirations from on high. We borrow the Golden Rule from Confucius after it has seen service for centuries and copyright it without a blush. When we want a Deluge we go away back to hoary Babylon and borrow it, and are as proud of it and as satisfied with it as if it had been worth the trouble. We still revere it and admire it today and claim that it came to us direct from the mouth of the Deity; whereas we know that Noah's flood never happened, and couldn't have happened. The flood is a favorite with Bible makers. If there is a Bible—or even a tribe of savages—that lacks a General Deluge it is only because the religious scheme that lacks it hadn't any handy source to borrow it from.

Another prime favorite with the authors of sacred literature and founders of religions is the Immaculate Conception. It had been worn threadbare before we adopted it as a fresh new idea—and we admire it as much now as did the original conceiver of it when his mind was delivered of it a million years ago. The Hindus prized it ages ago when they acquired Krishna by the Immaculate process. The Buddhists were happy when they acquired Gautama by the same process twenty-five hundred years ago. The Greeks of the same period had great joy in it when their Supreme Being and his cabinet used to come down and people Greece with mongrels half human and half divine. The Romans borrowed the idea from Greece and found great happiness in Jupiter's Immaculate Conception products. We got it direct from Heaven, by way of Rome. We are still charmed with it. And only a fortnight ago, when an Episcopal clergyman in Rochester was summoned before the governing body of his church to answer the charge of intimating that he did not believe that the Savior was miraculously conceived, the Rev. Dr. Briggs, who is perhaps the most daringly broad-minded religious person now occupying an American pulpit, took up the cudgels in favor of the Immaculate Conception in an article in the *North American Review,* and from the tone of that article it seemed apparent that he believed he had settled that vexed question once and for all.[1] His idea was that there could be no doubt about it, for the reason that the Virgin Mary knew it was authentic because the Angel of the Annunciation told her so. Also, it must have been so, for the additional reason that Jude—a later son of Mary, the Virgin, and born in wedlock—was still living and associating with the adherents of the early church many years after the event, and that he said quite decidedly that it was a case of

[1] The article is "Criticism and Dogma," by Charles Augustus Briggs, Vol. 182, June 1906, pp. 861–74. Briggs does not mention a Rochester clergyman, nor does he "take up the cudgels" in any apparent sense. More important, he does not once mention the doctrine of the Immaculate Conception. Instead, he discusses the doctrine of the Virgin Birth at length and in detail, although not, to my mind, coherently. Clemens, on the other hand, discusses the Immaculate Conception, and does so as if it were identical with the Virgin Birth. Apparently he missed the point that the Immaculate Conception refers to the conception of Mary and not to that of Jesus. In his *Mark Twain in Eruption* (p. 317) DeVoto noted, "Throughout Mark Twain's writing, he confuses the doctrine of the Immaculate Conception with that of the Virgin Birth of Christ."—C.N.

Immaculate Conception; therefore it must be true, for Jude was right there in the family and in a position to know.

If there is anything more amusing than the Immaculate Conception doctrine it is the quaint reasonings whereby ostensibly intelligent human beings persuade themselves that the impossible fact is proven.

If Dr. Briggs were asked to believe in the Immaculate Conception process as exercised in the cases of Krishna, Osiris, Buddha and the rest of the tribe he would decline with thanks and probably be offended. If pushed, he would probably say that it would be childish to believe in those cases, for the reason that they were supported by none but human testimony and that it would be impossible to prove such a thing by human testimony, because if the entire human race were present at a case of Immaculate Conception they wouldn't be able to tell when it happened, nor whether it happened at all—and yet this bright man with the temporarily muddy mind is quite able to believe an impossibility whose authenticity rests entirely upon human testimony—the testimony of but one human being, the Virgin herself, a witness not disinterested, but powerfully interested; a witness incapable of knowing the fact as a fact, but getting all that she supposed she knew about it at second hand—at second hand from an entire stranger, an alleged angel, who could have been an angel, perhaps, but also could have been a tax collector. It is not likely that she had ever seen an angel before or knew their trade-marks. He was a stranger. He brought no credentials. His evidence was worth nothing at all to anybody else in the community. It is worth nothing today to any but minds which are like Dr. Briggs's—which have lost their clarity through mulling over absurdities in the pious wish to dig something sane and rational out of them. The Immaculate Conception rests wholly upon the testimony of a single witness—a witness whose testimony is without value—a witness whose very existence has nothing to rest upon but the assertion of the young peasant wife whose husband needed to be pacified. Mary's testimony satisfied him but that is because he lived in Nazareth instead of New York. There isn't any carpenter in New York that would take the testimony at par. If the Immaculate Conception could be repeated in New York today there isn't a man, woman or child of those four millions who would believe in it—except perhaps some addled Christian Scientists. A person who can believe in Mother Eddy wouldn't strain at an

Immaculate Conception, or six of them in a bunch. The Immaculate Conception could not be repeated successfully in New York in our day. It would produce laughter, not reverence and adoration.

To a person who doesn't believe in it, it seems a most puerile invention. It could occur to nobody but a god that it was a large and ingenious arrangement and had dignity in it. It could occur to nobody but a god that a divine Son procured through promiscuous relations with a peasant family in a village could improve the purity of the product, yet that is the very idea. The product acquires purity —purity absolute—purity from all stain or blemish—through a gross violation of both human and divine law, as set forth in the constitution and by-laws of the Bible. Thus the Christian religion, which requires everybody to be moral and to obey the laws, has its very beginning in immorality and in disobedience to law. You couldn't purify a tomcat by the Immaculate Conception process.

Apparently as a pious stage-property it is still useful, still workable, although it is so bent with age and so nearly exhausted by overwork. It is another case of begats. What's-his-name begat Krishna, Krishna begat Buddha, Buddha begat Osiris, Osiris begat the Babylonian deities, they begat God, He begat Jesus, Jesus begat Mrs. Eddy. If she is going to continue the line and do her proper share of the begatting, she must get at it, for she is already an antiquity.

There is one notable thing about our Christianity: bad, bloody, merciless, money-grabbing and predatory as it is—in our country particularly, and in all other Christian countries in a somewhat modified degree—it is still a hundred times better than the Christianity of the Bible, with its prodigious crime—the invention of Hell. Measured by our Christianity of today, bad as it is, hypocritical as it is, empty and hollow as it is, neither the Deity nor His Son is a Christian, nor qualified for that moderately high place. Ours is a terrible religion. The fleets of the world could swim in spacious comfort in the innocent blood it has spilt.

Three

For two years now Christianity has been repeating in Russia the sort of industries in the way of massacre and mutilation with which it has been successfully persuading Christendom in every century for nineteen hundred years that it is the only right and true religion—the one and only religion of peace and love. For two years now the ultra-Christian Government of Russia had been officially ordering and conducting massacres of its Jewish subjects. These massacres have been so frequent that we have become almost indifferent to them. The accounts of them hardly affect us more than do accounts of corners in a railroad stock in which we have no money invested. We have become so used to their described horrors that we hardly shudder now when we read of them.

Here are some of the particulars of one of the latest efforts of these humble Twentieth Century disciples to persuade the unbeliever to come into the fold of the meek and gentle Savior.[2]

Horrible details have been sent out by the correspondent of the Bourse Gazette, who arrived in Bialystok in company with Deputy Schepkin on Saturday, and who managed to send his story by a messenger Sunday afternoon. The correspondent, who accompanied Schepkin directly to the hospital escorted by a Corporal's guard, says he was utterly unnerved by the sights he witnessed there.

"Merely saying that the bodies were mutilated," the correspondent writes, "fails to describe the awful facts. The faces of the dead have lost all human resemblance. The body of Teacher Apstein lay on the grass with the hands tied. In the face and eyes had been hammered three-inch nails. Rioters entered his home, killing him thus, and then murdered the rest of his family of seven. When the body arrived at the hospital it was also marked with bayonet thrusts.

"Beside the body of Apstein lay that of a child of 10 years, whose leg

[2] The name and date of the newspaper from which the following clipping was taken are not given. The clipping no doubt referred to the massacre of Jews, June 15, 1906, in Bialystok, instigated by government officials.—C.N.

had been chopped off with an axe. Here also were the dead from the Schlachter home, where, according to witnesses, soldiers came and plundered the house and killed the wife, son, and a neighbor's daughter and seriously wounded Schlachter and his two daughters.

"I am told that soldiers entered the apartments of the Lapidus brothers, which were crowded with people who had fled from the streets for safety, and ordered the Christians to separate themselves from the Jews. A Christian student named Dikar protested and was killed on the spot. Then all of the Jews were shot."

From the wounded in the hospital the correspondent heard many pitiable stories, all of the same general tenor. Here is the account of a badly wounded merchant named Nevyazhiky:

"I live in the suburbs. Learning of the pogrom, I tried to reach the town through the fields, but was intercepted by roughs. My brother was killed, my arm and leg were broken, my skull was fractured, and I was stabbed twice in the side. I fainted from loss of blood, and revived to find a soldier standing over me, who asked: 'What, are you still alive! Shall I bayonet you?' I begged him to spare my life. The roughs again came, but spared me, saying: 'He will die; let him suffer longer.' "

The correspondent, who adopts the bitterest tone toward the government, holds that the pogrom undoubtedly was provoked, and attributes the responsibility to Police Lieutenant Sheremetieff. He declares that not only the soldiers, but their officers, participated, and that he himself was a witness as late as Saturday to the shooting down of a Jewish girl from the window of a hotel by Lieut. Miller of the Vladimir Regiment. The Governor of the Province of Grodno, who happened to be passing at the moment, ordered an investigation.

The pulpit and the optimist are always talking about the human race's steady march toward ultimate perfection. As usual, they leave out the statistics. It is the pulpit's way—the optimist's way.

Is there any discoverable advance toward moderation between the massacre of the Albigenses and these massacres of Russian Jews? There is one difference. In elaborate cruelty and brutality the modern massacre exceeds the ancient one. Is any advance discoverable between Batholomew's Day and these Jewish massacres? Yes. The same difference again appears: the modern Russian Christian and his Czar have advanced to an extravagance of bloody and bestial atrocity undreamed of by their crude brethren of three hundred and thirty-five years ago.

The Gospel of Peace is always making a good deal of noise with its mouth; always rejoicing in the progress it is making toward final perfection, and always diligently neglecting to furnish the statistics. George the Third reigned sixty years, the longest reign in English history up to his time. When his revered successor, Victoria, turned the sixty-year corner—thus scoring a new long-reign record—the event was celebrated with great pomp and circumstance and public rejoicing in England and her colonies. Among the statistics fetched out for general admiration were these: that for each year of the sixty of her reign Victoria's Christian soldiers had fought in a separate and distinct war. Meantime the possessions of England had swollen to such a degree by depredations committed upon helpless and godless pagans that there were not figures enough in Great Britain to set down the stolen acreage and they had to import a lot from other countries.

There are no peaceful nations now except those unhappy ones whose borders have not been invaded by the Gospel of Peace. All Christendom is a soldier-camp. During all the past generation the Christian poor have been taxed almost to starvation-point to support the giant armaments which the Christian Governments have built up, each to protect itself from the rest of the brotherhood and, incidentally, to snatch any patch of real estate left exposed by its savage owner. King Leopold II of Belgium—probably the most intensely Christian monarch, except Alexander the Sixth,[3] that has escaped Hell thus far—has stolen an entire kingdom in Africa, and in the fourteen years of Christian endeavor there has reduced the population of thirty millions to fifteen by murder, mutilation, overwork, robbery, rapine—confiscating the helpless native's very labor and giving him nothing in return but salvation and a home in Heaven, furnished at the last moment by the Christian priest.[4]

Within this last generation each Christian power has turned the bulk of its attention to finding out newer and still newer and more and more effective ways of killing Christians—and, incidentally, a pagan now and then—and the surest way to get rich quickly in

---

[3] It is not clear to whom Clemens was referring here. The reigning Russian monarch was Nicholas II, son of Alexander III.—C.N.

[4] See "King Leopold's Soliloquy," a biting pamphlet by Clemens, reprinted in my *Life As I Find It* [by *Mark Twain*, ed. *Charles Neider.* Hanover House, 1961]. Clemens's figures regarding the reduction of the native population may have been exaggerated, but his case in general was well substantiated.—C.N.

Christ's earthly kingdom is to invent a gun that can kill more Christians at one shot than any other existing gun.

Also, during the same generation each Christian Government has played with its neighbors a continuous poker game in the naval line. In this game France puts up a battleship; England sees that battleship and goes it one battleship better; Russia comes in and raises it a battleship or two—*did,* before the untaught stranger entered the game and reduced her stately pile of chips to a damaged ferryboat and a cruiser that can't cruise. We are in it ourselves now. This game goes on and on and on. There is never a new shuffle; never a new deal. No player ever calls another's hand. It is merely an unending game of put up and put up and put up; and by the law of probabilities a day is coming when no Christians will be left on the land, except the women. The men will all be at sea, manning the fleets.

This singular game, which is so costly and so ruinous and so silly, is called statesmanship—which is different from assmanship on account of the spelling. Anybody but a statesman could invent some way to reduce these vast armaments to rational and sensible and safe police proportions, with the result that thenceforth all Christians could sleep in their beds unafraid, and even the Savior could come down and walk on the seas, foreigner as He is, without dread of being chased by Christian battleships.

Has the Bible done something still worse than drench the planet with innocent blood? To my mind it has—but this is only an opinion, and it may be a mistaken one. There has never been a Protestant boy or a Protestant girl whose mind the Bible has not soiled. No Protestant child ever comes clean from association with the Bible. This association cannot be prevented. Sometimes the parents try to prevent it by not allowing the children to have access to the Bible's awful obscenities, but this only whets the child's desire to taste that forbidden fruit, and it does taste it—seeks it out secretly and devours it with a strong and grateful appetite. The Bible does its baleful work in the propagation of vice among children, and vicious and unclean ideas, daily and constantly, in every Protestant family in Christendom. It does more of this deadly work than all the other unclean books in Christendom put together; and not only more, but a thousandfold more. It is easy to protect the young from those other books, and they are protected from them. But they have no protection against the deadly Bible.

Is it doubted that the young people hunt out the forbidden passages privately and study them with pleasure? If my reader were here present—let him be of either sex or any age, between ten and ninety —I would make him answer this question himself—and he could answer it in only one way. He would be obliged to say that by his own knowledge and experience of the days of his early youth he knows positively that the Bible defiles all Protestant children, without a single exception.

Do I think the Christian religion is here to stay? Why should I think so? There had been a thousand religions before it was born. They are all dead. There had been millions of gods before ours was invented. Swarms of them are dead and forgotten long ago. Ours is by long odds the worst God that the ingenuity of man has begotten from his insane imagination—and shall He and His Christianity be immortal against the great array of probabilities furnished by the theological history of the past? No. I think that Christianity and its God must follow the rule. They must pass on in their turn and make room for another God and a stupider religion. Or perhaps a better than this? No. That is not likely. History shows that in the matter of religions we progress backward and not the other way. No matter, there will be a new God and a new religion. They will be introduced to popularity and accepted with the only arguments that have ever persuaded any people in this earth to adopt Christianity, or any other religion that they were not born to: the Bible, the sword, the torch and the axe—the only missionaries that have ever scored a single victory since gods and religions began in the world. After the new God and the new religion have become established in the usual proportions—one-fifth of the world's population ostensible adherents, the four-fifths pagan missionary field, with the missionary scratching its continental back complacently and inefficiently—will the new converts believe in them? Certainly they will. They have always believed in the million gods and religions that have been stuffed down their midriffs. There isn't anything so grotesque or so incredible that the average human being can't believe it. At this very day there are thousands upon thousands of Americans of average intelligence who fully believe in *Science and Health,* although they can't understand a line of it, and who also worship the sordid and ignorant old purloiner of that gospel—Mrs. Mary Baker G. Eddy, whom they do absolutely believe to be a member by adoption of the

Holy Family and on the way to push the Savior to third place and assume occupancy of His present place and continue that occupancy during the rest of eternity.

Four

Let us now consider the real God, the genuine God, the great God, the sublime and supreme God, the authentic Creator of the *real* universe, whose remotenesses are visited by comets only—comets unto which incredibly distant Neptune is merely an outpost, a Sandy Hook to homeward-bound spectres of the deeps of space that have not glimpsed it before for generations—a universe not made with hands and suited to an astronomical nursery, but spread abroad through the illimitable reaches of space by the fiat of the real God just mentioned; that God of unthinkable grandeur and majesty, by comparison with whom all the other gods whose myriads infest the feeble imaginations of men are as a swarm of gnats scattered and lost in the infinitudes of the empty sky.

When we think of such a God as this we cannot associate with Him anything trivial, anything lacking dignity, anything lacking grandeur. We cannot conceive of His passing by Sirius to choose our potato for a footstool. We cannot conceive of His interesting Himself in the affairs of the microscopic human race and enjoying its Sunday flatteries and experiencing pangs of jealousy when the flatteries grow lax or fail, any more than we can conceive of the Emperor of China being interested in a bottle of microbes and pathetically anxious to stand well with them and harvest their impertinent compliments. If we could conceive of the Emperor of China taking an intemperate interest in his bottle of microbes we should have to draw the line there; we could not by any stretch of imagination conceive of his selecting from these innumerable millions a quarter of a thimbleful of Jew microbes—the least attractive of the whole swarm—and making pets of them and nominating them as his chosen germs and carrying his infatuation for them so far as to resolve to keep and coddle them alone and damn all the rest.

When we examine the myriad wonders and glories and charms and perfections of this infinite universe (as we know the universe now), and perceive that there is not a detail of it—from the blade of grass to the giant trees of California, nor from the obscure mountain rivulet to the measureless ocean; nor from the ebb and flow of the tides to the stately motions of the planets—that is not the slave of a system of exact and inflexible law, we seem to know—not suppose nor conjecture, but *know*—that the God that brought this stupendous fabric into being with a flash of thought and framed its laws with another flash of thought is endowed with limitless power. We seem to know that whatever thing He wishes to do, He can do that thing without anybody's assistance. We also seem to know that when He flashed the universe into being He foresaw everything that would happen in it from that moment until the end of time.

Do we also know that He is a moral being, according to our standard of morals? No. If we know anything at all about it we know that He is destitute of morals—at least of the human pattern. Do we know that He is just, charitable, kindly, gentle, merciful, compassionate? No. There is no evidence that He is any of these things—whereas each and every day as it passes furnishes us a thousand volumes of evidence, and indeed proof, that He possesses none of these qualities.

When we pray, when we beg, when we implore, does He listen? Does He answer? There is not a single authentic instance of it in human history. Does He silently refuse to listen—refuse to answer? There is nothing resembling proof that He has ever done anything else. From the beginning of time priests, who have imagined themselves to be His appointed and salaried servants, have gathered together their full numerical strength and simultaneously prayed for rain and never once got it when it was not due according to the eternal laws of Nature. Whenever they got it, if they had had a competent Weather Bureau they could have saved themselves the trouble of praying for that rain, because the Bureau could have told them it was coming anyhow within twenty-four hours, whether they prayed or saved their sacred wind.

From the beginning of time whenever a king has lain dangerously ill the priesthood and some part of the nation have prayed in unison that the king be spared to his grieving and anxious people (in case they were grieving and anxious, which was not usually the rule) and in no instance was their prayer ever answered. When Mr. Garfield lay near to death, the physicians and surgeons knew that nothing could save him, yet at an appointed signal all the pulpits in the United States broke forth with one simultaneous and supplicating appeal for the President's restoration to health. They did this with the same old innocent confidence with which the primeval savage had prayed to his imaginary devils to spare his perishing chief—for that day will never come when facts and experience can teach a pulpit anything useful. Of course the President died just the same.

Great Britain has a population of forty-one millions. She has eighty thousand pulpits. The Boer population was a hundred and fifty thousand, with a battery of two hundred and ten pulpits. In the beginning of the Boer war, at a signal from the Primate of all England the eighty thousand English pulpits thundered forth a titanic simultaneous supplication to their God to give the embattled English in South Africa the victory. The little Boer battery of two hundred and ten guns replied with a simultaneous supplication to the same God to give the Boers the victory. If the eighty thousand English clergy had left their prayers unshed and gone to the field they would have got it—whereas the victory went the other way and the English forces suffered defeat after defeat at the hands of the Boers. The English pulpit kept discreetly quiet about the result of its effort, but the indiscreet Boer pulpit proclaimed with a loud and exultant voice that it was *its* prayers that had conferred the victory upon the Boers.

The British Government had more confidence in soldiers than in prayer—therefore instead of doubling and trebling the numerical strength of the clergy it doubled and trebled the strength of its forces in the field. Then the thing happened that always happens—the English whipped the fight, a rather plain indication that the Lord had not listened to either side and was as indifferent as to who should win as He had always been, from the day that He was evolved down to the present time—there being no instance on record where He has shown any interest at all in any human squabble, nor whether the good cause won out or lost.

Has this experience taught the pulpit anything? It has not. When the Boer prayers achieved victory—as the Boers believed—the Boers were confirmed once more in their trust in the power of prayer.

When a crushing finality of defeat overwhelmed them later in the face of their confident supplications, their attitude was not altered, nor their confidence in the righteousness and intelligence of God impaired.

Often we see a mother who has been despoiled little by little of everything she held dear in life but a sole remaining dying child; we have seen her, I say, kneeling by its bed and pouring out from a breaking heart beseechings to God for mercy that would get glad and instant answer from any man who had the power to save that child— yet no such prayer has ever moved a God to pity. Has that mother been convinced? Sometimes—but only for a little while. She was merely a human being and like the rest—ready to pray again in the next emergency; ready to believe again that she would be heard.

We know that the real God, the Supreme God, the actual Maker of the universe, made everything that is in it. We know that He made all the creatures, from the microbe and the brontosaur down to man and the monkey, and that He knew what would happen to each and every one of them from the beginning of time to the end of it. In the case of each creature, big or little, He made it an unchanging law that that creature should suffer wanton and unnecessary pains and miseries every day of its life—that by that law these pains and miseries could not be avoided by any diplomacy exercisable by the creature; that its way, from birth to death, should be beset by traps, pitfalls and gins, ingeniously planned and ingeniously concealed; and that by another law every transgression of a law of Nature, either ignorantly or wittingly committed, should in every instance be visited by a punishment ten-thousandfold out of proportion of the transgression. We stand astonished at the all-comprehensive malice which could patiently descend to the contriving of elaborate tortures for the meanest and pitifulest of the countless kinds of creatures that were to inhabit the earth. The spider was so contrived that she would not eat grass but must catch flies and such things and inflict a slow and horrible death upon them, unaware that her turn would come next. The wasp was so contrived that he also would decline grass and stab the spider, not conferring upon her a swift and merciful death, but merely half-paralyzing her, then ramming her down into the wasp den, there to live and suffer for days while the wasp babies should chew her legs off at their leisure. In turn, there was a murderer provided for the wasp, and another murderer for the wasp's murderer, and so on throughout the whole scheme of living creatures in the earth. There isn't one of them that was not designed and appointed to inflict misery and murder on some fellow creature and suffer the same in turn from some other murderous fellow creature. In flying into the web the fly is merely guilty of an indiscretion—not a breach of any law—yet the fly's punishment is ten-thousandfold out of proportion to that little indiscretion.

The ten-thousandfold law of punishment is rigorously enforced against every creature, man included. The debt, whether made innocently or guiltily, is promptly collected by Nature—and in this world, without waiting for the ten-billionfold additional penalty appointed—in the case of man—for collection in the next.

This system of atrocious punishments for somethings and nothings begins upon the helpless baby on its first day in the world and never ceases until its last one. Is there a father who would persecute his baby with unearned colics and the unearned miseries of teething, and follow these with mumps, measles, scarlet-fever and the hundred other persecutions appointed for the unoffending creature? And then follow these, from youth to the grave, with a multitude of ten-thousandfold punishments for laws broken either by intention or indiscretion? With a fine sarcasm we ennoble God with the title of Father— yet we know quite well that we should hang His style of father wherever we might catch him.

The pulpit's explanation of and apology for these crimes is pathetically destitute of ingenuity. It says that they are committed for the benefit of the sufferer. They are to discipline him, purify him, elevate him, train him for the society of the Deity and the angels—send him up sanctified with cancers, tumors, smallpox and the rest of the educational plant; whereas the pulpit knows that it is stultifying itself, if it knows anything at all. It knows that if this kind of discipline is wise and salutary, we are insane not to adopt it ourselves and apply it to our children.

Does the pulpit really believe that we can improve a purifying and elevating breed of culture invented by the Almighty? It seems to me that if the pulpit honestly believed what it is preaching in this regard it would recommend every father to imitate the Almighty's methods.

When the pulpit has succeeded in persuading its congregation that this system has been really wisely and mercifully contrived by the Almighty to discipline and purify and elevate His children whom He so loves, the pulpit judiciously closes its mouth. It doesn't venture further and explain why these same crimes and cruelties are inflicted upon the higher animals—the alligators, the tigers and the rest. It even proclaims that the beasts perish—meaning that their sorrowful life begins and ends here; that they go no further; that there is no Heaven for them; that neither God nor the angels nor the redeemed desire their society on the other side. It puts the pulpit in a comical situation, because in spite of all its ingenuities of explanation and apology it convicts its God of being a wanton and pitiless tyrant in the case of the unoffending beasts. At any rate, and beyond cavil or argument, by its silence it condemns Him irrevocably as a malignant master, after having persuaded the congregation that He is constructed entirely out of compassion, righteousness and all-pervading love. The pulpit doesn't know how to reconcile these grotesque contradictions and it doesn't try.

In His destitution of one and all of the qualities which could grace a God and invite respect for Him and reverence and worship, the real God, the genuine God, the Maker of the mighty universe is just like all the other gods in the list. He proves every day that He takes no interest in man, nor in the other animals, further than to torture them, slay them and get out of this pastime such entertainment as it may afford—and do what He can not to get weary of the eternal and changeless monotony of it.

Five

Monday, June 25, 1906

It is to these celestial bandits that the naïve and confiding and illogical human rabbit looks for a Heaven of eternal bliss, which is to be his reward for patiently enduring the want and sufferings inflicted upon him here below—unearned sufferings covering terms of two or three years in some cases; five or ten years in others; thirty, forty or fifty in others; sixty, seventy, eighty in others. As usual, where the Deity is Judge the rewards are vastly out of proportion to the sufferings—and there is no system about the matter anyhow. You do not get any more Heaven for suffering eighty years than you get if you die of the measles at three.

There is no evidence that there is to be a Heaven hereafter. If we should find, somewhere, an ancient book in which a dozen unknown men professed to tell all about a blooming and beautiful tropical Paradise secreted in an inaccessible valley in the center of the eternal icebergs which constitute the Antarctic continent—not claiming that they had seen it themselves, but had acquired an intimate knowledge of it through a revelation from God—no Geographical Society in the earth would take any stock in that book; yet that book would be quite as authentic, quite as trustworthy, quite as valuable evidence as is the Bible. The Bible is just like it. Its Heaven exists solely upon hearsay evidence—evidence furnished by unknown persons; persons who did not prove that they had ever been there.

If Christ had really been God He could have proved it, since nothing is impossible with God. He could have proved it to every individual of His own time and of our time and of all future time. When God wants to prove that the sun and the moon may be depended upon to do their appointed work every day and every night He has no difficulty about it. When He wants to prove that man may depend upon finding the constellations in their places every night— although they vanish and seem lost to us every day—He has no difficulty about it. When He wants to prove that the seasons may be depended upon to come and go according to a fixed law, year after year, He has no difficulty about it. Apparently He has desired to prove to us beyond cavil or doubt many millions of things, and He has had no difficulty about proving them all. It is only when He apparently wants to prove a future life to us that His invention fails and He comes up against a problem which is beyond the reach of His alleged omnipotence. With a message to deliver to men which is of infinitely more importance than all those other messages put together, which He has delivered without difficulty, He can think of no better medium than the poorest of all contrivances—a book. A book written in two languages—to convey a message to a thousand nations—which in the course of the dragging centuries and eons must change and change and become finally wholly unintelligible. And even if they remained fixed, like a dead language, it would never be possible to translate the message with perfect clearness into any one of the thousand tongues, at any time.

According to the hearsay evidence the character of every conspicuous god is made up of love, justice, compassion, forgiveness, sorrow for all suffering and desire to extinguish it. Opposed to this beautiful character—built wholly upon valueless hearsay evidence—it is the absolutely authentic evidence furnished us every day in the year, and verifiable by our eyes and our other senses, that the real character of these gods is destitute of love, mercy, compassion, justice and other gentle and excellent qualities, and is made up of all imaginable cruelties, persecutions and injustices. The hearsay character rests upon evidence only—exceedingly doubtful evidence. The real character rests upon proof—proof unassailable.

Is it logical to expect of gods, whose unceasing and unchanging pastime is the malignant persecution of innocent men and animals, that they are going to provide an eternity of bliss, presently, for these very same creatures? If King Leopold II, the Butcher, should proclaim that out of each hundred innocent and unoffending Congo negroes he is going to save one from humiliation, starvation and assassination, and fetch that one home to Belgium to live with him in his palace and feed at his table, how many people would believe it? Everybody would say "A person's character is a permanent thing. His act would not be in accordance with that butcher's character. Leopold's character is established beyond possibility of change and it could never occur to him to do this kindly thing."

Leopold's character *is* established. The character of the conspicuous gods is also established. It is distinctly illogical to suppose that either Leopold of Belgium or the Heavenly Leopolds are ever going to think of inviting any fraction of their victims to the royal table and the comforts and conveniences of the regal palace.

According to hearsay evidence the conspicuous gods make a pet of one victim in a hundred—select him arbitrarily, without regard to whether he's any better than the other ninety-nine or not—but damn the ninety-nine through all eternity without examining into their case. But for one slight defect this would be logical and would properly reflect the known character of the gods—that defect is the gratuitous and unplausible suggestion that one in a hundred is permitted to pull through. It is not likely that there will be a Heaven hereafter. It is exceedingly likely that there will be a Hell—and it is nearly dead certain that nobody is going to escape it.

As to the human race. There are many pretty and winning things about the human race. It is perhaps the poorest of all the inventions of all the gods but it has never suspected it once. There is nothing prettier than its naïve and complacent appreciation of itself. It comes out frankly and proclaims without bashfulness or any sign of a blush that it is the noblest work of God. It has had a billion opportunities to know better, but all signs fail with this ass. I could say harsh things about it but I cannot bring myself to do it—it is like hitting a child.

Man is not to blame for what he is. He didn't make himself. He has no control over himself. All the control is vested in his temperament—which he did not create—and in the circumstances which hedge him round from the cradle to the grave and which he did not devise and cannot change by any act of his will, for the reason that he has no will. He is as purely a piece of automatic mechanism as is a watch, and can no more dictate or influence his actions than can the watch.[5] He is a subject for pity, not blame—and not contempt. He is flung head over heels into this world without ever a chance to decline, and straightway he conceives and accepts the notion that he is in some mysterious way under obligations to the unknown Power that inflicted this outrage upon him—and thenceforth he considers himself responsible to that Power for every act of his life, and punishable for such of his acts as do not meet with the approval of that Power—yet that same man would argue quite differently if a human tyrant should capture him and put chains upon him of any kind and require obedience: argue that the tyrant had no right to do that; that the tyrant had no right to put commands upon him of any kind and require obedience; that the tyrant had no right to compel him to commit murder and then put the responsibility for the murder upon him. Man constantly makes a most strange distinction between man and his Maker in the matter of morals. He requires of his fellow man obedience to a very creditable code of morals but he observes without shame or disapproval his God's utter destitution of morals.

God ingeniously contrived man in such a way that he could not escape obedience to the laws of his passions, his appetites and his

---

[5] See "What Is Man?" for a more explicit statement of Clemens's belief in determinism. Elsewhere I have written: "It is interesting to speculate how he would have reacted to twentieth-century science, in which the principle of indeterminacy of quantum physics has lent support to the doctrine of free will, the opposite of his favorite doctrine. This principle asserts that the behavior of particles within the atom is not determinable except in terms of broad statistics and probability."—C.N.

various unpleasant and undesirable qualities. God has so contrived him that all his goings outs and comings in are beset by traps which he cannot possibly avoid and which compel him to commit what are called sins—and then God punishes him for doing these very things which from the beginning of time He had always intended that he should do. Man is a machine and God made it—without invitation from any one. Whoever makes a machine here below is responsible for that machine's performance. No one would think of such a thing as trying to put the responsibility upon the machine itself. We all know perfectly well—though we all conceal it, just as I am doing, until I shall be dead and out of reach of public opinion—we all know, I say, that God, and God alone, is responsible for every act and word of a human being's life between cradle and grave. We know it perfectly well. In our secret hearts we haven't the slightest doubt of it. In our secret hearts we have no hesitation in proclaiming as an unthinking fool anybody who thinks he believes that he is by any possibility capable of committing a sin against God—or who thinks he thinks he is under obligations to God and owes Him thanks, reverence and worship.

1601

OR

CONVERSATION AS IT WAS
BY THE SOCIAL FIRESIDE IN
THE TIME OF THE TUDORS

Yesternight toke her maiste ye queene a fantasie such as she sometimes hath, and hadde to her closet certain that doe write playes,
bokes, and such like, these being my lord Bacon, his worship Sr
Walter Ralegh, Mr. Ben Jonson, and ye childe Francis Beaumonte,
which being but sixteen, hath yet turned his hande to ye doing of ye
Lattin masters into our Englishe tong, wh grete discretion and much
applaus. Also came wh these ye famous Shaxpur. A righte straunge
mixing truly of mightie blode wh mean, ye more in especial since ye
queenes grace was present, as likewise these following, to wit: Ye
Duchess of Bilgewater, twenty-two yeres of age; ye Countesse of
Granby, twenty-six; her doter, ye Lady Helen, fifteen; as also these
two maides of honour, to wit: ye Lady Margery Boothy, sixty-five,
and ye Lady Alice Dilberry, turned seventy, she being two yeres ye
queenes graces elder.

I being her maistes cup-bearer, hadde no choice but to remaine
and beholde rank forgot, and ye high holde converse wh ye low as
uppon equal termes, a grete scandal did ye world heare therof.

In ye heat of ye talk it befel yt one did breake wynde, yielding an
exceding mightie and distresful stink, wherat all did laffe full sore,
and then—

Ye Queene.—Verily in mine eight and sixty yeres have I not heard
the fellow to this fart. Meseemeth, by ye grete sounde and clamour of

it, it was male; yet ye belly it did lurk behinde shoulde now fall leane and flat against ye spine of him yt hath bene delivered of so stately and so vaste a bulk, wheras ye guts of them yt doe quiff-splitters beare, stande comely still and rounde. Prithee let ye author confes ye offspring. Will my Lady Alice testify?

Lady Alice.—Good your grace, an' I hadde room for such a thunderbust within mine ancient bowels, 'tis not in reason I coulde discharge ye same and live to thank God for yt He did choose handmaide so humble wherby to shew his power. Nay, 'tis not I yt have broughte forth this rich o'ermastering fog, this fragrant bloom, so pray ye seeke ye further.

Ye Queene.—Mayhap ye Lady Margery hath done ye companie this favour?

Lady Margery.—So please ye madam, my limbs are feeble wh ye weighte and drouth of five and sixty winters, and it behoveth yt I be tender unto them. In ye good providence of God, an' *I* hadde contained this wonder, forsoothe wolde I have gi'en ye whole evening of my sinking life to ye dribbling of it forth, wh trembling and uneasy soul, not launched it sudden in its matchless might, taking mine own life wh violence, rending my weak frame like rotten rags. It was not I, your maiste.

Ye Queene.—O' God's name who hath favoured us? Hath it come to pass yt a fart shall fart *itself?* Not such a one as this, I trow. Young Master Beaumonte—but no; 'twolde have wafted him to heav'n like downe of gooses boddy. 'Twas not ye little Lady Helen—nay, ne'er blush, my childe; thoul't tickle thy tender maidenhedde with many a mousie-squeak before thou learnest to blow a harricane like this. Was't you, my learned and ingenious Jonson?

Jonson.—So fell a blast hath ne'er mine ears saluted, nor yet a stench so all-pervading and immortal. 'Twas not a novice did it, good your maiste, but one of veteran experience—else hadde he failed of confidence. In soothe it was not I.

Ye Queene.—My lord Bacon?

Lord Bacon.—Not from mine leane entrailes hath this prodigie burst forth, so pleas your grace. Naught doth so befit ye grete as grete performance; and haply shall ye finde yt 'tis not from mediocrity this miracle hath issued.

[Tho' ye subject be but a fart, yet will this tedious sink of learning pondrously phillosophize. Meantime did the foul and deadly stink pervade all places to that degree, yt never smelt I ye like, yet dare I not to leave ye presence, albeit I was like to suffocate.]

Ye Queene.—What saith ye worshipful Master Shaxpur?

Shaxpur.—In the grete hand of God I stande and so proclaim mine innocence. Though ye sinless hosts of heav'n hadde foretolde ye coming of this most desolating breath, proclaiming it a work of uninspired man, its quaking thunders, its firmament-clogging rottenness, its own achievement in due course of nature, yet hadde not I believed it; but hadde said the pit itself hath furnished forth the stink, and heav'ns artillery hath shook the globe in admiration of it.

[Then there was a silence, and each did turn him toward the worshipful Sr Walter Ralegh that browned, embattled, bloody swashbuckler, who rising up did smile, and simpering say]

Sr W.—Most gracious maiste, 'twas I that did it, but indeed it was so poor and frail a note, compared wh such as I am wont to furnish, yt in sooth I was ashamed to call the weakling mine in so august a presence. It was nothing—less than nothing, madam—I did it but to clear my nether throat; but hadde I come prepared, then hadde I delivered something worthie. Bear wh me, pleas your grace, till I can make amends.

[Then delivered he himself of such a godless and rock-shivering blast that all were fain to stoppe their ears, and following it did come so dense and foul a stink that yt which went before did seem a poor and trifling thing beside it. Then saith he, feigning that he blushed and was confused, *I perceive that I am weak to-day, and cannot justice do unto my powers:* and sat him down as who shoulde say, *There it is not much; yet he yt hath an arse to spare, let him fellow yt, an think he can.* By God, an I were ye Queene, I wolde e'en tip this swaggering braggart out o' the court, and let him air his grandeurs and break his intolerable wynde before ye deaf and such as suffocation pleaseth.]

Then felle they to talk about ye manners and customs of many peoples, and Master Shaxpur spake of ye boke of ye sieur Michael de Montaine, wherein was mention of ye customs of widows of Perigord to wear uppon ye headdress, in signe of widowhood, a jewel in ye similitude of a man's member wilted and limber, wherat ye queene did laffe and say, *Widows in England doe wear prickes too, but betwixt the thighs, and not wilted neither, till coition hath done that office for them.* Master Shaxpur did likewise observe how yt ye sieur de Montaine hath also spoken of a certain emperor of such mightie prowess yt he did take ten maidenheddes in ye compass of a single night, ye while his empress did entertain two and twenty lusty knights between her sheetes, yet was not satisfied; wherat ye merrie Countesse Granby saith a ram is yet ye emperor's superior, sith he will tup a hundred yewes 'twixt sun and sun; and after, if he can have none more to shag, will masturbate until he hath enrich'd whole acres wh his seed.

Then spake ye damned windmill, Sr Walter, of a people in ye utermost parts of America, yt copulate not until they be five and thirty yeres of age, ye women being eight and twenty, and do it then but once in seven yeres.

Ye Queene.—How doth yt like mine little Lady Helen? Shall we send thee thither and preserve thy belly?

Lady Helen.—Please your highness grace, mine old nurse hath told me there are more ways of serving God than by locking the thighs together; yet am I willing to serve him yt way too, sith your highnesses grace hath set ye ensample.

Ye Queene.—God's wowndes, a good answer, childe.

Lady Alice.—Mayhap 'twill weaken when ye hair sprouts below ye navel.

Lady Helen.—Nay, it sprouted two yeres syne. I can scarce more than cover it with my hand now.

Ye Queene.—Hear ye that, my little Beaumonte? Have ye not a little birde about ye yt stirs at hearing tell of so sweete a neste?

Beaumonte.—'Tis not insensible, illustrious madam; but mousing owls and bats of low degree may not aspire to bliss so whelming and ecstatic as is founde in ye downie nestes of birdes of Paradise.

Ye Queene.—By ye gullet of God, 'tis a neat-turned compliment. With such a tong as thine, lad, thou'lt spread the ivory thighs of many a willing maide in thy good time, an thy cod-piece be as handie as thy speeche.

Then spake ye queene of how she met olde Rabelais when she was turned of fifteen, and he did tell her of a man his father knew yt hadde a double pair of bollocks, wheron a controversy followed as concerning the most just way to spell the word, ye contention running high betwixt ye learned Bacon and ye ingenious Jonson, until at last ye olde Lady Margery, wearying of it all, saith, *Gentles, what mattereth it how ye shall spell the word? I warrant ye when ye use your*

*bollocks ye shall not think of it; and my Lady Granby, be ye content;
let the spelling be, ye shall enjoy the beating of them on your buttocks
just the same, I trow. Before I hadde gained my fourteenth yere I
hadde learned yt them yt wolde explore a cunte stop't not to consider
the spelling o't.*

Sr W.—In soothe, when a shift's turned uppe, delay is mete for
naught but dalliance. Boccaccio hath a story of a prieste yt did beguile a maide into his cell, then knelt him in a corner to praye for
grace to be rightly thankful for this tender maidenhedde ye Lord
hath sent him; but ye abbot, spying through ye key-hole, did see a
tuft of brownish hair with fair white flesh about it, wherfore when ye
priestes prayer was done, his chance was gone, forasmuch as ye little
maide hadde but ye one cunte, and yt was already occupied to her
content.

Then conversed they of religion, and ye mightie work ye olde dead
Luther did doe by ye grace of God. Then next about poetry, and
Master Shaxpur did rede a part of his King Henry IV, ye which, it
seemeth unto me, is not of the value of an arseful of ashes, yet they
praised it bravely, one and all.

Ye same did rede a portion of his "Venus and Adonis" to their
prodigious admiration, wheras I, being sleepy and fatigued withal,
did deme it but paltrie stuff, and was the more discomfited in yt ye
blodie bucanier hadde got his secconde wynde, and did turn his mind
to farting wh such villain zeal that presently I was like to choke once
more. God damn this wyndie ruffian and all his breed. I wolde yt hell
mighte get him.

They talked about ye wonderful defense which olde Sr Nicholas
Throgmorton did make for himself before ye judges in ye time of
Mary; which was an unlucky matter to broach, sith it fetched out ye
queene wh a *Pity yt he, having so much wit, hadde yet not enough to
save his doter's maidenhedde sounde for her marriage-bedde.* And ye
queene did give ye damn'd Sr Walter a look yt made hym wince—for
she hath not forgot he was her own lover in yt olde day. There was
silent uncomfortableness now; 'twas not a good turn for talk to take,
sith if ye queene must find offense in a little harmless debauching,
when prickes were stiff and cuntes not loath to take ye stiffness out of
them, who of this companie was sinless? Beholde, was not ye wife of
Master Shaxpur four months gone wh childe when she stood uppe
before ye altar? Was not her Grace of Bilgewater roger'd by four

lords before she hadde a husband? Was not ye little Lady Helen borne on her mother's wedding-day? And, beholde, were not ye Lady Alice and ye Lady Margery there, mouthing religion, whores from ye cradle?

In time came they to discourse of Cervantes, and of the new painter, Rubens, that is beginning to be heard of. Fine words and dainty-wrought phrases from the ladies now, one or two of them being, in other days, pupils of yt poor arse, Lille himself; and I marked how that Jonson and Shaxpur did fidget to discharge some venom of sarcasm, yet dared they not in the presence, ye queenes grace being ye very flower of ye Euphuists herself. But beholde, these be they yt, having a specialtie, and admiring in it themselves, be jealous when a neighbour doth essaye it, nor can abide it in them long. Wherfore 'twas observable yt ye queene waxed uncontent; and in time a labor'd grandiose speeche out of ye mouthe of Lady Alice, who manifestly did mightily pride herself theron, did quite exhauste ye queenes endurance, who listened till ye gaudie speeche was done, then lifted uppe her brows, and wh vaste ironie, mincing saith, *O shitte!* Wherat they alle did laffe, but not ye Lady Alice, yt olde foolish bitche.

Now was Sr Walter minded of a tale he once did heare ye ingenious Margarette of Navarre relate, about a maide, which being like to suffer rape by an olde archbishoppe, did smartly contrive a device to save her maidenhedde, and said to him, *First, my lord, I prithee, take out thy holy tool and pisse before me;* which doing, lo! his member felle, and wolde not rise again.

SCIENCE OF ONANISM

My gifted predecessor has warned you against the "social evil—adultery." In his able paper he exhausted that subject. He left absolutely nothing more to be said on it. But I will continue his good work in the cause of morality by cautioning you against that species of recreation called self-abuse, to which I perceive that you are too much addicted.

All great writers upon health and morals, both ancient and modern, have struggled with this stately subject. This shows its dignity and importance. Some of these writers have taken one side, some the other.

Homer, in the second book of the *Iliad,* says with fine enthusiasm, "Give me masturbation or give me death!" Caesar, in his *Commentaries,* says, "To the lonely it is company. To the forsaken it is a friend. To the aged and impotent it is a benefactor. They that be penniless are yet rich in that they still have this majestic diversion." In another place this excellent observer has said, "There are times when I prefer it to sodomy."

Robinson Crusoe says, "I cannot describe what I owe to this gentle art." Queen Elizabeth said, "It is the bulwark of virginity." Cetewayo, the Zulu hero, remarked that "a jerk in the hand is worth two in the bush." The immortal Franklin has said, "Masturbation is the mother of invention." He also said, "Masturbation is the best policy."

Michelangelo and all the other Old Masters—Old Masters, I will remark, is an abbreviation, a contraction—have used similar language. Michelangelo said to Pope Julius II, "Self-negation is noble. Self-culture is beneficent. Self-possession is manly. But to the truly great and inspiring soul they are poor and tame compared to self-abuse."

Mr. Brown, here, in one of his latest and most graceful poems refers to it in an eloquent line which is destined to live to the end of time—"None know it but to love it, None name it but to praise."

Such are the utterances of the most illustrious of the masters of this renowned science and apologists for it. The name of those who decry it and oppose it is legion. They have made strong arguments and uttered bitter speeches against it. But there is not room to repeat them here in much detail.

Brigham Young, an expert of incontestable authority, said, "As compared with the other thing, it is the difference between the lightning bug and the lightning."

Solomon said, "There is nothing to recommend it but its cheapness."

Galen said, "It is shameful to degrade to such bestial use that grand limb, that formidable member, which we votaries of science dub the 'Major Maxillary'—when they dub it at all—which is seldom. It would be better to decapitate the Major than to use him so. It would be better to amputate the *os frontis* than to put it to such a use."

The great statistician, Smith, in his report to Parliament says, "In my opinion more children have been wasted in this way than in any other."

It cannot be denied that the high authority of this art entitles it to our respect. But at the same time I think that its harmfulness demands our condemnation. Mr. Darwin was grieved to feel obliged to give up his theory that the monkey was the connecting link between man and the lower animals. I think he was too hasty. The monkey is the only animal except man that practices this science. Hence he is our brother. There is a bond of sympathy and relationship between us. Give this ingenious animal an audience of the proper kind and he will straightaway put aside his other affairs and take a whet. And you will see by the contortions and his ecstatic expression that he takes an intelligent and human interest in his performance.

The signs of excessive indulgence in this destructive pastime are easily detectable. They are these. A disposition to eat, to drink, to smoke, to meet together convivially, to laugh, to joke and tell indelicate stories—and mainly a yearning to paint pictures. The results of the habit are: loss of memory, loss of virility, loss of cheerfulness, loss of hopefulness, loss of character and loss of progeny. Of all the various kinds of sexual intercourse this has least to recommend it.

As an amusement it is too fleeting. As an occupation it is too wearing. As a public exhibition there is no money in it. It is unsuited to the drawing room. And in the most cultured society it has long since been banished from the social board. It has at last, in our day of progress and improvement, been degraded to brotherhood with flatulence. Among the best bred these two arts are now indulged only in private. Though by consent of the whole company, when only males are present, it is still permissible in good society to remove the embargo upon the fundamental sigh.

My illustrious predecessor has taught you that all forms of the "social evil" are bad. I would teach you that some of those forms are more to be avoided than others. So in concluding I say, "If you *must* gamble away your lives sexually, don't play a Lone Hand too much." When you feel a revolutionary uprising in your system get your Vendôme Column down some other way—don't jerk it down.

1879

EXTRACT FROM CAPTAIN STORMFIELD'S VISIT TO HEAVEN

1

Well, when I had been dead about thirty years, I begun to get a little anxious. Mind you, I had been whizzing through space all that time, like a comet. *Like* a comet! Why, Peters, I laid over the lot of them. Of course there warn't any of them going my way, as a steady thing, you know, because they travel in a long circle like the loop of a lasso, whereas I was pointed as straight as a dart for the Hereafter; but I happened on one every now and then that was going my way for an hour or so, and then we had a bit of a brush together. But it was generally pretty one-sided, because I sailed by them the same as if they were standing still. An ordinary comet don't make more than about 200,000 miles a minute. Of course when I came across one of that sort—like Encke's and Halley's comets, for instance—it warn't anything but just a flash and a vanish, you see. You couldn't rightly call it a race. It was as if the comet was a gravel-train and I was a telegraph despatch. But after I got outside of our astronomical system, I used to flush a comet occasionally that was something *like. We* haven't got any such comets—ours don't begin. One night I was swinging along at a good round gait, everything taut and trim, and the wind in my favor—I judged I was going about a million miles a minute—it might have been more, it couldn't have been less—when I flushed a most uncommonly big one about three points off my starboard bow. By his stern lights I judged he was bearing about north-east-and-by-north-half-east. Well, it was so near my course that I wouldn't throw away the chance; so I fell off a point, steadied my helm, and went for him. You should have heard me whiz, and seen the electric fur fly! In about a minute and a half I was fringed out with an electrical nimbus that flamed around for miles and miles and lit up all space like broad day. The comet was burning blue in the distance, like a sickly torch, when I first sighted him, but he begun to grow bigger and bigger as I crept up on him. I slipped up on him so fast that when I had gone about 150,000,000 miles I was close enough to be swallowed up in the phosphorescent glory of his wake, and I couldn't see anything for the glare. Thinks I, it won't do to run into him, so I shunted to one side and tore along. By and by I closed up abreast of his tail. Do you know what it was like? It was like a gnat closing up on the continent of America. I forged along. By and by I had sailed along his coast for a little upwards of a hundred and fifty million miles, and then I could see by the shape of him that I hadn't even got up to his waistband yet. Why, Peters, *we* don't know anything about comets, down here. If you want to see comets that *are* comets, you've got to go outside of our solar system—where there's room for them, you understand. My friend, I've seen comets out there that couldn't even lay down inside the *orbits* of our noblest comets without their tails hanging over.

Well, I boomed along another hundred and fifty million miles, and got up abreast his shoulder, as you may say. I was feeling pretty fine, I tell you; but just then I noticed the officer of the deck come to the side and hoist his glass in my direction. Straight off I heard him sing out—

"Below there, ahoy! Shake her up, shake her up! Heave on a hundred million billion tons of brimstone!"

"Ay—ay, sir!"

"Pipe the starboard watch! All hands on deck!"

"Ay—ay, sir!"

"Send two hundred thousand million men aloft to shake out royals and sky-scrapers!"

"Ay—ay, sir!"

"Hand the stuns'ls! Hang out every rag you've got! Clothe her from stem to rudder-post!"

"Ay—ay, sir!"

In about a second I begun to see I'd woke up a pretty ugly customer, Peters. In less than ten seconds that comet was just a blazing cloud of red-hot canvas. It was piled up into the heavens clean out of sight—the old thing seemed to swell out and occupy all space; the sulphur smoke from the furnaces—oh, well, nobody can describe the way it rolled and tumbled up into the skies, and nobody can half describe the way it smelt. Neither can anybody begin to describe the way that monstrous craft begun to crash along. And such another powwow—thousands of bo's'n's whistles screaming at once, and a crew like the populations of a hundred thousand worlds like ours all swearing at once. Well, I never heard the like of it before.

We roared and thundred along side by side, both doing our level best, because I'd never struck a comet before that could lay over me, and so I was bound to beat this one or break something. I judged I had some reputation in space, and I calculated to keep it. I noticed I wasn't gaining as fast, now, as I was before, but still I was gaining. There was a power of excitement on board the comet. Upwards of a hundred billion passengers swarmed up from below and rushed to the side and begun to bet on the race. Of course this careened her and damaged her speed. My, but wasn't the mate mad! He jumped at that crowd, with his trumpet in his hand, and sung out—

"Amidships! amidships, you——!¹ or I'll brain the last idiot of you!"

Well, sir, I gained and gained, little by little, till at last I went skimming sweetly by the magnificent old conflagration's nose. By this time the captain of the comet had been rousted out, and he stood there in the red glare for'ard, by the mate, in his shirtsleeves and slippers, his hair all rats' nests and one suspender hanging, and how sick those two men did look! I just simply couldn't help putting my thumb to my nose as I glided away and singing out:

"Ta-ta! ta-ta! Any word to send to your family?"

Peters, it was a mistake. Yes, sir, I've often regretted that—it was a mistake. You see, the captain had given up the race, but that remark was too tedious for him—he couldn't stand it. He turned to the mate, and says he—

"Have we got brimstone enough of our own to make the trip?"

"Yes, sir."

"Sure?"

"Yes, sir—more than enough."

"How much have we got in cargo for Satan?"

"Eighteen hundred thousand billion quintillions of kazarks."

"Very well, then, let his boarders freeze till the next comet comes.

¹ The Captain could not remember what this word was. He said it was in a foreign tongue.

Lighten ship! Lively, now, lively, men! Heave the whole cargo overboard!"

Peters, look me in the eye, and be calm. I found out, over there,
that a kazark is exactly the bulk of a *hundred and sixty-nine worlds
like ours!* They hove all that load overboard. When it fell it wiped
out a considerable raft of stars just as clean as if they'd been candles
and somebody blowed them out. As for the race, that was at an end.
The minute she was lightened the comet swung along by me the
same as if I was anchored. The captain stood on the stern, by the
after-davits, and put his thumb to his nose and sung out—

"Ta-ta! ta-ta! Maybe *you've* got some message to send your friends
in the Everlasting Tropics!"

Then he hove up his other suspender and started for'ard, and
inside of three-quarters of an hour his craft was only a pale torch
again in the distance. Yes, it was a mistake, Peters—that remark of
mine. I don't reckon I'll ever get over being sorry about it. I'd 'a'
beat the bully of the firmament if I'd kept my mouth shut.

But I've wandered a little off the track of my tale; I'll get back on
my course again. Now you see what kind of speed I was making. So,
as I said, when I had been tearing along this way about thirty years I
begun to get uneasy. Oh, it was pleasant enough, with a good deal to
find out, but then it was kind of lonesome, you know. Besides, I
wanted to get somewhere. I hadn't shipped with the idea of cruising
forever. First off, I liked the delay, because I judged I was going to
fetch up in pretty warm quarters when I got through; but towards
the last I begun to feel that I'd rather go to—well, most any place, so
as to finish up the uncertainty.

Well, one night—it was always night, except when I was rushing
by some star that was occupying the whole universe with its fire and
its glare—light enough then, of course, but I necessarily left it behind
in a minute or two and plunged into a solid week of darkness again.
The stars ain't so close together as they look to be. Where was I? Oh
yes; one night I was sailing along, when I discovered a tremendous
long row of blinking lights away on the horizon ahead. As I approached, they begun to tower and swell and look like mighty furnaces. Says I to myself—

"By George, I've arrived at last—and at the wrong place, just as I
expected!"

Then I fainted. I don't know how long I was insensible, but it must have been a good while, for, when I came to, the darkness was all gone and there was the loveliest sunshine and the balmiest, fragrantest air in its place. And there was such a marvelous world spread out before me—such a glowing, beautiful, bewitching country. The things I took for furnaces were gates, miles high, made all of flashing jewels, and they pierced a wall of solid gold that you couldn't see the top of, nor yet the end of, in either direction. I was pointed straight for one of these gates, and a-coming like a house afire. Now I noticed that the skies were black with millions of people, pointed for those gates. What a roar they made, rushing through the air! The ground was as thick as ants with people, too—billions of them, I judge.

I lit. I drifted up to a gate with a swarm of people, and when it was my turn the head clerk says, in a businesslike way—

"Well, quick! Where are you from?"

"San Francisco," says I.

"San Fran—*what?*" says he.

"San Francisco."

He scratched his head and looked puzzled, then he says—

"Is it a planet?"

By George, Peters, think of it! *"Planet?"* says I; "it's a city. And moreover, it's one of the biggest and finest and—"

"There, there!" says he, "no time here for conversation. We don't deal in cities here. Where are you from in a *general* way?"

"Oh," I says, "I beg your pardon. Put me down for California."

I had him *again,* Peters! He puzzled a second, then he says, sharp and irritable—

"I don't know any such planet—is it a constellation?"

"Oh, my goodness!" says I. "Constellation, says you? No—it's a State."

"Man, we don't deal in States here. *Will* you tell me where you are from *in general—at large,* don't you understand?"

"Oh, now I get your idea," I says. "I'm from America—the United States of America."

Peters, do you know I had him *again?* If I hadn't I'm a clam! His face was as blank as a target after a militia shooting-match. He turned to an under clerk and says—

"Where is America? *What* is America?"

The under clerk answered up prompt and says—
"There ain't any such orb."

"*Orb?*" says I. "Why, what are you talking about, young man? It ain't an orb; it's a country; it's a continent. Columbus discovered it; I reckon likely you've heard of *him,* anyway. America—why, sir, America—"

"Silence!" says the head clerk. "Once for all, where—are—you—*from?*"

"Well," says I, "I don't know anything more to say—unless I lump things, and just say I'm from the world."

"Ah," says he, brightening up, "now that's something like! *What* world?"

Peters, he had *me,* that time. I looked at him, puzzled, he looked at me, worried. Then he burst out—

"Come, come, what world?"

Says I, "Why, *the* world, of course."

"*The* world!" he says. "H'm! there's billions of them! . . . Next!"

That meant for me to stand aside. I done so, and a sky-blue man with seven heads and only one leg hopped into my place. I took a walk. It just occurred to me, then, that all the myriads I had seen swarming to that gate, up to this time, were just like that creature. I tried to run across somebody I was acquainted with, but they were out of acquaintances of mine just then. So I thought the thing all over and finally sidled back there pretty meek and feeling rather stumped, as you may say.

"Well?" said the head clerk.

"Well, sir," I says, pretty humble, "I don't seem to make out which world it is I'm from. But you may know it from this—it's the one the Saviour saved."

He bent his head at the Name. Then he says, gently—

"The worlds He has saved are like to the gates of heaven in number—none can count them. What astronomical system is your world in?—perhaps that may assist."

"It's the one that has the sun in it—and the moon—and Mars"— he shook his head at each name—hadn't ever heard of them, you see —"and Neptune—and Uranus—and Jupiter—"

"Hold on!" says he—"hold on a minute! Jupiter . . . Jupiter . . . Seems to me we had a man from there eight or nine hundred years ago—but people from that system very seldom enter by this gate." All of a sudden he begun to look me so straight in the eye that I thought he was going to bore through me. Then he says, very deliberate, "Did you come *straight here* from your system?"

"Yes, sir," I says—but I blushed the least little bit in the world when I said it.

He looked at me very stern, and says—

"That is not true; and this is not the place for prevarication. You wandered from your course. How did that happen?"

Says I, blushing again—

"I'm sorry, and I take back what I said, and confess. I raced a little with a comet one day—only just the least little bit—only the tiniest lit—"

"So—so," says he—and without any sugar in his voice to speak of. I went on, and says—

"But I only fell off just a bare point, and I went right back on my course again the minute the race was over."

"No matter—that divergence has made all this trouble. It has brought you to a gate that is billions of leagues from the right one. If you had gone to your own gate they would have known all about your world at once and there would have been no delay. But we will try to accommodate you." He turned to an under clerk and says—

"What system is Jupiter in?"

"I don't remember, sir, but I think there is such a planet in one of the little new systems away out in one of the thinly worlded corners of the universe. I will see."

He got a balloon and sailed up and up and up, in front of a map that was as big as Rhode Island. He went on up till he was out of sight, and by and by he came down and got something to eat and went up again. To cut a long story short, he kept on doing this for a day or two, and finally he came down and said he thought he had found that solar system, but it might be fly-specks. So he got a microscope and went back. It turned out better than he feared. He had rousted out our system, sure enough. He got me to describe our planet and its distance from the sun, and then he says to his chief—

"Oh, I know the one he means, now, sir. It is on the map. It is called the Wart."

Says I to myself, "Young man, it wouldn't be wholesome for you to go down *there* and call it the Wart."

Well, they let me in, then, and told me I was safe forever and wouldn't have any more trouble.

Then they turned from me and went on with their work, the same as if they considered my case all complete and shipshape. I was a good deal surprised at this, but I was diffident about speaking up and reminding them. I did so hate to do it, you know; it seemed a pity to bother them, they had so much on their hands. Twice I thought I would give up and let the thing go; so twice I started to leave, but immediately I thought what a figure I should cut stepping out amongst the redeemed in such a rig, and that made me hang back and come to anchor again. People got to eying me—clerks, you know —wondering why I didn't get under way. I couldn't stand this long —it was too uncomfortable. So at last I plucked up courage and tipped the head clerk a signal. He says—

"What! you here yet? What's wanting?"

Says I, in a low voice and very confidential, making a trumpet with my hands at his ear—

"I beg pardon, and you mustn't mind my reminding you, and seeming to meddle, but hain't you forgot something?"

He studied a second, and says—

"Forgot something? . . . No, not that I know of."

"Think," says I.

He thought. Then he says—

"No, I can't seem to have forgot anything. What is it?"

"Look at me," says I, "look me all over."

He done it.

"Well?" says he.

"Well," says I, "you don't notice anything? If I branched out amongst the elect looking like this, wouldn't I attract considerable attention?—wouldn't I be a little conspicuous?"

"Well," he says, "I don't see anything the matter. What do you lack?"

"Lack! Why, I lack my harp, and my wreath, and my halo, and my hymn-book, and my palm branch—I lack everything that a body naturally requires up here, my friend."

Puzzled? Peters, he was the worst puzzled man you ever saw. Finally he says—

"Well, you seem to be a curiosity every way a body takes you. I never heard of these things before."

I looked at the man awhile in solid astonishment; then I says—

"Now, I hope you don't take it as an offence, for I don't mean any, but really, for a man that has been in the Kingdom as long as I reckon you have, you do seem to know powerful little about its customs."

"Its customs!" says he. "Heaven is a large place, good friend. Large empires have many and diverse customs. Even small dominions have, as you doubtless know by what you have seen of the matter on a small scale in the Wart. How can you imagine I could ever learn the varied customs of the countless kingdoms of heaven? It makes my head ache to think of it. I know the customs that prevail in those portions inhabited by peoples that are appointed to enter by my own gate—and hark ye, that is quite enough knowledge for one individual to try to pack into his head in the thirty-seven millions of years I have devoted night and day to that study. But the idea of learning the customs of the whole appalling expanse of heaven—O man, how insanely you talk! Now I don't doubt that this odd costume you talk about is the fashion in that district of heaven you belong to, but you won't be conspicuous in this section without it."

I felt all right, if that was the case, so I bade him good-day and left. All day I walked towards the far end of the prodigious hall of the office, hoping to come out into heaven any moment, but it was a mistake. That hall was built on the general heavenly plan—it naturally couldn't be small. At last I got so tired I couldn't go any farther; so I sat down to rest, and begun to tackle the queerest sort of strangers and ask for information, but I didn't get any; they couldn't understand my language, and I could not understand theirs. I got dreadfully lonesome. I was so downhearted and homesick I wished a hundred times I never had died. I turned back, of course. About noon next day, I got back at last and was on hand at the booking-office once more. Says I to the head clerk—

"I begin to see that a man's got to be in his own heaven to be happy."

"Perfectly correct," says he. "Did you imagine the same heaven would suit all sorts of men?"

"Well, I had that idea—but I see the foolishness of it. Which way am I to go to get to my district?"

He called the under clerk that had examined the map, and he gave me general directions. I thanked him and started; but he says—

"Wait a minute; it is millions of leagues from here. Go outside and stand on that red wishing-carpet; shut your eyes, hold your breath, and wish yourself there."

"I'm much obliged," says I; "why didn't you dart me through when I first arrived?"

"We have a good deal to think of here; it was your place to think of it and ask for it. Good-by; we probably sha'n't see you in this region for a thousand centuries or so."

"In that case, *o revoor,*" says I.

I hopped onto the carpet and held my breath and shut my eyes and wished I was in the booking-office of my own section. The very next instant a voice I knew sung out in a business kind of a way—

"A harp and a hymn-book, pair of wings and a halo, size 13, for Cap'n Eli Stormfield, of San Francisco!—make him out a clean bill of health, and let him in."

I opened my eyes. Sure enough, it was a Pi Ute Injun I used to know in Tulare County; mighty good fellow—I remembered being at his funeral, which consisted of him being burnt and the other Injuns gauming their faces with his ashes and howling like wild-cats. He was powerful glad to see me, and you may make up your mind I was just as glad to see him, and felt that I was in the right kind of a heaven at last.

Just as far as your eye could reach, there was swarms of clerks, running and bustling around, tricking out thousands of Yanks and Mexicans and English and Arabs, and all sorts of people in their new outfits; and when they gave me my kit and I put on my halo and I took a look in the glass, I could have jumped over a house for joy, I was so happy. "Now *this* is something like!" says I. "Now," says I, "I'm all right—show me a cloud."

Inside of fifteen minutes I was a mile on my way towards the cloud-banks and about a million people along with me. Most of us tried to fly, but some got crippled and nobody made a success of it. So we concluded to walk, for the present, till we had had some wing practice.

We begun to meet swarms of folks who were coming back. Some had harps and nothing else; some had hymn-books and nothing else; some had nothing at all; all of them looked meek and uncomfortable; one young fellow hadn't anything left but his halo, and he was carrying that in his hand; all of a sudden he offered it to me and says—

"Will you hold it for me a minute?"

Then he disappeared in the crowd. I went on. A woman asked me to hold her palm branch, and then *she* disappeared. A girl got me to hold her harp for her, and by George, *she* disappeared; and so on and so on, till I was about loaded down to the guards. Then comes a smiling old gentleman and asked me to hold *his* things. I swabbed off the perspiration and says, pretty tart—

"I'll have to get you to excuse me, my friend—*I* ain't no hat-rack."

About this time I begun to run across piles of those traps, lying in the road. I just quietly dumped my extra cargo along with them. I looked around, and, Peters, that whole nation that was following me were loaded down the same as I'd been. The return crowd had got them to hold their things a minute, you see. They all dumped their loads, too, and we went on.

When I found myself perched on a cloud, with a million other people, I never felt so good in my life. Says I, "Now this is according to the promises; I've been having my doubts, but now I *am* in heaven, sure enough." I gave my palm branch a wave or two, for luck, and then I tautened up my harp-strings and struck in. Well, Peters, you can't imagine anything like the row we made. It was grand to listen to, and made a body thrill all over, but there was considerable many tunes going on at once, and that was a drawback to the harmony, you understand; and then there was a lot of Injun tribes, and they kept up such another war-whooping that they kind of took the tuck out of the music. By and by I quit performing, and judged I'd take a rest. There was quite a nice mild old gentleman sitting next to me, and I noticed he didn't take a hand; I encouraged him, but he said he was naturally bashful, and was afraid to try before so many people. By and by the old gentleman said he never could seem to enjoy music somehow. The fact was, I was beginning to feel the same way; but I didn't say anything. Him and I had a considerable long silence, then, but of course it warn't noticeable in that place. After about sixteen or seventeen hours, during which I played and sung a little, now and then—always the same tune, because I didn't know any other—I laid down my harp and begun to fan myself with my palm branch. Then we both got to sighing pretty regular. Finally, says he—

"Don't you know any tune but the one you've been pegging at all day?"

"Not another blessed one," says I.

"Don't you reckon you could learn another one?" says he.

"Never," says I; "I've tried to, but I couldn't manage it."

"It's a long time to hang to the one—eternity, you know."

"Don't break my heart," says I; "I'm getting low-spirited enough already."

After another long silence, says he—

"Are you glad to be here?"

Says I, "Old man, I'll be frank with you. This *ain't* just as near my idea of bliss as I thought it was going to be, when I used to go to church."

Says he, "What do you say to knocking off and calling it half a day?"

"That's me," says I. "I never wanted to get off watch so bad in my life."

So we started. Millions were coming to the cloud-bank all the time, happy and hosannahing; millions were leaving it all the time, looking mighty quiet, I tell you. We laid for the new-comers, and pretty soon I'd got them to hold all my things a minute, and then I was a free man again and most outrageously happy. Just then I ran across old Sam Bartlett, who had been dead a long time, and stopped to have a talk with him. Says I—

"Now tell me—is this to go on forever? Ain't there anything else for a change?"

Says he—

"I'll set you right on that point very quick. People take the figurative language of the Bible and the allegories for literal, and the first thing they ask for when they get here is a halo and a harp, and so on. Nothing that's harmless and reasonable is refused a body here, if he asks it in the right spirit. So they are outfitted with these things without a word. They go and sing and play just about one day, and that's the last you'll ever see them in the choir. They don't need anybody to tell them that that sort of thing wouldn't make a heaven —at least not a heaven that a sane man could stand a week and remain sane. That cloud-bank is placed where the noise can't disturb the old inhabitants, and so there ain't any harm in letting everybody get up there and cure himself as soon as he comes.

"Now you just remember this—heaven is as blissful and lovely as it can be; but it's just the busiest place you ever heard of. There ain't any idle people here after the first day. Singing hymns and waving palm branches through all eternity is pretty when you hear about it in the pulpit, but it's as poor a way to put in valuable time as a body could contrive. It would just make a heaven of warbling ignoramuses, don't you see? Eternal Rest sounds comforting in the pulpit, too. Well, you try it once, and see how heavy time will hang on your hands. Why, Stormfield, a man like you, that had been active and stirring all his life, would go mad in six months in a heaven where he hadn't anything to do. Heaven is the very last place to come to *rest* in —and don't you be afraid to bet on that!"

Says I—

"Sam, I'm as glad to hear it as I thought I'd be sorry. I'm glad I come, now."

Says he—

"Cap'n, ain't you pretty physically tired?"

Says I—

"Sam, it ain't any name for it! I'm dog-tired."

"Just so—just so. You've earned a good sleep, and you'll get it. You've earned a good appetite, and you'll enjoy your dinner. It's the same here as it is on earth—you've got to earn a thing, square and honest, before you enjoy it. You can't enjoy first and earn afterwards. But there's this difference, here: you can choose your own occupation, and all the powers of heaven will be put forth to help you make a success of it, if you do your level best. The shoemaker on earth that had the soul of a poet in him won't have to make shoes here."

"Now that's all reasonable and right," says I. "Plenty of work, and the kind you hanker after; no more pain, no more suffering—"

"Oh, hold on; there's plenty of pain here—but it don't kill. There's plenty of suffering here, but it don't last. You see, happiness ain't a *thing in itself*—it's only a *contrast* with something that ain't pleasant. That's all it is. There ain't a thing you can mention that is happiness in its own self—it's only so by contrast with the other thing. And so, as soon as the novelty is over and the force of the contrast dulled, it ain't happiness any longer, and you have to get something fresh. Well, there's plenty of pain and suffering in heaven—consequently there's plenty of contrasts, and just no end of happiness."

Says I, "It's the sensiblest heaven I've heard of yet, Sam, though it's about as different from the one I was brought up on as a live princess is different from her own wax figger."

Along in the first months I knocked around about the Kingdom, making friends and looking at the country, and finally settled down in a pretty likely region, to have a rest before taking another start. I went on making acquaintances and gathering up information. I had a good deal of talk with an old bald-headed angel by the name of Sandy McWilliams. He was from somewhere in New Jersey. I went about with him, considerable. We used to lay around, warm afternoons, in the shade of a rock, on some meadow-ground that was pretty high and out of the marshy slush of his cranberry-farm, and there we used to talk about all kinds of things, and smoke pipes. One day, says I—

"About how old might you be, Sandy?"

"Seventy-two."

"I judged so. How long you been in heaven?"

"Twenty-seven years, come Christmas."

"How old was you when you come up?"

"Why, seventy-two, of course."

"You can't mean it!"

"Why can't I mean it?"

"Because, if you was seventy-two then, you are naturally ninety-nine now."

"No, but I ain't. I stay the same age I was when I come."

"Well," says I, "come to think, there's something just here that I want to ask about. Down below, I always had an idea that in heaven we would all be young, and bright, and spry."

"Well, you *can* be young if you want to. You've only got to wish."

"Well, then, why didn't you wish?"

"I did. They all do. You'll try it, some day, like enough; but you'll get tired of the change pretty soon."

"Why?"

"Well, I'll tell you. Now you've always been a sailor; did you ever try some other business?"

"Yes, I tried keeping grocery, once, up in the mines; but I couldn't stand it; it was too dull—no stir, no storm, no life about it; it was like being part dead and part alive, both at the same time. I wanted to be one thing or t'other. I shut up shop pretty quick and went to sea."

"That's it. Grocery people like it, but you couldn't. You see you wasn't used to it. Well, I wasn't used to being young, and I couldn't seem to take any interest in it. I was strong, and handsome, and had curly hair—yes, and wings, too!—gay wings like a butterfly. I went to picnics and dances and parties with the fellows, and tried to carry on and talk nonsense with the girls, but it wasn't any use; I couldn't take to it—fact is, it was an awful bore. What I wanted was early to bed and early to rise, and something to *do;* and when my work was done, I wanted to sit quiet, and smoke and think—not tear around with a parcel of giddy young kids. You can't think what I suffered whilst I was young."

"How long was you young?"

"Only two weeks. That was plenty for me. Laws, I was so lonesome! You see, I was full of the knowledge and experience of seventy-two years; the deepest subject those young folks could strike was only *a-b-c* to me. And to hear them argue—oh, my! it would have been funny, if it hadn't been so pitiful. Well, I was so hungry for the ways and the sober talk I was used to, that I tried to ring in with the old people, but they wouldn't have it. They considered me a conceited young upstart, and gave me the cold shoulder. Two weeks was a-plenty for me. I was glad to get back my bald head again, and my pipe, and my old drowsy reflections in the shade of a rock or a tree."

"Well," says I, "do you mean to say you're going to stand still at seventy-two, forever?"

"I don't know, and I ain't particular. But I ain't going to drop back to twenty-five any more—I know that, mighty well. I know a sight more than I did twenty-seven years ago, and I enjoy learning, all the time, but I don't seem to get any older. That is, bodily—my mind gets older, and stronger, and better seasoned, and more satisfactory."

Says I, "If a man comes here at ninety, don't he ever set himself back?"

"Of course he does. He sets himself back to fourteen; tries it a couple of hours, and feels like a fool; sets himself forward to twenty; it ain't much improvement; tries thirty, fifty, eighty, and finally ninety—finds he is more at home and comfortable at the same old figure he is used to than any other way. Or, if his mind begun to fail him on earth at eighty, that's where he finally sticks up here. He sticks at the place where his mind was last at its best, for there's where his enjoyment is best, and his ways most set and established."

"Does a chap of twenty-five stay always twenty-five, and look it?"

"If he is a fool, yes. But if he is bright, and ambitious and industrious, the knowledge he gains and the experience he has, change his ways and thoughts and likings, and make him find his best pleasure in the company of people above that age; so he allows his body to take on that look of as many added years as he needs to make him comfortable and proper in that sort of society; he lets his body go on taking the look of age, according as he progresses, and by and by he will be bald and wrinkled outside, and wise and deep within."

"Babies the same?"

"Babies the same. Laws, what asses we used to be, on earth, about these things! We said we'd be always young in heaven. We didn't say *how* young—we didn't think of that, perhaps—that is, we didn't all think alike, anyway. When I was a boy of seven, I suppose I thought we'd all be twelve, in heaven; when I was twelve, I suppose I thought we'd all be eighteen or twenty in heaven; when I was forty, I begun to go back; I remember I hoped we'd all be about *thirty* years old in heaven. Neither a man nor a boy ever thinks the age he *has* is exactly the best one—he puts the *right* age a few years older or a few years younger than he is. Then he makes the ideal age the general age of the heavenly people. And he expects everybody to *stick* at that age— stand stock-still—and expects them to enjoy it!— Now just think of the idea of standing still in heaven! Think of a heaven made up entirely of hoop-rolling, marble-playing cubs of seven years!—or of awkward, diffident, sentimental immaturities of nineteen!—or of vigorous people of thirty, healthy-minded, brimming with ambition, but chained hand and foot to that one age and its limitations like so many helpless galley-slaves! Think of the dull sameness of a society made up of people all of one age and one set of looks, habits, tastes and feelings. Think how superior to it earth would be, with its variety of types and faces and ages, and the enlivening attrition of the myriad interests that come into pleasant collision in such a variegated society."

"Look here," says I, "do you know what you're doing?"

"Well, what am I doing?"

"You are making heaven pretty comfortable in one way, but you are playing the mischief with it in another."

"How d'you mean?"

"Well," I says, "take a young mother that's lost her child, and—"

" 'Sh!" he says. "Look!"

It was a woman. Middle-aged, and had grizzled hair. She was walking slow, and her head was bent down, and her wings hanging limp and droopy; and she looked ever so tired, and was crying, poor thing! She passed along by, with her head down, that way, and the tears running down her face, and didn't see us. Then Sandy said, low and gentle, and full of pity:

"*She's* hunting for her child! No, *found* it, I reckon. Lord, how she's changed! But I recognized her in a minute, though it's twenty-seven years since I saw her. A young mother she was, about twenty-two or four, or along there; and blooming and lovely and sweet—oh, just a flower! And all her heart and all her soul was wrapped up in her child, her little girl, two years old. And it died, and she went wild with grief, just wild! Well, the only comfort she had was that she'd see her child again, in heaven—'never more to part,' she said, and kept on saying it over and over, 'never more to part.' And the words made her happy; yes, they did; they made her joyful; and when I was dying, twenty-seven years ago, she told me to find her child the first thing, and say she was coming—'soon, soon, *very* soon, she hoped and believed!' "

"Why, it's pitiful, Sandy."

He didn't say anything for a while, but sat looking at the ground, thinking. Then he says, kind of mournful:

"And now she's come!"

"Well? Go on."

"Stormfield, maybe she hasn't found the child, but *I* think she has. Looks so to me. I've seen cases before. You see, she's kept that child in her head just the same as it was when she jounced it in her arms a little chubby thing. But here it didn't elect to *stay* a child. No, it elected to grow up, which it did. And in these twenty-seven years it has learned all the deep scientific learning there is to learn, and is studying and studying and learning and learning more and more, all the time, and don't give a damn for anything *but* learning; just learning, and discussing gigantic problems with people like herself."

"Well?"

"Stormfield, don't you see? Her mother knows *cranberries,* and how to tend them, and pick them, and put them up, and market them; and not another blamed thing! Her and her daughter can't be any more company for each other *now* than mud turtle and bird o' paradise. Poor thing, she was looking for a baby to jounce; *I* think she's struck a disapp'intment."

"Sandy, what will they do—stay unhappy forever in heaven?"

"No, they'll come together and get adjusted by and by. But not this year, and not next. By and by."

2

I had been having considerable trouble with my wings. The day after I helped the choir I made a dash or two with them, but was not lucky. First off, I flew thirty yards, and then fouled an Irishman and brought him down—brought us both down, in fact. Next, I had a collision with a Bishop—and bowled him down, of course. We had some sharp words, and I felt pretty cheap, to come banging into a grave old person like that, with a million strangers looking on and smiling to themselves.

I saw I hadn't got the hang of the steering, and so couldn't rightly tell where I was going to bring up when I started. I went afoot the rest of the day, and let my wings hang. Early next morning I went to a private place to have some practice. I got up on a pretty high rock, and got a good start, and went swooping down, aiming for a bush a little over three hundred yards off; but I couldn't seem to calculate for the wind, which was about two points abaft my beam. I could see I was going considerable to looard of the bush, so I worked my starboard wing slow and went ahead strong on the port one, but it wouldn't answer; I could see I was going to broach to, so I slowed down on both, and lit. I went back to the rock and took another chance at it. I aimed two or three points to starboard of the bush— yes, more than that—enough so as to make it nearly a head-wind. I done well enough, but made pretty poor time. I could see, plain enough, that on a head-wind, wings was a mistake. I could see that a body could sail pretty close to the wind, but he couldn't go in the wind's eye. I could see that if I wanted to go a-visiting any distance from home, and the wind was ahead, I might have to wait days, maybe, for a change; and I could see, too, that these things could not be any use at all in a gale; if you tried to run before the wind, you would make a mess of it, for there isn't any way to shorten sail—like reefing, you know—you have to take it *all* in—shut your feathers down flat to your sides. That would *land* you, of course. You could lay to, with your head to the wind—that is the best you could do, and right hard work you'd find it, too. If you tried any other game, you would founder, sure.

I judge it was about a couple of weeks or so after this that I dropped old Sandy McWilliams a note one day—it was a Tuesday—and asked him to come over and take his manna and quails with me next day; and the first thing he did when he stepped in was to twinkle his eye in a sly way, and say—

"Well, Cap, what you done with your wings?"

I saw in a minute that there was some sarcasm done up in that rag somewheres, but I never let on. I only says—

"Gone to the wash."

"Yes," he says, in a dry sort of way, "they mostly go to the wash—about this time—I've often noticed it. Fresh angels are powerful neat. When do you look for 'em back?"

"Day after tomorrow," says I.

He winked at me, and smiled.

Says I—

"Sandy, out with it. Come—no secrets among friends. I notice you don't ever wear wings—and plenty others don't. I've been making an ass of myself—is that it?"

"That is about the size of it. But it is no harm. We all do it at first. It's perfectly natural. You see, on earth we jumped to such foolish conclusions as to things up here. In the pictures we always saw the angels with wings on—and that was all right; but we jumped to the conclusion that that was their way of getting around—and that was all wrong. The wings ain't anything but a uniform, that's all. When they are in the field—so to speak—they always wear them; you never see an angel going with a message anywhere without his wings, any more than you would see a military officer presiding at a court-martial without his uniform, or a postman delivering letters, or a policeman walking his beat, in plain clothes. But they ain't to *fly* with! The wings are for show, not for use. Old experienced angels are like officers of the regular army—they dress plain, when they are off duty. New angels are like the militia—never shed the uniform—always fluttering and floundering around in their wings, butting peo-

ple down, flapping here, and there, and everywhere, always imagining they are attracting the admiring eye—well, they just think they
are the very most important people in heaven. And when you see one
of them come sailing around with one wing tipped up and t'other
down, you make up your mind he is saying to himself: 'I wish Mary
Ann in Arkansaw could see me now. I reckon she'd wish she hadn't
shook me.' No, they're just for show, that's all—only just for show."

"I judge you've got it about right, Sandy," says I.

"Why, look at it yourself," says he. "*You* ain't built for wings—no
man is. You know what a grist of years it took you to come here from
the earth—and yet you were booming along faster than any cannon-
ball could go. Suppose you had to fly that distance with your wings
—wouldn't eternity have been over before you got here? Certainly.
Well, angels have to go to the earth every day—millions of them—to
appear in visions to dying children and good people, you know—it's
the heft of their business. They appear with their wings, of course,
because they are on official service, and because the dying persons
wouldn't know they were angels if they hadn't wings—but do you
reckon they fly with them? It stands to reason they don't. The wings
would wear out before they got half-way; even the pinfeathers would
be gone; the wing frames would be as bare as kite sticks before the
paper is pasted on. The distances in heaven are billions of times
greater; angels have to go all over heaven every day; could they do it
with their wings alone? No, indeed; they wear the wings for style, but
they travel any distance in an instant by *wishing*. The wishing-carpet
of the Arabian Nights was a sensible idea—but our earthly idea of
angels flying these awful distances with their clumsy wings was foolish.

"Our young saints, of both sexes, wear wings all the time—blazing
red ones, and blue and green, and gold, and variegated, and
rainbowed, and ring-streaked-and-striped ones—and nobody finds
fault. It is suitable to their time of life. The things are beautiful, and
they set the young people off. They are the most striking and lovely
part of their outfit—a halo don't *begin*."

"Well," says I, "I've tucked mine away in the cupboard, and I
allow to let them lay there till there's mud."

"Yes—or a reception."

"What's that?"

"Well, you can see one tonight if you want to. There's a barkeeper from Jersey City going to be received."

"Go on—tell me about it."

"This barkeeper got converted at a Moody and Sankey meeting, in New York, and started home on the ferryboat, and there was a collision and he got drowned. He is of a class that thinks all heaven goes wild with joy when a particularly hard lot like him is saved; they think all heaven turns out hosannahing to welcome them; they think there isn't anything talked about in the realms of the blest but their case, for that day. This barkeeper thinks there hasn't been such another stir here in years, as his coming is going to raise.— And I've always noticed this peculiarity about a dead barkeeper—he not only expects all hands to turn out when he arrives, but he expects to be received with a torchlight procession."

"I reckon he is disappointed, then."

"No, he isn't. No man is allowed to be disappointed here. Whatever he wants, when he comes—that is, any reasonable and unsacrilegious thing—he can have. There's always a few millions or billions of young folks around who don't want any better entertainment than to fill up their lungs and swarm out with their torches and have a high time over a barkeeper. It tickles the barkeeper till he can't rest, it makes a charming lark for the young folks, it don't do anybody any harm, it don't cost a rap, and it keeps up the place's reputation for making all comers happy and content."

"Very good. I'll be on hand and see them land the barkeeper."

"It is manners to go in full dress. You want to wear your wings, you know, and your other things."

"Which ones?"

"Halo, and harp, and palm branch, and all that."

"Well," says I, "I reckon I ought to be ashamed of myself, but the fact is I left them laying around that day I resigned from the choir. I haven't got a rag to wear but this robe and the wings."

"That's all right. You'll find they've been raked up and saved for you. Send for them."

"I'll do it, Sandy. But what was it you was saying about unsacrilegious things, which people expect to get, and will be disappointed about?"

"Oh, there are a lot of such things that people expect and don't get. For instance, there's a Brooklyn preacher by the name of Talmage, who is laying up a considerable disappointment for himself. He says, every now and then in his sermons, that the first thing he does when he gets to heaven, will be to fling his arms around Abraham, Isaac and Jacob, and kiss them and weep on them. There's millions of people down there on earth that are promising themselves the same thing. As many as sixty thousand people arrive here every single day, that want to run straight to Abraham, Isaac and Jacob, and hug them and weep on them. Now mind you, sixty thousand a day is a pretty heavy contract for those old people. If they were a mind to allow it, they wouldn't ever have anything to do, year in and year out, but stand up and be hugged and wept on thirty-two hours in the twenty-four. They would be tired out and as wet as muskrats all the time. What would heaven be, to *them?* It would be a mighty good place to get out of—you know that, yourself. Those are kind and gentle old Jews, but they ain't any fonder of kissing the emotional high-lights of Brooklyn than you be. You mark my words, Mr. T.'s endearments are going to be declined, with thanks. There are limits to the privileges of the elect, even in heaven. Why, if Adam was to show himself to every new comer that wants to call and gaze at him and strike him for his autograph, he would never have time to do anything else but just that. Talmage has said he is going to give Adam some of his attentions, as well as A., I. and J. But he will have to change his mind about that."

"Do you think Talmage will really come here?"

"Why, certainly, he will; but don't you be alarmed; he will run with his own kind, and there's plenty of them. That is the main charm of heaven—there's all kinds here—which wouldn't be the case if you let the preachers tell it. Anybody can find the sort he prefers, here, and he just lets the others alone, and they let him alone. When the Deity builds a heaven, it is built right, and on a liberal plan."

Sandy sent home for his things, and I sent for mine, and about nine in the evening we begun to dress. Sandy says—

"This is going to be a grand time for you, Stormy. Like as not some of the patriarchs will turn out."

"No, but will they?"

"Like as not. Of course they are pretty exclusive. They hardly ever show themselves to the common public. I believe they never turn out except for an eleventh-hour convert. They wouldn't do it then, only earthly tradition makes a grand show pretty necessary on that kind of an occasion."

"Do they all turn out, Sandy?"

"Who?—all the patriarchs? Oh, no—hardly ever more than a couple. You will be here fifty thousand years—maybe more—before you get a glimpse of all the patriarchs and prophets. Since I have been here, Job has been to the front once, and once Ham and Jeremiah both at the same time. But the finest thing that has happened in my day was a year or so ago; that was Charles Peace's reception—him they called 'the Bannercross Murderer'—an Englishman. There were four patriarchs and two prophets on the Grand Stand that time— there hasn't been anything like it since Captain Kidd came; Abel was there—the first time in twelve hundred years. A report got around that Adam was coming; well, of course, Abel was enough to bring a crowd, all by himself, but there is nobody that can draw like Adam. It was a false report, but it got around, anyway, as I say, and it will be a long day before I see the like of it again. The reception was in the English department, of course, which is eight hundred and eleven million miles from the New Jersey line. I went, along with a good many of my neighbors, and it was a sight to see, I can tell you. Flocks came from all the departments. I saw Esquimaux there, and Tartars, Negroes, Chinamen—people from everywhere. You see a mixture like that in the Grand Choir, the first day you land here, but you hardly ever see it again. There were billions of people; when they were singing or hosannahing, the noise was wonderful; and even when their tongues were still the drumming of the wings was nearly enough to burst your head, for all the sky was as thick as if it was snowing angels. Although Adam was not there, it was a great time anyway, because we had three archangels on the Grand Stand—it is a seldom thing that even one comes out."

"What did they look like, Sandy?"

"Well, they had shining faces, and shining robes, and wonderful rainbow wings, and they stood eighteen feet high, and wore swords, and held their heads up in a noble way, and looked like soldiers."

"Did they have halos?"

"No—anyway, not the hoop kind. The archangels and the upper-class patriarchs wear a finer thing than that. It is a round, solid, splendid glory of gold, that is blinding to look at. You have often seen a patriarch in a picture, on earth, with that thing on—you remember it?—he looks as if he had his head in a brass platter. That don't give you the right idea of it at all—it is much more shining and beautiful."

"Did you talk with those archangels and patriarchs, Sandy?"

"Who—*I?* Why, what can you be thinking about, Stormy? I ain't worthy to speak to such as they."

"Is Talmage?"

"Of course not. You have got the same mixed-up idea about these things that everybody had down there. I had it once, but I got over it. Down there they talk of the heavenly King—and that is right—but then they go right on speaking as if this was a republic and everybody was on a dead level with everybody else, and privileged to fling his arms around anybody he comes across, and be hail-fellow-well-met with all the elect, from the highest down. How tangled up and absurd that is! How are you going to have a republic under a king? How are you going to have a republic at all, where the head of the government is absolute, holds his place forever, and has no parliament, no council to meddle or make in his affairs, nobody voted for, nobody elected, nobody in the whole universe with a voice in the government, nobody asked to take a hand in its matters, and nobody *allowed* to do it? Fine republic, ain't it?"

"Well, yes—it *is* a little different from the idea I had—but I thought I might go around and get acquainted with the grandees, anyway—not exactly splice the main-brace with them, you know, but shake hands and pass the time of day."

"Could Tom, Dick and Harry call on the Cabinet of Russia and do that?—on Prince Gortschakoff, for instance?"

"I reckon not, Sandy."

"Well, this is Russia—only more so. There's not the shadow of a republic about it anywhere. There are ranks, here. There are viceroys, princes, governors, sub-governors, sub-sub-governors, and a hundred orders of nobility, grading along down from grand-ducal archangels, stage by stage, till the general level is struck, where there ain't any titles. Do you know what a prince of the blood is, on earth?"

"No."

"Well, a prince of the blood don't belong to the royal family exactly, and he don't belong to the mere nobility of the kingdom; he is lower than the one, and higher than t'other. That's about the position of the patriarchs and prophets here. There's some mighty high nobility here—people that you and I ain't worthy to polish sandals for—and *they* ain't worthy to polish sandals for the patriarchs and prophets. That gives you a kind of an idea of their rank, don't it? You begin to see how high up they are, don't you? Just to get a two-minute glimpse of one of them is a thing for a body to remember and tell about for a thousand years. Why, Captain, just think of this: if Abraham was to set his foot down here by this door, there would be a railing set up around that foot-track right away, and a shelter put over it, and people would flock here from all over heaven, for hundreds and hundreds of years, to look at it. Abraham is one of the parties that Mr. Talmage, of Brooklyn, is going to embrace, and kiss, and weep on, when he comes. He wants to lay in a good stock of tears, you know, or five to one he will go dry before he gets a chance to do it."

"Sandy," says I, "I had an idea that *I* was going to be equal with everybody here, too, but I will let that drop. It don't matter, and I am plenty happy enough anyway."

"Captain, you are happier than you would be, the other way. These old patriarchs and prophets have got ages the start of you; they know more in two minutes than you know in a year. Did you ever try to have a sociable improving-time discussing winds, and currents and variations of compass with an undertaker?"

"I get your idea, Sandy. He couldn't interest me. He would be an ignoramus in such things—he would bore me, and I would bore him."

"You have got it. You would bore the patriarchs when you talked, and when they talked they would shoot over your head. By and by you would say, 'Good morning, your Eminence, I will call again'— but you wouldn't. Did you ever ask the slush-boy to come up in the cabin and take dinner with you?"

"I get your drift again, Sandy. I wouldn't be used to such grand people as the patriarchs and prophets, and I would be sheepish and tongue-tied in their company, and mighty glad to get out of it. Sandy, which is the highest rank, patriarch or prophet?"

"Oh, the prophets hold over the patriarchs. The newest prophet, even, is of a sight more consequence than the oldest patriarch. Yes, sir, Adam himself has to walk behind Shakespeare."

"Was Shakespeare a prophet?"

"Of course he was; and so was Homer, and heaps more. But Shakespeare and the rest have to walk behind a common tailor from Tennessee, by the name of Billings; and behind a horse-doctor named Sakka, from Afghanistan. Jeremiah, and Billings and Buddha walk together, side by side, right behind a crowd from planets not in our astronomy; next come a dozen or two from Jupiter and other worlds; next come Daniel, and Sakka and Confucius; next a lot from systems outside of ours; next come Ezekiel, and Mahomet, Zoroaster, and a knife-grinder from ancient Egypt; then there is a long string, and after them, away down toward the bottom, come Shakespeare and Homer, and a shoemaker named Marais, from the back settlements of France."

"Have they really rung in Mahomet and all those other heathens?"

"Yes—they all had their message, and they all get their reward. The man who don't get his reward on earth, needn't bother—he will get it here, sure."

"But why did they throw off on Shakespeare, that way, and put him away down there below those shoemakers and horse-doctors and knife-grinders—a lot of people nobody ever heard of?"

"That is the heavenly justice of it—they warn't rewarded according to their deserts, on earth, but here they get their rightful rank. That tailor Billings, from Tennessee, wrote poetry that Homer and Shakespeare couldn't begin to come up to; but nobody would print it, nobody read it but his neighbors, an ignorant lot, and they laughed at it. Whenever the village had a drunken frolic and a dance, they would drag him in and crown him with cabbage leaves, and pretend to bow down to him; and one night when he was sick and nearly starved to death, they had him out and crowned him, and then they rode him on a rail about the village, and everybody followed along, beating tin pans and yelling. Well, he died before morning. He wasn't ever expecting to go to heaven, much less that there was going to be any fuss made over him, so I reckon he was a good deal surprised when the reception broke on him."

"Was you there, Sandy?"

"Bless you, no!"

"Why? Didn't you know it was going to come off?"

"Well, I judge I did. It was the talk of these realms—not for a day, like this barkeeper business, but for twenty years before the man died."

"Why the mischief didn't you go, then?"

"Now how you talk! The like of me go meddling around at the reception of a prophet? A mudsill like me trying to push in and help receive an awful grandee like Edward J. Billings? Why, I should have been laughed at for a billion miles around. I shouldn't ever heard the last of it."

"Well, who did go, then?"

"Mighty few people that you and I will ever get a chance to see, Captain. Not a solitary commoner ever has the luck to see a reception of a prophet, I can tell you. All the nobility, and all the patriarchs and prophets—every last one of them—and all the archangels, and all the princes and governors and viceroys, were there and *no* small fry—not a single one. And mind you, I'm not talking about only the grandees from *our* world, but the princes and patriarchs and so on from *all* the worlds that shine in our sky, and from billions more that belong in systems upon systems away outside of the one our sun is in. There were some prophets and patriarchs there that ours ain't a circumstance to, for rank and illustriousness and all that. Some were from Jupiter and other worlds in our own system, but the most celebrated were three poets, Saa, Bo and Soof, from great planets in three different and very remote systems. These three names are common and familiar in every nook and corner of heaven, clear from one end of it to the other—fully as well known as the eighty Supreme Archangels, in fact—whereas our Moses, and Adam, and the rest, have not been heard of outside of our world's little corner of heaven, except by a few very learned men scattered here and there—and they always spell their names wrong, and get the performances of one mixed up with the doings of another, and they almost always locate them simply *in our solar system,* and think that is enough without going into little details such as naming the particular world they are from. It is like a learned Hindoo showing off how much he knows by saying Longfellow lived in the United States—as if he lived all over the United States, and as if the country was so small you couldn't throw a brick there without hitting him. Between you and me, it does gravel me, the cool way people from those monster worlds outside our system snub our little world, and even our system. Of course we think a good deal of Jupiter, because our world is only a potato to it, for size; but then there are worlds in other systems that Jupiter isn't even a mustard-seed to—like the planet Goobra, for instance, which you couldn't squeeze inside the orbit of Halley's comet without straining the rivets. Tourists from Goobra (I mean parties that lived and died there—natives) come here, now and then, and inquire about our world, and when they find out it is so little that a streak of lightning can flash clear around it in the eighth of a second, they have to lean up against something to laugh. Then they screw a glass into their eye and go to examining *us,* as if we were a curious kind of foreign bug, or something of that sort. One of them asked me how long our day was; and when I told him it was twelve hours long, as a general thing, he asked me if people where I was from considered it worth while to get up and wash for such a day as that. That is the way with those Goobra people—they can't seem to let a chance go by to throw it in your face that their day is three hundred and twenty-two of our years long. This young snob was just of age—he was six or seven thousands of his days old—say two million of our years—and he had all the puppy airs that belong to that time of life —that turning-point when a person has got over being a boy and yet ain't quite a man exactly. If it had been anywhere else but in heaven, I would have given him a piece of my mind. Well, anyway, Billings had the grandest reception that has been seen in thousands of centuries, and I think it will have a good effect. His name will be carried pretty far, and it will make our system talked about, and maybe our world, too, and raise us in the respect of the general public of heaven. Why, look here—Shakespeare walked backwards before that tailor from Tennessee, and scattered flowers for him to walk on, and Homer stood behind his chair and waited on him at the banquet. Of course that didn't go for much *there,* amongst all those big foreigners from other systems, as they hadn't heard of Shakespeare or Homer either, but it would amount to considerable down there on our little earth if they could know about it. I wish there was something *in* that miserable spiritualism, so we could send them word. That Tennessee village would set up a monument to Billings, then, and his autograph would outsell Satan's. Well, they had grand times at that reception— a small-fry noble from Hoboken told me all about it—Sir Richard Duffer, Baronet."

"What, Sandy, a nobleman from Hoboken? How is that?"

"Easy enough. Duffer kept a sausage-shop and never saved a cent in his life because he used to give all his spare meat to the poor, in a quiet way. Not tramps—no, the other sort—the sort that will starve before they will beg—honest square people out of work. Dick used to watch hungry-looking men and women and children, and track them home, and find out all about them from the neighbors, and then feed them and find them work. As nobody ever *saw* him give anything to anybody, he had the reputation of being mean; he died with it, too, and everybody said it was a good riddance; but the minute he landed here, they made him a baronet, and the very first words Dick the sausage-maker of Hoboken heard when he stepped upon the heavenly shore were, 'Welcome, Sir Richard Duffer!' It surprised him some, because he thought he had reasons to believe he was pointed for a warmer climate than this one."

All of a sudden the whole region fairly rocked under the crash of eleven hundred and one thunder blasts, all let off at once, and Sandy says—

"There, that's for the barkeep."

I jumped up and says—

"Then let's be moving along, Sandy; we don't want to miss any of this thing, you know."

"Keep your seat," he says; "he is only just telegraphed, that is all."

"How?"

"That blast only means that he has been sighted from the signal station. He is off Sandy Hook. The committees will go down to meet him, now, and escort him in. There will be ceremonies and delays; they won't be coming up the Bay for a considerable time, yet. It is several billion miles away, anyway."

"*I* could have been a barkeeper and a hard lot just as well as not," says I, remembering the lonesome way I arrived, and how there wasn't any committee nor anything.

"I notice some regret in your voice," says Sandy, "and it is natural enough; but let bygones be bygones; you went according to your lights, and it is too late now to mend the thing."

"No, let it slide, Sandy, I don't mind. But you've got a Sandy Hook *here*, too, have you?"

"We've got everything here, just as it is below. All the States and Territories of the Union, and all the kingdoms of the earth and the islands of the sea are laid out here just as they are on the globe—all the same shape they are down there, and all graded to the relative size, only each State and realm and island is a good many billion times bigger here than it is below. There goes another blast."

"What is that one for?"

"That is only another fort answering the first one. They each fire eleven hundred and one thunder blasts at a single dash—it is the usual salute for an eleventh-hour guest; a hundred for each hour and an extra one for the guest's sex; if it was a woman we would know it by their leaving off the extra gun."

"How do we know there's eleven hundred and one, Sandy, when they all go off at once?—and yet we certainly do know."

"Our intellects are a good deal sharpened up, here, in some ways, and that is one of them. Numbers and sizes and distances are so great, here, that we have to be made so we can *feel* them—our old ways of counting and measuring and ciphering wouldn't ever give us an idea of them, but would only confuse and oppress us and make our heads ache."

After some more talk about this, I says: "Sandy, I notice that I hardly ever see a white angel; where I run across one white angel, I strike as many as a hundred million copper-colored ones—people that can't speak English. How is that?"

"Well, you will find it the same in any State or Territory of the American corner of heaven you choose to go to. I have shot along, a whole week on a stretch, and gone millions and millions of miles, through perfect swarms of angels, without ever seeing a single white one, or hearing a word I could understand. You see, America was occupied a billion years and more, by Injuns and Aztecs, and that sort of folks, before a white man ever set his foot in it. During the first three hundred years after Columbus's discovery, there wasn't ever more than one good lecture audience of white people, all put together, in America—I mean the whole thing, British Possessions and all; in the beginning of our century there were only 6,000,000 or 7,000,000—say seven; 12,000,000 or 14,000,000 in 1825; say 23,000,000 in 1850; 40,000,000 in 1875. Our death-rate has always been 20 in 1000 per annum. Well, 140,000 died the first year of the century; 280,000 the twenty-fifth year; 500,000 the fiftieth year; about a million the seventy-fifth year. Now I am going to be liberal about this thing, and consider that fifty million whites have died in America from the beginning up to today—make it sixty, if you want to; make it a hundred million—it's no difference about a few millions

one way or t'other. Well, now, you can see, yourself, that when you
come to spread a little dab of people like that over these hundreds of
billions of miles of American territory here in heaven, it is like scattering a ten-cent box of homoeopathic pills over the Great Sahara
and expecting to find them again. You can't expect us to amount to
anything in heaven, and we *don't*—now that is the simple fact, and
we have got to do the best we can with it. The learned men from
other planets and other systems come here and hang around a while,
when they are touring around the Kingdom, and then go back to
their own section of heaven and write a book of travels, and they give
America about five lines in it. And what do they say about us? They
say this wilderness is populated with a scattering few hundred thousand billions of red angels, with now and then a curiously com-
plected *diseased* one. You see, they think we whites and the occasional nigger are Injuns that have been bleached out or blackened by
some leprous disease or other—for some peculiarly rascally *sin*, mind
you. It is a mighty sour pill for us all, my friend—even the modestest
of us, let alone the other kind, that think they are going to be received like a long-lost government bond, and hug Abraham into the
bargain. I haven't asked you any of the particulars, Captain, but I
judge it goes without saying—if my experience is worth anything—
that there wasn't much of a hooraw made over you when you arrived
—now was there?"

"Don't mention it, Sandy," says I, coloring up a little; "I wouldn't
have had the family see it for any amount you are a mind to name.
Change the subject, Sandy, change the subject."

"Well, do you think of settling in the California department of
bliss?"

"I don't know. I wasn't calculating on doing anything really definite in that direction till the family come. I thought I would just look
around, meantime, in a quiet way, and make up my mind. Besides, I
know a good many dead people, and I was calculating to hunt them
up and swap a little gossip with them about friends, and old times,
and one thing or another, and ask them how they like it here, as far
as they have got. I reckon my wife will want to camp in the California range, though, because most all her departed will be there, and
she likes to be with folks she knows."

"Don't you let her. You see what the Jersey district of heaven is,
for whites; well, the California district is a thousand times worse. It

swarms with a mean kind of leather-headed mud-colored angels—
and your nearest white neighbors is likely to be a million miles away.
What a man mostly misses, in heaven, is company—company of his
own sort and color and language. I have come near settling in the
European part of heaven once or twice on that account."

"Well, why didn't you, Sandy?"

"Oh, various reasons. For one thing, although you *see* plenty of
whites there, you can't understand any of them hardly, and so you
go about as hungry for talk as you do here. I like to look at a Russian
or a German or an Italian—I even like to look at a Frenchman if I
ever have the luck to catch him engaged in anything that ain't indelicate—but *looking* don't cure the hunger—what you want is talk."

"Well, there's England, Sandy—the English district of heaven."

"Yes, but it is not so very much better than this end of the heavenly domain. As long as you run across Englishmen born this side of
three hundred years ago, you are all right; but the minute you get
back of Elizabeth's time the language begins to fog up, and the further back you go the foggier it gets. I had some talk with one Lang-
land and a man by the name of Chaucer—old-time poets—but it was
no use, I couldn't quite understand them and they couldn't quite
understand me. I have had letters from them since, but it is such
broken English I can't make it out. Back of those men's time the
English are just simply foreigners, nothing more, nothing less; they
talk Danish, German, Norman French, and sometimes a mixture of
all three; back of *them*, they talk Latin, and ancient British, Irish,
and Gaelic; and then back of these come billions and billions of pure
savages that talk a gibberish that Satan himself couldn't understand.
The fact is, where you strike one man in the English settlements that
you can understand, you wade through awful swarms that talk something you can't make head nor tail of. You see, every country on
earth has been overlaid so often, in the course of a billion years, with
different kinds of people and different sorts of languages, that this
sort of mongrel business was bound to be the result in heaven."

"Sandy," says I, "did you see a good many of the great people
history tells about?"

"Yes—plenty. I saw kings and all sorts of distinguished people."

"Do the kings rank just as they did below?"

"No; a body can't bring his rank up here with him. Divine right is
a good-enough earthly romance, but it don't go, here. Kings drop

down to the general level as soon as they reach the realms of grace. I knew Charles the Second very well—one of the most popular comedians in the English section—draws first rate. There are better, of course—people that were never heard of on earth—but Charles is making a very good reputation indeed, and is considered a rising man. Richard the Lion-hearted is in the prize-ring, and coming into considerable favor. Henry the Eighth is a tragedian, and the scenes where he kills people are done to the very life. Henry the Sixth keeps a religious-book stand."

"Did you ever see Napoleon, Sandy?"

"Often—sometimes in the Corsican range, sometimes in the French. He always hunts up a conspicuous place, and goes frowning around with his arms folded and his field-glass under his arm, looking as grand, gloomy and peculiar as his reputation calls for, and very much bothered because he don't stand as high, here, for a soldier, as he expected to."

"Why, who stands higher?"

"Oh, a *lot* of people *we* never heard of before—the shoemaker and horse-doctor and knife-grinder kind, you know—clodhoppers from goodness knows where, that never handled a sword or fired a shot in their lives—but the soldiership was in them, though they never had a chance to show it. But here they take their right place, and Caesar and Napoleon and Alexander have to take a back seat. The greatest military genius our world ever produced was a bricklayer from somewhere back of Boston—died during the Revolution—by the name of Absalom Jones. Wherever he goes, crowds flock to see him. You see, everybody knows that if he had had a chance he would have shown the world some generalship that would have made all generalship before look like child's play and 'prentice work. But he never got a chance; he tried heaps of times to enlist as a private, but he had lost both thumbs and a couple of front teeth, and the recruiting sergeant wouldn't pass him. However, as I say, everybody knows, now, what he *would* have been, and so they flock by the million to get a glimpse of him whenever they hear he is going to be anywhere. Caesar, and Hannibal, and Alexander, and Napoleon are all on his staff, and ever so many more great generals; but the public hardly care to look at *them* when *he* is around. Boom! There goes another salute. The barkeeper's off quarantine now."

Sandy and I put on our things. Then we made a wish, and in a second we were at the reception-place. We stood on the edge of the ocean of space, and looked out over the dimness, but couldn't make out anything. Close by us was the Grand Stand—tier on tier of dim thrones rising up toward the zenith. From each side of it spread away the tiers of seats for the general public. They spread away for leagues and leagues—you couldn't see the ends. They were empty and still, and hadn't a cheerful look, but looked dreary, like a theater before anybody comes—gas turned down. Sandy says—

"We'll sit down here and wait. We'll see the head of the procession come in sight away off yonder pretty soon, now."

Says I—

"It's pretty lonesome, Sandy; I reckon there's a hitch somewheres. Nobody but just you and me—it ain't much of a display for the barkeeper."

"Don't you fret, it's all right. There'll be one more gun-fire—then you'll see."

In a little while we noticed a sort of lightish flush, away off on the horizon.

"Head of the torchlight procession," says Sandy.

It spread, and got lighter and brighter; soon it had a strong glare like a locomotive headlight; it kept on getting brighter and brighter till it was like the sun peeping above the horizon-line at sea—the big red rays shot high up into the sky.

"Keep your eyes on the Grand Stand and the miles of seats—sharp!" says Sandy, "and listen for the gun-fire."

Just then it burst out, "Boom-boom-boom!" like a million thunderstorms in one, and made the whole heavens rock. Then there was a sudden and awful glare of light all about us, and in that very instant every one of the millions of seats was occupied, and as far as you could see, in both directions, was just a solid pack of people, and the place was all splendidly lit up! It was enough to take a body's breath away. Sandy says—

"That is the way we do it here. No time fooled away; nobody straggling in after the curtain's up. Wishing is quicker work than traveling. A quarter of a second ago these folks were millions of miles from here. When they heard the last signal, all they had to do was to wish, and here they are."

The prodigious choir struck up—

> *We long to hear thy voice,*
> *To see thee face to face.*

It was noble music, but the uneducated chipped in and spoilt it, just as the congregations used to do on earth.

The head of the procession begun to pass, now, and it was a wonderful sight. It swept along, thick and solid, five hundred thousand angels abreast, and every angel carrying a torch and singing—the whirring thunder of the wings made a body's head ache. You could follow the line of the procession back, and slanting upward into the sky, far away in a glittering snaky rope, till it was only a faint streak in the distance. The rush went on and on, for a long time, and at last, sure enough, along comes the barkeeper, and then everybody rose, and a cheer went up that made the heavens shake, I tell you! He was all smiles, and had his halo tilted over one ear in a cocky way, and was the most satisfied-looking saint I ever saw. While he marched up the steps of the Grand Stand, the choir struck up—

> *The whole wide heaven groans,*
> *And waits to hear that voice.*

There were four gorgeous tents standing side by side in the place of honor, on a broad railed platform in the center of the Grand Stand, with a shining guard of honor round about them. The tents had been shut up all this time. As the barkeeper climbed along up, bowing and smiling to everybody, and at last got to the platform, these tents were jerked up aloft all of a sudden, and we saw four noble thrones of gold, all caked with jewels, and in the two middle ones sat old white-whiskered men, and in the two others a couple of the most glorious and gaudy giants, with platter halos and beautiful armor. All the millions went down on their knees, and stared, and looked glad, and burst out into a joyful kind of murmurs. They said—

"Two archangels!—that is splendid. Who can the others be?"

The archangels gave the barkeeper a stiff little military bow; the two old men rose; one of them said, "Moses and Esau welcome thee!" and then all the four vanished, and the thrones were empty.

The barkeeper looked a little disappointed, for he was calculating to hug those old people, I judge; but it was the gladdest and proudest multitude you ever saw—because they had seen Moses and Esau.

Everybody was saying, "Did you see them?—I did—Esau's side face was to me, but I saw Moses full in the face, just as plain as I see you this minute!"

The procession took up the barkeeper and moved on with him again, and the crowd broke up and scattered. As we went along home, Sandy said it was a great success, and the barkeeper would have a right to be proud of it forever. And he said *we* were in luck, too; said we might attend receptions for forty thousand years to come, and not have a chance to see a brace of such grand moguls as Moses and Esau. We found afterwards that we had come near seeing another patriarch, and likewise a genuine prophet besides, but at the last moment they sent regrets. Sandy said there would be a monument put up there, where Moses and Esau had stood, with the date and circumstances, and all about the whole business, and travelers would come for thousands of years and gawk at it, and climb over it, and scribble their names on it.

1907

OPEN LETTER TO
COMMODORE VANDERBILT[1]

How my heart goes out in sympathy to you! how I do pity you, Commodore Vanderbilt! Most men have at least a few friends, whose devotion is a comfort and a solace to them, but you seem to be the idol of only a crawling swarm of small souls, who love to glorify your most flagrant unworthinesses in print; or praise your vast possessions worshippingly; or sing of your unimportant private habits and sayings and doings, as if your millions gave them dignity; friends who applaud your superhuman stinginess with the same gusto that they do your most magnificent displays of commercial genius and daring, and likewise your most lawless violations of commercial honor—for these infatuated worshippers of dollars not their own seem to make no distinctions, but swing their hats and shout hallelujah every time you do *anything*, no matter what it is. I do pity you. I would pity any man with such friends as these.

I should think you would hate the sight of a newspaper. I should think you would not dare to glance at one, for fear you would find in it one of these distressing eulogies of something you had been doing, which was either infinitely trivial or else a matter you ought to be ashamed of. Unacquainted with you as I am, my honest compassion for you still gives me a right to speak in this way.

Now, have you ever thought calmly over your newspaper reputation? Have you ever dissected it, to see what it was made of? It would interest you. One day one of your subjects comes out with a column or two detailing your rise from penury to affluence, and praising you as if you were the last and noblest work of God, but unconsciously telling how exquisitely mean a man has to be in order

[1] Mark Twain had a remarkable gift of invective, which he liberally displayed in his *Autobiography*, written in his later years. The present essay is a brilliant early example. —C.N.

to achieve what you have achieved. Then another subject tells how you drive in the Park, with your scornful head down, never deigning to look to the right or the left, and make glad the thousands who covet a glance of your eye, but driving straight ahead, heedlessly and recklessly, taking the road by force, with a bearing which plainly says, "Let these people get out of the way if they can; but if they can't, and I run over them, and kill them, no matter, I'll pay for them." And then how the retailer of the pleasant anecdote does grovel in the dust and glorify you, Vanderbilt!

Next, a subject of yours prints a long article to show how, in some shrewd, underhanded way, you have "come it" over the public with some Erie dodge or other, and added another million or so to your greasy greenbacks; and behold! *he* praises you, and never hints that immoral practices, in so prominent a place as you occupy, are a damning example to the rising commercial generation—more, a damning thing to the whole nation, while there are insects like your subjects to make virtues of them in print. Next, a subject tells a most laughable joke in *Harpers* of how a lady laid a wager of a pair of gloves that she could touch your heart with the needs of some noble public charity, which unselfish people were building up for the succoring of the helpless and the unfortunate, and so persuade you to spare a generous billow to it from your broad ocean of wealth, and how you listened to the story of want and suffering, and then—then what?—gave the lady a paltry dollar (the act in itself an insult to your sister or mine, coming from a stranger) and said, "Tell your opponent you have won the gloves." And, having told his little anecdote, how your loving subject did shake his sides at the bare idea of *your* having generosity enough to be persuaded by any tender womanly pleader into giving a manly lift to any helpless creature under the sun! What precious friends you do have, Vanderbilt!

And next, a subject tells how when you owned the California line of steamers you used to have your pursers make out false lists of passengers, and thus carry some hundreds more than the law allowed—in this way breaking the laws of your country and jeopardizing the lives of your passengers by overcrowding them during a long, sweltering voyage over tropical seas, and through a disease-poisoned atmosphere. And this shrewdness was duly glorified too.

But I remember how those misused passengers used to revile you and curse you when they got to the Isthmus—and especially the women and young girls, who were forced to sleep on your steerage floors, side by side with strange men, who were the offscourings of creation, and even in the steerage beds with them, if the poor wretches told the truth; and I do assure you that nobody who lived in California at that time disbelieved them—O, praised and envied Vanderbilt! These women were nothing to you and me; but if they had been, we might have been shamed and angered at this treatment, mightn't we? We cannot rightly judge of matters like these till we sit down and try to fancy these women related to us by ties of blood and affection, but *then* the rare joke of it melts away, and the indignant tides go surging through our veins, poor little Commodore!

There are other anecdotes told of you by your glorifying subjects, but let us pass them by, they only damage you. They only show how unfortunate and how narrowing a thing it is for a man to have wealth who makes a god of it instead of a servant. They only show how soulless it can make him—like that pretty anecdote that tells how a young lawyer charged you $500 for a service, and how you deemed the charge too high, and so went shrewdly to work and won his confidence, and persuaded him to borrow money and put it in Erie, when you knew the stock was going down, and so held him in the trap till he was a ruined man, and then you were revenged; and you gloated over it; and, as usual, your admiring friends told the story in print, and lauded you to the skies. No, let us drop the anecdotes. I don't remember ever reading anything about you which you oughtn't be ashamed of.

All I wish to urge upon you now is, that you crush out your native instincts and go and do something *worthy* of praise—go and do something you need not blush to see in print—do something that may rouse one solitary good impulse in the breasts of your horde of worshippers; prove one solitary good example to the thousands of young men who emulate your energy and your industry; shine as one solitary grain of pure gold upon the heaped rubbish of your life. Do this, I beseech you, else through your example we shall shortly have in our midst five hundred Vanderbilts, which God forbid! Go, now please go, and do one worthy act. Go, boldly, grandly, nobly, and give four dollars to some great public charity. It will break your heart, no doubt; but no matter, you have but a little while to live, and it is better to die suddenly and nobly than live a century longer the same Vanderbilt you are now. Do this, and I declare *I* will praise you too.

Poor Vanderbilt. How I do pity you; and this is honest. You are an old man, and ought to have some rest; and yet you have to struggle and struggle, and deny yourself, and rob yourself of restful sleep and peace of mind, because you need money so badly. I always feel for a man who is so poverty ridden as you. Don't misunderstand me, Vanderbilt. I know you own seventy millions; but then you know and I know that it isn't what a man has that constitutes wealth. No—it is to be *satisfied* with what one has; that is wealth. As long as one sorely *needs* a certain additional amount, that man isn't rich. Seventy times seventy millions can't make him rich as long as his poor heart is breaking for more. I am just about rich enough to buy the least valuable horse in your stable, perhaps, but I cannot sincerely and honestly take an oath that I need any more now. And so I am rich. But you! you have got seventy millions, and you *need* five hundred millions, and are really suffering for it. Your poverty is something appalling. I tell you truly that I do not believe I could live twenty-four hours with the awful weight of four hundred and thirty millions of abject want crushing down upon me. I should die under it. My soul is so wrought upon by your hapless pauperism, that if you came by me now I would freely put ten cents in your tin cup, if you carry one, and say, "God pity you, poor unfortunate!"

Now, I pray you take kindly all that I have said, Vanderbilt, for I assure you I have meant it kindly, and it is said in an honester spirit than you are accustomed to find in what is said to you or about you. And *do* go, now, and do something that isn't shameful. Do go and do something worthy of a man possessed of seventy millions—a man whose most trifling act is remembered and imitated all over the country by younger men than you.

Do not be deceived into the notion that everything you do and say is wonderful, simply because those asses who publish you so much make it appear so. Do not deceive yourself. Very often an idea of yours is possessed of no innate magnificence, but is simply shining with the reflected splendor of your seventy millions. Now, think of it. I have tried to imitate you and become famous; all the young men do it; but, bless you, my performances attracted no attention. I gave a crippled beggar girl a two-cent piece and humorously told her to go to the Fifth Avenue Hotel and board a week; but nobody published it. If you had done that it would have been regarded as one of the funniest things that ever happened; because you *can* say the flattest things that ever I heard of, Vanderbilt, and have them magnified into wit and wisdom in the papers. And the other day, in Chicago, I talked of buying the entire Union Pacific Railroad, clear to the Rocky Mountains, and running it on my own hook. It was as splendid an idea and as bold an enterprise as ever entered that over-praised brain of yours, but did it excite any newspaper applause? No. If you had conceived it, though, the newspaper world would have gone wild over it.

No, sir; other men think and talk as brilliantly as you do, but they don't do it in the glare of seventy millions; so pray do not be deceived by the laudation you receive; more of it belongs to your millions than to you. I say this to warn you against becoming vainglorious on a false basis, and an unsound one—for if your millions were to pass from you you might be surprised and grieved to notice what flat and uncelebrated things you were capable of saying and doing forever afterwards.

You observe that I don't say anything about your soul, Vanderbilt. It is because I have evidence that you haven't any. It would be impossible to convince me that a man of your matchless financial ability would overlook so dazzling an "operation," if you had a soul to save, as the purchasing of millions of years of Paradise, and rest, and peace, and pleasure, for so trifling a sum as ten years blamelessly lived on earth—for you probably haven't longer than that to live now, you know, you are very old. Well, I don't know, after all, possibly you *have* got a soul. But I know you, Vanderbilt—I know you well. You will try to get the purchase cheaper. You will want those millions of years of rest and pleasure, and you will try to make the trade and get the superb stock; but you will wait till you are on your death-bed, and then offer *an hour and forty minutes* for it. I know you so well, Vanderbilt! Still worse men than you do this. The people we hang always send for a priest at the last moment.

I assure you, Vanderbilt, that I mean what I am saying for your good—not to make you mad. Why, the way you are going on, you are no better than those Astors. No, I won't say that; for it is better to be a mean *live* man than a stick—even a gold-headed stick. And now my lesson is done. It is bound to refresh you and make you feel good; for you must necessarily get sick of puling flattery and sycophancy sometimes, and sigh for a paragraph of honest criticism and abuse for a change.

And in parting, I say that, surely, standing as you do upon the pinnacle of moneyed magnificence in America you must certainly feel a vague desire in you sometimes to do some splendid deed in the interest of commercial probity, or of human charity, or of manly honor and dignity, that shall flash into instant celebrity over the whole nation, and be rehearsed to ambitious boys by their mothers a century after you are dead. I say you must feel so sometimes, for it is only natural, and therefore I urge you to congeal that thought into an act.

Go and surprise the whole country by doing something right. Cease to do and say unworthy things, and excessively *little* things, for those reptile friends of yours to magnify in the papers. Snub them thus, or else throttle them.

Yours truly,

Mark Twain

1869

GOLDSMITH'S FRIEND
ABROAD AGAIN

NOTE.—No experience is set down in the following letters which had to be invented. Fancy is not needed to give variety to the history of a Chinaman's sojourn in America. Plain fact is amply sufficient.—M.T.

Letter 1

Shanghai, 18—

Dear Ching-Foo:

It is all settled, and I am to leave my oppressed and overburdened native land and cross the sea to that noble realm where all are free and all equal, and none reviled or abused—America! America, whose precious privilege it is to call herself the Land of the Free and the Home of the Brave. We and all that are about us here look over the waves longingly, contrasting the privations of this our birthplace with the opulent comfort of that happy refuge. We know how America has welcomed the Germans and the Frenchmen and the stricken and sorrowing Irish, and we know how she has given them bread and work and liberty, and how grateful they are. And we know that America stands ready to welcome all other oppressed peoples and offer her abundance to all that come, without asking what their nationality is, or their creed or color. And, without being told it, we know that the foreign sufferers she has rescued from oppression and starvation are the most eager of her children to welcome us, because, having suffered themselves, they know what suffering is, and having been generously succored, they long to be generous to other unfortunates and thus show that magnanimity is not wasted upon them.

Ah Song Hi

Letter 2

At Sea, 18—

Dear Ching-Foo:

We are far away at sea now, on our way to the beautiful Land of the Free and Home of the Brave. We shall soon be where all men are alike, and where sorrow is not known.

The good American who hired me to go to his country is to pay me $12 a month, which is immense wages, you know—twenty times as much as one gets in China. My passage in the ship is a very large sum—indeed, it is a fortune—and this I must pay myself eventually, but I am allowed ample time to make it good to my employer in, he advancing it now. For a mere form, I have turned over my wife, my boy, and my two daughters to my employer's partner for security for the payment of the ship fare. But my employer says they are in no danger of being sold, for he knows I will be faithful to him, and that is the main security.

I thought I would have twelve dollars to begin life with in America, but the American Consul took two of them for making a certificate that I was shipped on the steamer. He has no right to do more than charge the ship two dollars for *one* certificate for the *ship*, with the number of her Chinese passengers set down in it; but he chooses to force a certificate upon each and every Chinaman and put the two dollars in his pocket. As 1300 of my countrymen are in this vessel, the Consul received $2600 for certificates. My employer tells me that the Government at Washington know of this fraud, and are so bitterly opposed to the existence of such a wrong that they tried hard to have the extor——the fee, I mean, legalized by the last Congress,[1] but as the bill did not pass, the Consul will have to take the fee dishonestly until next Congress makes it legitimate. It is a great and good and noble country, and hates all forms of vice and chicanery.

We are in that part of the vessel always reserved for my countrymen. It is called the steerage. It is kept for us, my employer says, because it is not subject to changes of temperature and dangerous drafts of air. It is only another instance of the loving and unselfish-

[1] Pacific and Mediterranean steamship bills.—M.T

ness of the Americans for all unfortunate foreigners. The steerage is a little crowded, and rather warm and close, but no doubt it is best for us that it should be so.

Yesterday our people got to quarrelling among themselves, and the captain turned a volume of hot steam upon a mass of them and scalded eighty or ninety of them more or less severely. Flakes and ribbons of skin came off some of them. There was wild shrieking and struggling while the vapor enveloped the great throng, and so some who were not scalded got trampled upon and hurt. We do not complain, for my employer says this is the usual way of quieting disturbances on board the ship, and that it is done in the cabins among the Americans every day or two.

Congratulate me, Ching-Foo! In ten days more I shall step upon the shore of America, and be received by her great-hearted people; and I shall straighten myself up and feel that I am a free man among freemen.

                                                                    Ah Song Hi

Letter 3

San Francisco, 18——

Dear Ching-Foo:

I stepped ashore jubilant! I wanted to dance, shout, sing, worship the generous Land of the Free and Home of the Brave. But as I walked from the gang-plank a man in a gray uniform[2] kicked me violently behind and told me to look out—so my employer translated it. As I turned, another officer of the same kind struck me with a short club and also instructed me to look out. I was about to take hold of my end of the pole which had mine and Hong-Wo's basket and things suspended from it, when a third officer hit me with his club to signify that I was to drop it, and then kicked me to signify that he was satisfied with my promptness. Another person came now, and searched all through our basket and bundles, emptying everything out on the dirty wharf. Then this person and another

[2] Policeman.—M.T.

searched us all over. They found a little package of opium sewed into the artificial part of Hong-Wo's queue, and they took that, and also they made him prisoner and handed him over to an officer, who marched him away. They took his luggage, too, because of his crime, and as our luggage was so mixed together that they could not tell mine from his, they took it all. When I offered to help divide it, they kicked me and desired me to look out.

Having now no baggage and no companion, I told my employer that if he was willing, I would walk about a little and see the city and the people until he needed me. I did not like to seem disappointed with my reception in the good land of refuge for the oppressed, and so I looked and spoke as cheerily as I could. But he said, wait a minute—I must be vaccinated to prevent my taking the small-pox. I smiled and said I had already had the small-pox, as he could see by the marks, and so I need not wait to be "vaccinated," as he called it. But he said it was the law, and I must be vaccinated anyhow. The doctor would never let me pass, for the law obliged him to vaccinate all Chinamen and charge them *ten dollars apiece* for it, and I might be sure that no doctor who would be the servant of that law would let a fee slip through his fingers to accommodate any absurd fool who had seen fit to have the disease in some other country. And presently the doctor came and did his work and took my last penny —my ten dollars which were the hard savings of nearly a year and a half of labor and privation. Ah, if the law-makers had only known there were plenty of doctors in the city glad of a chance to vaccinate people for a dollar or two, they would never have put the price up so high against poor friendless Irish, or Italian, or Chinese pauper flee-ing to the good land to escape hunger and hard times.

                                                            Ah Song Hi

Letter 4

San Francisco, 18—

Dear Ching-Foo:

I have been here about a month now, and am learning a little of the language every day. My employer was disappointed in the matter of hiring us out to service on the plantations in the far eastern portion of this continent. His enterprise was a failure, and so he set us all free, merely taking measures to secure to himself the repayment of the passage money which he paid for us. We are to make this good to him out of the first moneys we earn here. He says it is sixty dollars apiece.

We were thus set free about two weeks after we reached here. We had been massed together in some small houses up to that time, waiting. I walked forth to seek my fortune. I was to begin life a stranger in a strange land, without a friend, or a penny, or any clothes but those I had on my back. I had not any advantage on my side in the world—not one, except good health and the lack of any necessity to waste any time or anxiety on the watching of my baggage. No, I forget. I reflected that I had one prodigious advantage over paupers in other lands—I was in America! I was in the heaven-provided refuge of the oppressed and the forsaken!

Just as that comforting thought passed through my mind, some young men set a fierce dog on me. I tried to defend myself, but could do nothing. I retreated to the recess of a closed doorway, and there the dog had me at his mercy, flying at my throat and face or any part of my body that presented itself. I shrieked for help, but the young men only jeered and laughed. Two men in gray uniforms (policemen is their official title) looked on for a minute and then walked leisurely away. But a man stopped them and brought them back and told them it was a shame to leave me in such distress. Then the two policemen beat off the dog with small clubs, and a comfort it was to be rid of him, though I was just rags and blood from head to foot. The man who brought the policemen asked the young men why they abused me in that way, and they said they didn't want any of his meddling. And they said to him:

"This Ching divil comes till Ameriky to take the bread out o' dacent intilligent white men's mouths, and whin they try to defind their rights there's a dale o' fuss made about it."

They began to threaten my benefactor, and as he saw no friendliness in the faces that had gathered meanwhile, he went on his way. He got many a curse when he was gone. The policmen now told me I was under arrest and must go with them. I asked one of them what wrong I had done to any one that I should be arrested, and he only struck me with his club and ordered me to "hold my yop." With a jeering crowd of street boys and loafers at my heels, I was taken up an alley and into a stone-paved dungeon which had large cells all down one side of it, with iron gates to them. I stood up by a desk while a man behind it wrote down certain things about me on a slate. One of my captors said:

"Enter a charge against this Chinaman of being disorderly and disturbing the peace."

I attempted to say a word, but he said:

"Silence! Now ye had better go slow, my good fellow. This is two or three times you've tried to get off some of your damned insolence. Lip won't do here. You've *got* to simmer down, and if you don't take to it paceable we'll see if we can't make you. Fat's your name?"

"Ah Song Hi."

"*Alias* what?"

I said I did not understand, and he said what he wanted was my *true* name, for he guessed I picked up this one since I stole my last chickens. They all laughed loudly at that.

Then they searched me. They found nothing, of course. They seemed very angry and asked who I supposed would "go my bail or pay my fine." When they explained these things to me, I said I had done nobody any harm, and why should I need to have bail or pay a fine? Both of them kicked me and warned me that I would find it to my advantage to try and be as civil as convenient. I protested that I had not meant anything disrespectful. Then one of them took me to one side and said:

"Now look here, Johnny, it's no use you playing softy wid us. We mane business, ye know; and the sooner ye put us on the scent of a

V, the asier ye'll save yerself from a dale of trouble. Ye can't get out o' this for anny less. Who's your frinds?"

I told him I had not a single friend in all the land of America, and that I was far from home and help, and very poor. And I begged him to let me go.

He gathered the slack of my blouse collar in his grip and jerked and shoved and hauled at me across the dungeon, and then unlocking an iron cell-gate thrust me in with a kick and said:

"Rot there, ye furrin spawn, till ye lairn that there's no room in America for the likes of ye or your nation."

Ah Song Hi

Letter 5

San Francisco, 18—

Dear Ching-Foo:

You will remember that I had just been thrust violently into a cell in the city prison when I wrote last. I stumbled and fell on some one. I got a blow and a curse; and on top of these a kick or two and a shove. In a second or two it was plain that I was in a nest of prisoners and was being "passed around"—for the instant I was knocked out of the way of one I fell on the head or heels of another and was promptly ejected, only to land on a third prisoner and get a new contribution of kicks and curses and a new destination. I brought up at last in an unoccupied corner, very much battered and bruised and sore, but glad enough to be let alone for a little while. I was on the flag-stones, for there was no furniture in the den except a long, broad board, or combination of boards, like a barn door, and this bed was accommodating five or six persons, and that was its full capacity. They lay stretched side by side, snoring—when not fighting. One end of the board was four inches higher than the other, and so the slant answered for a pillow. There were no blankets, and the night was a little chilly; the nights are always a little chilly in San Francisco, though never severely cold. The board was a deal more comfortable than the stones, and occasionally some flag-stone plebeian like me

would try to creep to a place on it; and then the aristocrats would
hammer him good and make him think a flag pavement was a nice
enough place after all.

I lay quiet in my corner, stroking my bruises and listening to the
revelations the prisoners made to each other—and to me—for some
that were near me talked to me a good deal. I had long had an idea
that Americans, being free, had no need of prisons, which are a
contrivance of despots for keeping restless patriots out of mischief.
So I was considerable surprised to find out my mistake.

Ours was a big general cell, it seemed, for the temporary accom-
modation of all comers whose crimes were trifling. Among us there
were two Americans, two "Greasers" (Mexicans), a Frenchman, a
German, four Irishmen, a Chilenean (and, in the next cell, only separated from us by a grating, two women), all drunk, and all more or
less noisy; and as night fell and advanced, they grew more and more
discontented and disorderly, occasionally shaking the prison bars
and glaring through them at the slowly pacing officer, and cursing
him with all their hearts.

The two women were nearly middle-aged, and they had only had
enough liquor to stimulate instead of stupefy them. Consequently
they would fondle and kiss each other for some minutes, and then
fall to fighting and keep it up till they were just two grotesque tangles
of rags and blood and tumbled hair. Then they would rest awhile,
and pant and swear. While they were affectionate they always spoke
of each other as "ladies," but while they were fighting "strumpet"
was the mildest name they could think of—and they could only
make that do by tacking some sounding profanity to it.

In their last fight, which was toward midnight, one of them bit off
the other's finger, and then the officer interfered and put the
"Greaser" into the "dark cell" to answer for it—because the woman
that did it laid it on him, and the other woman did not deny it
because, as she said afterward, she "wanted another crack at the
huzzy when her finger quit hurting," and so she did not want her
removed. By this time those two women had mutilated each other's
clothes to that extent that there was not sufficient left to cover their
nakedness.

I found that one of these creatures had spent nine years in the
county jail, and that the other one had spent about four or five years
in the same place. They had done it from choice. As soon as they

were discharged from captivity they would go straight and get drunk, and then steal some trifling thing while an officer was observing them. That would entitle them to another two months in jail, and there they would occupy clean, airy apartments, and have good food in plenty, and being at no expense at all, they could make shirts for the clothiers at half a dollar apiece and thus keep themselves in smoking tobacco and such other luxuries as they wanted. When the two months were up, they would go just as straight as they could walk to Mother Leonard's and get drunk; and from there to Kearny Street and steal something; and thence to this city prison, and next day back to the old quarters in the county jail again. One of them had really kept this up for nine years and the other four or five, and both said they meant to end their days in that prison.[1]

Finally, both these creatures fell upon me while I was dozing with my head against their grating, and battered me considerably, because they discovered that I was a Chinaman, and they said I was "a bloody interlopin' loafer come from the divil's own country to take the bread out of dacent people's mouths and put down the wages for work whin it was all a Christian could do to kape body and sowl together as it was." "Loafer" means one who will not work.

Ah Song Hi

Letter 6

San Francisco, 18—

Dear Ching-Foo:

To continue—the two women became reconciled to each other again through the common bond of interest and sympathy created between them by pounding me in partnership, and when they had finished me they fell to embracing each other again and swearing more eternal affection like that which had subsisted between them all the evening, barring occasional interruptions. They agreed to swear the finger-biting on the Greaser in open court, and get him sent to the penitentiary for the crime of mayhem.

[1] The former of the two did.—M.T.

Another of our company was a boy of fourteen who had been watched for some time by officers and teachers, and repeatedly detected in enticing young girls from the public schools to the lodgings of gentlemen down town. He had been furnished with lures in the form of pictures and books of a peculiar kind, and these he had distributed among his clients. There were likenesses of fifteen of these young girls on exhibition (only to prominent citizens and persons in authority, it was said, though most people came to get a sight) at the police headquarters, but no punishment at all was to be inflicted on the poor little misses. The boy was afterward sent into captivity at the House of Correction for some months, and there was a strong disposition to punish the gentlemen who had employed the boy to entice the girls, but as that could not be done without making public the names of those gentlemen and thus injuring them socially, the idea was finally given up.

There was also in our cell that night a photographer (a kind of artist who makes likenesses of people with a machine), who had been for some time patching the pictured heads of well-known and respectable young ladies to the nude, pictured bodies of another class of women; then from this patched creation he would make photographs and sell them privately at high prices to rowdies and blackguards, averring that these, the best young ladies of the city, had hired him to take their likenesses in that unclad condition. What a lecture the police judge read that photographer when he was convicted! He told him his crime was little less than an outrage. He abused that photographer till he almost made him sink through the floor, and then he fined him a hundred dollars. And he told him he might consider himself lucky that he didn't fine him a hundred and twenty-five dollars. They are awfully severe on crime here.

About two or two and a half hours after midnight, of that first experience of mine in the city prison, such of us as were dozing were awakened by a noise of beating and dragging and groaning, and in a little while a man was pushed into our den with a "There, damn you, soak there a spell!"—and then the gate was closed and the officers went away again. The man who was thrust among us fell limp and helpless by the grating, but as nobody could reach him with a kick without the trouble of hitching along toward him or getting fairly up to deliver it, our people only grumbled at him, and cursed him, and called him insulting names—for misery and hardship do not make

their victims gentle or charitable toward each other. But as he neither tried humbly to conciliate our people nor swore back at them,
his unnatural conduct created surprise, and several of the party
crawled to him where he lay in the dim light that came through the
grating, and examined into his case. His head was very bloody and
his wits were gone. After about an hour, he sat up and stared around;
then his eyes grew more natural and he began to tell how that he was
going along with a bag on his shoulder and a brace of policemen
ordered him to stop, which he did not do—was chased and caught,
beaten ferociously about the head on the way to the prison and after
arrival there, and finally thrown into our den like a dog. And in a
few seconds he sank down again and grew flighty of speech. One of
our people was at last penetrated with something vaguely akin to
compassion, may be, for he looked out through the gratings at the
guardian officer pacing to and fro, and said:

"Say, Mickey, this shrimp's goin' to die."

"Stop your noise!" was all the answer he got. But presently our
man tried it again. He drew himself to the gratings, grasping them
with his hands, and looking out through them, sat waiting till the
officer was passing once more, and then said:

"Sweetness, you'd better mind your eye, now, because you beats
have killed this cuss. You've busted his head and he'll pass in his
checks before sun-up. You better go for a doctor, now, you bet you
had."

The officer delivered a sudden rap on our man's knuckles with his
club, that sent him scampering and howling among the sleeping
forms on the flag-stones, and an answering burst of laughter came
from the half dozen policemen idling about the railed desk in the
middle of the dungeon.

But there was a putting of heads together out there presently, and
a conversing in low voices, which seemd to show that our man's talk
had made an impression; and presently an officer went away in a
hurry, and shortly came back with a person who entered our cell and
felt the bruised man's pulse and threw the glare of a lantern on his
drawn face, striped with blood, and his glassy eyes, fixed and vacant.
The doctor examined the man's broken head also, and presently said:

"If you'd called me an hour ago I might have saved this man, may
be—too late now."

Then he walked out into the dungeon and the officers surrounded him, and they kept up a low and earnest buzzing of conversation for fifteen minutes, I should think, and then the doctor took his departure from the prison. Several of the officers now came in and worked a little with the wounded man, but toward daylight he died.

It was the longest, longest night! And when the daylight came filtering reluctantly into the dungeon at last, it was the grayest, dreariest, saddest daylight! And yet, when an officer by and by turned off the sickly yellow gas flame, and immediately the gray of dawn became fresh and white, there was a lifting of my spirits that acknowledged and believed that the night *was* gone, and straightway I fell to stretching my sore limbs, and looking about me with a grateful sense of relief and a returning interest in life. About me lay the evidences that what seemed now a feverish dream and a nightmare was the memory of a reality instead. For on the boards lay four frowsy, ragged, bearded vagabonds, snoring—one turned end-for-end and resting an unclean foot, in a ruined stocking, on the hairy breast of a neighbor; the young boy was uneasy, and lay moaning in his sleep; other forms lay half revealed and half concealed about the floor; in the furthest corner the gray light fell upon a sheet, whose elevations and depressions indicated the places of the dead man's face and feet and folded hands; and through the dividing bars one could discern the almost nude forms of the two exiles from the county jail twined together in a drunken embrace, and sodden with sleep.

By and by all the animals in all the cages awoke, and stretched themselves, and exchanged a few cuffs and curses, and then began to clamor for breakfast. Breakfast was brought in at last—bread and beefsteak on tin plates, and black coffee in tin cups, and no grabbing allowed. And after several dreary hours of waiting, after this, we were all marched out into the dungeon and joined there by all manner of vagrants and vagabonds, of all shades and colors and nationalities, from the other cells and cages of the place; and pretty soon our whole menagerie was marched upstairs and locked fast behind a high railing in a dirty room with a dirty audience in it. And this audience stared at us, and at a man seated on high behind what they call a pulpit in this country, and at some clerks and other officials seated below him—and waited. This was the police court.

The court opened. Pretty soon I was compelled to notice that a culprit's nationality made for or against him in this court. Overwhelming proofs were necessary to convict an Irishman of crime, and even then his punishment amounted to little; Frenchmen, Spaniards, and Italians had strict and unprejudiced justice meted out to them, in exact accordance with the evidence; negroes were promptly punished, when there was the slightest preponderance of testimony against them; but Chinamen were punished *always,* apparently. Now this gave me some uneasiness, I confess. I knew that this state of things must of necessity be accidental, because in this country all men were free and equal, and one person could not take to himself an advantage not accorded to all other individuals. I knew that, and yet in spite of it I was uneasy.

And I grew still more uneasy when I found that any succored and befriended refugee from Ireland or elsewhere could stand up before that judge and swear away the life or liberty or character of a refugee from China; but that by the law of the land *the Chinaman could not testify against the Irishman.* I was really and truly uneasy, but still my faith in the universal liberty that America accords and defends, and my deep veneration for the land that offered all distressed outcasts a home and protection, was strong within me, and I said to myself that it would all come out right yet.

Ah Song Hi

Letter 7

San Francisco, 18—

Dear Ching-Foo:

I was glad enough when my case came up. An hour's experience had made me as tired of the police court as of the dungeon. I was not uneasy about the result of the trial, but on the contrary felt that as soon as the large auditory of Americans present should hear how that the rowdies had set the dogs on me when I was going peacefully along the street, and how, when I was all torn and bleeding, the officers arrested *me* and put me in jail and let the rowdies go free, the gallant hatred of oppression which is part of the very flesh and blood of every American would be stirred to its utmost, and I should be instantly set at liberty. In truth I began to fear for the other side. There in full view stood the ruffians who had misused me, and I began to fear that in the first burst of generous anger occasioned by the revealment of what they had done, they might be harshly handled, and possibly even banished the country as having dishonored her and being no longer worthy to remain upon her sacred soil.

The official interpreter of the court asked my name, and then spoke it aloud so that all could hear. Supposing that all was now ready, I cleared my throat and began—in Chinese, because of my imperfect English:

"Hear, O high and mighty mandarin, and believe! As I went about my peaceful business in the street, behold certain men set a dog on me, and——"

"Silence!"

It was the judge that spoke. The interpreter whispered to me that I must keep perfectly still. He said that no statement would be received from me—I must only talk through my lawyer.

I had no lawyer. In the early morning a police lawyer (termed, in the higher circles of society, a "shyster") had come into our den in the prison and offered his services to me, but I had been obliged to go without them because I could not pay in advance or give security. I told the interpreter how the matter stood. He said I must take my chances on the witnesses then. I glanced around, and my failing confidence revived.

"Call those four Chinamen yonder," I said. "They saw it all. I remember their faces perfectly. They will prove that the white men set the dog on me when I was not harming them."

"That won't work," said he. "In this country white men can testify against Chinamen all they want to, but *Chinamen ain't allowed to testify against white men!*"

What a chill went through me! And then I felt the indignant blood rise to my cheek at this libel upon the Home of the Oppressed, where all men are free and equal—perfectly equal—perfectly free and perfectly equal. I despised this Chinese-speaking Spaniard for his mean slander of the land that was sheltering and feeding him. I sorely wanted to sear his eyes with that sentence from the great and good American Declaration of Independence which we have copied in letters of gold in China and keep hung up over our family altars and in our temples—I mean the one about all men being created free and equal.

But woe is me, Ching-Foo, the man was right. He was right, after all. There were my witnesses, but I could not use them. But now came a new hope. I saw my white friend come in, and I felt that he had come there purposely to help me. I may almost say I knew it. So I grew easier. He passed near enough to me to say under his breath, "Don't be afraid," and then I had no more fear. But presently the rowdies recognized him and began to scowl at him in no friendly way, and to make threatening signs at him. The two officers that arrested me fixed their eyes steadily on his; he bore it well, but gave in presently, and dropped his eyes. They still gazed at his eyebrows, and every time he raised his eyes he encountered their winkless stare —until after a minute or two he ceased to lift his head at all. The judge had been giving some instructions privately to some one for a little while, but now he was ready to resume business. Then the trial so unspeakably important to me, and freighted with such prodigious consequence to my wife and children, began, progressed, ended, was recorded in the books, noted down by the newspaper reporters, and *forgotten* by everybody but me—all in the little space of two minutes!

"Ah Song Hi, Chinaman. Officers O'Flannigan and O'Flaherty, witnesses. Come forward, Officer O'Flannigan."

OFFICER—"He was making a disturbance in Kearny Street."

JUDGE—"Any witnesses on the other side?"

No response. The white friend raised his eyes—encountered Officer O'Flaherty's—blushed a little—got up and left the courtroom, avoiding all glances and not taking his own from the floor.

JUDGE—"Give him five dollars or ten days."

In my desolation there was a glad surprise in the words; but it passed away when I found that he only meant that I was to be fined five dollars or imprisoned ten days longer in default of it.

There were twelve or fifteen Chinamen in our crowd of prisoners, charged with all manner of little thefts and misdemeanors, and their cases were quickly disposed of, as a general thing. When the charge came from a policeman or other white man, he made his statement and that was the end of it, unless the Chinaman's lawyer could find some white person to testify in his client's behalf; for, neither the accused Chinaman nor his countrymen being allowed to say anything, the statement of the officers or other white person was amply sufficient to convict. So, as I said, the Chinamen's cases were quickly disposed of, and fines and imprisonment promptly distributed among them. In one or two of the cases the charges against Chinamen were brought by Chinamen themselves, and in those cases Chinamen testified against Chinamen, through the interpreter; but the fixed rule of the court being that the *preponderance* of testimony in such cases should determine the prisoner's guilt or innocence, and there being nothing very binding about an oath administered to the lower orders of our people without the ancient solemnity of cutting off a chicken's head and burning some yellow paper at the same time, the interested parties naturally drum up a cloud of witnesses who are cheerfully willing to give evidence without ever knowing anything about the matter in hand. The judge has a custom of rattling through with as much of this testimony as his patience will stand, and then shutting off the rest and striking an average.

By noon all the business of the court was finished, and then several of us who had not fared well were remanded to prison; the judge went home; the lawyers, and officers, and spectators departed their several ways, and left the uncomely court-room to silence, solitude, and Stiggers, the newspaper reporter, which latter would now write up his items (said an ancient Chinaman to me), in which he would praise all the policemen indiscriminately and abuse the Chinamen and dead people.

Ah Song Hi
1870–71

THE INDIGNITY
PUT UPON THE REMAINS
OF GEORGE HOLLAND
BY THE REV. MR. SABINE

What a ludicrous satire it was upon Christian charity!—even upon the vague, theoretical idea of it which doubtless this small saint mouths from his own pulpit every Sunday. Contemplate this freak of Nature, and think what a Cardiff giant of self-righteousness is crowded into his pigmy skin. If we probe, and dissect, and lay open this diseased, this cancerous piety of his, we are forced to the conviction that it is the production of an impression on his part that his guild do about all the good that is done in the earth, and hence are better than common clay—hence are competent to say to such as George Holland, "You are unworthy; you are a play-actor, and consequently a sinner; I cannot take the responsibility of recommending you to the mercy of Heaven." It must have had its origin in that impression, else he would have thought, "We are all instruments for the carrying out of God's purposes; it is not for me to pass judgment upon your appointed share of the work, or to praise or to revile it; I have divine authority for it that we are *all* sinners, and therefore it is not for me to discriminate and say we will supplicate for this sinner, for he was a merchant prince or a banker, but we will beseech no forgiveness for this other one, for he was a play-actor."

It surely requires the furthest possible reach of self-righteousness to enable a man to lift his scornful nose in the air and turn his back upon so poor and pitiable a thing as a dead stranger come to beg the last kindness that humanity can do in its behalf. This creature has violated the letter of the gospel and judged George Holland—not George Holland either, but his *profession*—through him. Then it is in a measure fair that we judge this creature's guild through *him*. In effect he has said, "We are the salt of the earth; we do all the good work that is done; to learn how to be good and do good, men must come to us; actors and such are obstacles to moral progress."[1]

Pray look at the thing reasonably for a moment, laying aside all biases of education and custom. If a common public impression is fair evidence of a thing, then this minister's legitimate, recognized, and acceptable business is to *tell* people calmly, coldly, and in stiff, written sentences, from the pulpit, to go and do right, be just, be merciful, be charitable. And his congregation forget it all between church and home. But for fifty years it was George Holland's business, on the stage, to *make* his audience go and do right, and be just, merciful, and charitable—because by his living, breathing, feeling pictures, he showed them what it *was* to do these things, and *how* to do them, and how instant and ample was the reward! Is it not a singular teacher of men, this reverend gentleman who is so poorly informed himself as to put the whole stage under ban, and say, "I do not think it teaches moral lessons"?

Where was ever a sermon preached that could make filial ingratitude so hateful to men as the sinful play of *King Lear?* Or where was there ever a sermon that could so convince men of the wrong and the cruelty of harboring a pampered and unanalyzed jealousy as the sinful play of *Othello?* And where are there ten preachers who can stand in the pulpit teaching heroism, unselfish devotion, and lofty patriotism, and hold their own against any one of five hundred William Tells that can be raised up upon five hundred stages in the land at a day's notice? It is almost fair and just to aver (although it is profanity) that nine-tenths of all the kindness and forbearance and Christian charity and generosity in the hearts of the American people today, got there by being filtered down from their fountain-head, the gospel of Christ, *through dramas and tragedies and comedies on*

---

[1] Reporter—What answer did you make, Mr. Sabine?

Mr. Sabine—I said that I had a distaste for officiating at such a funeral, and that I did not care to be mixed up in it. I said to the gentleman that I was willing to bury the deceased from his house, but that I objected to having the funeral solemnized at a church.

Reporter—Is it one of the laws of the Protestant Episcopal Church that a deceased theatrical performer shall not be buried from the church?

Mr. Sabine—It is not: but I have always warned the professing members of my congregation to keep away from theaters and not to have anything to do with them. I don't think that they teach moral lessons.—*New York Times.*

the stage, and through the despised novel and the Christmas story, and through the thousand and one lessons, suggestions, and narratives of generous deeds that stir the pulses, and exalt and augment the nobility of the nation day by day from the teeming columns of ten thousand newspapers, and NOT from the drowsy pulpit!

All that is great and good in our particular civilization came straight from the hand of Jesus Christ, and many creatures, and of divers sorts, were doubtless appointed to disseminate it; and let us believe that *this seed and the result* are the main thing, and not the cut of the sower's garment; and that whosoever, in his way and according to his opportunity, sows the one and produces the other, has done high service and worthy. And further, let us try with all our strength to believe that whenever old simple-hearted George Holland sowed his seed, and reared his crop of broader charities and better impulses in men's hearts, it was just as acceptable before the Throne as if the seed had been scattered in vapid platitudes from the pulpit of the ineffable Sabine himself.

Am I saying that the pulpit does not do its share toward disseminating the marrow, the *meat* of the gospel of Christ? (For we are not talking of ceremonies and wire-drawn creeds now, but the living heart and soul of what is pretty often only a spectre.)

No, I am not saying that. The pulpit teaches assemblages of people twice a week—nearly two hours, altogether—and does what it can in that time. The theater teaches large audiences seven times a week—28 or 30 hours altogether; and the novels and newspapers plead, and argue, and illustrate, stir, move, thrill, thunder, urge, persuade, and supplicate, at the feet of millions and millions of people every single day, and all day long, and far into the night; and so these vast agencies till *nine-tenths* of the vineyard, and the pulpit tills the other tenth. Yet now and then some complacent blind idiot says, "You unanointed are coarse clay and useless; you are not as we, the regenerators of the world; go, bury yourselves elsewhere, for we cannot take the responsibility of recommending idlers and sinners to the yearning mercy of Heaven." How *does* a soul like that stay in a carcass without getting mixed with the secretions and sweated out through the pores? Think of this insect condemning the whole theatrical service as a disseminator of bad morals because it has Black Crooks in it; forgetting that if that were sufficient ground, people would condemn the pulpit because it had Cooks, and Kallochs, and Sabines in it.

No, I am not trying to rob the pulpit of any atom of its full share and credit in the work of disseminating the meat and marrow of the gospel of Christ; but I am trying to get a moment's hearing for worthy agencies in the same work, that with overwrought modesty seldom or never claim a recognition of their great services. I am aware that the pulpit does its excellent one-tenth (and credits itself with it now and then, though most of the time a press of business causes it to forget it); I am aware that in its honest and well-meaning way it bores the people with uninflammable truisms about doing good; bores them with correct compositions on charity; bores them, chloroforms them, stupefies them with argumentative mercy without a flaw in the grammar, or an emotion which the minister could put in in the right place if he turned his back and took his finger off the manuscript. And in doing these things the pulpit is doing its duty, and let us believe that it is likewise doing its best, and doing it in the most harmless and respectable way. And so I have said, and shall keep on saying, let us give the pulpit its full share of credit in elevating and ennobling the people; but when a pulpit takes to itself authority to pass judgment upon the work and the worth of just as legitimate an instrument of God as itself, who spent a long life preaching from the stage the self-same gospel without the alteration of a single sentiment or a single axiom of right, it is fair and just that somebody who believes that actors were made for a high and good purpose, and that they *accomplish the object of their creation* and accomplish it well, protest. And having protested, it is also fair and just—being driven to it, as it were—to whisper to the Sabine pattern of clergyman, under the breath, a simple, instructive truth, and say, "Ministers are not the only servants of God upon earth, nor His most efficient ones either, by a very, very long distance!" Sensible ministers already know this, and it may do the other kind good to find it out.

But to cease teaching and go back to the beginning again, was it not pitiable, that spectacle? Honored and honorable old George Holland, whose theatrical ministry had for fifty years softened hard hearts, bred generosity in cold ones, kindled emotion in dead ones, uplifted base ones, broadened bigoted ones, and made many and many a stricken one glad and filled it brim full of gratitude, figuratively spit upon in his unoffending coffin by this crawling, slimy, sanctimonious, self-righteous reptile!

1871

JOHN CAMDEN HOTTEN[1]

To the Editor of *The Spectator.*

Sir:

I only venture to intrude upon you because I come, in some sense, in the interest of public morality, and this makes my mission respectable. Mr. John Camden Hotten, of London, has, of his own individual motion, republished several of my books in England. I do not protest against this, for there is no law that could give effect to the protest; and, besides, publishers are not accountable to the laws of heaven and earth in any country, as I understand it.

But my grievance is this: My books are bad enough just as they are written, then what must they be after Mr. John Camden Hotten has composed half-a-dozen chapters and added the same to them? I feel that all true hearts will bleed for an author whose volumes have fallen under such a dispensation as this. If a friend of yours, or even if you yourself, were to write a book and send it adrift among the people, with the gravest apprehensions that it was not up to what it ought to be intellectually, how would you like to have John Camden Hotten sit down and stimulate his powers, and drool two or three original chapters on to the end of that book? Would not the world seem cold and hollow to you? Would you not feel that you wanted to die and be at rest? Little the world knows of true suffering.

And suppose he should entitle these chapters, "Holiday Literature," "True Stories of Chicago," "On Children," "Train Up a Child, and Away He Goes," and "Vengeance," and then, on the strength of having evolved these marvels from his own consciousness, go and "Copyright" the entire book, and put on the title-page a picture of a man with his hand in another man's pocket and the legend "All

---

[1] For a time Hotten regularly pirated Mark Twain's works in England. He was not alone in this activity. Clemens was also for a while the victim of extensive piracy in Canada.—C.N.

Rights Reserved" (I only suppose the picture; still it would be rather a neat thing).

And, further, suppose that in the kindness of his heart and the exuberance of his untaught fancy this thoroughly well-meaning innocent should expunge the modest title which you had given your book and replace it with so foul an invention as this, "Screamers and Eye-Openers," and went and got *that* copyrighted, too. And suppose that on top of all this he continually and persistently forgot to offer you a single penny or even send you a copy of your mutilated book to burn. Let us suppose all this. Let him suppose it with strength enough, and then he will know something about woe.

Sometimes when I read one of those additional chapters constructed by John Camden Hotten I feel as if I wanted to take a broom-straw and go and knock that man's brains out. Not in anger, for I feel none. Oh! not in anger; but only to see, that is all. Mere idle curiosity.

And Mr. Hotten says that one *nom de plume* of mine is "Carl Byng." I hold that there is no affliction in this world that makes a man feel so downtrodden and abused as the giving him a name that does not belong to him. How would this sinful aborigine feel if I were to call him John Camden Hottentot, and come out in the papers and say he was entitled to it by divine right? I do honestly believe it would throw him into a brain fever, if there were not an insuperable obstacle in the way.

Yes—to come to the original subject, which is the sorrow that is slowly but surely undermining my health—Mr. Hotten prints unrevised, uncorrected, and in some respects spurious books, with my name to them as author and thus embitters his customers against one of the most innocent of men. Messrs. George Routledge and Sons are the only English publishers who pay me any copyright, and therefore if my books are to disseminate either suffering or crime among the readers of our language, I would ever so much rather they did it through that house, and then I could contemplate the spectacle calmly as the dividends came in.

I am sir, etc.,
Samuel L. Clemens

London, September 20, 1872.

MR. DUNCAN OF THE *QUAKER CITY*

To the Editor of *The World*.

Sir:

I see by your report of a lecture delivered in your neighborhood very recently that a bit of my private personal history has been revealed to the public. The lecturer was head-waiter of the Quaker City Excursion of ten years ago. I do not repeat his name for the reason that I think he wants a little notoriety as a basis for introduction to the lecture platform, and I don't wish to contribute. I harbor this suspicion because he calls himself "captain" of that expedition.

The truth is, that as soon as the ship was fairly at sea, he was degraded from his captaincy by Mr. Leary (owner of the vessel) and Mr. Bunsley (executive officer). As he was not a passenger, and had now ceased to be an officer, it was something of a puzzle to define his position. However, as he still had authority to discharge waiter-boys —an authority which the passengers did not possess—it was presently decided, privately, that he must naturally be the "headwaiter"; and thus was he dubbed. During the voyage he gave orders to none but his under-waiters; all the excursionists will testify to this. It may be humorous enough to call himself "captain," but then it is calculated to deceive the public.

The "captain" says that when I came to engage passage in the *Quaker City* I "seemed to be full of whiskey, or something," and filled his office with the "fumes of bad whiskey." I hope this is true, but I cannot say, because it is so long ago; at the same time I am not depraved enough to deny that for a ceaseless, tireless, forty-year public advocate of total abstinence the "captain" is a mighty good judge of whiskey at second-hand.

He charges that I couldn't tell the *Quaker City* tea from coffee. Am I a god, that I can solve the impossible?

He charges that I uttered a libel when I said he made this speech at a Fourth of July dinner on shipboard: "Ladies and gentlemen, may you all live long and prosper; steward, pass up another basket of champagne."

Well, the truth is often a libel, and this may be one; yet it is the truth nevertheless. I did not publish it with malicious intent, but because it showed that even a total-abstinence gladiator can have gentle instincts when he is removed from hampering home influences.

The "captain" charges that when I came to his office to engage passage I represented myself to be a Baptist minister cruising after health. No; Mr. Edward H. House told him that, without giving me any warning that he was going to do it. But no matter, I should have done it myself if I had thought of it. Therefore I lift this crime from Mr. House's shoulders and transfer it to mine. I was without conscience in those old days. It had been my purpose to represent that I was a son of the captain's whom he had never met, and consequently hadn't classified, and by this means I hoped to get a free passage; but I was saved from this great villainy by the happy accident of Mr. House's getting in his milder rascality ahead of me. I often shudder to think how near I came to saddling an old father on to myself forever whom I never could have made any use of after that excursion was finished. Still, if I had him now, I would make him lecture his head off at his customary 25 cents before I would support him in idleness. I consider idleness an immoral thing for the aged.

Certain of my friends in New York have been so distressed by the "captain's" charges against me that they have simply forced me to come out in print. But I find myself in a great difficulty by reason of the fact that I don't find anything in the charges that discomforts me. Why should I worry over the "bad whiskey?" I was poor—I couldn't afford good whiskey. How could I know that the "captain" was so particular about the quality of a man's liquor? I didn't know he was a purist in that matter, and that the difference between 5-cent and 40-cent toddy would remain a rankling memory with him for ten years.

The tea and champagne items do not trouble me—both being true and harmless. The Baptist minister fraud does not give me any anguish, since I did not invent it.

What I need, now that I am going into print, is a text. These little things do not furnish it. Why does the "captain" make no mention of the highway robbery which I committed on the road between Jerusalem and the Dead Sea? He must have heard of it—the land was full of it. Why does he make no mention of the fact that during the entire excursion I never drew a sober breath except by proxy? Why does he conceal the fact that I killed a cripple in Cairo because I thought he had an unpleasant gait? Why is he silent about my skinning a leper in Smyrna in order that I might have a little something to start a museum with when I got home? What is the use of making "charges" out of a man's few little virtuous actions when that man has committed real indiscretions by the dozen?

But where is the use in bothering about what a man's character was ten years ago, anyway? Perhaps the "captain" values his character of ten years ago? I never have heard of any reason why he should; but still he may possibly value it. No matter. I do not value my character of ten years ago. I can go out any time and buy a better one for half it cost me. In truth, my character was simply in course of construction then. I hadn't anything up but the scaffolding, so to speak. But I have finished the edifice now and taken down that worm-eaten scaffolding. I have finished my moral edifice, and frescoed it and furnished it, and I am obliged to admit that it is one of the neatest and sweetest things of the kind that I have ever encountered. I greatly value it, and I would feel like resenting any damage done to it. But that old scaffolding is no longer of any use to me; and inasmuch as the "captain" seems able to use it to advantage, I hereby make him a present of it. It is a little shaky, of course, but if he will patch it here and there he will find that it is still superior to anything of the kind he can scare up upon his own premises.

Mark Twain

February 14.

Postscript—Two Days Later

The following paragraph from the *New York Times* has just reached my hands:

THE SHIP-OWNERS AND MR. DUNCAN

The Ship-owners' Association have sent a long communication to the Senate Committee on Commerce, in support of the "Ward Amendments" bill. It recites that the old law gives no right of appeal from the

Shipping Commissioner's decision except to the appointing power. It charges Commissioner Duncan with appropriating to his own use large amounts received as fees, in direct violation of the law, and says that it was decided that the law contains no provision to compel him to refund. It accuses him of paying salaries to his four sons and others, grossly in excess of the services rendered; of being arbitrary and unjust in his decisions; of refusing to recognize exemptions specified in the law, and of renting his offices from the Seamen's Association, of which he is President, at a price four times greater than is just, the amount paid being exactly the sum required to pay the interest on the mortgage and unpaid taxes and assessments of the building owned by the Seamen's Association. It quotes a number of contradictory decisions given by courts in various localities as to the spirit of sections of the law, and mentions several points of the Amendatory bill, which give assurance that its passage will overcome all future troubles.—*New York Times.*

They do say that people who live in glass houses should not throw stones. Mr. Duncan has neglected his own character of today to hunt down mine of ten years ago. What my character was in that day can be a matter of importance to no one—not even me; but what the present character of the Shipping Commissioner of the great port of New York is, is a matter of serious importance to the whole public. What the character of the President of the Seamen's Association and master of the Sailors' Savings Bank connected with it is, is matter of similarly serious importance to the public. That character—Mr. Duncan's character—is vividly suggested by the charges recited in the above extract. I have known and observed Mr. Duncan for ten years, and I think I have good reason for believing him to be wholly without principle, without moral sense, without honor of any kind. I think I am justified in believing that he is cruel enough and heartless enough to rob any sailor or sailor's widow or orphan he can get his clutches upon; and I know him to be coward enough. I know him to be a canting hypocrite, filled to the chin with sham godliness, and forever oozing and dripping false piety and pharisaical prayers. I know his word to be worthless.

It is a shame and a disgrace to the civil service that such a man was permitted to worm himself into an office of trust and high responsibility. It is a greater shame and disgrace that he has been permitted to remain in it after he was found out and published, more than three years ago (for the present charges were made against him and printed as long ago as that).

If any one imagines that I am moved to speak in this way by Mr. Duncan's "charges" against me, I beg that he will dismiss that idea. A charge made by Mr. Duncan must naturally fall dead, for the source it emanates from is amply sufficient to sap it of effect.

Samuel L. Clemens
(Mark Twain)

Hartford, February 16.

MR. DUNCAN ONCE MORE

To the Editor of *The World*.

Sir:

If you should glance over the letters which have come to me from New York and Brooklyn since last Sunday you would be surprised to perceive how general is the knowledge of Mr. Chas. C. Duncan's character in those cities, and how frank and outspoken the abhorrence of it. It seems that everybody has known for four or five years that this Shipping Commissioner was diligently and constantly robbing the till of his office, with the exception of the brief intervals of time which he devoted to the Sunday-school of which he was (and is) Superintendent. And yet he has been allowed to keep his place. This ought to delight those sarcastic people who say we do not live under a "form of government" in America, but under a "system of organized imbecility."

I think that Mr. Duncan's strength has lain in the fact that he robs nobody but sailors and the United States Government. Nobody is personally interested in the protection of these, else the newspapers would have been flooded with the complaints of sufferers, and Mr. Duncan would have been driven from his office long ago.

Penning newspaper letters about this over-pious miscreant is not agreeable work, and I would much prefer to leave the present one unwritten; but one correspondent desires to know something about the law which made Mr. Duncan a Shipping Commissioner, and I am sure that there are others who would like to see a synopsis of its provisions. That law was devised by Mr. Duncan himself. It is plainly and simply a Black Flag, and the man who has sailed under it all these years is—but name him yourself.

That infamous law was most ably dissected and its purpose exposed four or five years ago, in a pamphlet published by Messrs. Morris & Wilder, attorneys, of New York. That pamphlet will destroy Mr. Duncan and his law if the judiciary committees of Congress can be brought to read it.

The title of Mr. Duncan's law is a blistering sarcasm: "An Act for the Further Protection of Seamen." Further along the reader will see what "protection" means in a Shipping Commissioner's dictionary.

1. Under all previous laws the injured sailor could bring his case in a court of equity. His only recourse now is to a court of law; "his only remedy lies in the inflexible terms of a statute of which the court is compelled to be a strict and rigid interpreter." No more equity is permitted, no more "exercise of discretion in view of all the circumstances of a case."

2. Under the old laws a sailor's rights were clearly defined and his remedy was simple and inexpensive. Under the new, the process is cumbered by all sorts of complications and obstructions, and the expenses increased to a prohibitory degree. "The maze of technicalities to which the seaman is now compelled to conform could not have been more cunningly devised by an organized band of conspirators intent upon perplexing and robbing him!"

3. This new law gives the sailor not a single right or privilege which he did not possess before; but it takes from him certain rights and privileges of inestimable value which he did possess before.

4. The new law creates a disease called a Shipping Commissioner, who is to "superintend" the shipping and discharge of sailors, and charge a fee for each man shipped or discharged. All these fees come eventually out of the sailor's pocket—and they have always gone into Mr. Duncan's.

5. The Shipping Commissioner "may refuse to proceed with any engagement or discharge unless the fees thereon are first paid." That is a quotation from the law! Jack may finish his voyage, but if he is unable to pay his fee he can remain the property of the ship-owner; for Mr. Duncan will not release him! This is "protection"—to the Shipping Commissioner.

6. The law gives the Shipping Commissioner $5000 a year for "superintending"; but he has charged the country more than $160,000 in four years for that needless service, by pocketing the fees.

7. "All acts done by a clerk or deputy shall be as valid and binding as if done by the Shipping Commissioner himself." Was ever a law

more ingeniously devised for the coddling of a lazy pilferer? He was not even willing to take the trouble to do the pilfering himself.

8. A penalty is provided for the punishment of any one who shall solicit a seaman's custom for a sailor boarding-house. That looks well, on its face, but—

9. "Every payment of wages to a seaman shall be valid in law, notwithstanding any previous sale or assignment of such wages; and no assignment or sale of such wages shall bind the party making the same." This is not a quotation from the rules and by-laws of a band of highwaymen, but is the exact wording of this most disgraceful statute. Its plain meaning is that the Government denies to the sailor the common human right to do as he pleases with his own! The effect is this: Formerly those dreadful boarding-house landlords fed and lodged the sailor on credit when his money was all gone, taking an assignment of his first advance-money (when he should next get a berth) as their security. The new law forbids the sailor to give such security now by making such security valueless; so the boarding-houses promptly turn him adrift when his money is gone, and—the Shipping Commissioner takes care of him? Suppose you apply at the Sunday-school in Brooklyn and ask Mr. Duncan that sarcastic question. No—Jack becomes a tramp. This law has filled the country with tramps. It ought to have been entitled "An act for the creation of a pirate and for the multiplication of tramps."

Everybody has heard of that horrible process of kidnapping sailors, called "shanghaeing"; everybody has loathed it, everybody has cursed it. Could anybody but a Duncan dream of so foul a crime as the creation of a law to legalize shanghaeing? Could anybody but a Duncan be heartless enough, cruel enough, shameless enough? I ask you to read this extract from the law framed by this bowelless Commissioner, and see if you can realize the fact that such a statute as this has blackened the code of America for five years (and almost unchallenged):

10. Whenever any seaman neglects or refuses to join, or deserts from or refuses to proceed to sea in any ship in which he is duly engaged to serve, or is found otherwise absenting himself therefrom without leave, the master, or any mate, or the owner, or consignee may in any place in the United States, with or without the assistance of the local public officers or constables (who are hereby directed to give their assistance, if required), apprehend him without first pro-

curing a warrant, and may thereupon in any case, and shall, in case he so requires, and it is practicable, convey him before any court of justice, &c., and may, for the purpose of conveying him before such court of justice, detain him in custody for a period not exceeding twenty-four hours, or may, if he does not so require, or if there is no such court at or near the place, at once convey him on board.

Let us suppose a case. A shanghaier has engaged to procure a crew for an outgoing vessel. He comes, with his little gang of assistants, to an isolated place and seizes a man he never saw before—Mr. Longfellow, for instance. An officer of the law interferes. Kidnapper —I have been formally constituted mate of the Osprey, and this man is one of my crew—a deserter. I propose to take him on board. Here is the law—read it for yourself.

Officer—He says he never shipped. You must convey him before a court of justice—he requires you to do it.

Kidnapper—I answer, according to the law, that "it is not practicable." There is no such court "near this place."

Officer—You have no warrant for his seizure.

Kidnapper—I require none—see the law.

Officer—You are right. Take him along.

Let me give an extract from the pamphlet I have before referred to:

Once on board, the mariner is secure. If the voyage be to the East Indies then the shanghaed sailor is left to shirk for himself at Bombay or Calcutta, lest if he returned home in the vessel he might seek to have the mate who kidnapped him punished. It is claimed that shanghaeing is prevented by section 53, which provides that if a sailor be carried to sea without entering into an agreement as prescribed by the act, that the ship shall be held liable, and for each offense shall incur a penalty not exceeding $200!!!

Without questioning here the soundness of so novel a doctrine as that a vessel is liable for the torts or crimes of a mate hired perhaps of a charterer, where is the protection against shanghaeing? Section 53 does not prohibit kidnapping, but says, in effect: "Kidnapping is permissible, provided you pay from $100 to $200 apiece for the kidnapped." And this money does not go to the sailor, but to the Government.

At this rate kidnapping is the cheapest way to get a crew for a long voyage, especially as the chances are that the vessel will not have to pay anything at all if the kidnapped sailors are forced to desert in a foreign port. The incentive to the master to force his crew to desert is not only to save the vessel from the penalty, but to hire cheaper crews abroad.

One further fact deserves to be considered in this connection. What becomes of the wages accrued and due to a crew at the time of their desertion? The answer is that, according to all maritime law, these, of course, are forfeited. Thus the horrible truth creeps over the mind that in the desertion of the seaman lies an actual source of revenue to the master's private pocket; then the still more horrible suspicion that that seaman's desertion has been, possibly, reckoned upon, calculated, forced upon him—that human ingenuity has been at work devising new methods of cruelty for the express purpose of driving this man, or this crew, to desertion. Should the port be favorable to the securing of cheap substitutes, the law offers every facility for "securing them on board." If not, then under section 53 it offers equal facilities for "securing" the runaways. But the wages of the latter are in either case forfeited. What a premium is thus placed upon cruelty! What deliberate perils are laid against the mariner's life! With what dignity does law now invest the brutal violence of his despot!

Please read a paragraph from the summing up of the same pamphlet:

The whole truth is that in not one line of this act can the intelligent reader find for the seaman "protection." Sixty sections are devoted to creating unnecessary officers, fixing their salaries, fees and perquisites, crushing all who might come in competition with their gains, and then binding the mariner, hand and foot, through their instrumentality, to the very class against whom he most needs protection. Of the eight remaining sections of the act, one alone, the sixty-first, bestows upon him, as we have seen above, the privilege of protecting himself by swindling all with whom he comes in contact. It is a noteworthy feature of this "benevolent" law that the only protection afforded by it to the sailor lies in a provision that he shall not suffer by his own fraudulent act. But the ship-owner is "protected" in the possession of his men, and protected also from paying them the high rates of wages hitherto paid them under the guidance of their landlords; the master is "protected" in his violence and brutality to them, as well as "protected" in the enjoyment of their wages when that violence has driven them from him; the mates are "protected" in the pursuit and recapture of them; both master and mates are "protected" in kidnapping sailors at all times, and "protected" always from the interference of local magistrates; and, above all and most of all, the Shipping Commissioner is "protected" in the exclusive enjoyment of the shipping business of his port and all the emoluments arising therefrom. But the sailor? As well call a lie the truth, or blasphemy pious, as to call this act, either in whole or in detail, "protection" to him. Such a prostitution of one of the noblest words of the English language to an act begotten in jobbery, chicanery and selfishness is absolutely without parallel.

Still further, this act is obnoxious not only in its centralizing tendencies, in its interference with the legitimate callings of citizens of the various seaports, in its multiplying Federal officers, and in its grinding effect upon the mariner, but, as a natural sequence of all this, it overreaches itself and infringes upon the constitutional and fundamental law. So far as the sailor is concerned, it is one continuous suspension of the habeas corpus! It deprives him of liberty without due process of law, "without first procuring a warrant." And it adds the infamous permission that this may be done by a mere private citizen.

This law is a curiosity in every possible way. It makes Mr. Duncan arbitrator between the sailor and his employer in cases of dispute. I judge that Mr. Duncan is a person whose decision is easily purchasable. This law makes this person's decision final and absolute! The sailor cannot appeal from it! Perhaps the reader now perceives the sarcasm which lurks in the title of the law—"for the further protection of seamen."

Perhaps no more infamous law than this has ever defiled the code of any Christian land in any age, and yet it is the work of a man whose stock in trade is sham temperance, sham benevolence, religious hypocrisy, and a ceaseless, unctuous drip of buttery prayers.

Samuel L. Clemens
(Mark Twain) *1877*

Hartford, February 22.

IS SHAKESPEARE DEAD?

(FROM MY AUTOBIOGRAPHY)

1

Scattered here and there through the stacks of unpublished manuscript which constitute this formidable Autobiography and Diary of mine, certain chapters will in some distant future be found which deal with "Claimants"—claimants historically notorious: Satan, Claimant; the Golden Calf, Claimant; the Veiled Prophet of Khorassan, Claimant; Louis XVII, Claimant; William Shakespeare, Claimant; Arthur Orton, Claimant; Mary Baker G. Eddy, Claimant—and the rest of them. Eminent Claimants, successful Claimants, defeated Claimants, royal Claimants, pleb Claimants, showy Claimants, shabby Claimants, revered Claimants, despised Claimants, twinkle star-like here and there and yonder through the mists of history and legend and tradition—and, oh, all the darling tribe are clothed in mystery and romance, and we read about them with deep interest and discuss them with loving sympathy or with rancorous resentment, according to which side we hitch ourselves to.

It has always been so with the human race. There was never a Claimant that couldn't get a hearing, nor one that couldn't accumulate a rapturous following, no matter how flimsy and apparently unauthentic his claim might be. Arthur Orton's claim that he was the lost Tichborne baronet come to life again was as flimsy as Mrs. Eddy's that she wrote *Science and Health* from the direct dictation of the Deity; yet in England near forty years ago Orton had a huge army of devotees and incorrigible adherents, many of whom remained stubbornly unconvinced after their fat god had been proven an impostor and jailed as a perjurer, and today Mrs. Eddy's following is not only immense, but is daily augmenting in numbers and enthusiasm. Orton had many fine and educated minds among his

adherents, Mrs. Eddy has had the like among hers from the beginning. Her Church is as well equipped in those particulars as is any
other Church.

Claimants can always count upon a following, it doesn't matter
who they are, nor what they claim, nor whether they come with
documents or without. It was always so. Down out of the long-
vanished past, across the abyss of the ages, if you listen you can still
hear the believing multitudes shouting for Perkin Warbeck and Lam-
bert Simnel.

A friend has sent me a new book, from England—*The Shakespeare Problem Restated*—well restated and closely reasoned; and my
fifty years' interest in that matter—asleep for the last three years—is
excited once more. It is an interest which was born of Delia Bacon's
book—away back in that ancient day—1857, or maybe 1856. About
a year later my pilot-master, Bixby, transferred me from his own
steamboat to the *Pennsylvania,* and placed me under the orders and
instructions of George Ealer—dead now, these many, many years. I
steered for him a good many months—as was the humble duty of the
pilot-apprentice: stood a daylight watch and spun the wheel under
the severe superintendence and correction of the master.

He was a prime chess-player and an idolater of Shakespeare. He
would play chess with anybody; even with me, and it cost his official
dignity something to do that. Also—quite uninvited—he would read
Shakespeare to me; not just casually, but by the hour, when it was
his watch and I was steering. He read well, but not profitably for me,
because he constanty injected commands into the text. That broke it
all up, mixed it all up, tangled it all up—to that degree, in fact, that if
we were in a risky and difficult piece of river an ignorant person
couldn't have told, sometimes, which observations were Shakespeare's and which were Ealer's. For instance:

> What man dare, *I* dare!
> Approach thou *what* are you laying in the leads for? what a hell of an
> idea! like the rugged ease her off a little, ease her off! rugged Russian
> bear, the armed rhinoceros or the *there* she goes! meet her, meet her!
> didn't you *know* she'd smell the reef if you crowded it like that? Hyrcan
> tiger; take any shape but that and my firm nerves she'll be in the *woods*
> the first you know! stop the starboard! come ahead strong on the lar-
> board! back the starboard! . . . *Now* then, you're all right; come ahead
> on the starboard; straighten up and go 'long, never tremble: or be alive

again, and dare me to the desert *damnation* can't you keep away from that greasy water? pull her down! snatch her! snatch her baldheaded! with thy sword; if trembling I inhabit then, lay in the leads!—no, only the starboard one, leave the other alone, protest me the baby of a girl. Hence horrible shadow! eight bells—that watchman's asleep again, I reckon, go down and call Brown yourself, unreal mockery, hence!

He certainly was a good reader, and splendidly thrilling and stormy and tragic, but it was a damage to me, because I have never since been able to read Shakespeare in a calm and sane way. I cannot rid it of his explosive interlardings, they break in everywhere with their irrelevant, "What in hell are you up to *now!* pull her down! more! *more!*—there now, steady as you go," and the other disorganizing interruptions that were always leaping from his mouth. When I read Shakespeare now I can hear them as plainly as I did in that long-departed time—fifty-one years ago. I never regarded Ealer's readings as educational. Indeed, they were a detriment to me.

His contributions to the text seldom improved it, but barring that detail he was a good reader; I can say that much for him. He did not use the book, and did not need to; he knew his Shakespeare as well as Euclid ever knew his multiplication table.

Did he have something to say—this Shakespeare-adoring Mississippi pilot—anent Delia Bacon's book?

Yes. And he said it; said it all the time, for months—in the morning watch, the middle watch, and dog watch; and probably kept it going in his sleep. He bought the literature of the dispute as fast as it appeared, and we discussed it all through thirteen hundred miles of river four times traversed in every thirty-five days—the time required by that swift boat to achieve two round trips. We discussed, and discussed, and discussed, and disputed and disputed and disputed; at any rate, *he* did, and I got in a word now and then when he slipped a cog and there was a vacancy. He did his arguing with heat, with energy, with violence; and I did mine with the reserve and moderation of a subordinate who does not like to be flung out of a pilot-house that is perched forty feet above the water. He was fiercely loyal to Shakespeare and cordially scornful of Bacon and of all the pretensions of the Baconians. So was I—at first. And at first he was glad that that was my attitude. There were even indications that he admired it; indications dimmed, it is true, by the distance that lay between the lofty boss-pilotical altitude and my lowly one, yet perceptible to me; perceptible, and translatable into a compliment—compliment coming down from above the snow-line and not well thawed in the transit, and not likely to set anything afire, not even a cub-pilot's self-conceit; still a detectable compliment, and precious.

Naturally it flattered me into being more loyal to Shakespeare—if possible—than I was before, and more prejudiced against Bacon—if possible—than I was before. And so we discussed and discussed, both on the same side, and were happy. For a while. Only for a while. Only for a very little while, a very, very, very little while. Then the atmosphere began to change; began to cool off.

A brighter person would have seen what the trouble was, earlier than I did, perhaps, but I saw it early enough for all practical purposes. You see, he was of an argumentative disposition. Therefore it took him but a little time to get tired of arguing with a person who agreed with everything he said and consequently never furnished him a provocative to flare up and show what he could do when it came to clear, cold, hard, rose-cut, hundred-faceted, diamond-flashing *reasoning*. That was his name for it. It has been applied since, with complacency, as many as several times, in the Bacon-Shakespeare scuffle. On the Shakespeare side.

Then the thing happened which has happened to more persons than to me when principle and personal interest found themselves in opposition to each other and a choice had to be made: I let principle go, and went over to the other side. Not the entire way, but far enough to answer the requirements of the case. That is to say, I took this attitude—to wit, I only *believed* Bacon wrote Shakespeare, whereas I *knew* Shakespeare didn't. Ealer was satisfied with that, and the war broke loose. Study, practice, experience in handling my end of the matter presently enabled me to take my new position almost seriously; a little bit later, utterly seriously; a little later still, lovingly, gratefully, devotedly; finally: fiercely, rabidly, uncompromisingly.

After that I was welded to my faith, I was theoretically ready to die for it, and I looked down with compassion not unmixed with scorn upon everybody else's faith that didn't tally with mine. That faith, imposed upon me by self-interest in that ancient day, remains my faith today, and in it I find comfort, solace, peace, and never-failing joy. You see how curiously theological it is. The "rice Christian" of the Orient goes through the very same steps, when he is after rice and the missionary is after *him;* he goes for rice, and remains to worship.

Ealer did a lot of our "reasoning"—not to say substantially all of it. The slaves of his cult have a passion for calling it by that large name. We others do not call our inductions and deductions and reductions by any name at all. They show for themselves what they are, and we can with tranquil confidence leave the world to ennoble them with a title of its own choosing.

Now and then when Ealer had to stop to cough, I pulled my induction-talents together and hove the controversial lead myself: always getting eight feet, eight and a half, often nine, sometimes even quarter-less-twain—as *I* believed; but always "no bottom," as *he* said.

I got the best of him only once. I prepared myself. I wrote out a passage from Shakespeare—it may have been the very one I quoted awhile ago, I don't remember—and riddled it with his wild steamboatful interlardings. When an unrisky opportunity offered, one lovely summer day, when we had sounded and buoyed a tangled patch of crossings known as Hell's Half Acre, and were aboard again and he had sneaked the *Pennsylvania* triumphantly through it without once scraping sand, and the *A. T. Lacey* had followed in our wake and got stuck, and he was feeling good, I showed it to him. It amused him. I asked him to fire it off—*read* it; read it, I diplomatically added, as only *he* could read dramatic poetry. The compliment touched him where he lived. He did read it; read it with surpassing fire and spirit; read it as it will never be read again; for *he* knew how to put the right music into those thunderous interlardings and make them seem a part of the text, make them sound as if they were bursting from Shakespeare's own soul, each one of them a golden inspiration and not to be left out without damage to the massed and magnificent whole.

I waited a week, to let the incident fade; waited longer; waited until he brought up for reasonings and vituperation my pet position, my pet argument, the one which I was fondest of, the one which I prized far above all others in my ammunition-wagon—to wit, that Shakespeare couldn't have written Shakespeare's works, for the reason that the man who wrote them was limitlessly familiar with the laws, and the law-courts, and law-proceedings, and lawyer-talk, and lawyer-ways—and if Shakespeare was possessed of the infinitely divided star-dust that constituted this vast wealth, *how* did he get it, and *where*, and *when?*

"From books."

From books! That was always the idea. I answered as my readings of the champions of my side of the great controversy had taught me to answer: that a man can't handle glibly and easily and comfortably and successfully the argot of a trade at which he has not personally served. He will make mistakes; he will not, and cannot, get the trade-phrasings precisely and exactly right; and the moment he departs, by even a shade, from a common trade-form, the reader who has served that trade will know the writer *hasn't.*

Ealer would not be convinced; he said a man could learn how to correctly handle the subtleties and mysteries and free-masonries of *any* trade by careful reading and studying. But when I got him to read again the passage from Shakespeare with the interlardings, he perceived, himself, that books couldn't teach a student a bewildering multitude of pilot-phrases so thoroughly and perfectly that he could talk them off in book and play or conversation and make no mistake that a pilot would not immediately discover. It was a triumph for me. He was silent awhile, and I knew what was happening—he was losing his temper. And I knew he would presently close the session with the same old argument that was always his stay and his support in time of need; the same old argument, the one I couldn't answer, because I dasn't—the argument that I was an ass, and better shut up. He delivered it, and I obeyed.

Oh dear, how long ago it was—how pathetically long ago! And here am I, old, forsaken, forlorn, and alone, arranging to get that argument out of somebody again.

When a man has a passion for Shakespeare, it goes without saying that he keeps company with other standard authors. Ealer always had several high-class books in the pilot-house, and he read the same ones over and over again, and did not care to change to newer and fresher ones. He played well on the flute, and greatly enjoyed hearing himself play. So did I. He had a notion that a flute would keep its health better if you took it apart when it was not standing a watch; and so, when it was not on duty it took its rest, disjointed, on the compass-shelf under the breastboard.

When the *Pennsylvania* blew up and became a drifting rack-heap freighted with wounded and dying poor souls (my young brother

Henry among them), pilot Brown had the watch below, and was probably asleep and never knew what killed him; but Ealer escaped unhurt. He and his pilot-house were shot up into the air; then they fell, and Ealer sank through the ragged cavern where the hurricane-deck and the boiler-deck had been, and landed in a nest of ruins on the main deck, on top of one of the unexploded boilers, where he lay prone in a fog of scald and deadly steam. But not for long. He did not lose his head—long familiarity with danger had taught him to keep it, in any and all emergencies. He held his coat-lapels to his nose with one hand, to keep out the steam, and scrabbled around with the other till he found the joints of his flute, then he took measures to save himself alive, and was successful.

I was not on board. I had been put ashore in New Orleans by Captain Klinefelter. The reason—however, I have told all about it in the book called *Old Times on the Mississippi,* and it isn't important, anyway, it is so long ago.

2

When I was a Sunday-school scholar, something more than sixty years ago, I became interested in Satan, and wanted to find out all I could about him. I began to ask questions, but my class-teacher, Mr. Barclay, the stone-mason, was reluctant about answering them, it seemed to me. I was anxious to be praised for turning my thoughts to serious subjects when there wasn't another boy in the village who could be hired to do such a thing. I was greatly interested in the incident of Eve and the serpent, and thought Eve's calmness was perfectly noble. I asked Mr. Barclay if he had ever heard of another woman who, being approached by a serpent, would not excuse herself and break for the nearest timber. He did not answer my question, but rebuked me for inquiring into matters above my age and comprehension. I will say for Mr. Barclay that he was willing to tell me the facts of Satan's history, but he stopped there: he wouldn't allow any discussion of them.

In the course of time we exhausted the facts. There were only five or six of them; you could set them all down on a visiting-card. I was disappointed. I had been meditating a biography, and was grieved to find that there were no materials. I said as much, with the tears running down. Mr. Barclay's sympathy and compassion were aroused, for he was a most kind and gentle-spirited man, and he patted me on the head and cheered me up by saying there was a whole vast ocean of materials! I can still feel the happy thrill which these blessed words shot through me.

Then he began to bail out that ocean's riches for my encouragement and joy. Like this: it was "conjectured"—though not established—that Satan was originally an angel in heaven; that he fell; that he rebelled, and brought on a war; that he was defeated, and banished to perdition. Also, "we have reason to believe" that later he did so and so; that "we are warranted in supposing" that at a subsequent time he traveled extensively, seeking whom he might devour; that a couple of centuries afterward, "as tradition instructs us," he took up the cruel trade of tempting people to their ruin, with vast and fearful results; that by and by, "as the probabilities seem to indicate," he may have done certain things, he might have done certain other things, he must have done still other things.

And so on and so on. We set down the five known facts by themselves, on a piece of paper, and numbered it "page 1"; then on fifteen hundred other pieces of paper we set down the "conjectures," and "suppositions," and "maybes," and "perhapses," and "doubtlesses," and "rumors" and "guesses," and "probabilities," and "likelihoods," and "we are permitted to thinks," and "we are warranted in believings," and "might have beens," and "could have beens," and "must have beens," and "unquestionablys," and "without a shadow of doubts"—and behold!

Materials? Why, we had enough to build a biography of Shakespeare!

Yet he made me put away my pen; he would not let me write the history of Satan. Why? Because, as he said, he had suspicions—suspicions that my attitude in this matter was not reverent, and that a person must be reverent when writing about the sacred characters. He said any one who spoke flippantly of Satan would be frowned upon by the religious world and also be brought to account.

I assured him, in earnest and sincere words, that he had wholly misconceived my attitude; that I had the highest respect for Satan, and that my reverence for him equaled, and possibly even exceeded, that of any member of any church. I said it wounded me deeply to perceive by his words that he thought I would make fun of Satan, and deride him, laugh at him, scoff at him; whereas in truth I had never thought of such a thing, but had only a warm desire to make fun of those others and laugh at *them.* "What others?" "Why, the Supposers, the Perhapsers, the Might-Have-Beeners, the Could-Have-Beeners, the Must-Have-Beeners, the Without-a-Shadow-of-Doubters, the We-Are-Warranted-in-Believingers, and all that funny crop of solemn architects who have taken a good solid foundation of five indisputable and unimportant facts and built upon it a Conjectural Satan thirty miles high."

What did Mr. Barclay do then? Was he disarmed? Was he silenced? No. He was shocked. He was so shocked that he visibly shuddered. He said the Satanic Traditioners and Perhapsers and Conjecturers were *themselves* sacred! As sacred as their work. So sacred that whoso ventured to mock them or make fun of their work, could not afterward enter any respectable house, even by the back door.

How true were his words, and how wise! How fortunate it would have been for me if I had heeded them. But I was young, I was but seven years of age, and vain, foolish, and anxious to attract attention. I wrote the biography, and have never been in a respectable house since.

3

How curious and interesting is the parallel—as far as poverty of biographical details is concerned—between Satan and Shakespeare. It is wonderful, it is unique, it stands quite alone, there is nothing resembling it in history, nothing resembling it in romance, nothing approaching it even in tradition. How sublime is their position, and how over-topping, how sky-reaching, how supreme—the two Great Unknowns, the two Illustrious Conjecturabilities! They are the best-known unknown persons that have ever drawn breath upon the planet.

For the instruction of the ignorant I will make a list, now, of those details of Shakespeare's history which are *facts*—verified facts, established facts, undisputed facts.

FACTS

He was born on the 23d of April, 1564.

Of good farmer-class parents who could not read, could not write, could not sign their names.

At Stratford, a small back settlement which in that day was shabby and unclean, and densely illiterate. Of the nineteen important men charged with the government of the town, thirteen had to "make their mark" in attesting important documents, because they could not write their names.

Of the first eighteen years of his life *nothing* is known. They are a blank.

On the 27th of November (1582) William Shakespeare took out a license to marry Anne Whateley.

Next day William Shakespeare took out a license to marry Anne Hathaway. She was eight years his senior.

William Shakespeare married Anne Hathaway. In a hurry. By grace of a reluctantly granted dispensation there was but one publication of the banns.

Within six months the first child was born.

About two (blank) years followed, during which period *nothing at all happened to Shakespeare,* so far as anybody knows.

Then came twins—1585. February.

Two blanks years follow.

Then—1587—he makes a ten-year visit to London, leaving the family behind.

Five blank years follow. During this period *nothing happened to him,* as far as anybody actually knows.

Then—1592—there is mention of him as an actor.

Next year—1593—his name appears in the official list of players.

Next year—1594—he played before the queen. A detail of no consequence: other obscurities did it every year of the forty-five of her reign. And remained obscure.

Three pretty full years follow. Full of play-acting. Then

In 1597 he bought New Place, Stratford.

Thirteen or fourteen busy years follow; years in which he accumulated money, and also reputation as actor and manager.

Meantime his name, liberally and variously spelt, had become associated with a number of great plays and poems, as (ostensibly) author of the same.

Some of these, in these years and later, were pirated, but he made no protest.

Then—1610–11—he returned to Stratford and settled down for good and all, and busied himself in lending money, trading in tithes, trading in land and houses; shirking a debt of forty-one shillings, borrowed by his wife during his long desertion of his family; suing debtors for shillings and coppers; being sued himself for shillings and coppers; and acting as confederate to a neighbor who tried to rob the town of its rights in a certain common, and did not succeed.

He lived five or six years—till 1616—in the joy of these elevated pursuits. Then he made a will, and signed each of its three pages with his name.

A thoroughgoing business man's will. It named in minute detail every item of property he owned in the world—houses, lands, sword, silver-gilt bowl, and so on—all the way down to his "second-best bed" and its furniture.

It carefully and calculatingly distributed his riches among the members of his family, overlooking no individual of it. Not even his wife: the wife he had been enabled to marry in a hurry by urgent grace of a special dispensation before he was nineteen; the wife whom he had left husbandless so many years; the wife who had had to borrow forty-one shillings in her need, and which the lender was never able to collect of the prosperous husband, but died at last with the money still lacking. No, even this wife was remembered in Shakespeare's will.

He left her that "second-best bed."

And *not another thing;* not even a penny to bless her lucky widowhood with.

It was eminently and conspicuously a business man's will, not a poet's.

It mentioned *not a single book.*

Books were much more precious than swords and silver-gilt bowls and second-best beds in those days, and when a departing person owned one he gave it a high place in his will.

The will mentioned *not a play, not a poem, not an unfinished literary work, not a scrap of manuscript of any kind.*

Many poets have died poor, but this is the only one in history that has died *this* poor; the others all left literary remains behind. Also a book. Maybe two.

If Shakespeare had owned a dog—but we need not go into that: we know he would have mentioned it in his will. If a good dog, Susanna would have got it; if an inferior one his wife would have got a dower interest in it. I wish he had had a dog, just so we could see how painstakingly he would have divided that dog among the family, in his careful business way.

He signed the will in three places.

In earlier years he signed two other official documents.

These five signatures still exist.

There are *no other specimens of his penmanship in existence.* Not a line.

Was he prejudiced against the art? His granddaughter, whom he loved, was eight years old when he died, yet she had had no teaching, he left no provision for her education, although he was rich, and in her mature womanhood she couldn't write and couldn't tell her husband's manuscript from anybody else's—she thought it was Shakespeare's.

When Shakespeare died in Stratford *it was not an event.* It made no more stir in England than the death of any other forgotten theater-actor would have made. Nobody came down from London; there were no lamenting poems, no eulogies, no national tears—there was merely silence, and nothing more. A striking contrast with what happened when Ben Jonson, and Francis Bacon, and Spenser, and Raleigh, and the other distinguished literary folk of Shakespeare's time passed from life! No praiseful voice was lifted for the lost Bard of Avon; even Ben Jonson waited seven years before he lifted his.

So far as anybody actually knows and can prove, Shakespeare of Stratford-on-Avon never wrote a play in his life.

So far as anybody knows and can prove, he never wrote a letter to anybody in his life.

So far as any one knows, he received only one letter during his life.

So far as any one *knows and can prove,* Shakespeare of Stratford wrote only one poem during his life. This one is authentic. He did write that one—a fact which stands undisputed; he wrote the whole of it; he wrote the whole of it out of his own head. He commanded that this work of art be engraved upon his tomb, and he was obeyed. There it abides to this day. This is it:

> *Good friend for Iesus sake forbeare*
> *To digg the dust encloased heare:*
> *Blest be ye man yt spares thes stones*
> *And curst be he yt moves my bones.*

In the list as above set down will be found *every positively known* fact of Shakespeare's life, lean and meager as the invoice is. Beyond these details we know *not a thing* about him. All the rest of his vast history, as furnished by the biographers, is built up, course upon course, of guesses, inferences, theories, conjectures—an Eiffel Tower of artificialities rising sky-high from a very flat and very thin foundation of inconsequential facts.

4

Conjectures

The historians "suppose" that Shakespeare attended the Free School in Stratford from the time he was seven years old till he was thirteen. There is no *evidence* in existence that he ever went to school at all.

The historians "infer" that he got his Latin in that school—the school which they "suppose" he attended.

They "suppose" his father's declining fortunes made it necessary for him to leave the school they supposed he attended, and get to work and help support his parents and their ten children. But there is no evidence that he ever entered or returned from the school they suppose he attended.

They "suppose" he assisted his father in the butchering business; and that, being only a boy, he didn't have to do full-grown butchering, but only slaughtered calves. Also, that whenever he killed a calf he made a high-flown speech over it. This supposition rests upon the testimony of a man who wasn't there at the time; a man who got it from a man who could have been there, but did not say whether he was or not; and neither of them thought to mention it for decades, and decades, and decades, and two more decades after Shakespeare's death (until old age and mental decay had refreshed and vivified their memories). They hadn't two facts in stock about the long-dead distinguished citizen, but only just the one: he slaughtered calves and broke into oratory while he was at it.

Curious. They had only one fact, yet the distinguished citizen had spent twenty-six years in that little town—just half his lifetime. However, rightly viewed, it was the most important fact, indeed almost the only important fact, of Shakespeare's life in Stratford. Rightly viewed. For experience is an author's most valuable asset; experience is the thing that puts the muscle and the breath and the warm blood into the book he writes. Rightly viewed, calf-butchering accounts for "Titus Andronicus," the only play—ain't it?—that the Stratford Shakespeare ever wrote; and yet it is the only one everybody tries to chouse him out of, the Baconians included.

The historians find themselves "justified in believing" that the young Shakespeare poached upon Sir Thomas Lucy's deer preserves and got haled before that magistrate for it. But there is no shred of respectworthy evidence that anything of the kind happened.

The historians, having argued the thing that *might* have happened into the thing that *did* happen, found no trouble in turning Sir Thomas Lucy into Mr. Justice Shallow. They have long ago convinced the world—on surmise and without trustworthy evidence—that Shallow *is* Sir Thomas.

The next addition to the young Shakespeare's Stratford history comes easy. The historian builds it out of the surmised deer-stealing, and the surmised trial before the magistrate, and the surmised vengeance-prompted satire upon the magistrate in the play: result, the young Shakespeare was a wild, wild, wild, oh, *such* a wild young scamp, and that gratuitous slander is established for all time! It is the very way Professor Osborn and I built the colossal skeleton brontosaur that stands fifty-seven feet long and sixteen feet high in the Natural History Museum, the awe and admiration of all the world, the stateliest skeleton that exists on the planet. We had nine bones, and we built the rest of him out of plaster of Paris. We ran short of plaster of Paris, or we'd have built a brontosaur that could sit down beside the Stratford Shakespeare and none but an expert could tell which was biggest or contained the most plaster.

Shakespeare pronounced "Venus and Adonis" "the first heir of his invention," apparently implying that it was his first effort at literary composition. He should not have said it. It has been an embarrassment to his historians these many, many years. They have to make him write that graceful and polished and flawless and beautiful poem before he escaped from Stratford and his family—1586 or '87—age, twenty-two, or along there; because within the next five years he wrote five great plays, and could not have found time to write another line.

It is sorely embarrassing. If he began to slaughter calves, and poach deer, and rollick around, and learn English, at the earliest likely moment—say at thirteen, when he was supposedly wrenched from that school where he was supposedly storing up Latin for future literary use—he had his youthful hands full, and much more than full. He must have had to put aside his Warwickshire dialect, which wouldn't be understood in London, and study English very hard. Very hard indeed; incredibly hard, almost, if the result of that labor was to be the smooth and rounded and flexible and letter-perfect English of the "Venus and Adonis" in the space of ten years; and at the same time learn great and fine and unsurpassable literary *form.*

However, it is "conjectured" that he accomplished all this and more, much more: learned law and its intricacies; and the complex procedure of the law-courts; and all about soldiering, and sailoring, and the manners and customs and ways of royal courts and aristocratic society; and likewise accumulated in his one head every kind of knowledge the learned then possessed, and every kind of humble knowledge possessed by the lowly and the ignorant; and added thereto a wider and more intimate knowledge of the world's great literatures, ancient and modern, than was possessed by any other man of his time—for he was going to make brilliant and easy and admiration-compelling use of these splendid treasures the moment he got to London. And according to the surmisers, that is what he did. Yes, although there was no one in Stratford able to teach him these things, and no library in the little village to dig them out of. His father could not read, and even the surmisers surmise that he did not keep a library.

It is surmised by the biographers that the young Shakespeare got his vast knowledge of the law and his familiar and accurate acquaintance with the manners and customs and shop-talk of lawyers through being for a time the *clerk of a Stratford court;* just as a bright lad like me, reared in a village on the banks of the Mississippi, might become perfect in knowledge of the Bering Strait whale-fishery and the shop-talk of the veteran exercises of that adventure-bristling trade through catching catfish with a "trot-line" Sundays. But the surmise is damaged by the fact that there is no evidence—and not even tradition—that the young Shakespeare was ever clerk of a law-court.

It is further surmised that the young Shakespeare accumulated his law-treasures in the first years of his sojourn in London, through "amusing himself" by learning book-law in his garret and by picking up lawyer-talk and the rest of it through loitering about the law-courts and listening. But it is only surmise; there is no *evidence* that he ever did either of those things. They are merely a couple of chunks of plaster of Paris.

There is a legend that he got his bread and butter by holding horses in front of the London theaters, mornings and afternoons. Maybe he did. If he did, it seriously shortened his law-study hours and his recreation-time in the courts. In those very days he was writing great plays, and needed all the time he could get. The horse-holding legend ought to be strangled; it too formidably increases the historian's difficulty in accounting for the young Shakespeare's erudition—an erudition which he was acquiring, hunk by hunk and chunk by chunk, every day in those strenuous times, and emptying each day's catch into next day's imperishable drama.

He had to acquire a knowledge of war at the same time; and a knowledge of soldier-people and sailor-people and their ways and talk; also a knowledge of some foreign lands and their languages: for he was daily emptying fluent streams of these various knowledges, too, into his dramas. How did he acquire these rich assets?

In the usual way: by surmise. It is *surmised* that he traveled in Italy and Germany and around, and qualified himself to put their scenic and social aspects upon paper; that he perfected himself in French, Italian, and Spanish on the road; that he went in Leicester's expedition to the Low Countries, as soldier or sutler or something, for several months or years—or whatever length of time a surmiser needs in his business—and thus became familiar with soldiership and soldier-ways and soldier-talk and generalship and general-ways and general-talk, and seamanship and sailor-ways and sailor-talk.

Maybe he did all these things, but I would like to know who held the horses in the mean time; and who studied the books in the garret; and who frollicked in the law-courts for recreation. Also, who did the call-boying and the play-acting.

For he became a call-boy; and as early as '93 he became a "vagabond"—the law's ungentle term for an unlisted actor; and in '94 a "regular" and properly and officially listed member of that (in those days) lightly valued and not much respected profession.

Right soon thereafter he became a stockholder in two theaters, and manager of them. Thenceforward he was a busy and flourishing business man, and was raking in money with both hands for twenty years. Then in a noble frenzy of poetic inspiration he wrote his one poem—his only poem, his darling—and laid him down and died:

> *Good friend for Iesus sake forbeare*
> *To digg the dust encloased heare:*
> *Blest be ye man yt spares thes stones*
> *And curst be he yt moves my bones.*

He was probably dead when he wrote it. Still, this is only conjecture. We have only circumstantial evidence. Internal evidence.

Shall I set down the rest of the Conjectures which constitute the giant Biography of William Shakespeare? It would strain the Unabridged Dictionary to hold them. He is a brontosaur: nine bones and six hundred barrels of plaster of Paris.

5

"We May Assume"

In the Assuming trade three separate and independent cults are transacting business. Two of these cults are known as the Shakespearites and the Baconians, and I am the other one—the Brontosaurian.

The Shakespearite knows that Shakespeare wrote Shakespeare's Works; the Baconian knows that Francis Bacon wrote them; the Brontosaurian doesn't really know which of them did it, but is quite composedly and contentedly sure that Shakespeare *didn't,* and strongly suspects that Bacon *did.* We all have to do a good deal of assuming, but I am fairly certain that in every case I can call to mind the Baconian assumers have come out ahead of the Shakespearites. Both parties handle the same materials, but the Baconians seem to me to get much more reasonable and rational and persuasive results out of them than is the case with the Shakespearites. The Shakespearite conducts his assuming upon a definite principle, an unchanging and immutable law: which is: 2 and 8 and 7 and 14, added together, make 165. I believe this to be an error. No matter, you cannot get a habit-sodden Shakespearite to cipher-up his materials upon any other basis. With the Baconian it is different. If you place before him the above figures and set him to adding them up, he will never in any case get more than 45 out of them, and in nine cases out of ten he will get just the proper 31.

Let me try to illustrate the two systems in a simple and homely way calculated to bring the idea within the grasp of the ignorant and unintelligent. We will suppose a case: take a lap-bred, house-fed, uneducated, inexperienced kitten; take a rugged old Tom that's scarred from stem to rudder-post with the memorials of strenuous experience, and is so cultured, so educated, so limitlessly erudite that one may say of him "all cat-knowledge is his province"; also, take a mouse. Lock the three up in a holeless, crackless, exitless, prison-cell. Wait half an hour, then open the cell, introduce a Shakespearite and a Baconian, and let them cipher and assume. The mouse is missing: the question to be decided is, where is it? You can guess both verdicts beforehand. One verdict will say the kitten contains the mouse; the other will as certainly say the mouse is in the tom-cat.

The Shakespearite will Reason like this—(that is not my word, it is his). He will say the kitten *may have been* attending school when nobody was noticing; therefore *we are warranted in assuming* that it did so; also, it *could have been* training in a court-clerk's office when no one was noticing; since that could have happened, *we are justified in assuming* that it did happen; it *could have studied catology in a garret* when no one was noticing—therefore it *did;* it *could have* attended cat-assizes on the shed-roof nights, for recreation, when no one was noticing, and have harvested a knowledge of cat court-forms and cat lawyer-talk in that way: it *could* have done it, therefore without a doubt it *did;* it *could have* gone soldiering with a war-tribe when no one was noticing, and learned soldier-wiles and soldier-ways, and what to do with a mouse when opportunity offers; the plain inference, therefore, is that that is what it *did*. Since all these manifold things *could* have occurred, we have *every right to believe* they did occur. These patiently and painstakingly accumulated vast acquirements and competences needed but one thing more—opportunity—to convert themselves into triumphant action. The opportunity came, we have the result; *beyond shadow of question* the mouse is in the kitten.

It is proper to remark that when we of the three cults plant a *"We think we may assume,"* we expect it, under careful watering and fertilizing and tending, to grow up into a strong and hardy and weather-defying *"there isn't a shadow of a doubt"* at last—and it usually happens.

We know what the Baconian's verdict would be: *"There is not a rag of evidence that the kitten has had any training, any education, any experience qualifying it for the present occasion, or is indeed equipped for any achievement above lifting such unclaimed milk as comes its way; but there is abundant evidence—unassailable proof, in fact—that the other animal is equipped, to the last detail, with every qualification necessary for the event. Without shadow of doubt the tom-cat contains the mouse."*

6

When Shakespeare died, in 1616, great literary productions attributed to him as author had been before the London world and in high
favor for twenty-five years. Yet his death was not an event. It made
no stir, it attracted no attention. Apparently his eminent literary
contemporaries did not realize that a celebrated poet had passed
from their midst. Perhaps they knew a play-actor of minor rank had
disappeared, but did not regard him as the author of his Works. "We
are justified in assuming" this.

His death was not even an event in the little town of Stratford.
Does this mean that in Stratford he was not regarded as a celebrity of
any kind?

"We are privileged to assume"—no, we are indeed *obliged* to assume—that such was the case. He had spent the first twenty-two or
twenty-three years of his life there, and of course knew everybody
and was known by everybody of that day in the town, including the
dogs and the cats and the horses. He had spent the last five or six
years of his life there, diligently trading in every big and little thing
that had money in it; so we are compelled to assume that many of
the folk there in those said latter days knew him personally, and the
rest by sight and hearsay. But not as a *celebrity?* Apparently not. For
everybody soon forgot to remember any contact with him or any
incident connected with him. The dozens of townspeople, still alive,
who had known of him or known about him in the first twenty-three
years of his life were in the same unremembering condition: if they
knew of any incident connected with that period of his life they
didn't tell about it. Would they if they had been asked? It is most
likely. Were they asked? It is pretty apparent that they were not.
Why weren't they? It is a very plausible guess that nobody there or
elsewhere was interested to know.

For seven years after Shakespeare's death nobody seems to have
been interested in him. Then the quarto[1] was published, and Ben

---

[1] A slip. Clemens meant to say "folio."—C.N.

Jonson awoke out of his long indifference and sang a song of praise and put it in the front of the book. Then silence fell *again.*

For sixty years. Then inquiries into Shakespeare's Stratford life began to be made, of Stratfordians. Of Stratfordians who had known Shakespeare or had seen him? No. Then of Stratfordians who had seen people who had known or seen people who had seen Shakespeare? No. Apparently the inquiries were only made of Stratfordians who were not Stratfordians of Shakespeare's day, but later comers; and what they had learned had come to them from persons who had not seen Shakespeare; and what they had learned was not claimed as *fact,* but only as legend—dim and fading and indefinite legend; legend of the calf-slaughtering rank, and not worth remembering either as history or fiction.

Has it ever happened before—or since—that a celebrated person who had spent exactly half of a fairly long life in the village where he was born and reared, was able to slip out of this world and leave that village voiceless and gossipless behind him—utterly voiceless, utterly gossipless? And permanently so? I don't believe it has happened in any case except Shakespeare's. And couldn't and wouldn't have happened in his case if he had been regarded as a celebrity at the time of his death.

When I examine my own case—but let us do that, and see if it will not be recognizable as exhibiting a condition of things quite likely to result, most likely to result, indeed substantially *sure* to result in the case of a celebrated person, a benefactor of the human race. Like me.

My parents brought me to the village of Hannibal, Missouri, on the banks of the Mississippi, when I was two and a half years old. I entered school at five years of age, and drifted from one school to another in the village during nine and a half years. Then my father died, leaving his family in exceedingly straitened circumstances; wherefore my book-education came to a standstill forever, and I became a printer's apprentice, on board and clothes, and when the clothes failed I got a hymn-book in place of them. This for summer wear, probably. I lived in Hannibal fifteen and a half years, altogether, then ran away, according to the custom of persons who are intending to become celebrated. I never lived there afterward. Four years later I became a "cub" on a Mississippi steamboat in the St. Louis and New Orleans trade, and after a year and a half of hard study and hard work the U.S. inspectors rigorously examined me through a couple of long sittings and decided that I knew every inch of the Mississippi—thirteen hundred miles—in the dark and in the day—as well as a baby knows the way to its mother's paps day or night. So they licensed me as a pilot—knighted me, so to speak—and I rose up clothed with authority, a responsible servant of the United States Government.

Now then. Shakespeare died young—he was only fifty-two. He had lived in his native village twenty-six years, or about that. He died celebrated (if you believe everything you read in the books). Yet when he died nobody there or elsewhere took any notice of it; and for sixty years afterward no townsman remembered to say anything about him or about his life in Stratford. When the inquirer came at last he got but one fact—no, *legend*—and got that one at second hand, from a person who had only heard it as a rumor and didn't claim copyright in it as a production of his own. He couldn't, very well, for its date antedated his own birth-date. But necessarily a number of persons were still alive in Stratford who, in the days of their youth, had seen Shakespeare nearly every day in the last five years of his life, and they would have been able to tell that inquirer some first-hand things about him if he had in those last days been a celebrity and therefore a person of interest to the villagers. Why did not the inquirer hunt them up and interview them? Wasn't it worth while? Wasn't the matter of sufficient consequence? Had the inquirer an engagement to see a dog-fight and couldn't spare the time?

It all seems to mean that he never had any literary celebrity, there or elsewhere, and no considerable repute as actor and manager.

Now then, I am away along in life—my seventy-third year being already well behind me—yet *sixteen* of my Hannibal schoolmates are still alive today, and can tell—and do tell—inquirers dozens and dozens of incidents of their young lives and mine together; things that happened to us in the morning of life, in the blossom of our youth, in the good days, the dear days, "the days when we went gipsying, a long time ago." Most of them creditable to me, too. One child to whom I paid court when she was five years old and I eight still lives in Hannibal, and she visited me last summer, traversing the necessary ten or twelve hundred miles of railroad without damage to her patience or to her old-young vigor. Another little lassie to whom I paid attention in Hannibal when she was nine years old and I the same, is still alive—in London—and hale and hearty, just as I am.

And on the few surviving steamboats—those lingering ghosts and remembrancers of great fleets that plied the big river in the beginning of my water-career—which is exactly as long ago as the whole invoice of the life-years of Shakespeare numbers—there are still findable two or three river-pilots who saw me do creditable things in those ancient days; and several white-headed engineers; and several roustabouts and mates; and several deck-hands who used to heave the lead for me and send up on the still night air the "Six—feet— *scant!"* that made me shudder, and the *"M-a-r-k—twain!"* that took the shudder away, and presently the darling "By the d-e-e-p—*four!"* that lifted me to heaven for joy.[2] They know about me, and can tell. And so do printers, from St. Louis to New York; and so do newspaper reporters, from Nevada to San Francisco. And so do the police. If Shakespeare had really been celebrated, like me, Stratford could have told things about him; and if my experience goes for anything, they'd have done it.

7

If I had under my superintendence a controversy appointed to decide whether Shakespeare wrote Shakespeare or not, I believe I would place before the debaters only the one question, *Was Shakespeare ever a practising lawyer?* and leave everything else out.

It is maintained that the man who wrote the plays was not merely myriad-minded, but also myriad-accomplished; that he not only knew some thousands of things about human life in all its shades and grades, and about the hundred arts and trades and crafts and professions which men busy themselves in, but that he could *talk* about the men and their grades and trades accurately, making no mistakes. Maybe it is so, but have the experts spoken, or is it only Tom, Dick, and Harry? Does the exhibit stand upon wide, and loose, and eloquent generalizing—which is not evidence, and not proof—or upon details, particulars, statistics, illustrations, demonstrations?

Experts of unchallengeable authority have testified definitely as to only one of Shakespeare's multifarious craft-equipments, so far as

[2] Four fathoms—twenty-four feet.—M.T.

my recollections of Shakespeare-Bacon talk abide with me—his law-equipment. I do not remember that Wellington or Napoleon ever examined Shakespeare's battles and sieges and strategies, and then decided and established for good and all that they were militarily flawless; I do not remember that any Nelson, or Drake, or Cook ever examined his seamanship and said it showed profound and accurate familiarity with that art; I don't remember that any king or prince or duke has ever testified that Shakespeare was letter-perfect in his handling of royal court-manners and the talk and manners of aristocracies; I don't remember that any illustrious Latinist or Grecian or Frenchman or Spaniard or Italian has proclaimed him a past-master in those languages; I don't remember—well, I don't remember that there is *testimony*—great testimony—imposing testimony—unanswerable and unattackable testimony as to any of Shakespeare's hundred specialties, except one: the law.

Other things change, with time, and the student cannot trace back with certainty the changes that various trades and their processes and technicalities have undergone in the long stretch of a century or two and find out what their processes and technicalities were in those early days, but with the law it is different: it is mile-stoned and documented all the way back, and the master of that wonderful trade, that complex and intricate trade, that awe-compelling trade, has competent ways of knowing whether Shakespeare-law is good law or not; and whether his law-court procedure is correct or not, and whether his legal shop-talk is the shop-talk of a veteran practitioner or only a machine-made counterfeit of it gathered from books and from occasional loiterings in Westminster.

Richard H. Dana served two years before the mast, and had every experience that falls to the lot of the sailor before the mast of our day. His sailor-talk flows from his pen with the sure touch and the ease and confidence of a person who has *lived* what he is talking about, not gathered it from books and random listenings. Hear him:

> Having hove short, cast off the gaskets, and made the bunt of each sail fast by the jigger, with a man on each yard, at the word the whole canvas of the ship was loosed, and with the greatest rapidity possible everything was sheeted home and hoisted up, the anchor tripped and cat-headed, and the ship under headway.

Again:

> The royal yards were all crossed at once, and royals and sky-sails set, and, as we had the wind free, the booms were run out, and all were aloft, active as cats, laying out on the yards and booms, reeving the studding-sail gear; and sail after sail the captain piled upon her, until she was covered with canvas, her sails looking like a great white cloud resting upon a black speck.

Once more. A race in the Pacific:

> Our antagonist was in her best trim. Being clear of the point, the breeze became stiff, and the royal-masts bent under our sails, but we would not take them in until we saw three boys spring into the rigging of the *California;* then they were all furled at once, but with orders to our boys to stay aloft at the top-gallant mast-heads and loose them again at the word. It was my duty to furl the fore-royal; and while standing by to loose it again, I had a fine view of the scene. From where I stood, the two vessels seemed nothing but spars and sails, while their narrow decks, far below, slanting over by the force of the wind aloft, appeared hardly capable of supporting the great fabrics raised upon them. The *California* was to windward of us, and had every advantage; yet, while the breeze was stiff we held our own. As soon as it began to slacken she ranged a little ahead, and the order was given to loose the royals. In an instant the gaskets were off and the bunt dropped. "Sheet home the fore-royal!"—"Weather sheet's home!"—"Lee sheet's home!"—"Hoist away, sir!" is bawled from aloft. "Overhaul your clew-lines!" shouts the mate. "Aye-aye, sir, all clear!"—"Taut leech! belay! Well the lee brace; haul taut to windward!" and the royals are set.

What would the captain of any sailing-vessel of our time say to that? He would say, "The man that wrote that didn't learn his trade out of a book, he has *been* there!" But would this same captain be competent to sit in judgment upon Shakespeare's seamanship—considering the changes in ships and ship-talk that have necessarily taken place, unrecorded, unremembered, and lost to history in the last three hundred years? It is my conviction that Shakespeare's sailor-talk would be Choctaw to him. For instance—from "The Tempest":

> *Master.* Boatswain!
> *Boatswain.* Here, master; what cheer?

Master. Good, speak to the mariners: fall to 't, yarely, or we run ourselves to ground; bestir, bestir!

(Enter mariners.)

Boatswain. Heigh, my hearts! cheerly, cheerly, my hearts! yare, yare! Take in the topsail. Tend to the master's whistle. . . . Down with the topmast! yare! lower, lower! Bring her to try wi' the main course. . . . Lay her a-hold, a-hold! Set her two courses. Off to sea again; lay her off.

That will do, for the present; let us yare a little, now, for a change.

If a man should write a book and in it make one of his characters say, "Here, devil, empty the quoins into the standing galley and the imposing-stone into the hell-box; assemble the comps around the frisket and let them jeff for takes and be quick about it," I should recognize a mistake or two in the phrasing, and would know that the writer was only a printer theoretically, not practically.

I have been a quartz miner in the silver regions—a pretty hard life; I know all the palaver of that business. I know all about discovery claims and the subordinate claims; I know all about lodes, ledges, outcroppings, dips, spurs, angles, shafts, drifts, inclines, levels, tunnels, air-shafts, "horses," clay casings, granite casings; quartz mills and their batteries; arastras, and how to charge them with quicksilver and sulphate of copper; and how to clean them up, and how to reduce the resulting amalgam in the retorts, and how to cast the bullion into pigs; and finally I know how to screen tailings, and also how to hunt for something less robust to do, and find it. I know the argot of the quartz-mining and milling industry familiarly; and so whenever Bret Harte introduces that industry into a story, the first time one of his miners opens his mouth I recognize from his phrasing that Harte got the phrasing by listening—like Shakespeare—I mean the Stratford one—not by experience. No one can talk the quartz dialect correctly without learning it with pick and shovel and drill and fuse.

I have been a surface miner—gold—and I know all its mysteries, and the dialect that belongs with them; and whenever Harte introduces that industry into a story I know by the phrasing of his characters that neither he nor they have ever served that trade.

I have been a "pocket" miner—a sort of gold mining not findable in any but one little spot in the world, so far as I know. I know how, with horn and water, to find the trail of a pocket and trace it step by step and stage by stage up the mountain to its source, and find the compact little nest of yellow metal reposing in its secret home under the ground. I know the language of that trade, that capricious trade, that fascinating buried-treasure trade, and can catch any writer who tries to use it without having learned it by the sweat of his brow and the labor of his hands.

I know several other trades and the argot that goes with them; and whenever a person tries to talk the talk peculiar to any of them without having learned it at its source I can trap him always before he gets far on his road.

And so, as I have already remarked, if I were required to superintend a Bacon-Shakespeare controversy, I would narrow the matter down to a single question—the only one, so far as the previous controversies have informed me, concerning which illustrious experts of unimpeachable competency have testified: *Was the author of Shakespeare's Works a lawyer?*—a lawyer deeply read and of limitless experience? I would put aside the guesses and surmises, and perhapses, and might-have-beens, and could-have-beens, and must-have-beens, and we-are-justified-in-presumings, and the rest of those vague specters and shadows and indefinitenesses, and stand or fall, win or lose, by the verdict rendered by the jury upon that single question. If the verdict was Yes, I should feel quite convinced that the Stratford Shakespeare, the actor, manager, and trader who died so obscure, so forgotten, so destitute of even village consequence, that sixty years afterward no fellow-citizen and friend of his later days remembered to tell anything about him, did not write the Works.

Chapter XIII of *The Shakespeare Problem Restated* bears the heading "Shakespeare as a Lawyer," and comprises some fifty pages of expert testimony, with comments thereon, and I will copy the first nine, as being sufficient all by themselves, as it seems to me, to settle the question which I have conceived to be the master-key to the Shakespeare-Bacon puzzle.

8

Shakespeare as a Lawyer[3]

The Plays and Poems of Shakespeare supply ample evidence that their author not only had a very extensive and accurate knowledge of law, but that he was well acquainted with the manners and customs of members of the Inns of Court and with legal life generally.

"While novelists and dramatists are constantly making mistakes as to the laws of marriage, of wills, and inheritance, to Shakespeare's law, lavishly as he expounds it, there can neither be demurrer, nor bill of exceptions, nor writ of error." Such was the testimony borne by one of the most distinguished lawyers of the nineteenth century who was raised to the high office of Lord Chief Justice in 1850, and subsequently became Lord Chancellor. Its weight will, doubtless, be more appreciated by lawyers than by laymen, for only lawyers know how impossible it is for those who have not served an apprenticeship to the law to avoid displaying their ignorance if they venture to employ legal terms and to discuss legal doctrines. "There is nothing so dangerous," wrote Lord Campbell, "as for one not of the craft to tamper with our freemasonry." A layman is certain to betray himself by using some expression which a lawyer would never employ. Mr. Sidney Lee himself supplies us with an example of this. He writes (p. 164): "On February 15, 1609, Shakespeare . . . obtained judgment from a jury against Addenbroke for the payment of No. 6, and No. 1, 5s. 0d. costs." Now a lawyer would never have spoken of obtaining "judgment from a jury," for it is the function of a jury not to deliver judgment (which is the prerogative of the court), but to find a verdict on the facts. The error is, indeed, a venial one, but it is just one of those little things which at once enable a lawyer to know if the writer is a layman or "one of the craft."

But when a layman ventures to plunge deeply into legal subjects, he is naturally apt to make an exhibition of his incompetence. "Let a non-professional man, however acute," writes Lord Campbell again, "presume to talk law, or to draw illustrations from legal science in discussing other subjects, and he will speedily fall into laughable absurdity."

And what does the same high authority say about Shakespeare? He

[3] From Chapter XIII of *The Shakespeare Problem Restated.* By George G. Greenwood, M.P. John Lane Company, publishers.

had "a deep technical knowledge of the law," and an easy familiarity
with "some of the most abstruse proceedings in English jurisprudence."
And again: "Whenever he indulges this propensity he uniformly lays
down good law." Of *Henry IV,* Part 2, he says: "If Lord Eldon could be
supposed to have written the play, I do not see how he could be charge-
able with having forgotten any of his law while writing it." Charles and
Mary Cowden Clarke speak of "the marvelous intimacy which he displays with legal terms, his frequent adoption of them in illustration, and
his curiously technical knowledge of their form and force." Malone,
himself a lawyer, wrote: "His knowledge of legal terms is not merely
such as might be acquired by the casual observation of even his all-
comprehending mind; it has the appearance of technical skill." Another
lawyer and well-known Shakespearian, Richard Grant White, says:
"No dramatist of the time, not even Beaumont, who was the younger
son of a judge of the Common Pleas, and who after studying in the Inns
of Court abandoned law for the drama, used legal phrases with Shakespeare's readiness and exactness. And the significance of this fact is
heightened by another, that it is only to the language of the law that he
exhibits this inclination. The phrases peculiar to other occupations
serve him on rare occasions by way of description, comparison, or illustration, generally when something in the scene suggests them, but legal
phrases flow from his pen as part of his vocabulary and parcel of his
thought. Take the word 'purchase' for instance, which, in ordinary use,
means to acquire by giving value, but applies in law to all legal modes of
obtaining property except by inheritance or descent, and in this peculiar
sense the word occurs five times in Shakespeare's thirty-four plays, and
only in one single instance in the fifty-four plays of Beaumont and
Fletcher. It has been suggested that it was in attendance upon the
courts in London that he picked up his legal vocabulary. But this supposition not only fails to account for Shakespeare's peculiar freedom
and exactness in the use of that phraseology, it does not even place him
in the way of learning those terms his use of which is most remarkable,
which are not such as he would have heard at ordinary proceedings at
nisi prius, but such as refer to the tenure or transfer of real property,
'fine and recovery,' 'statutes merchant,' 'purchase,' 'indenture,' 'tenure,'
'double voucher,' 'fee simple,' 'fee farm,' 'remainder,' 'reversion,' 'forfeiture,' etc. This conveyancer's jargon could not have been picked up
by hanging round the courts of law in London two hundred and fifty
years ago, when suits as to the title of real property were comparatively
rare. And besides, Shakespeare uses his law just as freely in his first
plays, written in his first London years, as in those produced at a later
period. Just as exactly, too; for the correctness and propriety with

which these terms are introduced have compelled the admiration of a Chief Justice and a Lord Chancellor."

Senator Davis wrote: "We seem to have something more than a sciolist's temerity of indulgence in the terms of an unfamiliar art. No legal solecisms will be found. The abstrusest elements of the common law are impressed into a disciplined service. Over and over again, where such knowledge is unexampled in writers unlearned in the law, Shakespeare appears in perfect possession of it. In the law of real property, its rules of tenure and descents, its entails, its fines and recoveries, their vouchers and double vouchers, in the procedure of the Courts, the method of bringing writs and arrests, the nature of actions, the rules of pleading, the law of escapes and of contempt of court, in the principles of evidence, both technical and philosophical, in the distinction between the temporal and spiritual tribunals, in the law of attainder and forfeiture, in the requisites of a valid marriage, in the presumption of legitimacy, in the learning of the law of prerogative, in the inalienable character of the Crown, this mastership appears with surprising authority."

To all this testimony (and there is much more which I have not cited) may now be added that of a great lawyer of our own times, *viz.:* Sir James Plaisted Wilde, Q.C. 1855, created a Baron of the Exchequer in 1860, promoted to the post of Judge-Ordinary and Judge of the Courts of Probate and Divorce in 1863, and better known to the world as Lord Penzance, to which dignity he was raised in 1869. Lord Penzance, as all lawyers know, and as the late Mr. Inderwick, K.C., has testified, was one of the first legal authorities of his day, famous for his "remarkable grasp of legal principles," and "endowed by nature with a remarkable facility for marshaling facts, and for a clear expression of his views."

Lord Penzance speaks of Shakespeare's "perfect familiarity with not only the principles, axioms, and maxims, but the technicalities of English law, a knowledge so perfect and intimate that he was never incorrect and never at fault. . . . The mode in which this knowledge was pressed into service on all occasions to express his meaning and illustrate his thoughts was quite unexampled. He seems to have had a special pleasure in his complete and ready mastership of it in all its branches. As manifested in the plays, this legal knowledge and learning had therefore a special character which places it on a wholly different footing from the rest of the multifarious knowledge which is exhibited in page after page of the plays. At every turn and point at which the author required a metaphor, simile, or illustration, his mind ever turned *first* to the law. He seems almost to have *thought* in legal phrases, the commonest of legal expressions were ever at the end of his pen in description or illustration. That he should have descanted in lawyer language when he had a forensic subject in hand, such as Shylock's bond, was to be expected, but the knowledge of law in 'Shakespeare' was exhibited in a far different manner: it protruded itself on all occasions, appropriate or inappropriate, and mingled itself with strains of thought widely divergent from forensic subjects." Again: "To acquire a perfect familiarity with legal principles, and an accurate and ready use of the technical terms and phrases not only of the conveyancer's office, but of the pleader's chambers and the Courts at Westminster, nothing short of employment in some career involving constant contact with legal questions and general legal work would be requisite. But a continuous employment involves the element of time, and time was just what the manager of two theaters had not at his disposal. In what portion of Shakespeare's *(i.e.,* Shakspere's) career would it be possible to point out that time could be found for the interposition of a legal employment in the chambers or offices of practising lawyers?"

Stratfordians, as is well known, casting about for some possible explanation of Shakespeare's extraordinary knowledge of law, have made the suggestion that Shakespeare might, conceivably, have been a clerk in an attorney's office before he came to London. Mr. Collier wrote to Lord Campbell to ask his opinion as to the probability of this being true. His answer was as follows: "You require us to believe implicitly a fact, of which, if true, positive and irrefragable evidence in his own handwriting might have been forthcoming to establish it. Not having been actually enrolled as an attorney, neither the records of the local court at Stratford nor of the superior Courts at Westminster would present his name as being concerned in any suit as an attorney, but it might reasonably have been expected that there would be deeds or wills witnessed by him still extant, and after a very diligent search none such can be discovered."

Upon this Lord Penzance comments: "It cannot be doubted that Lord Campbell was right in this. No young man could have been at work in an attorney's office without being called upon continually to act as a witness, and in many other ways leaving traces of his work and name." There is not a single fact or incident in all that is known of Shakespeare, even by rumor or tradition, which supports this notion of a clerkship. And after much argument and surmise which has been indulged in on this subject, we may, I think, safely put the notion on one side, for no less an authority than Mr. Grant White says finally that the idea of his having been clerk to an attorney has been "blown to pieces."

It is altogether characteristic of Mr. Churton Collins that he, nevertheless, adopts this exploded myth. "That Shakespeare was in early life employed as a clerk in an attorney's office may be correct. At Stratford there was by royal charter a Court of Record sitting every fortnight, with six attorneys, besides the town clerk, belonging to it, and it is certainly not straining probability to suppose that the young Shakespeare may have had employment in one of them. There is, it is true, no tradition to this effect, but such traditions as we have about Shakespeare's occupation between the time of leaving school and going to London are so loose and baseless that no confidence can be placed in them. It is, to say the least, more probable that he was in an attorney's office than that he was a butcher killing calves 'in a high style,' and making speeches over them."

This is a charming specimen of Stratfordian argument. There is, as we have seen, a very old tradition that Shakespeare was a butcher's apprentice. John Dowdall, who made a tour in Warwickshire in 1693, testifies to it as coming from the old clerk who showed him over the church, and it is unhesitatingly accepted as true by Mr. Halliwell-Phillipps. (Vol. I, p. 11, and Vol. II, pp. 71, 72.) Mr. Sidney Lee sees nothing improbable in it, and it is supported by Aubrey, who must have written his account some time before 1680, when his manuscript was completed. Of the attorney's clerk hypothesis, on the other hand, there is not the faintest vestige of a tradition. It has been evolved out of the fertile imaginations of embarrassed Stratfordians, seeking for some explanation of the Stratford rustic's marvelous acquaintance with law and legal terms and legal life. But Mr. Churton Collins has not the least hesitation in throwing over the tradition which has the warrant of antiquity and setting up in its stead this ridiculous invention, for which not only is there no shred of positive evidence, but which, as Lord Campbell and Lord Penzance point out, is really put out of court by the negative evidence, since "no young man could have been at work in an attorney's office without being called upon continually to act as a witness, and in many other ways leaving traces of his work and name." And as Mr. Edwards further points out, since the day when Lord Campbell's book was published (between forty and fifty years ago), "every old deed or will, to say nothing of other legal papers, dated during the period of William Shakespeare's youth, has been scrutinized over half a dozen shires, and not one signature of the young man has been found."

Moreover, if Shakespeare had served as clerk in an attorney's office it is clear that he must have so served for a considerable period in order to have gained (if, indeed, it is credible that he could have so gained) his remarkable knowledge of law. Can we then for a moment believe that, if this had been so, tradition would have been absolutely silent on the matter? That Dowdall's old clerk, over eighty years of age, should have never heard of it (though he was sure enough about the butcher's apprentice), and that all the other ancient witnesses should be in similar ignorance!

But such are the methods of Stratfordian controversy. Tradition is to be scouted when it is found inconvenient, but cited as irrefragable truth when it suits the case. Shakespeare of Stratford was the author of the Plays and Poems, but the author of the Plays and Poems could not have been a butcher's apprentice. Away, therefore, with tradition. But the author of the Plays and Poems *must* have had a very large and a very accurate knowledge of the law. Therefore, Shakespeare of Stratford must have been an attorney's clerk! The method is simplicity itself. By similar reasoning Shakespeare has been made a country schoolmaster, a soldier, a physician, a printer, and a good many other things besides, according to the inclination and the exigencies of the commentator. It would not be in the least surprising to find that he was studying Latin as a schoolmaster and law in an attorney's office at the same time.

However, we must do Mr. Collins the justice of saying that he has fully recognized, what is indeed tolerably obvious, that Shakespeare must have had a sound legal training. "It may, of course, be urged," he writes, "that Shakespeare's knowledge of medicine, and particularly that branch of it which related to morbid psychology, is equally remarkable, and that no one has ever contended that he was a physician. (Here Mr. Collins is wrong; that contention also has been put forward.) It may be urged that his acquaintance with the technicalities of other crafts and callings, notably of marine and military affairs, was also extraordinary, and yet no one has suspected him of being a sailor or a soldier. (Wrong again. Why, even Messrs. Garnett and Gosse "suspect" that he was a soldier!) This may be conceded, but the concession hardly furnishes an analogy. To these and all other subjects he recurs occasionally, and in season, but with reminiscences of the law his memory, as is abundantly clear, was simply saturated. In season and out of season now in manifest, now in recondite application, he presses it into the service of expression and illustration. At least a third of his myriad metaphors are derived from it. It would indeed be difficult to find a single act in any of his dramas, nay, in some of them, a single scene, the diction and imagery of which are not colored by it. Much of his law may have been acquired from three books easily accessible to him— namely, Tottell's *Precedents* (1572), Pulton's *Statutes* (1578), and Fraunce's *Lawier's Logike* (1588), works with which he certainly seems to have been familiar; but much of it could only have come from one who had an intimate acquaintance with legal proceedings. We quite agree with Mr. Castle that Shakespeare's legal knowledge is not what could have been picked up in an attorney's office, but could only have been learned by an actual attendance at the Courts, at a Pleader's Chambers, and on circuit, or by associating intimately with members of the Bench and Bar."

This is excellent. But what is Mr. Collins's explanation? "Perhaps the simplest solution of the problem is to accept the hypothesis that in early life he was in an attorney's office (!), that he there contracted a love for the law which never left him, that as a young man in London he continued to study or dabble in it for his amusement, to stroll in leisure hours into the Courts, and to frequent the society of lawyers. On no other supposition is it possible to explain the attraction which the law evidently had for him, and his minute and undeviating accuracy in a subject where no layman who has indulged in such copious and ostentatious display of legal technicalities has ever yet succeeded in keeping himself from tripping."

A lame conclusion. "No other supposition" indeed! Yes, there is another, and a very obvious supposition—namely, that Shakespeare was himself a lawyer, well versed in his trade, versed in all the ways of the courts, and living in close intimacy with judges and members of the Inns of Court.

One is, of course, thankful that Mr. Collins has appreciated the fact that Shakespeare must have had a sound legal training, but I may be forgiven if I do not attach quite so much importance to his pronouncements on this branch of the subject as to those of Malone, Lord Campbell, Judge Holmes, Mr. Castle, K.C., Lord Penzance, Mr. Grant White, and other lawyers, who have expressed their opinion on the matter of Shakespeare's legal acquirements. . . .

Here it may, perhaps, be worth while to quote again from Lord Penzance's book as to the suggestion that Shakespeare had somehow or other managed "to acquire a perfect familiarity with legal principles, and an accurate and ready use of the technical terms and phrases, not only of the conveyancer's office, but of the pleader's chambers and the Courts at Westminster." This, as Lord Penzance points out, "would require nothing short of employment in some career involving *constant contact* with legal questions and general legal work." But "in what portion of Shakespeare's career would it be possible to point out that time could be found for the interposition of a legal employment in the chambers or offices of practising lawyers? . . . It is beyond doubt that at an early period he was called upon to abandon his attendance at school and assist his father, and was soon after, at the age of sixteen, bound apprentice to a trade. While under the obligation of this bond he could not have pursued any other employment. Then he leaves Stratford and comes to London. He has to provide himself with the means of a livelihood, and this he did in some capacity at the theater. No one doubts that. The holding of horses is scouted by many, and perhaps with justice, as being unlikely and certainly unproved; but whatever the nature of his employment was at the theater, there is hardly room for the belief that it could have been other than continuous, for his progress there was so rapid. Ere long he had been taken into the company as an actor, and was soon spoken of as a 'Johannes Factotum.' His rapid accumulation of wealth speaks volumes for the constancy and activity of his services. One fails to see when there could be a break in the current of his life at this period of it, giving room or opportunity for legal or indeed any other employment. 'In 1589,' says Knight, 'we have undeniable evidence that he had not only a casual engagement, was not only a salaried servant, as many players were, but was a shareholder in the company of the Queen's players with other shareholders below him on the list.' This (1589) would be within two years after his arrival in London, which is placed by White and Halliwell-Phillipps about the year 1587. The difficulty in supposing that, starting with a state of ignorance in 1587, when he is supposed to have come to London, he was induced to enter upon a course of most extended study and mental culture, is almost insuperable. Still it was physically possible, provided always that he could have had access to the needful books. But this legal training seems to me to stand on a different footing. It is not only unaccountable and incredible, but it is actually negatived by the known facts of his career." Lord Penzance then refers to the fact that "by 1592 (according to the best authority, Mr. Grant White) several of the plays had been written. *The Comedy of Errors* in 1589, *Love's Labour's Lost* in 1589, *Two Gentlemen of Verona* in 1589 or 1590," and so forth, and then asks, "with this catalogue of dramatic work on hand . . . was it possible that he could have taken a leading part in the management and conduct of two theaters, and if Mr. Phillipps is to be relied upon, taken his share in the performances of the provincial tours of his company— and at the same time devoted himself to the study of the law in all its branches so efficiently as to make himself complete master of its principles and practice, and saturate his mind with all its most technical terms?"

I have cited this passage from Lord Penzance's book, because it lay before me, and I had already quoted from it on the matter of Shakespeare's legal knowledge; but other writers have still better set forth the insuperable difficulties, as they seem to me, which beset the idea that Shakespeare might have found time in some unknown period of early life, amid multifarious other occupations, for the study of classics, literature, and law, to say nothing of languages and a few other matters. Lord Penzance further asks his readers: "Did you ever meet with or hear of an instance in which a young man in this country gave himself up to legal studies and engaged in legal employments, which is the only way of becoming familiar with the technicalities of practice, unless with the view of practising in that profession? I do not believe that it would be easy, or indeed possible, to produce an instance in which the law has been seriously studied in all its branches, except as a qualification for practice in the legal profession."

This testimony is so strong, so direct, so authoritative; and so uncheapened, unwatered by guesses, and surmises, and maybe-so's, and might-have-beens, and could-have-beens, and must-have-beens, and the rest of that ton of plaster of Paris out of which biographers have built the colossal brontosaur which goes by the Stratford actor's name, that it quite convinces me that the man who wrote Shakespeare's Works knew all about law and lawyers. Also, that that man could not have been the Stratford Shakespeare—and *wasn't.*

Who did write these Works, then?

I wish I knew.

9

Did Francis Bacon write Shakespeare's Works?

Nobody knows.

We cannot say we *know* a thing when that thing has not been proved. *Know* is too strong a word to use when the evidence is not final and absolutely conclusive. We can infer, if we want to, like those slaves. . . . No, I will not write that word, it is not kind, it is not courteous. The upholders of the Stratford-Shakespeare superstition call *us* the hardest names they can think of, and they keep doing it all the time; very well, if they like to descend to that level, let them do it, but I will not so undignify myself as to follow them. I cannot call them harsh names; the most I can do is to indicate them by terms reflecting my disapproval; and this without malice, without venom.

To resume. What I was about to say was, those thugs have built their entire superstition upon *inferences,* not upon known and established facts. It is a weak method, and poor, and I am glad to be able to say our side never resorts to it while there is anything else to resort to.

But when we must, we must; and we have now arrived at a place of that sort. . . . Since the Stratford Shakespeare couldn't have written the Works, we infer that somebody did. Who was it, then? This requires some more inferring.

Ordinarily when an unsigned poem sweeps across the continent like a tidal wave whose roar and boom and thunder are made up of admiration, delight, and applause, a dozen obscure people rise up and claim the authorship. Why a dozen, instead of only one or two? One reason is, because there are a dozen that are recognizably competent to do that poem. Do you remember "Beautiful Snow"? Do you remember "Rock Me to Sleep, Mother, Rock Me to Sleep"? Do you remember "Backward, turn backward, O Time, in thy flight! Make me a child again just for tonight"? I remember them very well. Their authorship was claimed by most of the grown-up people who were alive at the time, and every claimant had one plausible argument in his favor, at least—to wit, he could have done the authoring; he was competent.

Have the Works been claimed by a dozen? They haven't. There was good reason. The world knows there was but one man on the planet at the time who was competent—not a dozen, and not two. A long time ago the dwellers in a far country used now and then to find a procession of prodigious footprints stretching across the plain—footprints that were three miles apart, each footprint a third of a mile long and a furlong deep, and with forests and villages mashed to mush in it. Was there any doubt as to who made that mighty trail? Were there a dozen claimants? Were there two? No—the people knew who it was that had been along there: there was only one Hercules.

There has been only one Shakespeare. There couldn't be two; certainly there couldn't be two at the same time. It takes ages to bring forth a Shakespeare, and some more ages to match him. This one was not matched before his time; nor during his time; and hasn't been matched since. The prospect of matching him in our time is not bright.

The Baconians claim that the Stratford Shakespeare was not qualified to write the Works, and that Francis Bacon was. They claim that Bacon possessed the stupendous equipment—both natural and acquired—for the miracle; and that no other Englishman of his day possessed the like; or, indeed, anything closely approaching it.

Macaulay, in his Essay, has much to say about the splendor and horizonless magnitude of that equipment. Also, he has synopsized Bacon's history—a thing which cannot be done for the Stratford Shakespeare, for he hasn't any history to synopsize. Bacon's history is open to the world, from his boyhood to his death in old age—a history consisting of known facts, displayed in minute and multitudinous detail: *facts*, not guesses and conjectures and might-have-beens.

Whereby it appears that he was born of a race of statesmen, and had a Lord Chancellor for his father, and a mother who was "distinguished both as a linguist and a theologian: she corresponded in Greek with Bishop Jewell, and translated his *Apologia* from the Latin so correctly that neither he nor Archbishop Parker could suggest a single alteration." It is the atmosphere we are reared in that determines how our inclinations and aspirations shall tend. The atmosphere furnished by the parents to the son in this present case was an atmosphere saturated with learning; with thinkings and ponderings upon deep subjects; and with polite culture. It had its natural effect. Shakespeare of Stratford was reared in a house which had no use for books, since its owners, his parents, were without education. This may have had an effect upon the son, but we do not know, because we have no history of him of an informing sort. There were but few books anywhere, in that day, and only the well-to-do and highly educated possessed them, they being almost confined to the dead languages. "All the valuable books then extant in all the vernacular dialects of Europe would hardly have filled a single shelf"—imagine it! The few existing books were in the Latin tongue mainly. "A person who was ignorant of it was shut out from all acquaintance—not merely with Cicero and Virgil, but with the most interesting memoirs, state papers, and pamphlets of his own time"—a literature necessary to the Stratford lad, for his fictitious reputation's sake, since the writer of his Works would begin to use it wholesale and in a most masterly way before the lad was hardly more than out of his teens and into his twenties.

At fifteen Bacon was sent to the university, and he spent three years there. Thence he went to Paris in the train of the English

Ambassador, and there he mingled daily with the wise, the cultured, the great, and the aristocracy of fashion, during another three years. A total of six years spent at the sources of knowledge; knowledge both of books and of men. The three spent at the university were coeval with the second and last three spent by the little Stratford lad at Stratford school supposedly, and perhapsedly, and maybe, and by inference—with nothing to infer from. The second three of the Baconian six were "presumably" spent by the Stratford lad as apprentice to a butcher. That is, the thugs presume it—on no evidence of any kind. Which is their way, when they want a historical fact. Fact and presumption are, for business purposes, all the same to them. They know the difference, but they also know how to blink it. They know, too, that while in history-building a fact is better than a presumption, it doesn't take a presumption long to bloom into a fact when *they* have the handling of it. They know by old experience that when they get hold of a presumption-tadpole he is not going to *stay* tadpole in their history-tank; no, they know how to develop him into the giant four-legged bullfrog of *fact*, and make him sit up on his hams, and puff out his chin, and look important and insolent and come-to-stay; and assert his genuine simon-pure authenticity with a thundering bellow that will convince everybody because it is so loud. The thug is aware that loudness convinces sixty persons where reasoning convinces but one. I wouldn't be a thug, not even if—but never mind about that, it has nothing to do with the argument, and it is not noble in spirit besides. If I am better than a thug, is the merit mine? No, it is His. Then to Him be the praise. That is the right spirit.

They "presume" the lad severed his "presumed" connection with the Stratford school to become apprentice to a butcher. They also "presume" that the butcher was his father. They don't know. There is no written record of it, nor any other actual evidence. If it would have helped their case any, they would have apprenticed him to thirty butchers, to fifty butchers, to a wilderness of butchers—all by their patented method "presumption." If it will help their case they will do it yet; and if it will further help it, they will "presume" that all those butchers were his father. And the week after, they will *say* it. Why, it is just like being the past tense of the compound reflexive adverbial incandescent hypodermic irregular accusative Noun of Multitude; which is father to the expression which the grammarians call Verb. It is like a whole ancestry, with only one posterity.

To resume. Next, the young Bacon took up the study of law, and mastered that abstruse science. From that day to the end of his life he was daily in close contact with lawyers and judges; not as a casual onlooker in intervals between holding horses in front of a theater, but as a practising lawyer—a great and successful one, a renowned one, a Launcelot of the bar, the most formidable lance in the high brotherhood of the legal Table Round; he lived in the law's atmosphere thenceforth, all his years, and by sheer ability forced his way up its difficult steeps to its supremest summit, the Lord-Chancellorship, leaving behind him no fellow-craftsman qualified to challenge his divine right to that majestic place.

When we read the praises bestowed by Lord Penzance and the other illustrious experts upon the legal condition and legal aptnesses, brilliances, profundities, and felicities so prodigally displayed in the Plays, and try to fit them to the historyless Stratford stage-manager, they sound wild, strange, incredible, ludicrous; but when we put them in the mouth of Bacon they do not sound strange, they seem in their natural and rightful place, they seem at home there. Please turn back and read them again. Attributed to Shakespeare of Stratford they are meaningless, they are inebriate extravagancies—intemperate admirations of the dark side of the moon, so to speak; attributed to Bacon, they are admirations of the golden glories of the moon's front side, the moon at the full—and not intemperate, not overwrought, but sane and right, and justified. "At every turn and point at which the author required a metaphor, simile, or illustration, his mind ever turned *first* to the law; he seems almost to have *thought* in legal phrases; the commonest legal phrases, the commonest of legal expressions, were ever at the end of his pen." That could hapen to no one but a person whose *trade* was the law; it could not happen to a dabbler in it. Veteran mariners fill their conversation with sailor-phrases and draw all their similes from the ship and the sea and the storm, but no mere *passenger* ever does it, be he of Stratford or elsewhere; or could do it with anything resembling accuracy, if he were hardy enough to try. Please read again what Lord Campbell and the other great authorities have said about Bacon when they thought they were saying it about Shakespeare of Stratford.

10

The Rest of the Equipment

The author of the Plays was equipped, beyond every other man of his time, with wisdom, erudition, imagination, capaciousness of mind, grace, and majesty of expression. Every one has said it, no one doubts it. Also, he had humor, humor in rich abundance, and always wanting to break out. We have no evidence of any kind that Shakespeare of Stratford possessed any of these gifts or any of these acquirements. The only lines he ever wrote, so far as we know, are substantially barren of them—barren of all of them.

> Good friend for Iesus sake forbeare
> To digg the dust encloased heare:
> Blest be ye man yt spares thes stones
> And curst be he yt moves my bones.

Ben Jonson says of Bacon, as orator:

His language, *where he could spare and pass by a jest,* was nobly censorious. No man ever spoke more neatly, more pressly, more weightily, or suffered less emptiness, less idleness, in what he uttered. No member of his speech but consisted of his (its) own graces. . . . The fear of every man that heard him was lest he should make an end.

From Macaulay:

He continued to distinguish himself in Parliament, particularly by his exertions in favor of one excellent measure on which the King's heart was set—the union of England and Scotland. It was not difficult for such an intellect to discover many irresistible arguments in favor of such a scheme. He conducted the great case of the *Post Nati* in the Exchequer Chamber; and the decision of the judges—a decision the legality of which may be questioned, but the beneficial effect of which must be acknowledged—was in a great measure attributed to his dexterous management.

Again:

> While actively engaged in the House of Commons and in the courts
> of law, he still found leisure for letters and philosophy. The noble trea-
> tise on the *Advancement of Learning,* which at a later period was ex-
> panded into the *De Augmentis,* appeared in 1605.
>
> The *Wisdom of the Ancients,* a work which, if it had proceeded from
> any other writer, would have been considered as a masterpiece of wit
> and learning, was printed in 1609.
>
> In the mean time the *Novum Organum* was slowly proceeding. Sev-
> eral distinguished men of learning had been permitted to see portions of
> that extraordinary book, and they spoke with the greatest admiration of
> his genius.
>
> Even Sir Thomas Bodley, after perusing the *Cogitata et Visa,* one of
> the most precious of those scattered leaves out of which the great oracu-
> lar volume was afterward made up, acknowledged that "in all proposals
> and plots in that book, Bacon showed himself a master workman"; and
> that "it could not be gainsaid but all the treatise over did abound with
> choice conceits of the present state of learning, and with worthy con-
> templations of the means to procure it."
>
> In 1612 a new edition of the *Essays* appeared, with additions surpass-
> ing the original collection both in bulk and quality.
>
> Nor did these pursuits distract Bacon's attention from a work the
> most arduous, the most glorious, and the most useful that even his
> mighty powers could have achieved, "the reducing and recompiling," to
> use his own phrase, "of the laws of England."

To serve the exacting and laborious offices of Attorney-General
and Solicitor-General would have satisfied the appetite of any other
man for hard work, but Bacon had to add the vast literary industries
just described, to satisfy his. He was a born worker.

> The service which he rendered to letters during the last five years of
> his life, amid ten thousand distractions and vexations, increase the re-
> gret with which we think on the many years which he had wasted, to
> use the words of Sir Thomas Bodley, "on such study as was not worthy
> such a student."
>
> He commenced a digest of the laws of England, a History of England
> under the Princes of the House of Tudor, a body of National History, a
> Philosophical Romance. He made extensive and valuable additions to
> his Essays. He published the inestimable *Treatise De Augmentis Scien-
> tiarum.*

Did these labors of Hercules fill up his time to his contentment, and quiet his appetite for work? Not entirely:

> The trifles with which he amused himself in hours of pain and languor bore the mark of his mind. *The best jest-book in the world* is that which he dictated from memory, without referring to any book, on a day on which illness had rendered him incapable of serious study.

Here are some scattered remarks (from Macaulay) which throw light upon Bacon, and seem to indicate—and maybe demonstrate that he was competent to write the Plays and Poems:

> With great minuteness of observation he had an amplitude of comprehension such as has never yet been vouchsafed to any other human being.

> The *Essays* contain abundant proofs that no nice feature of character, no peculiarity in the ordering of a house, a garden, or a court-masque, could escape the notice of one whose mind was capable of taking in the whole world of knowledge.

> His understanding resembled the tent which the fairy Paribanou gave to Prince Ahmed: fold it, and it seemed a toy for the hand of a lady; spread it, and the armies of powerful Sultans might repose beneath its shade.

> The knowledge in which Bacon excelled all men was a knowledge of the mutual relations of all departments of knowledge.

> In a letter written when he was only thirty-one, to his uncle, Lord Burleigh, he said, "I have taken all knowledge to be my province."

> Though Bacon did not arm his philosophy with the weapons of logic, he adorned her profusely with all the richest decorations of rhetoric.

> The practical faculty was powerful in Bacon; but not, like his wit, so powerful as occasionally to usurp the place of his reason and to tyrannize over the whole man.

There are too many places in the Plays where this happens. Poor old dying John of Gaunt volleying second-rate puns at his own name, is a pathetic instance of it. "We may assume" that it is Bacon's fault, but the Stratford Shakespeare has to bear the blame.

> No imagination was ever at once so strong and so thoroughly subjugated. It stopped at the first check from good sense.

In truth, much of Bacon's life was passed in a visionary world—amid things as strange as any that are described in the *Arabian Tales* . . . amid buildings more sumptuous than the palace of Aladdin, fountains more wonderful than the golden water of Parizade, conveyances more rapid than the hippogryph of Ruggiero, arms more formidable than the lance of Astolfo, remedies more efficacious than the balsam of Fierabras. Yet in his magnificent day-dreams there was nothing wild—nothing but what sober reason sanctioned.

Bacon's greatest performance is the first book of the *Novum Organum.* . . . Every part of it blazes with wit, but with wit which is employed only to illustrate and decorate truth. No book ever made so great a revolution in the mode of thinking, overthrew so many prejudices, introduced so many new opinions.

But what we most admire is the vast capacity of that intellect which, without effort, takes in at once all the domains of science—all the past, the present and the future, all the errors of two thousand years, all the encouraging signs of the passing times, all the bright hopes of the coming age.

He had a wonderful talent for packing thought close and rendering it portable.

His eloquence would alone have entitled him to a high rank in literature.

It is evident that he had each and every one of the mental gifts and each and every one of the acquirements that are so prodigally displayed in the Plays and Poems, and in much higher and richer degree than any other man of his time or of any previous time. He was a genius without a mate, a prodigy not matable. There was only one of him; the planet could not produce two of him at one birth, nor in one age. He could have written anything that is in the Plays and Poems. He could have written this:

> *The cloud-cap'd towers, the gorgeous palaces,*
> *The solemn temples, the great globe itself,*
> *Yea, all which it inherit, shall dissolve,*
> *And, like an insubstantial pageant faded,*
> *Leave not a rack behind. We are such stuff*
> *As dreams are made on, and our little life*
> *Is rounded with a sleep.*

Also, he could have written this, but he refrained:

> *Good friend for Iesus sake forbeare*
> *To digg the dust encloased heare:*
> *Blest be ye man yt spares thes stones*
> *And curst be he yt moves my bones.*

When a person reads the noble verses about the cloud-cap'd towers, he ought not to follow it immediately with Good friend for Iesus sake forbeare, because he will find the transition from great poetry to poor prose too violent for comfort. It will give him a shock. You never notice how commonplace and unpoetic gravel is until you bite into a layer of it in a pie.

11

Am I trying to convince anybody that Shakespeare did not write Shakespeare's Works? Ah, now, what do you take me for? Would I be so soft as that, after having known the human race familiarly for nearly seventy-four years? It would grieve me to know that any one could think so injuriously of me, so uncomplimentarily, so unadmiringly of me. No, no, I am aware that when even the brightest mind in our world has been trained up from childhood in a superstition of any kind, it will never be possible for that mind, in its maturity, to examine sincerely, dispassionately, and conscientiously any evidence or any circumstance which shall seem to cast a doubt upon the validity of that superstition. I doubt if I could do it myself. We always get at second hand our notions about systems of government; and high tariff and low tariff; and prohibition and anti-prohibition; and the holiness of peace and the glories of war; and codes of honor and codes of morals; and approval of the duel and disapproval of it; and our beliefs concerning the nature of cats; and our ideas as to whether the murder of helpless wild animals is base or is heroic; and our preferences in the matter of religious and political parties; and our acceptance or rejection of the Shakespeares and the Arthur Ortons and the Mrs. Eddys. We get them all at second hand, we reason none of them out for ourselves. It is the way we are made. It is the way we are all made, and we can't help it, we can't change it. And whenever we have been furnished a fetish, and have been taught to believe in it, and love it and worship it, and refrain from examining it, there is no evidence, howsoever clear and strong, that can persuade us to withdraw from it our loyalty and our devotion. In morals, conduct, and beliefs we take the color of our environment and associations, and it is a color that can safely be warranted to wash. Whenever we have been furnished with a tar baby ostensibly stuffed with jewels, and warned that it will be dishonorable and irreverent to disembowel it and test the jewels, we keep our sacrilegious hands off it. We submit, not reluctantly, but rather gladly, for we are privately afraid we should find, upon examination, that the jewels are of the sort that are manufactured at North Adams, Mass.

I haven't any idea that Shakespeare will have to vacate his pedestal this side of the year 2209. Disbelief in him cannot come swiftly, disbelief in a healthy and deeply-loved tar baby has never been known to disintegrate swiftly; it is a very slow process. It took several thousand years to convince our fine race—including every splendid intellect in it—that there is no such thing as a witch; it has taken several thousand years to convince that same fine race—including every splendid intellect in it—that there is no such person as Satan; it has taken several centuries to remove perdition from the Protestant Church's program of post-mortem entertainments; it has taken a weary long time to persuade American Presbyterians to give up infant damnation and try to bear it the best they can; and it looks as if their Scotch brethren will still be burning babies in the everlasting fires when Shakespeare comes down from his perch.

We are The Reasoning Race. We can't prove it by the above examples, and we can't prove it by the miraculous "histories" built by those Stratfordolaters out of a hatful of rags and a barrel of sawdust, but there is a plenty of other things we can prove it by, if I could think of them. We are The Reasoning Race, and when we find a vague file of chipmunk-tracks stringing through the dust of Stratford village, we know by our reasoning powers that Hercules has been along there. I feel that our fetish is safe for three centuries yet. The bust, too—there in the Stratford Church. The precious bust, the priceless bust, the calm bust, the serene bust, the emotionless bust, with the dandy mustache, and the putty face, unseamed of care— that face which has looked passionlessly down upon the awed pilgrim for a hundred and fifty years and will still look down upon the awed pilgrim three hundred more, with the deep, deep, deep, subtle, subtle, subtle, expression of a bladder.

12

Irreverence

One of the most trying defects which I find in these—these—what shall I call them? for I will not apply injurious epithets to them, the way they do to us, such violations of courtesy being repugnant to my nature and my dignity. The farthest I can go in that direction is to call them by names of limited reverence—names merely descriptive, never unkind, never offensive, never tainted by harsh feeling. If *they* would do like this, they would feel better in their hearts. Very well, then—to proceed. One of the most trying defects which I find in these Stratfordolaters, these Shakesperiods, these thugs, these bangalores, these troglodytes, these herumfrodites, these blatherskites, these buccaneers, these bandoleers, is their spirit of irreverence. It is detectable in every utterance of theirs when they are talking about us. I am thankful that in me there is nothing of that spirit. When a thing is sacred to me it is impossible for me to be irreverent toward it. I cannot call to mind a single instance where I have ever been irreverent, except toward the things which were sacred to other people. Am I in the right? I think so. But I ask no one to take my unsupported word; no, look at the dictionary; let the dictionary decide. Here is the definition:

> *Irreverence.* The quality or condition of irreverence toward God and sacred things.

What does the Hindu say? He says it is correct. He says irreverence is lack of respect for Vishnu, and Brahma, and Chrishna, and his other gods, and for his sacred cattle, and for his temples and the things within them. He indorses the definition, you see; and there are 300,000,000 Hindus or their equivalents back of him.

The dictionary had the acute idea that by using the capital G it could restrict irreverence to lack of reverence for *our* Deity and our sacred things, but that ingenious and rather sly idea miscarried: for by the simple process of spelling *his* deities with capitals the Hindu confiscates the definition and restricts it to his own sects, thus making it clearly compulsory upon us to revere *his* gods and *his* sacred things, and nobody's else. We can't say a world, for he has our own dictionary at his back, and its decision is final.

This law, reduced to its simplest terms, is this: 1. Whatever is sacred to the Christian must be held in reverence by everybody else; 2. whatever is sacred to the Hindu must be held in reverence by everybody else; 3. therefore, by consequence, logically, and indisputably, whatever is sacred to *me* must be held in reverence by everybody else.

Now then, what aggravates me is that these troglodytes and muscovites and bandoleers and buccaneers are *also* trying to crowd in and share the benefit of the law, and compel everybody to revere their Shakespeare and hold him sacred. We can't have that: there's enough of us already. If you go on widening and spreading and inflating the privilege, it will presently come to be conceded that each man's sacred things are the *only* ones, and the rest of the human race will have to be humbly reverent toward them or suffer for it. That can surely happen, and when it happens, the word Irreverence will be regarded as the most meaningless, and foolish, and self-conceited, and insolent, and impudent, and dictatorial word in the language. And people will say, "Whose business is it what gods I worship and what things hold sacred? Who has the right to dictate to my conscience, and where did he get that right?"

We cannot afford to let that calamity come upon us. We must save the world from this destruction. There is but one way to do it, and that is to stop the spread of the privilege and strictly confine it to its present limits—that is, to all the Christian sects, to all the Hindu sects, and me. We do not need any more, the stock is watered enough, just as it is.

It would be better if the privilege were limited to me alone. I think so because I am the only sect that knows how to employ it gently, kindly, charitably, dispassionately. The other sects lack the quality of self-restraint. The Catholic Church says the most irreverent things about matters which are sacred to the Protestants, and the Protestant Church retorts in kind about the confessional and other matters which Catholics hold sacred; then both of these irreverencers turn upon Thomas Paine and charge *him* with irreverence. This is all unfortunate, because it makes it difficult for students equipped with only a low grade of mentality to find out what Irreverence really *is*.

It will surely be much better all around if the privilege of regulating the irreverent and keeping them in order shall eventually be withdrawn from all the sects but me. Then there will be no more quarreling, no more bandying of disrespectful epithets, no more heartburnings.

There will then be nothing sacred involved in this Bacon-Shakespeare controversy except what is sacred to me. That will simplify the whole matter, and trouble will cease. There will be irreverence no longer, because I will not allow it. The first time those criminals charge me with irreverence for calling their Stratford myth an Arthur-Orton-Mary-Baker-Thompson-Eddy-Louis-the-Seventeenth-Veiled-Prophet-of-Khorassan will be the last. Taught by the methods found effective in extinguishing earlier offenders by the Inquisition, of holy memory, I shall know how to quiet them.

13

Isn't it odd, when you think of it, that you may list all the celebrated Englishmen, Irishmen, and Scotchmen of modern times, clear back to the first Tudors—a list containing five hundred names, shall we say?—and you can go to the histories, biographies, and cyclopedias and learn the particulars of the lives of every one of them. Every one of them except one—the most famous, the most renowned—by far the most illustrious of them all—Shakespeare! You can get the details of the lives of all the celebrated ecclesiastics in the list; all the celebrated tragedians, comedians, singers, dancers, orators, judges, lawyers, poets, dramatists, historians, biographers, editors, inventors, reformers, statesmen, generals, admirals, discoverers, prize-fighters, murderers, pirates, conspirators, horse-jockeys, bunco-steerers, misers, swindlers, explorers, adventurers by land and sea, bankers, financiers, astronomers, naturalists, claimants, impostors, chemists, biologists, geologists, philologists, college presidents and professors, architects, engineers, painters, sculptors, politicians, agitators, rebels, revolutionists, patriots, demagogues, clowns, cooks, freaks, philosophers, burglars, highwaymen, journalists, physicians, surgeons—you can get the life-histories of all of them but *one*. Just *one*—the most extraordinary and the most celebrated of them all—Shakespeare!

You may add to the list the thousand celebrated persons furnished by the rest of Christendom in the past four centuries, and you can find out the life-histories of all those people, too. You will then have listed fifteen hundred celebrities, and you can trace the authentic life-histories of the whole of them. Save one—far and away the most colossal prodigy of the entire accumulation—Shakespeare! About him you can find out *nothing*. Nothing of even the slightest importance. Nothing worth the trouble of stowing away in your memory. Nothing that even remotely indicates that he was ever anything more than a distinctly commonplace person—a manager, an actor of inferior grade, a small trader in a small village that did not regard him as a person of any consequence, and had forgotten all about him before he was fairly cold in his grave. We can go to the records and find out the life-history of every renowned *race-horse* of modern times—but not Shakespeare's! There are many reasons why, and they have been furnished in cart-loads (of guess and conjecture) by those troglodytes; but there is one that is worth all the rest of the reasons put together, and is abundantly sufficient all by itself—*he hadn't any history to record.* There is no way of getting around that deadly fact. And no sane way has yet been discovered of getting around its formidable significance.

Its quite plain significance—to any but those thugs (I do not use the term unkindly) is, that Shakespeare had no prominence while he lived, and none until he had been dead two or three generations. The Plays enjoyed high fame from the beginning; and if he wrote them it seems a pity the world did not find it out. He ought to have explained that he was the author, and not merely a *nom de plume* for another man to hide behind. If he had been less intemperately solicitous about his bones, and more solicitous about his Works, it would have been better for his good name, and a kindness to us. The bones were not important. They will moulder away, they will turn to dust, but the Works will endure until the last sun goes down.

Mark Twain.

P.S. March 25. About two months ago I was illuminating this Autobiography with some notions of mine concerning the Bacon-Shakespeare controversy, and I then took occasion to air the opinion that the Stratford Shakespeare was a person of no public consequence or celebrity during his lifetime, but was utterly obscure and unimportant. And not only in great London, but also in the little village where he was born, where he lived a quarter of a century, and where he died and was buried. I argued that if he had been a person of any note at all, aged villagers would have had much to tell about him many and many a year after his death, instead of being unable to furnish inquirers a single fact connected with him. I believed, and I still believe, that if he had been famous, his notoriety would have lasted as long as mine has lasted in my native village out in Missouri. It is a good argument, a prodigiously strong one, and a most formidable one for even the most gifted and ingenious and plausible Stratfordolater to get around or explain away. Today a Hannibal *Courier-Post* of recent date has reached me, with an article in it which reinforces my contention that a really celebrated person cannot be forgotten in his village in the short space of sixty years. I will make an extract from it:

> Hannibal, as a city, may have many sins to answer for, but ingratitude is not one of them, or reverence for the great men she has produced, and as the years go by her greatest son, Mark Twain, or S. L. Clemens as a few of the unlettered call him, grows in the estimation and regard of the residents of the town he made famous and the town that made him famous. His name is associated with every old building that is torn down to make way for the modern structures demanded by a rapidly growing city, and with every hill or cave over or through which he might by any possibility have roamed, while the many points of interest which he wove into his stories, such as Holiday Hill, Jackson's Island, or Mark Twain Cave, are now monuments to his genius. Hannibal is glad of any opportunity to do him honor as he has honored her.
>
> So it has happened that the "old timers" who went to school with Mark or were with him on some of his usual escapades have been honored with large audiences whenever they were in a reminiscent mood and condescended to tell of their intimacy with the ordinary boy who came to be a very extraordinary humorist and whose every boyish act is now seen to have been indicative of what was to come. Like Aunt Becky and Mrs. Clemens, they can now see that Mark was hardly appreciated when he lived here and that the things he did as a boy and

was whipped for doing were not all bad, after all. So they have been in no hesitancy about drawing out the bad things he did as well as the good in their efforts to get a "Mark Twain story," all incidents being viewed in the light of his present fame, until the volume of "Twainiana" is already considerable and growing in proportion as the "old timers" drop away and the stories are retold second and third hand by their descendants. With some seventy-three years young and living in a villa instead of a house, he is a fair target, and let him incorporate, copyright, or patent himself as he will, there are some of his "works" that will go swooping up Hannibal chimneys as long as graybeards gather about the fires and begin with, "I've heard father tell," or possibly, "Once when I."

The Mrs. Clemens referred to is my mother—*was* my mother.

And here is another extract from a Hannibal paper, of date twenty days ago:

> Miss Becca Blankenship died at the home of William Dickason, 408 Rock Street, at 2.30 o'clock yesterday afternoon, aged 72 years. The deceased was a sister of "Huckleberry Finn," one of the famous characters in Mark Twain's *Tom Sawyer.* She had been a member of the Dickason family—the housekeeper—for nearly forty-five years, and was a highly respected lady. For the past eight years she had been an invalid, but was as well cared for by Mr. Dickason and his family as if she had been a near relative. She was a member of the Park Methodist Church and a Christian woman.

I remember her well. I have a picture of her in my mind which was graven there, clear and sharp and vivid, sixty-three years ago. She was at that time nine years old, and I was about eleven. I remember where she stood, and how she looked; and I can still see her bare feet, her bare head, her brown face, and her short tow-linen frock. She was crying. What it was about I have long ago forgotten. But it was the tears that preserved the picture for me, no doubt. She was a good child, I can say that for her. She knew me nearly seventy years ago. Did she forget me, in the course of time? I think not. If she had lived in Stratford in Shakespeare's time, would she have forgotten him? Yes. For he was never famous during his lifetime, he was utterly obscure in Stratford, and there wouldn't be any occasion to remember him after he had been dead a week.

"Injun Joe," "Jimmy Finn," and "General Gaines" were prominent and very intemperate ne'er-do-weels in Hannibal two generations ago. Plenty of grayheads there remember them to this day, and can tell you about them. Isn't it curious that two "town drunkards" and one half-breed loafer should leave behind them, in a remote Missourian village, a fame a hundred times greater and several hundred times more particularized in the matter of definite facts than Shakespeare left behind him in the village where he had lived the half of his lifetime?

CHRISTIAN SCIENCE

WITH NOTES CONTAINING
CORRECTIONS TO DATE

Preface

Book I of this volume occupies a quarter or a third of the volume, and consists of matter written about four years ago, but not hitherto published in book form. It contained errors of judgment and of fact. I have now corrected these to the best of my ability and later knowledge.

Book II was written at the beginning of 1903, and has not until now appeared in any form. In it my purpose has been to present a character-portrait of Mrs. Eddy, drawn from her own acts and words solely, not from hearsay and rumor; and to explain the nature and scope of her Monarchy, as revealed in the Laws by which she governs it, and which she wrote herself.

Mark Twain

New York, January, 1907

BOOK I

"It is the first time since the dawn-days of Creation that a Voice
has gone crashing through space with such placid and complacent confidence and command."

Chapter 1

This last summer, when I was on my way back to Vienna from the
Appetite-Cure in the mountains, I fell over a cliff in the twilight and
broke some arms and legs and one thing or another, and by good
luck was found by some peasants who had lost an ass, and they
carried me to the nearest habitation, which was one of those large,
low, thatch-roofed farm houses, with apartments in the garret for the
family, and a cunning little porch under the deep gable decorated
with boxes of bright-colored flowers and cats; on the ground-floor a
large and light sitting-room, separated from the milch-cattle apart-
ment by a partition; and in the front yard rose stately and fine the
wealth and pride of the house, the manure-pile. That sentence is
Germanic, and shows that I am acquiring that sort of mastery of the
art and spirit of the language which enables a man to travel all day in
one sentence without changing cars.

There was a village a mile away, and a horse-doctor lived there,
but there was no surgeon. It seemed a bad outlook; mine was distinctly a surgery case. Then it was remembered that a lady from
Boston was summering in that village, and she was a Christian Science doctor and could cure anything. So she was sent for. It was
night by this time, and she could not conveniently come, but sent
word that it was no matter, there was no hurry, she would give me
"absent treatment" now, and come in the morning; meantime she

begged me to make myself tranquil and comfortable and remember
that there was nothing the matter with me. I thought there must be
some mistake.

"Did you tell her I walked off a cliff seventy-five feet high?"

"Yes."

"And struck a bowlder at the bottom and bounced?"

"Yes."

"And struck another one and bounced again?"

"Yes."

"And struck another one and bounced yet again?"

"Yes."

"And broke the bowlders?"

"Yes."

"That accounts for it; she is thinking of the bowlders. Why didn't
you tell her I got hurt, too?"

"I did. I told her what you told me to tell her: that you were now
but an incoherent series of compound fractures extending from your
scalp-lock to your heels, and that the comminuted projections caused
you to look like a hat-rack."

"And it was after this that she wished me to remember that there
was nothing the matter with me?"

"Those were her words."

"I do not understand it. I believe she has not diagnosed the case
with sufficient care. Did she look like a person who was theorizing,
or did she look like one who has fallen off precipices herself and
brings to the aid of abstract science the confirmations of personal
experience?"

"*Bitte?*"

It was too large a contract for the *Stubenmadchen's* vocabulary;
she couldn't call the hand. I allowed the subject to rest there, and
asked for something to eat and smoke, and something hot to drink,
and a basket to pile my legs in; but I could not have any of these
things.

"Why?"

"She said you would need nothing at all."

"But I am hungry and thirsty, and in desperate pain."

"She said you would have these delusions, but must pay no attention to them. She wants you to particularly remember that there are
no such things as hunger and thirst and pain."

"She does, does she?"

"It is what she said."

"Does she seem to be in full and functionable possession of her intellectual plant, such as it is?"

"*Bitte?*"

"Do they let her run at large, or do they tie her up?"

"Tie her up?"

"There, good night, run along, you are a good girl, but your mental *Geschirr* is not arranged for light and airy conversation. Leave me to my delusions."

Chapter 2

It was a night of anguish, of course—at least, I supposed it was, for it had all the symptoms of it—but it passed at last, and the Christian Scientist came, and I was glad. She was middle-aged, and large and bony, and erect, and had an austere face and a resolute jaw and a Roman beak and was a widow in the third degree, and her name was Fuller. I was eager to get to business and find relief, but she was distressingly deliberate. She unpinned and unhooked and uncoupled her upholsteries one by one, abolished the wrinkles with a flirt of her hand, and hung the articles up; peeled off her gloves and disposed of them, got a book out of her hand-bag, then drew a chair to the bedside, descended into it without hurry, and I hung out my tongue. She said, with pity but without passion:

"Return it to its receptacle. We deal with the mind only, not with its dumb servants."

I could not offer my pulse, because the connection was broken; but she detected the apology before I could word it, and indicated by a negative tilt of her head that the pulse was another dumb servant that she had no use for. Then I thought I would tell her my symptoms and how I felt, so that she would understand the case; but that was another inconsequence, she did not need to know those things; moreover, my remark about how I felt was an abuse of language, a misapplication of terms.

"One does not *feel*," she explained; "there is no such thing as feeling: therefore, to speak of a non-existent thing as existent is a contradiction. Matter has no existence; nothing exists but mind; the mind cannot feel pain, it can only imagine it."

"But if it hurts, just the same—"

"It doesn't. A thing which is unreal cannot exercise the functions of reality. Pain is unreal; hence, pain cannot hurt."

In making a sweeping gesture to indicate the act of shooing the illusion of pain out of the mind, she raked her hand on a pin in her dress, said "Ouch!" and went tranquilly on with her talk. "You should never allow yourself to speak of how you feel, nor permit others to ask you how you are feeling; you should never concede that you are ill, nor permit others to talk about disease or pain or death or similar non-existences in your presence. Such talk only encourages the mind to continue its empty imaginings." Just at that point the *Stubenmadchen* trod on the cat's tail, and the cat let fly a frenzy of cat-profanity. I asked, with caution:

"Is a cat's opinion about pain valuable?"

"A cat has no opinion; opinions proceed from mind only; the lower animals, being eternally perishable, have not been granted mind; without mind, opinion is impossible."

"She merely *imagined* she felt a pain—the cat?"

"She cannot imagine a pain, for imagining is an effect of mind; without mind, there is no imagination. A cat has no imagination."

"Then she had a *real* pain?"

"I have already told you there is no such *thing* as real pain."

"It is strange and interesting. I do wonder what was the matter with the cat. Because, there being no such thing as a real pain, and she not being able to imagine an imaginary one, it would seem that God in His pity has compensated the cat with some kind of a mysterious emotion usable when her tail is trodden on which, for the moment, joins cat and Christian in one common brotherhood of—"

She broke in with an irritated—

"Peace! The cat feels nothing, the Christian feels nothing. Your empty and foolish imaginings are profanation and blasphemy, and can do you an injury. It is wiser and better and holier to recognize and confess that there is no such thing as disease or pain or death."

"I am full of imaginary tortures," I said, "but I do not think I could be any more uncomfortable if they were real ones. What must I do to get rid of them?"

"There is no occasion to get rid of them, since they do not exist.

They are illusions propagated by matter, and matter has no existence; there is no such thing as matter."

"It sounds right and clear, but yet it seems in a degree elusive; it seems to slip through, just when you think you are getting a grip on it."

"Explain."

"Well, for instance: if there is no such thing as matter, how can matter propagate things?"

In her compassion she almost smiled. She would have smiled if there were any such thing as a smile.

"It is quite simple," she said; "the fundamental propositions of Christian Science explain it, and they are summarized in the four following self-evident propositions: 1. God is All in all. 2. God is good. Good is Mind. 3. God, Spirit, being all, nothing is matter. 4. Life, God, omnipotent Good, deny death, evil, sin, disease. There—now you see."

It seemed nebulous; it did not seem to say anything about the difficulty in hand—how non-existent matter can propagate illusions. I said, with some hesitancy:

"Does—does it explain?"

"*Doesn't* it? Even if read backward it will do it."

With a budding hope, I asked her to do it backward.

"Very well. Disease sin evil death deny Good omnipotent God life matter is nothing all being Spirit God Mind is Good good is God all in All is God. There—do you understand now?"

"It—it—well, it is plainer than it was before; still—"

"Well?"

"Could you try it some more ways?"

"As many as you like; it always means the same. Interchanged in any way you please it cannot be made to mean anything different from what it means when put in any other way. Because it is perfect. You can jumble it all up, and it makes no difference: it always comes out the way it was before. It was a marvellous mind that produced it. As a mental *tour de force* it is without a mate, it defies alike the simple, the concrete, and the occult."

"It seems to be a corker."

I blushed for the word, but it was out before I could stop it.

"A what?"

"A—wonderful structure—combination, so to speak, of profound thoughts—unthinkable ones—un—"

"It is true. Read backward, or forward, or perpendicularly, or at any given angle, these four propositions will always be found to agree in statement and proof."

"Ah—proof. Now we are coming at it. The *statements* agree; they agree with—with—anyway, they agree; I noticed that; but what is it they prove—I mean, in particular?"

"Why, nothing could be clearer. They prove: 1. GOD—Principle, Life, Truth, Love, Soul, Spirit, Mind. Do you get that?"

"I—well, I seem to. Go on, please."

"2. MAN—God's universal idea, individual, perfect, eternal. Is it clear?"

"It—I think so. Continue."

"3. IDEA—An image in Mind; the immediate object of understanding. There it is—the whole sublime Arcana of Christian Science in a nutshell. Do you find a weak place in it anywhere?"

"Well—no; it seems strong."

"Very well. There is more. Those three constitute the Scientific Definition of Immortal Mind. Next, we have the Scientific Definition of Mortal Mind. Thus. FIRST DEGREE: *Depravity.* 1. Physical—Passions and appetites, fear, depraved will, pride, envy, deceit, hatred, revenge, sin, disease, death."

"Phantasms, madam—unrealities, as I understand it."

"Every one. SECOND DEGREE: *Evil Disappearing.* 1. Moral—Honesty, affection, compassion, hope, faith, meekness, temperance. Is it clear?"

"Crystal."

"THIRD DEGREE: *Spiritual Salvation.* 1. Spiritual—Faith, wisdom, power, purity, understanding, health, love. You see how searchingly and co-ordinately interdependent and anthropomorphous it all is. In this Third Degree, as we know by the revelations of Christian Science, mortal mind disappears."

"Not earlier?"

"No, not until the teaching and preparation for the Third Degree are completed."

"It is not until then that one is enabled to take hold of Christian Science effectively, and with the right sense of sympathy and kinship, as I understand you. That is to say, it could not succeed during the processes of the Second Degree, because there would still be remains of mind left; and therefore—but I interrupted you. You were about to further explain the good results proceeding from the erosions and disintegrations effected by the Third Degree. It is very interesting; go on, please."

"Yes, as I was saying, in this Third Degree mortal mind disappears. Science so reverses the evidence before the corporeal human senses as to make this scriptural testimony true in our hearts, 'the last shall be first and the first shall be last,' that God and His Idea may be to us—what divinity really is, and must of necessity be—all-inclusive."

"It is beautiful. And with what exhaustive exactness your choice and arrangement of words confirm and establish what you have claimed for the powers and functions of the Third Degree. The Second could probably produce only temporary absence of mind; it is reserved to the Third to make it permanent. A sentence framed under the auspices of the Second could have a kind of meaning—a sort of deceptive semblance of it—whereas it is only under the magic of the Third that that defect would disappear. Also, without doubt, it is the Third Degree that contributes another remarkable specialty to Christian Science—viz., case and flow and lavishness of words, and rhythm and swing and smoothness. There must be a special reason for this?"

"Yes—God-all, all-God, good God, non-Matter, Matteration, Spirit, Bones, Truth."

"That explains it."

"There is nothing in Christian Science that is not explicable; for God is one, Time is one, Individuality is one, and may be one of a series, one of many, as an individual man, individual horse; whereas God is one, not one of a series, but one alone and without an equal."

"These are noble thoughts. They make one burn to know more. How does Christian Science explain the spiritual relation of systematic duality to incidental deflection?"

"Christian Science reverses the seeming relation of Soul and body —as astronomy reverses the human perception of the movement of the solar system—and makes body tributary to the Mind. As it is the earth which is in motion, while the sun is at rest, though in viewing the sun rise one finds it impossible to believe the sun not to be really rising, so the body is but the humble servant of the restful Mind,

though it seems otherwise to finite sense; but we shall never understand this while we admit that soul is in body, or mind in matter, and
that man is included in non-intelligence. Soul is God, unchangeable
and eternal; and man coexists with and reflects Soul, for the All-in-
all is the Altogether, and the Altogether embraces the All-one, Soul-
Mind, Mind-Soul, Love, Spirit, Bones, Liver, one of a series, alone
and without an equal."

"What is the origin of Christian Science? Is it a gift of God, or did
it just happen?"

"In a sense, it is a gift of God. That is to say, its powers are from
Him, but the credit of the discovery of the powers and what they are
for is due to an American lady."

"Indeed? When did this occur?"

"In 1866. That is the immortal date when pain and disease and
death disappeared from the earth to return no more forever. That is,
the fancies for which those terms stand disappeared. The things
themselves had never existed; therefore, as soon as it was perceived
that there were no such things, they were easily banished. The history and nature of the great discovery are set down in the book here,
and—"

"Did the lady write the book?"

"Yes, she wrote it all, herself. The title is *Science and Health, with
Key to the Scriptures*—for she explains the Scriptures; they were not
understood before. Not even by the twelve Disciples. She begins thus
—I will read it to you."

But she had forgotten to bring her glasses.

"Well, it is no matter," she said. "I remember the words—indeed,
all Christian Scientists know the book by heart; it is necessary in our
practice. We should otherwise make mistakes and do harm. She begins thus: 'In the year 1866 I discovered the Science of Metaphysical
Healing, and named it Christian Science.' And she says—quite beautifully, I think—'Through Christian Science, religion and medicine
are inspired with a diviner nature and essence, fresh pinions are
given to faith and understanding, and thoughts acquaint themselves
intelligently with God.' Her very words."

"It is elegant. And it is a fine thought, too—marrying religion to
medicine, instead of medicine to the undertaker in the old way; for
religion and medicine properly belong together, they being the basis

of all spiritual and physical health. What kind of medicine do you give for the ordinary diseases, such as—"

"We never give medicine in *any* circumstances whatever! We—"

"But, madam, it *says*—"

"I don't care what it says, and I don't wish to talk about it."

"I am sorry if I have offended, but you see the mention seemed in some way inconsistent, and—"

"There *are* no inconsistencies in Christian Science. The thing is impossible, for the Science is absolute. It cannot be otherwise, since it proceeds directly from the All-in-all and the Everything-in-Which, also Soul, Bones, Truth, one of a series, alone and without equal. It is Mathematics purified from material dross and made spiritual."

"I can see that, but—"

"It rests upon the immovable basis of an Apodictical Principle."

The word flattened itself against my mind in trying to get in, and disordered me a little, and before I could inquire into its pertinency, she was already throwing the needed light:

"This Apodictical Principle is the absolute Principle of Scientific Mind-healing, the sovereign Omnipotence which delivers the children of men from pain, disease, decay, and every ill that flesh is heir to."

"Surely not every ill, every decay?"

"Every one; there are no exceptions; there is no such thing as decay—it is an unreality, it has no existence."

"But without your glasses your failing eyesight does not permit you to—"

"My eyesight cannot fail; nothing can fail; the Mind is master, and the Mind permits no retrogression."

She was under the inspiration of the Third Degree, therefore there could be no profit in continuing this part of the subject. I shifted to other ground and inquired further concerning the Discoverer of the Science.

"Did the discovery come suddenly, like Klondike, or after long study and calculation, like America?"

"The comparisons are not respectful, since they refer to trivialities —but let it pass. I will answer in the Discoverer's own words: 'God had been graciously fitting me, during many years, for the reception of a final revelation of the absolute Principle of Scientific Mind-healing.'"

"Many years. How many?"

"Eighteen centuries!"

"All-God, God-good, good-God, Truth, Bones, Liver, one of a series, alone and without equal—it is amazing!"

"You may well say it, sir. Yet it is but the truth. This American lady, our revered and sacred Founder, is distinctly referred to, and her coming prophesied, in the twelfth chapter of the Apocalypse; she could not have been more plainly indicated by St. John without actually mentioning her name."

"How strange, how wonderful!"

"I will quote her own words, from her *Key to the Scriptures:* 'The twelfth chapter of the Apocalypse *has a special suggestiveness in connection with this nineteenth century.'* There—do you note that? Think—note it well."

"But—what does it mean?"

"Listen, and you will know. I quote her inspired words again: 'In the opening of the Sixth Seal, typical of six thousand years since Adam, there is one distinctive feature *which has special reference to the present age.* Thus:

" 'Revelation xii. 1. And there appeared a great wonder in heaven —a *woman* clothed with the sun, and the moon under her feet, and upon her head a crown of twelve stars.'

"That is our Head, our Chief, our Discoverer of Christian Science —nothing can be plainer, nothing surer. And note this:

" 'Revelation xii. 6. And the woman fled into the wilderness, where she had a place prepared of God.' "

"That is Boston. I recognize it, madam. These are sublime things, and impressive; I never understood these passages before; please go on with the—with the—proofs."

"Very well. Listen:

" 'And I saw another mighty angel come down from heaven, clothed with a cloud; and a rainbow was upon his head, and his face was as it were the sun, and his feet as pillars of fire. And he held in his hand *a little book.'*

"A little book, merely a little book—could words be modester? Yet how stupendous its importance! Do you know what book that was? Was it—"

"I hold it in my hand—Christian Science!"

"Love, Livers, Lights, Bones, Truth, Kidneys, one of a series, alone and without equal—it is beyond imagination for wonder!"

"Hear our Founder's eloquent words: 'Then will a voice from harmony cry, "Go and take the little book: take it and eat it up, and it shall make thy belly bitter; but it shall be in thy mouth sweet as honey." Mortal, obey the heavenly evangel. Take up Divine Science. Read it from beginning to end. Study it, ponder it. It will be, indeed, sweet at its first taste, when it heals you; but murmur not over Truth, if you find its digestion bitter.' You now know the history of our dear and holy Science, sir, and that its *origin* is not of this earth, but only its *discovery*. I will leave the book with you and will go, now; but give yourself no uneasiness—I will give you absent treatment from now till I go to bed."

Chapter 3

Under the powerful influence of the near treatment and the absent treatment together, my bones were gradually retreating inward and disappearing from view. The good work took a brisk start, now, and went on swiftly. My body was diligently straining and stretching, this way and that, to accommodate the processes of restoration, and every minute or two I heard a dull click inside and knew that the two ends of a fracture had been successfully joined. This muffled clicking and gritting and grinding and rasping continued during the next three hours, and then stopped—the connections had all been made. All except dislocations; there were only seven of these: hips, shoulders, knees, neck; so that was soon over; one after another they slipped into their sockets with a sound like pulling a distant cork, and I jumped up as good as new, as to framework, and sent for the horse-doctor.

I was obliged to do this because I had a stomach-ache and a cold in the head, and I was not willing to trust these things any longer in the hands of a woman whom I did not know, and in whose ability to successfully treat mere disease I had lost all confidence. My position was justified by the fact that the cold and the ache had been in her charge from the first, along with the fractures, but had experienced not a shade of relief; and, indeed, the ache was even growing worse and worse, and more and more bitter, now, probably on account of the protracted abstention from food and drink.

The horse-doctor came, a pleasant man and full of hope and professional interest in the case. In the matter of smell he was pretty aromatic—in fact, quite horsey—and I tried to arrange with him for absent treatment, but it was not in his line, so, out of delicacy, I did not press it. He looked at my teeth and examined my hock, and said my age and general condition were favorable to energetic measures; therefore he would give me something to turn the stomach-ache into the botts and the cold in the head into the blind staggers; then he should be on his own beat and would know what to do. He made up a bucket of bran-mash, and said a dipperful of it every two hours, alternated with a drench with turpentine and axle-grease in it, would either knock my ailments out of me in twenty-four hours, or so interest me in other ways as to make me forget they were on the premises. He administered my first dose himself, then took his leave, saying I was free to eat and drink anything I pleased and in any quantity I liked. But I was not hungry any more, and did not care for food.

I took up the Christian Science book and read half of it, then took a dipperful of drench and read the other half. The resulting experiences were full of interest and adventure. All through the rumblings and grindings and quakings and effervescings accompanying the evolution of the ache into the botts and the cold into the blind staggers I could note the generous struggle for mastery going on between the mash and the drench and the literature; and often I could tell which was ahead, and could easily distinguish the literature from the others when the others were separate, though not when they were mixed; for when a bran-mash and an eclectic drench are mixed together they look just like the Apodictical Principle out on a lark, and no one can tell it from that. The finish was reached at last, the evolutions were complete, and a fine success, but I think that this result could have been achieved with fewer materials. I believe the mash was necessary to the conversion of the stomach-ache into the botts, but I think one could develop the blind staggers out of the literature by itself; also, that blind staggers produced in this way would be of a better quality and more lasting than any produced by the artificial processes of the horse-doctor.

For of all the strange and frantic and incomprehensible and

uninterpretable books which the imagination of man has created, surely this one is the prize sample. It is written with a limitless confidence and complacency, and with a dash and stir and earnestness which often compel the effects of eloquence, even when the words do not seem to have any traceable meaning. There are plenty of people who imagine they understand the book; I know this, for I have talked with them; but in all cases they were people who also imagined that there were no such things as pain, sickness, and death, and no realities in the world; nothing actually existent but Mind. It seems to me to modify the value of their testimony. When these people talk about Christian Science they do as Mrs. Fuller did: they do not use their own language, but the book's; they pour out the book's showy incoherences, and leave you to find out later that they were not originating, but merely quoting; they seem to know the volume by heart, and to revere it as they would a Bible—another Bible, perhaps I ought to say. Plainly the book was written under the mental desolations of the Third Degree, and I feel sure that none but the membership of that Degree can discover meanings in it. When you read it you seem to be listening to a lively and aggressive and oracular speech delivered in an unknown tongue, a speech whose spirit you get but not the particulars; or, to change the figure, you seem to be listening to a vigorous instrument which is making a noise which it thinks is a tune, but which, to persons not members of the band, is only the martial tooting of a trombone, and merely stirs the soul through the noise, but does not convey a meaning.

The book's serenities of self-satisfaction do almost seem to smack of a heavenly origin—they have no blood-kin in the earth. It is more than human to be so placidly certain about things, and so finely superior, and so airily content with one's performance. Without ever presenting anything which may rightfully be called by the strong name of Evidence, and sometimes without even *mentioning* a reason for a deduction at all, it thunders out the startling words, "I have *Proved*" so and so. It takes the Pope and all the great guns of his Church in battery assembled to authoritatively settle and establish the meaning of a sole and single unclarified passage of Scripture, and this at vast cost of time and study and reflection, but the author of this work is superior to all that: she finds the whole Bible in an unclarified condition, and at small expense of time and no expense of mental effort she clarifies it from lid to lid, reorganizes and improves the meanings, then authoritatively settles and establishes them with formulas which you cannot tell from "Let there be light!" and "Here you have it!" It is the first time since the dawn-days of Creation that a Voice has gone crashing through space with such placid and complacent confidence and command.[1]

[1] *January,* 1903. The first reading of any book whose terminology is new and strange is nearly sure to leave the reader in a bewildered and sarcastic state of mind. But now that, during the past two months, I have, by diligence, gained a fair acquaintanceship with *Science and Health* technicalities, I no longer find the bulk of that work hard to understand.—M.T.

P. S. The wisdom harvested from the foregoing thoughts has already done me a service and saved me a sorrow. Nearly a month ago there came to me from one of the universities a tract by Dr. Edward Anthony Spitzka on the "Encephalic Anatomy of the Races." I judged that my opinion was desired by the university, and I was greatly pleased with this attention and wrote and said I would furnish it as soon as I could. That night I put my plodding and disheartening Christian Science mining aside and took hold of the matter. I wrote an eager chapter, and was expecting to finish my opinion the next day, but was called away for a week, and my mind was soon charged with other interests. It was not until today, after the lapse of nearly a month, that I happened upon my Encephalic chapter again. Meantime, the new wisdom had come to me, and I read it with shame. I recognized that I had entered upon that work in far from the right temper—far from the respectful and judicial spirit which was its due of reverence. I had begun upon it with the following paragraph for fuel:

"FISSURES OF THE PARIETAL AND OCCIPITAL LOBES (LATERAL SURFACE).—*The Postcentral Fissural Complex.*—In this hemicerebrum, the postcentral and subcentral are combined to form a continuous fissure, attaining a length of 8.5 cm. Dorsally, the fissure bifurcates, embracing the gyre indented by the caudal limb of the paracentral. The caudal limb of the postcentral is joined by a transparietal piece. In all, five additional rami spring from the combined fissure. A vadum separates it from the parietal; another from the central."

It humiliates me, now, to see how angry I got over that; and how scornful. I said that the style was disgraceful; that it was labored and tumultuous, and in places violent, that the treatment was involved and erratic, and almost, as a rule, bewildering; that to lack of simplicity was added a lack of vocabulary; that there was quite too much feeling shown; that if I had a dog that would get so excited and incoherent over a tranquil subject like Encephalic Anatomy I would not pay his tax; and at that point I got excited myself and spoke bitterly of these mongrel insanities, and said a person might as well try to understand *Science and Health.*

I know, now, where the trouble was, and am glad of the interruption! that saved me from sending my verdict to the university. It makes me cold to think what those people might have thought of me.—M.T.

Chapter 4

No one doubts—certainly not I—that the mind exercises a powerful influence over the body. From the beginning of time, the sorcerer, the interpreter of dreams, the fortune-teller, the charlatan, the quack, the wild medicine-man, the educated physician, the mesmerist, and the hypnotist have made use of the client's *imagination* to help them in their work. They have all recognized the potency and availability of that force. Physicians cure many patients with a bread pill; they know that where the disease is only a fancy, the patient's confidence in the doctor will make the bread pill effective.

Faith in the doctor. Perhaps that is the entire thing. It seems to look like it. In old times the King cured the king's evil by the touch of the royal hand. He frequently made extraordinary cures. Could his footman have done it? No—not in his own clothes. Disguised as the King, could he have done it? I think we may not doubt it. I think we may feel sure that it was not the King's touch that made the cure in any instance, but the patient's faith in the efficacy of a King's touch. Genuine and remarkable cures have been achieved through contact with the relics of a saint. Is it not likely that any other bones would have done as well if the substitution had been concealed from the patient?

When I was a boy a farmer's wife who lived five miles from our village had great fame as a faith-doctor—that was what she called herself. Sufferers came to her from all around, and she laid her hand upon them and said, "Have faith—it is all that is necessary," and they went away well of their ailments. She was not a religious woman, and pretended to no occult powers. She said that the patient's faith in her did the work. Several times I saw her make immediate cures of severe toothaches. My mother was the patient.

In Austria there is a peasant who drives a great trade in this sort of industry, and has both the high and the low for patients. He gets into prison every now and then for practising without a diploma, but his business is as brisk as ever when he gets out, for his work is unquestionably successful and keeps his reputation high. In Bavaria there is a man who performed so many great cures that he had to retire from his profession of stage-carpentering in order to meet the demand of his constantly increasing body of customers. He goes on from year to year doing his miracles, and has become very rich. He pretends to no religious helps, no supernatural aids, but thinks there is something in his make-up which inspires the confidence of his patients, and that it is this confidence which does the work, and not some mysterious power issuing from himself.[1]

Within the last quarter of a century, in America, several sects of curers have appeared under various names and have done notable things in the way of healing ailments without the use of medicines. There are the Mind Cure, the Faith Cure, the Prayer Cure, the Mental-Science Cure, and the Christian-Science Cure; and apparently they all do their miracles with the same old, powerful instrument—*the patient's imagination.* Differing names, but no difference in the process. But they do not give that instrument the credit; each sect claims that its way differs from the ways of the others.

They all achieve some cures, there is no question about it; and the Faith Cure and the Prayer Cure probably do no harm when they do no good, since they do not forbid the patient to help out the cure with medicines if he wants to; but the others bar medicines, and claim ability to cure every conceivable human ailment through the application of their mental forces alone. There would seem to be an element of danger here. It has the look of claiming too much, I think. Public confidence would probably be increased if less were claimed.[2]

The Christian Scientist was not able to cure my stomach-ache and my cold; but the horse-doctor did it. This convinces me that Christian Science claims too much. In my opinion it ought to let diseases alone and confine itself to surgery. There it would have everything its own way.

The horse-doctor charged me thirty kreutzers, and I paid him; in fact, I doubled it and gave him a shilling. Mrs. Fuller brought in an

---

[1] *January.* 1903. I have personal and intimate knowledge of the "miraculous" cure of a case of paralysis which had kept the patient helpless in bed during two years, in spite of all that the best medical science of New York could do. The travelling "quack" (that is what they called him), came on two successive mornings and lifted the patient out of bed and said "Walk!" and the patient walked. That was the end of it. It was forty-one years ago. The patient has walked ever since.—M.T.

[2] *February.* 1903. I find that Christian Science claims that the healing-force which it employs is radically different from the force used by any other party in the healing business. I shall talk about this towards the end of this work.—M.T.

itemized bill for a crate of broken bones mended in two hundred and thirty-four places—one dollar per fracture.

"Nothing exists but Mind?"

"Nothing," she answered. "All else is substanceless, all else is imaginary."

I gave her an imaginary check, and now she is suing me for substantial dollars. It looks inconsistent.

NOTE.—The foregoing chapters appeared originally in the *Cosmopolitan Magazine*, about three years ago.—M.T.

Chapter 5

Let us consider that we are all partially insane. It will explain us to each other; it will unriddle many riddles; it will make clear and simple many things which are involved in haunting and harassing difficulties and obscurities now.

Those of us who are not in the asylum, and not demonstrably due there, are nevertheless, no doubt, insane in one or two particulars. I think we must admit this; but I think that we are otherwise healthy-minded. I think that when we all see one thing alike, it is evidence that, as regards that one thing, our minds are perfectly sound. Now there are really several things which we do all see alike; things which we all accept, and about which we do not dispute. For instance, we who are outside of the asylum all agree that water seeks its level; that the sun gives light and heat; that fire consumes; that fog is damp; that six times six are thirty-six; that two from ten leaves eight; that eight and seven are fifteen. These are, perhaps, the only things we are agreed about; but, although they are so few, they are of inestimable value, because they make an infallible standard of sanity. Whosoever accepts them him we know to be substantially sane; sufficiently sane; in the working essentials, sane. Whoever disputes a single one of them him we know to be wholly insane, and qualified for the asylum.

Very well, the man who disputes none of them we concede to be entitled to go at large. But that is concession enough. We cannot go any further than that; for we know that in all matters of mere *opinion* that same man is insane—just as insane as we are; just as insane as

Shakespeare was. We know exactly where to put our finger upon his insanity: *it is where his opinion differs from ours.*

That is a simple rule, and easy to remember. When I, a thoughtful and unbiased Presbyterian, examine the Koran, I know that beyond any question every Mohammedan is insane; not in all things, but in religious matters. When a thoughtful and unbiased Mohammedan examines the Westminster Catechism, he knows that beyond any question I am spiritually insane. I cannot prove to him that he is insane, because you never can prove anything to a lunatic—for that is a part of his insanity and the evidence of it. He cannot prove to me that I am insane, for my mind has the same defect that afflicts his. All Democrats are insane, but not one of them knows it; none but the Republicans and Mugwumps know it. All the Republicans are insane, but only the Democrats and Mugwumps can perceive it. The rule is perfect: *in all matters of opinion our adversaries are insane.* When I look around me, I am often troubled to see how many people are mad. To mention only a few:

The Atheist,

The Infidel,

The Agnostic,

The Baptist,

The Methodist,

The Christian Scientist,

The Catholic, and the 115 Christian sects, the Presbyterian excepted,

The 72 Mohammedan sects,

The Buddhist,

The Blavatsky-Buddhist,

The Nationalist,

The Confucian,

The Spiritualist,

The 2000 East Indian sects,

The Peculiar People,

The Theosophists,

The Swedenborgians,

The Shakers,

The Millerites,

The Mormons,

The Laurence Oliphant Harrisites,

The Grand Lama's people,

The Monarchists,

The Imperialists,

The Democrats,

The Republicans (but not the Mugwumps),

The Mind-Curists,

The Faith-Curists,

The Mental Scientists,

The Allopaths,

The Homoeopaths,

The Electropaths,

The ———

But there's no end to the list; there are millions of them! And all insane; each in his own way; insane as to his pet fad or opinion, but otherwise sane and rational.

This should move us to be charitable towards one another's lunacies. I recognize that in his special belief the Christian Scientist is insane, because he does not believe as I do; but I hail him as my mate and fellow, because I am as insane as he—insane from his point of view, and his point of view is as authoritative as mine and worth as much. That is to say, worth a brass farthing. Upon a great religious or political question, the opinion of the dullest head in the world is worth the same as the opinion of the brightest head in the world—a brass farthing. How do we arrive at this? It is simple. The affirmative opinion of a stupid man is neutralized by the negative opinion of his stupid neighbor—no decision is reached; the affirmative opinion of the intellectual giant Gladstone is neutralized by the negative opinion of the intellectual giant Newman—no decision is reached. Opinions that prove nothing are, of course, without value—any but a dead person knows that much. This obliges us to admit the truth of the unpalatable proposition just mentioned above—that, in disputed matters political and religious, one man's opinion is worth no more than his peer's, and hence it follows that no man's opinion possesses any real value. It is a humbling thought, but there is no way to get around it: *all* opinions upon these great subjects are brass-farthing opinions.

It is a mere plain, simple fact—as clear and as certain as that eight and seven make fifteen. And by it we recognize that we are all insane, as concerns those matters. If we were sane, we should all see a political or religious doctrine alike; there would be no dispute: it would be a case of eight and seven—just as it is in heaven, where all are sane and none insane. There there is but one religion, one belief; the harmony is perfect; there is never a discordant note.

Under protection of these preliminaries, I suppose I may now repeat without offence that the Christian Scientist is insane. I mean him no discourtesy, and I am not charging—nor even imagining—that he is insaner than the rest of the human race. I think he is more picturesquely insane than some of us. At the same time, I am quite sure that in one important and splendid particular he is much saner than is the vast bulk of the race.

Why is he insane? I told you before: it is because his opinions are not ours. I know of no other reason, and I do not need any other; it is the only way we *have* of discovering insanity when it is not violent. It is merely the picturesqueness of his insanity that makes it more interesting than my kind or yours. For instance, consider his "little book"; the "little book" exposed in the sky eighteen centuries ago by the flaming angel of the Apocalypse, and handed down in our day to Mrs. Mary Baker G. Eddy, of New Hampshire, and translated by her, word for word, into English (with help of a polisher), and now published and distributed in hundreds of editions by her at a clear profit per volume, above cost, of seven hundred per cent![1]—a profit which distinctly belongs to the angel of the Apocalypse, and let him collect it if he can; a "little book" which the C.S. very frequently calls by just that name, and always enclosed in quotation-marks to keep its high origin exultantly in mind; a "little book" which "explains" and reconstructs and new-paints and decorates the Bible, and puts a mansard roof on it and a lightning-rod and all the other modern improvements; a "little book" which for the present affects to travel in yoke with the Bible and be friendly to it, and within half a century will hitch the Bible in the rear and thenceforth travel tandem, itself in the lead, in the coming great march of Christian Scientism through the Protestant dominions of the planet.

Chapter 6

> "Hungry ones throng to hear the Bible read in connection with the text-book of Christian Science, *Science and Health, with Key to the Scriptures,* by Mary Baker G. Eddy. *These* are our only preachers. *They* are the word of God."
> —*Christian Science Journal,* October, 1898.

Is that picturesque? A lady has told me that in a chapel of the Mosque in Boston there is a picture or image of Mrs. Eddy, and that before it burns a never-extinguished light.[2] Is that picturesque? How

---

[1] *February,* 1903. This has been disputed by novices. It is not possible that the copy possessed by me could have cost above thirty-seven and a half cents. I have been a printer and book-maker myself. I shall go into some particulars concerning this matter in a later chapter.—M.T.

[2] *February,* 1903. There is a dispute about that picture. I will render justice concerning it in the new half of this book.—M.T.

long do you think it will be before the Christian Scientist will be worshipping that picture or image and praying to it? How long do you think it will be before it is claimed that Mrs. Eddy is a Redeemer, a Christ, and Christ's equal?[3] Already her army of disciples speak of her reverently as "Our Mother." How long will it be before they place her on the steps of the Throne beside the Virgin—and, later, a step higher? First, Mary the Virgin and Mary the Matron; later, with a change of precedence, Mary the Matron and Mary the Virgin. Let the artist get ready with his canvas and his brushes; the new Renaissance is on its way, and there will be money in altar-canvases—a thousand times as much as the Popes and their Church ever spent on the Old Masters; for their riches were poverty as compared with what is going to pour into the treasure-chest of the Christian-Scientist Papacy by-and-by, let us not doubt it. We will examine the financial outlook presently and see what it promises. A favorite subject of the new Old Master will be the first verse of the twelfth chapter of Revelation— a verse which Mrs. Eddy says (in her Annex to the Scriptures) has "one distinctive feature which has special reference to the present age"—and to *her*, as is rather pointedly indicated:

"And there appeared a great wonder in heaven; a *woman* clothed with the sun, and the moon under her feet," etc.

The woman clothed with the sun will be a portrait of Mrs. Eddy.

Is it insanity to believe that Christian Scientism is destined to make the most formidable show that any new religion has made in the world since the birth and spread of Mohammedanism, and that within a century from now it may stand second to Rome only, in numbers and power in Christendom?

If this is a wild dream it will not be easy to prove it so just yet, I think. There seems argument that it may come true. The Christian-Science "boom," proper, is not yet five years old; yet already it has two hundred and fifty churches.[4]

It has its start, you see, and it is a phenomenally good one. Moreover, it is latterly spreading with a constantly accelerating swiftness. It has a better chance to grow and prosper and achieve permanency

[3] This suggestion has been scorned. I will examine the matter in the new half of the book.—M.T.

[4] *February, 1903.* Through misinformation I doubled those figures when I wrote this chapter four years ago.—M.T.

than any other existing "ism"; for it has *more to offer* than any other. The past teaches us that in order to succeed, a movement like this must not be a mere philosophy, it must be a religion; also, that it must not claim entire originality, but content itself with passing for an improvement on an *existing* religion, and show its hand later, when strong and prosperous—like Mohammedanism.

Next, there must be money—and plenty of it.

Next, the power and authority and capital must be concentrated in the grip of a small and irresponsible clique, with nobody outside privileged to ask questions or find fault.

Next, as before remarked, it must bait its hook with some new and attractive advantages over the baits offered by its competitors.

A new movement equipped with some of these endowments—like spiritualism, for instance—may count upon a considerable success; a new movement equipped with the bulk of them—like Mohammedanism, for instance—may count upon a widely extended conquest. Mormonism had all the requisites but one—it had nothing new and nothing valuable to bait with. Spiritualism lacked the important detail of concentration of money and authority in the hands of an irresponsible clique.

The above equipment is excellent, admirable, powerful, but not perfect. There is yet another detail which is worth the whole of it put together—and more; a detail which has never been joined (in the *beginning* of a religious movement) to a supremely good working equipment since the world began, until now: *a new personage to worship.*[5] Christianity had the Saviour, but at first and for generations it lacked money and concentrated power. In Mrs. Eddy, Christian Science possesses the new personage for worship, and in addition—here in the very beginning—a working equipment that has not a flaw in it. In the beginning, Mohammedanism had no money; and it has never had anything to offer its client but heaven—nothing here below that was valuable. In addition to heaven hereafter, Christian Science has *present health and a cheerful spirit* to offer; and in comparison with this bribe all other this-world bribes are poor and cheap. You recognize that this estimate is admissible, do you not?

To whom does Bellamy's "Nationalism" appeal? Necessarily to

[5] *That* has been disputed by a Christian-Science friend. This surprises me. I will examine this detail in the new half of the book.—M.T.

the few: people who read and dream, and are compassionate, and troubled for the poor and the hard-driven. To whom does Spiritualism appeal? Necessarily to the few; its "boom" has lasted for half a century, and I believe it claims short of four millions of adherents in America. Who are attracted by Swedenborgianism and some of the other fine and delicate "isms"? The few again: educated people, sensitively organized, with superior mental endowments, who seek lofty planes of thought and find their contentment there. And who are attracted by Christian Science? There is no limit; its field is horizonless; its appeal is as universal as is the appeal of Christianity itself. It appeals to the rich, the poor, the high, the low, the cultured, the ignorant, the gifted, the stupid, the modest, the vain, the wise, the silly, the soldier, the civilian, the hero, the coward, the idler, the worker, the godly, the godless, the freeman, the slave, the adult, the child; *they who are ailing in body or mind, they who have friends that are ailing in body or mind.* To mass it in a phrase, its clientage is the Human Race. Will it march? I think so.

Remember its principal great offer: to *rid the Race of pain and disease.* Can it do so? In large measure, yes. How much of the pain and disease in the world is created by the imaginations of the sufferers, and then kept alive by those same imaginations? Four-fifths? Not anything short of that, I should think. Can Christian Science banish that four-fifths? I think so. Can any other (organized) force do it? None that I know of. Would this be a new world when that was accomplished? And a pleasanter one—for us well people, as well as for those fussy and fretting sick ones? Would it seem as if there was not as much gloomy weather as there used to be? I think so.

In the meantime, would the Scientist kill off a good many patients? I think so. More than get killed off now by the legalized methods? I will take up that question presently.

At present, I wish to ask you to examine some of the Scientist's performances, as registered in his magazine, *The Christian Science Journal*—October number, 1898. First, a Baptist clergyman gives us this true picture of "the average orthodox Christian"—and he could have added that it is a true picture of the average (civilized) human being:

"He is a worried and fretted and fearful man; afraid of himself and his propensities, afraid of colds and fevers, afraid of treading on serpents or drinking deadly things."

Then he gives us this contrast:

"The average Christian Scientist has put all anxiety and fretting under his feet. He does have a victory over fear and care that is not achieved by the average orthodox Christian."

He has put all anxiety and fretting under his feet. What proportion of your earnings or income would you be willing to pay for that frame of mind, year in, year out? It really outvalues any price that can be put upon it. Where can you purchase it, at any outlay of any sort, in any Church or out of it, except the Scientist's?

Well, it is the anxiety and fretting about colds, and fevers, and draughts, and getting our feet wet, and about forbidden food eaten in terror of indigestion, that brings on the cold and the fever and the indigestion and the most of our other ailments; and so, if the Science can banish that anxiety from the world I think it can reduce the world's disease and pain about four-fifths.[6]

In this October number many of the redeemed testify and give thanks; and not coldly, but with passionate gratitude. As a rule they seem drunk with health, and with the surprise of it, the wonder of it, the unspeakable glory and splendor of it, after a long, sober spell spent in inventing imaginary diseases and concreting them with doctor-stuff. The first witness testifies that when "this most beautiful Truth first dawned on him" he had "nearly all the ills that flesh is heir to"; that those he did not have he thought he had—and this made the tale about complete. What was the natural result? Why, he was a dump-pit "for all the doctors, druggists, and patent medicines of the country." Christian Science came to his help, and "the old sick conditions passed away," and along with them the "dismal forebodings" which he had been accustomed to employ in conjuring up ailments. And so he was a healthy and cheerful man, now, and astonished.

But I am not astonished, for from other sources I know what must have been his method of applying Christian Science. If I am in the right, he watchfully and diligently *diverted his mind from unhealthy*

----

[6] *February*, 1903. In a letter to me, a distinguished New York physician finds fault with this notion. If four-fifths of our pains and diseases are not the result of unwholesome fears and imaginings, the Science has a smaller field than I was guessing; but I still think four-fifths is a sound guess.—M.T.

channels and compelled it to travel in healthy ones. Nothing contrivable by human invention could be more formidably effective than that, in banishing imaginary ailments and in closing the entrances against subsequent applicants of their breed. I think his method was to keep saying, "I am well! I am sound!—sound and well! well and sound! Perfectly sound, perfectly well! I have no pain; there's no such thing as pain! I have no disease; there's no such thing as disease! Nothing is real but Mind; all is Mind, All-Good-Good-Good, Life, Soul, Liver, Bones, one of a series, ante and pass the buck!"

I do not mean that that was exactly the formula used, but that it doubtless contains the spirit of it. The Scientist would attach value to the *exact* formula, no doubt, and to the religious spirit in which it was used. I should think that *any* formula that would divert the mind from unwholesome channels and force it into healthy ones would answer every purpose with some people, though not with all. I think it most likely that a very religious man would find the addition of the religious spirit a powerful reinforcement in his case.

The second witness testifies that the Science banished "an old organic trouble," which the doctor and the surgeon had been nursing with drugs and the knife for seven years.

He calls it his "claim." A surface-miner would think it was not *his* claim at all, but the property of the doctor and his pal the surgeon— for he would be misled by that word, which is Christian-Science slang for "ailment." The Christian Scientist *has* no ailment; to him there is no such thing, and he will not use the hateful word. All that happens to him is that upon his attention an imaginary disturbance sometimes obtrudes itself which *claims* to be an ailment but isn't.

This witness offers testimony for a clergyman seventy years old who had preached forty years in a Christian church, and has now gone over to the new sect. He was "almost blind and deaf." He was treated by the C. S. method, and "when he heard the voice of Truth he saw spiritually." Saw spiritually? It is a little indefinite; they had better treat him again. Indefinite testimonies might properly be waste-basketed, since there is evidently no lack of definite ones procurable; but this C. S. magazine is poorly edited, and so mistakes of this kind must be expected.

The next witness is a soldier of the Civil War. When Christian Science found him, he had in stock the following claims:

Indigestion,
Rheumatism,
Catarrh,
Chalky deposits in
   Shoulder-joints, ⎫
   Arm-joints, ⎬
   Hand-joints, ⎭
Insomnia,

Atrophy of the muscles
of
   Arms, ⎫
   Shoulders, ⎭
Stiffness of all those
   joints,
Excruciating pains
   most of the time.

These claims have a very substantial sound. They came of exposure in the campaigns. The doctors did all they could, but it was little. Prayers were tried, but "I never realized any physical relief from that source." After thirty years of torture, he went to a Christian Scientist and took an hour's treatment and went home painless. Two days later, he "began to eat like a well man." Then "the claims vanished—some at once, others more gradually"; finally, "they have almost entirely disappeared." And—a thing which is of still greater value—he is now *contented and happy.*" That is a detail which, as earlier remarked, is a Scientist-Church specialty. And, indeed, one may go further and assert with little or no exaggeration that it is a Christian-Science monopoly. With thirty-one years' effort, the Methodist Church had not succeeded in furnishing it to this harassed soldier.

And so the tale goes on. Witness after witness bulletins his claims, declares their prompt abolishment, and gives Mrs. Eddy's Discovery the praise. Milk-leg is cured; nervous prostration is cured; consumption is cured; and St. Vitus's dance is made a pastime. Even without a fiddle. And now and then an interesting new addition to the Science slang appears on the page. We have "demonstrations over chilblains" and such things. It seems to be a curtailed way of saying "demonstrations of the power of Christian-Science Truth over the fiction which masquerades under the name of Chilblains." The children, as well as the adults, share in the blessings of the Science. "Through the study of the 'little book' they are learning how to be healthful, peaceful, and wise." Sometimes they are cured of their little claims by the professional healer, and sometimes more advanced children say over the formula and cure themselves.

A little Far-Western girl of nine, equipped with an adult vocabulary, states her age and says, "I thought I would write a demonstration to you." She had a claim, derived from getting flung over a pony's head and landed on a rockpile. She saved herself from disaster by remembering to say "God is All" while she was in the air. I couldn't have done it. I shouldn't even have thought of it. I should have been too excited. Nothing but Christian Science could have enabled that child to do that calm and thoughtful and judicious thing in those circumstances. She came down on her head, and by all the rules she should have broken it; but the intervention of the formula prevented that, so the only claim resulting was a blackened eye. Monday morning it was still swollen and shut. At school "it hurt pretty badly—that is, it *seemed* to." So "I was excused, and went down to the basement and said, 'Now I am depending on mamma instead of God, and I *will* depend on God instead of mamma.'" No doubt this would have answered; but, to make sure, she added Mrs. Eddy to the team and recited "the Scientific Statement of Being," which is one of the principal incantations, I judge. Then "I felt my eye opening." Why, dear, it would have opened an oyster. I think it is one of the touchingest things in child-history, that pious little rat down cellar pumping away at the Scientific Statement of Being.

There is a page about another good child—little Gordon. Little Gordon "came into the world without the assistance of surgery or anaesthetics." He was a "demonstration." A painless one; therefore, his coming evoked "joy and thankfulness to God and the Discoverer of Christian Science." It is a noticeable feature of this literature—the so frequent linking together of the Two Beings in an equal bond; also of Their Two Bibles. When little Gordon was two years old, "he was playing horse on the bed, where I had left my 'little book.' I noticed him stop in his play, take the book carefully in his little hands, kiss it softly, then look about for the highest place of safety his arms could reach, and put it there." This pious act filled the mother "with such a train of thought as I had never experienced before. I thought of the sweet mother of long ago who kept things in her heart," etc. It is a bold comparison; however, unconscious profanations are about as common in the mouths of the lay membership of the new Church as are frank and open ones in the mouths of its consecrated chiefs.

Some days later, the family library—Christian-Science books— was lying in a deep-seated window. This was another chance for the holy child to show off. He left his play and went there and pushed all the books to one side, except the Annex. "*It* he took in both hands, slowly raised it to his lips, then removed it carefully, and seated himself in the window." It had seemed to the mother too wonderful to be true, that first time; but now she was convinced that "neither imagination nor accident had anything to do with it." Later, little Gordon let the author of his being see him do it. After that he did it frequently; probably every time anybody was looking. I would rather have that child than a chromo. If this tale has any object, it is to intimate that the inspired book was supernaturally able to convey a sense of its sacred and awful character to this innocent little creature, without the intervention of outside aids. The magazine is not edited with high-priced discretion. The editor has a "claim," and he ought to get it treated.

Among other witnesses there is one who had a "jumping toothache," which several times tempted her to "believe that there was sensation in matter, but each time it was overcome by the power of Truth." She would not allow the dentist to use cocaine, but sat there and let him punch and drill and split and crush the tooth, and tear and slash its ulcerations, and pull out the nerve, and dig out fragments of bone; and she wouldn't once confess that it hurt. And to this day she thinks it didn't, and I have not a doubt that she is nine-tenths right, and that her Christian-Science faith did her better service than she could have gotten out of cocaine.

There is an account of a boy who got broken all up into small bits by an accident, but said over the Scientific Statement of Being, or some of the other incantations, and got well and sound without having suffered any real pain and without the intrusion of a surgeon.

Also, there is an account of the restoration to perfect health, in a single night, of a fatally injured *horse,* by the application of Christian Science. I can stand a good deal, but I recognize that the ice is getting thin, here. That horse had as many as fifty claims; how could *he* demonstrate over them? Could he do the All-Good, Good-Good, Good-Gracious, Liver, Bones, Truth, All down but Nine, Set them up on the Other Alley? Could he intone the Scientific Statement of Being? Now, could he? Wouldn't it give him a relapse? Let us draw the line at horses. Horses and furniture.

There is plenty of other testimonies in the magazine, but these quoted samples will answer. They show the kind of trade the Science is driving. Now we come back to the question, Does the Science kill a patient here and there and now and then? We must concede it. Does it compensate for this? I am persuaded that it can make a plausible showing in that direction. For instance: when it lays its hand upon a soldier who has suffered thirty years of helpless torture and makes him whole in body and mind, what is the actual sum of that achievement? This, I think: that it has restored to life a subject who had essentially died ten deaths a year for thirty years, and each of them a long and painful one. But for its interference that man in the three years which have since elapsed, would have essentially died thirty times more. There are thousands of young people in the land who are now ready to enter upon a lifelong death similar to that man's. Every time the Science captures one of these and secures to him life-long immunity from imagination-manufactured disease, it may plausibly claim that in his person it has saved three hundred lives. Meantime, it will kill a man every now and then. But no matter, it will still be ahead on the credit side.

NOTE.—I have received several letters (two from educated and ostensibly intelligent persons) which contained, in substance, this protest: "I don't object to men and women chancing their lives with these people, but it is a burning shame that the law should allow them to trust their helpless little children in their deadly hands." Isn't it touching? Isn't it deep? Isn't it modest? It is as if the person said: "I know that to a parent his child is the core of his heart, the apple of his eye, a possession so dear, so precious that he will trust its life in no hands but those which he believes, with all his soul, to be the very best and the very safest, but it is a burning shame that the law does not require him to come to *me* to ask what kind of healer I will allow him to call." The public is merely a multiplied "me."—M.T.

Chapter 7[1]

"We consciously declare that *Science and Health, with Key to the Scriptures,* was foretold, *as well as its author,* Mary Baker Eddy, in Revelation x. She is the 'mighty angel,' or God's highest thought to this age (verse 1), giving us the spiritual interpretation of the Bible in the 'little book *open*' (verse 2). Thus we prove that Christian Science is the second coming of Christ—Truth—Spirit."

—*Lecture by Dr. George Tomkins, D.D. C.S.*

There you have it in plain speech. She is the mighty angel; she is the divinely and officially sent bearer of God's highest thought. For the present, she *brings* the Second Advent. We must expect that before

[1] Written in Europe in 1899, but not hitherto published in book form.—M.T.

she has been in her grave fifty years she will be regarded by her following as having been *herself* the Second Advent. She is already worshipped, and we must expect this feeling to spread, territorially, and also to deepen in intensity.[2]

Particularly after her death; for then, as any one can foresee, Eddy-Worship will be taught in the Sunday-schools and pulpits of the cult. Already whatever she puts her trade-mark on, though it be only a memorial-spoon, is holy and is eagerly and gratefully bought by the disciple, and becomes a fetich in his house. I say bought, for the Boston Christian-Science Trust gives nothing away; everything it has is for sale. And the terms are cash; and not only cash, but cash in advance. Its god is Mrs. Eddy first, then the Dollar. Not a spiritual Dollar, but a real one. From end to end of the Christian-Science literature not a single (material) thing in the world is conceded to be real, except the Dollar. But all through and through its advertisements that reality is eagerly and persistently recognized.

The Dollar is hunted down in all sorts of ways; the Christian-Science Mother-Church and Bargain-Counter in Boston peddles all kinds of spiritual wares to the faithful, and always on the one condition—*cash,* cash in advance. The Angel of the Apocalypse could not go there and get a copy of his own pirated book on credit. Many, many precious Christian-Science things are to be had there—for cash: Bible Lessons; Church Manual; C. S. Hymnal; History of the building of the Mother-Church; lot of Sermons; Communion Hymn, "Saw Ye My Saviour," by Mrs. Eddy, half a dollar a copy, "words used by special permission of Mrs. Eddy." Also we have Mrs. Eddy's and the Angel's little Bible-Annex in eight styles of binding at eight kinds of war-prices; among these a sweet thing in "levant, divinity circuit, leather lined to edge, round corners, gold edge, silk sewed, each, *prepaid,* $6," and if you take a million you get them a shilling cheaper—that is to say, "prepaid, $5.75." Also we have Mrs. Eddy's *Miscellaneous Writings,* at 'andsome big prices, the divinity-circuit style heading the extortions, shilling discount where you take an edition. Next comes *Christ and Christmas,* by the fertile Mrs. Eddy

---

[2] After *raising a dead child to life,* the disciple who did it writes an account of her performance to Mrs. Eddy, and closes it thus: "My prayer daily is to be more spiritual, that I may do more as you would have me do, . . . and may we all love you more, and so live it that the world may know that the Christ is come."—*Printed in the Concord, N. H., Independent Statesman, March 9, 1899.* If this is not worship, it is a good imitation of it.—M.T.

—a *poem*—would God I could see it!—price $3, cash in advance. Then follow five more books by Mrs. Eddy, at highwayman's rates, some of them in "leatherette covers," some of them in "pebbled cloth," with divinity-circuit, compensation-balance, twin-screw, and the other modern improvements; and at the same bargain-counter can be had *The Christian Science Journal.*

Christian-Science literary discharges are a monopoly of the Mother-Church Headquarters Factory in Boston; none genuine without the trade-mark of the Trust. You must apply there and not else where.[3]

The Trust has still other sources of income. Mrs. Eddy is president (and proprietor) of the Trust's Metaphysical College in Boston, where the student of C. S. healing learns the game by a three weeks' course, and pays *one hundred dollars* for it.[4] And I have a case among my statistics where the student had a three weeks' course and paid *three* hundred for it.

The Trust does love the Dollar, when it isn't a spiritual one.

In order to force the sale of Mrs. Eddy's Bible-Annex, no healer, Metaphysical-College-bred or other, is allowed to practise the game unless he possesses a copy of that book. That means a large and constantly augmenting income for the Trust. No C. S. family would consider itself loyal or pious or pain-proof without an Annex or two in the house. That means an income for the Trust, in the near future, of millions; not thousands—millions a year.

No member, young or old, of a branch Christian-Scientist church can acquire and retain membership in the Mother-Church unless he pay "capitation tax" (of "not less than a dollar," say the By-Laws) to the Boston Trust every year. That means an income for the Trust, in the near future, of—let us venture to say—millions more per year.

It is a reasonably safe guess that in America in 1920 there will be ten million[5] Christian Scientists, and three millions in Great Britain;

---

[3] *February,* 1903. I applied last month, but they returned my money, and wouldn't play. We are not on speaking terms now.—M.T.

[4] An error. For one hundred, read *three* hundred. That was for twelve brief lessons. But this cheapness only lasted until the end of 1888—fourteen years ago. [I am making this note in December, 1902]. Mrs. Eddy—over her own signature—then made a change; the new terms were three hundred dollars for *seven* lessons. See *Christian Science Journal* for December, 1888.—M.T.

[5] Written in 1899. It is intended to include men, women, and children. Although the calculation was based upon inflated statistics, I believe today that it is not far out.—M.T.

that these figures will be trebled in 1930; that in America in 1920 the Christian Scientists will be a political force, in 1930 politically formidable, and in 1940 the governing power in the Republic—to remain that, permanently. And I think it a reasonable guess that the Trust (which is already in our day pretty brusque in its ways) will then be the most insolent and unscrupulous and tyrannical politico-religious master that has dominated a people since the palmy days of the Inquisition. And a stronger master than the strongest of bygone times, because this one will have a financial strength not dreamed of by any predecessor; as effective a concentration of irresponsible power as any predecessor has had;[6] in the railway, the telegraph, and the subsidized newspaper, better facilities for watching and managing his empire than any predecessor has had; and, after a generation or two, he will probably divide Christendom with the Catholic Church.

The Roman Church has a perfect organization, and it has an effective centralization of power—but not of its cash. Its multitude of Bishops are rich, but their riches remain in large measure in their own hands. They collect from two hundred millions of people, but they keep the bulk of the result at home. The Boston Pope of by-and-by will draw his dollar-a-head capitation-tax from three hundred millions of the human race,[7] and the Annex and the rest of his bookshop stock will fetch in as much more; and his Metaphysical Colleges, the annual pilgrimage to Mrs. Eddy's tomb, from all over the world—admission, the Christian-Science Dollar (payable in advance)—purchases of consecrated glass beads, candles, memorial spoons, aureoled chromo-portraits and bogus autographs of Mrs. Eddy; cash offerings at her shrine—no crutches of cured cripples received, and no imitations of miraculously restored broken legs and necks allowed to be hung up except when made out of the Holy Metal and proved by fire-assay; cash for miracles worked at the tomb: these money-sources, with a thousand to be yet invented and ambushed upon the devotee, will bring the annual increment well up above a billion. And nobody but the Trust will have the handling of

---

[6] It can be put stronger than that and still be true.—M.T.

[7] In that day by force; it is voluntary now. In the new half of this book the reader will perceive that all imaginable compulsions are possible under the Mother-Church's body of Laws. Today more is expected than the one dollar. This is indicated in the wording of the By-Law. Much more comes, from many members.—M.T.

it. In that day, the Trust will monopolize the manufacture and sale of the Old and New Testaments as well as the Annex, and raise their price to Annex rates, and compel the devotee to buy (for even today a healer has to have the Annex *and* the Scriptures or he is not allowed to work the game), and that will bring several hundred million dollars more. In those days, the Trust will have an income approaching five million dollars a day, and no expenses to be taken out of it; no taxes to pay, and *no charities to support.* That last detail should not be lightly passed over by the reader; it is well entitled to attention.

No charities to support. No, nor even to contribute to. One searches in vain the Trust's advertisements and the utterances of its organs for any suggestion that it spends a penny on orphans, widows, discharged prisoners, hospitals, ragged schools, night missions, city missions, libraries, old people's homes, or any other object that appeals to a human being's purse through his heart.[8]

I have hunted, hunted, and hunted, by correspondence and otherwise, and have not yet got upon the track of a farthing that the Trust has spent upon any worthy object. Nothing makes a Scientist so uncomfortable as to ask him if he knows of a case where Christian Science has spent money on a benevolence, either among its own adherents or elsewhere. He is obliged to say "No." And then one discovers that the person questioned has been asked the question many times before, and that it is getting to be a sore subject with him. Why a sore subject? Because he has written his chiefs and asked with high confidence for an answer that will confound these questioners—and the chiefs did not reply. He has written again, and then again—not with confidence, but humbly, now—and has begged for defensive ammunition in the voice of supplication. A reply does at last come—to this effect: "We must have faith in Our Mother, and rest content in the conviction that whatever She[9] does with the money it is in accordance with orders from Heaven, for She does no act of any kind without first 'demonstrating over' it."

That settles it—as far as the disciple is concerned. His mind is satisfied with that answer; he gets down his Annex and does an

---

[8] In two years (1898–99) the membership of the Established Church in England gave voluntary contributions amounting to seventy-three millions of dollars to the Church's benevolent enterprises. Churches that give have nothing to hide.—M.T.

[9] I may be introducing the capital S a little early—still, it is on its way.—M.T.

incantation or two, and that mesmerizes his spirit and puts *that* to sleep—brings it peace. Peace and comfort and joy, until some inquirer punctures the old sore again.

Through friends in America I asked some questions, and in some cases got definite and informing answers; in other cases the answers were not definite and not valuable. To the question, "Does any of the money go to charities?" the answer from an authoritative source was: "No, *not in the sense usually conveyed by this word.*" (The italics are mine.) That answer is cautious. But definite, I think—utterly and unassailably definite—although quite Christian-Scientifically foggy in its phrasing. Christian-Science testimony is generally foggy, generally diffuse, generally garrulous. The writer was aware that the first word in his phrase answered the question which I was asking, but he could not help adding nine dark words. Meaningless ones, unless explained by him. It is quite likely, as intimated by him, that Christian Science has invented a new class of objects to apply the word "charity" to, but without an explanation we cannot know what they are. We quite easily and naturally and confidently guess that they are in all cases objects which will return five hundred per cent on the Trust's investment in them, but guessing is not knowledge; it is merely, in this case, a sort of nine-tenths certainty deducible from what we think we know of the Trust's trade principles and its sly and furtive and shifty ways.[10]

Sly? Deep? Judicious? The Trust understands its business. The Trust does not give itself away. It defeats all the attempts of us impertinents to get at its trade secrets. To this day, after all our diligence, we have not been able to get it to confess what it does with the money. It does not even let its own disciples find out. All it says is, that the matter has been "demonstrated over." Now and then a lay Scientist says, with a grateful exultation, that Mrs. Eddy is enormously rich, but he stops there; as to whether any of the money goes to other charities or not, he is obliged to admit that he does not know. However, the Trust is composed of human beings; and this justifies the conjecture that if it had a charity on its list which it was proud of, we should soon hear of it.

[10] *February,* 1903. A letter has come to me, this month, from a lady who says that while she was living in Boston, a few years ago, she visited the Mother-Church and offices and had speech with Judge Septimius J. Hanna, the "first reader," who "stated positively that the Church, as a body, does no philanthropic work whatever."—M.T.

"Without money and without price." Those used to be the terms. Mrs. Eddy's Annex cancels them. The motto of Christian Science is, "The laborer is worthy of his hire." And now that it has been "demonstrated over," we find its spiritual meaning to be, "Do anything and everything your hand may find to do; and charge cash for it, and collect the money in advance." The Scientist has on his tongue's end a cut-and-dried, Boston-supplied set of rather lean arguments, whose function is to show that it is a Heaven-commanded *duty* to do this, and that the croupiers of the game have no choice but to obey.[11]

---

[11] *February*, 1903. If I seem to be charging any one outside of the Trust with an exaggerated appetite for money, I have not meant to do it. The exactions of the ordinary C. S. "healer" are not exorbitant. If I have prejudices against the Trust—and I do feel that I have—they do not extend to the lay membership. "The laborer is worthy of his hire." And is entitled to receive it, too, and charge his own price (when he is laboring in a lawful calling). The great surgeon charges a thousand dollars, and no one is justified in objecting to it. The great preacher and teacher in religion receives a large salary, and is entitled to it; Henry Ward Beecher's was twenty thousand dollars. Mrs. Eddy's Metaphysical College was chartered by the State, and she had a legal right to charge amazing prices, and she did it. She allows only a few persons to *teach* Christian Science. The calling of these teachers is not illegal. Mrs. Eddy appoints the sum their students must pay, and it is a round one; but that is no matter, since they need not come unless they want to.

But when we come to the C. S. "healer," the *practitioner,* that is another thing. He exists by the hundred; his services are prized by his C. S. patient, they are preferred above all other human help, and are thankfully paid for. As I have just remarked, his prices are not large. But there is hardly a State wherein he can lawfully practise his profession. In the name of religion, of morals, and of Christ—represented on the earth by Mrs. Eddy—he enters upon his trade a commissioned law-breaker.

A law-breaker. It is curious, but if the Second Advent should happen now, Jesus could not heal the sick in the State of New York. He could not do it lawfully; therefore He could not do it morally; therefore He could not do it at all.—M.T.

March 12, 1903. While I am reading the final proofs of this book, the following letter has come to me. It is not marked private, therefore I suppose I may without impropriety insert it here, if I suppress the signature:

"Dear Sir,—In the *North American Review* for January is the statement, in effect, that Christian Scientists give nothing to charities. It has had wide reading and is doubtless credited. To produce a true impression, it seems as if other facts should have been stated in connection.

"With regret for adding anything to the burden of letters from strangers, I am impelled to write what I know from a limited acquaintance in the sect. I am not connected with it myself.

"The charity freely given by individual practitioners, so far as I know it, is at least equal to that of regular physicians. Charges are made with much more than equal consideration of the means of the patient. Of course druggists' bills and the enormous expenses involved in the employment of a trained nurse, exist in small degree or not at all.

"As to organized charities: It is hard to find one where the most intelligent laborers in it feel that they are reaching the root of an evil. They are putting a few plasters on a

The Trust seems to be a reincarnation. Exodus xxxii. 4.

I have no reverence for the Trust, but I am not lacking in reverence for the sincerities of the lay membership of the new Church. There is every evidence that the lay members are entirely sincere in their faith, and I think sincerity is always entitled to honor and respect, let the inspiration of the sincerity be what it may. Zeal and sincerity can carry a new religion further than any other missionary except fire and sword, and I believe that the new religion will conquer the half of Christendom in a hundred years. I am not intending this as a compliment to the human race; I am merely stating an opinion. And yet I think that perhaps it *is* a compliment to the race. I keep in mind that saying of an orthodox preacher—quoted further back. He conceded that this new Christianity frees its possessor's life from *frets, fears, vexations, bitterness, and all sorts of imagination-propagated maladies and pains, and fills his world with sunshine and his heart with gladness.* If Christian Science, with this stupendous equipment—and final salvation added—cannot win half the Christian globe, I must be badly mistaken in the make-up of the human race.

I think the Trust will be handed down like the other Papacy, and will always know how to handle its limitless cash. It will press the button; the zeal, the energy, the sincerity, the enthusiasm of its countless vassals will do the rest.

---

body of disease. Complaint is made, too, that the machinery, by which of necessity systematic charity must be administered, prevents the personal friendliness and sympathy which should pervade it throughout.

"Christian Science claims to be able to abolish the need for charity. The results of drunkenness make great demands upon the charitable. But the principle of Christian Science takes away the desire for strong drink. If sexual propensities were dominated, not only by reason, but by Christian love for both the living and the unborn—Christian Science is emphatic on this subject—many existing charitable societies would have no reason to be. So far as Christian Science prevents disease, the need for hospitals is lessened. Not only illness, but poverty, is a subject for the practice of Christian Science. If this evil were prevented there would be no occasion to alleviate its results.

"The faith, hope, and love which the few Christian Scientists I have known have lived and radiated, made conditions needing organized charity vanish before them.

"With renewed apology for intrusion upon one whose own 'Uncle Silas' was 'loved back' to sanity,

"I am, etc., etc.

"Woburn, Mass.,
"March 10, 1903."

Chapter 8

The power which a man's imagination has over his body to heal it or make it sick is a force which none of us is born without. The first man had it, the last one will possess it. If left to himself, a man is most likely to use only the mischievous half of the force—the half which invents imaginary ailments for him and cultivates them; and if he is one of these very wise people, he is quite likely to scoff at the beneficent half of the force and deny its existence. And so, to heal or help that man, *two* imaginations are required: his own and some outsider's. The outsider, B, must imagine that *his* incantations are the healing-power that is curing A, and A must imagine that this is so. I think it is not so, at all; but no matter, the cure is effected, and that is the main thing. The outsider's work is unquestionably valuable, so valuable that it may fairly be likened to the essential work performed by the engineer when he handles the throttle and turns on the steam; the actual power is lodged exclusively in the engine, but if the engine were left alone it would never start of itself. Whether the engineer be named Jim, or Bob, or Tom, it is all one—his services are necessary, and he is entitled to such wage as he can get you to pay. Whether he be named Christian Scientist, or Mental Scientist, or Mind Curist, or King's-Evil Expert, or Hypnotist, it is all one; he is merely the Engineer; he simply turns on the same old steam and the engine does the whole work.

The Christian-Scientist engineer drives exactly the same trade as the other engineers, yet he out-prospers the whole of them put together.[1]

Is it because he has captured the takingest name? I think that that is only a small part of it. I think that the secret of his high prosperity lies elsewhere.

The Christian Scientist has *organized* the business. Now that was certainly a gigantic idea. Electricity, in limitless volume, has existed in the air and the rocks and the earth and everywhere since time began—and was going to waste all the while. In our time we have *organized* that scattered and wandering force and set it to work, and

[1] *February*, 1903. As I have already remarked in a foot-note, the Scientist claims that he uses a force not used by any of the others.—M.T.

backed the business with capital, and concentrated it in few and competent hands, and the results are as we see.

The Christian Scientist has taken a force which has been lying idle in every member of the human race since time began, and has organized it, and backed the business with capital, and concentrated it at Boston headquarters in the hands of a small and very competent Trust, and there are results.

Therein lies the promise that this monopoly is going to extend its commerce wide in the earth. I think that if the business were conducted in the loose and disconnected fashion customary with such things, it would achieve but little more than the modest prosperity usually secured by unorganized great moral and commercial ventures; but I believe that so long as this one remains compactly organized and closely concentrated in a Trust, the spread of its dominion will continue.

Chapter 9

Four years ago I wrote the preceding chapters.[1] I was assured by the wise that Christian Science was a fleeting craze and would soon perish. This prompt and all-competent stripe of prophet is always to be had in the market at ground-floor rates. He does not stop to load, or consider, or take aim, but lets fly just as he stands. Facts are nothing to him, he has no use for such things; he works wholly by inspiration. And so, when he is asked why he considers a new movement a passing fad and quickly perishable, he finds himself unprepared with a reason and is more or less embarrassed. For a moment. Only for a moment. Then he waylays the first spectre of a reason that goes flitting through the desert places of his mind, and is at once serene again and ready for conflict. Serene and confident. Yet he should not be so, since he has had no chance to examine his catch, and cannot know whether it is going to help his contention or damage it.

The impromptu reason furnished by the early prophets of whom I have spoken was this:

"There is nothing *to* Christian Science; there is nothing about it

[1] That is to say, in 1898.

that appeals to the intellect; its market will be restricted to the unintelligent, the mentally inferior, the people who do not think."

They called that a reason why the cult would not flourish and endure. It seems the equivalent of saying:

"There is no money in tinware; there is nothing about it that appeals to the rich; its market will be restricted to the poor."

It is like bringing forward the best reason in the world why Christian Science should flourish and live, and then blandly offering it as a reason why it should sicken and die.

That reason was furnished me by the complacent and unfrightened prophets four years ago, and it has been furnished me again today. If conversions to new religions or to old ones were in any considerable degree achieved through the intellect, the aforesaid reason would be sound and sufficient, no doubt; the inquirer into Christian Science might go away unconvinced and unconverted. But we all know that conversions are seldom made in that way; that such a thing as a serious and painstaking and fairly competent inquiry into the claims of a religion or of a political dogma is a rare occurrence; and that the vast mass of men and women are far from being capable of making such an examination. They are not capable, for the reason that their minds, howsoever good they may be, are not trained for such examinations. The mind not trained for that work is no more competent to do it than are lawyers and farmers competent to make successful clothes without learning the tailor's trade. There are seventy-five million men and women among us who do not know how to cut out and make a dress-suit, and they would not think of trying; yet they all think they can competently think out a political or religious scheme without any apprenticeship to the business, and many of them believe they have actually worked that miracle. But, indeed, the truth is, almost all the men and women of our nation or of any other get their religion and their politics where they get their astronomy—entirely at second hand. Being untrained, they are no more able to intelligently examine a dogma or a policy than they are to calculate an eclipse.

Men are usually competent thinkers along the lines of their specialized training only. Within these limits alone are their opinions and judgments valuable; outside of these limits they grope and are lost—usually without knowing it. In a church assemblage of five hundred persons, there will be a man or two whose trained minds can seize upon each detail of a great manufacturing scheme and recognize its value or its lack of value promptly; and can pass the details in intelligent review, section by section, and finally as a whole, and then deliver a verdict upon the scheme which cannot be flippantly set aside nor easily answered. And there will be one or two other men there who can do the same thing with a great and complicated educational project; and one or two others who can do the like with a large scheme for applying electricity in a new and unheard-of way; and one or two others who can do it with a showy scheme for revolutionizing the scientific world's accepted notions regarding geology. And so on, and so on. But the manufacturing experts will not be competent to examine the educational scheme intelligently, and their opinion about it would not be valuable; neither of these two groups will be able to understand and pass upon the electrical scheme; none of these three batches of experts will be able to understand and pass upon the geological revolution; and probably not one man in the entire lot will be competent to examine, capably, the intricacies of a political or religious scheme, new or old, and deliver a judgment upon it which any one need regard as precious.

There you have the top crust. There will be four hundred and seventy-five men and women present who can draw upon their training and deliver incontrovertible judgments concerning cheese, and leather, and cattle, and hardware, and soap, and tar, and candles, and patent medicines, and dreams, and apparitions, and garden truck, and cats, and baby food, and warts, and hymns, and time-tables, and freight-rates, and summer resorts, and whiskey, and law, and surgery, and dentistry, and blacksmithing, and shoemaking, and dancing, and Huyler's candy, and mathematics, and dog fights, and obstetrics, and music, and sausages, and dry goods, and molasses, and railroad stocks, and horses, and literature, and labor unions, and vegetables, and morals, and lamb's fries, and etiquette, and agriculture. And not ten among the five hundred—let their minds be ever so good and bright—will be competent, by grace of the requisite specialized mental training, to take hold of a complex abstraction of any kind and make head or tail of it.

The whole five hundred are thinkers, and they are all capable thinkers—but only within the narrow limits of their specialized trainings. Four hundred and ninety of them cannot competently examine either a religious plan or a political one. A scattering few of them do examine both—that is, they think they do. With results as precious as when I examine the nebular theory and explain it to myself.

If the four hundred and ninety got their religion through their minds, and by weighed and measured detail, Christian Science would not be a scary apparition. But they don't; they get a little of it through their minds, more of it through their feelings, and the overwhelming bulk of it through their environment.

Environment is the chief thing to be considered when one is proposing to predict the future of Christian Science. It is not the ability to reason that makes the Presbyterian, or the Baptist, or the Methodist, or the Catholic, or the Mohammedan, or the Buddhist, or the Mormon; it is *environment*. If religions were got by reasoning, we should have the extraordinary spectacle of an American family with a Presbyterian in it, and a Baptist, a Methodist, a Catholic, a Mohammedan, a Buddhist, and a Mormon. A Presbyterian family does not produce Catholic families or other religious brands, it produces its own kind; and not by intellectual processes, but by association. And so also with Mohammedanism, the cult which in our day is spreading with the sweep of a world-conflagration through the Orient, that native home of profound thought and of subtle intellectual fence, that fertile womb whence has sprung every great religion that exists. Including our own; for with all our brains we cannot invent a religion and market it.

The language of my quoted prophets recurs to us now, and we wonder to think how small a space in the world the mighty Mohammedan Church would be occupying now, if a successful trade in its line of goods had been conditioned upon an exhibit that would "appeal to the intellect" instead of to "the unintelligent, the mentally inferior, the people who do not think."

The Christian Science Church, like the Mohammedan Church, makes no embarrassing appeal to the intellect, has no occasion to do it, and can get along quite well without it.

Provided. Provided what? That it can secure that thing which is worth two or three hundred thousand times more than an "appeal to the intellect"—an *environment*. Can it get that? Will it be a menace to regular Christianity if it gets that? Is it time for regular Christianity to get alarmed? Or shall regular Christianity smile a smile and turn over and take another nap? Won't it be wise and proper for regular Christianity to do the old way, the customary way, the historical way—lock the stable-door after the horse is gone? Just as Protestantism has smiled and nodded this long time (while the alert and diligent Catholic was slipping in and capturing the public schools), and is now beginning to hunt around for the key when it is too late?

Will Christian Science get a chance to show its wares? It has *already* secured that chance. Will it flourish and spread and prosper if it shall create for itself the one thing essential to those conditions—an environment? It has *already* created an environment. There are families of Christian Scientists in every community in America, and each family is a factory; each family turns out a Christian Science product at the customary intervals, and contributes it to the Cause in the only way in which contributions of recruits to Churches are ever made on a large scale—by the puissant forces of personal contact and association. Each family is an agency for the Cause, and makes converts among the neighbors, and starts some more factories.

Four years ago there were six Christian Scientists in a certain town that I am acquainted with; a year ago there were two hundred and fifty there; they have built a church, and its membership now numbers four hundred. This has all been quietly done; done without frenzied revivals, without uniforms, brass bands, street parades, corner oratory, or any of the other customary persuasions to a godly life. Christian Science, like Mohammedanism, is "restricted" to the "unintelligent, the people who do not think." There lies the danger. It makes Christian Science formidable. It is "restricted" to ninety-nine one-hundredths of the human race, and must be reckoned with by regular Christianity. And will be, as soon as it is too late.

BOOK II

There were remarkable things about the stranger called the Man-Mystery—things so very extraordinary that they monopolized attention and made *all* of him seem extraordinary; but this was not so, the most of his qualities being of the common, every-day size and like anybody else's. It was curious. He was of the ordinary stature, and had the ordinary aspects; yet in him were hidden such strange contradictions and disproportions! He was majestically fearless and heroic; he had the strength of thirty men and the daring of thirty thousand; handling armies, organizing states, administering governments—these were pastimes to him; he publicly and ostentatiously accepted the human race at its own valuation—as demigods—and privately and successfully dealt with it at quite another and juster valuation—as children and slaves; his ambitions were stupendous, and his dreams had no commerce with the humble plain, but moved with the cloud-rack among the snow-summits. These features of him were, indeed, extraordinary, but the rest of him was ordinary and usual. He was so mean-minded, in the matter of jealousy, that it was thought he was descended from a god; he was vain in little ways, and had a pride in trivialities; he doted on ballads about moonshine and bruised hearts; in education he was deficient, he was indifferent to literature, and knew nothing of art; he was dumb upon all subjects but one, indifferent to all except that one—the Nebular Theory. Upon that one his flow of words was full and free, he was a geyser. The official astronomers disputed his facts and derided his views, and said that he had invented both, they not being findable in any of the books. But many of the laity, who wanted their nebulosities fresh, admired his doctrine and adopted it, and it attained to great prosperity in spite of the hostility of the experts."

—The Legend of the Man-Mystery, ch. i.

Chapter 1

January, 1903. When we do not know a public man personally, we guess him out by the facts of his career. When it is Washington, we all arrive at about one and the same result. We agree that his words and his acts clearly interpret his character to us, and that they never leave us in doubt as to the motives whence the words and acts proceeded. It is the same with Joan of Arc, it is the same with two or three or five or six others among the immortals. But in the matter of motives and of a few details of character we agree to disagree upon Napoleon, Cromwell, and all the rest; and to this list we must add Mrs. Eddy. I think we can peacefully agree as to two or three extraordinary features of her make-up, but not upon the other features of it. We cannot peacefully agree as to her motives, therefore her character must remain crooked to some of us and straight to the others.

No matter, she is interesting enough without an amicable agreement. In several ways she is the most interesting woman that ever lived, and the most extraordinary. The same may be said of her career, and the same may be said of its chief result. She started from nothing. Her enemies charge that she surreptitiously took from Quimby a peculiar system of healing which was mind-cure with a Biblical basis. She and her friends deny that she took anything from him. This is a matter which we can discuss by-and-by. Whether she took it or invented it, it was—materially—a sawdust mine when she got it, and she has turned it into a Klondike; its spiritual dock had next to no custom, if any at all: from it she has launched a world-religion which has now six hundred and sixty-three churches, and she charters a new one every four days. When we do not know a person—and also when we do—we have to judge his size by the size and nature of his achievements, as compared with the achievements of others in his special line of business—there is no other way. Measured by this standard, it is thirteen hundred years since the world has produced anyone who could reach up to Mrs. Eddy's waistbelt.

Figuratively speaking, Mrs. Eddy is already as tall as the Eiffel

Tower. She is adding surprisingly to her stature every day. It is quite within the probabilities that a century hence she will be the most imposing figure that has cast its shadow across the globe since the inauguration of our era. I grant that after saying these strong things, it is necessary that I offer some details calculated to satisfactorily demonstrate the proportions which I have claimed for her. I will do that presently; but before exhibiting the matured *sequoia gigantea,* I believe it will be best to exhibit the sprout from which it sprang. It may save the reader from making miscalculations. The person who imagines that a Big Tree sprout is bigger than other kinds of sprouts is quite mistaken. It is the ordinary thing; it makes no show, it compels no notice, it hasn't a detectible quality in it that entitles it to attention, or suggests the future giant its sap is suckling. That is the kind of sprout Mrs. Eddy was. From her childhood days up to where she was running a half-century a close race and gaining on it, she was most humanly commonplace.

She is the witness I am drawing this from. She has revealed it in her autobiography. Not intentionally, of course—I am not claiming that. An autobiography is the most treacherous thing there is. It lets out every secret its author is trying to keep; it lets the truth shine unobstructed through every harmless little deception he tries to play; it pitilessly exposes him as a tin hero worshipping himself as Big Metal every time he tries to do the modest-unconsciousness act before the reader. This is not guessing; I am speaking from autobiographical personal experience; I was never able to refrain from mentioning, with a studied casualness that could deceive none but the most incautious reader, that an ancestor of mine was sent ambassador to Spain by Charles I, nor that in a remote branch of my family there exists a claimant to an earldom, nor that an uncle of mine used to own a dog that was descended from the dog that was in the Ark; and at the same time I was never able to persuade myself to call a gibbet by its right name when accounting for other ancestors of mine, but always spoke of it as the "platform"—puerilely intimating that they were out lecturing when it happened.

It is Mrs. Eddy over again. As regards her minor half, she is as commonplace as the rest of us. Vain of trivial things all the first half of her life, and still vain of them at seventy and recording them with naïve satisfaction—even rescuing some early rhymes of hers of the sort that we all scribble in the innocent days of our youth—rescuing

them and printing them without pity or apology, just as the weakest
and commonest of us do in our gray age. More—she still frankly
admires them; and in her introduction of them profanely confers
upon them the holy name of "poetry." Sample:

> And laud the land whose talents rock
>   The cradle of her power,
> And wreaths are twined round Plymouth Rock
>   From erudition's bower.
>
> Minerva's silver sandals still
>   Are loosed and not effete.

You note it is not a shade above the thing which all human beings
churn out in their youth.

You would not think that in a little wee primer—for that is what
the *Autobiography* is—a person with a tumultuous career of seventy
years behind her could find room for two or three pages of padding
of this kind, but such is the case. She evidently puts narrative together with difficulty and is not at home in it, and is glad to have
something ready-made to fill in with. Another sample:

> *Here fame-honored Hickory rears his bold form,*
> *And bears[1] a brave breast to the lightning and storm,*
> *While Palm, Bay, and Laurel in classical glee,*
> *Chase Tulip, Magnolia, and fragrant Fringe-tree.*

Vivid? You can fairly see those trees galloping around. That she
could still treasure up, and print, and manifestly admire those Poems, indicates that the most daring and masculine and masterful
woman that has appeared in the earth in centuries has the same soft,
girly-girly places in her that the rest of us have.

When it comes to selecting her ancestors she is still human, natural, vain, commonplace—as commonplace as I am myself when I am
sorting ancestors for my autobiography. She combs out some creditable Scots, and labels them and sets them aside for use, not overlooking the one to whom Sir William Wallace gave "a heavy sword en-
cased in a brass scabbard," and naïvely explaining *which* Sir William
Wallace it was, lest we get the wrong one by the hassock;[2] this is the
one "from whose patriotism and bravery comes that heart-stirring

---

[1] Meaning *bares?* I think so.—M.T.

[2] I am in some doubt as to what a hassock is, but any way it sounds good.—M.T.

air, 'Scots wha hae wi' Wallace bled.' " Hannah More was related to
her ancestors. She explains who Hannah More was.

Whenever a person informs us who Sir William Wallace was, or
who wrote *Hamlet*, or where the Declaration of Independence was
fought, it fills us with a suspicion wellnigh amounting to conviction,
that that person would not suspect us of being so empty of knowledge if he wasn't suffering from the same "claim" himself. Then we
turn to page 20 of the *Autobiography* and happen upon this passage,
and that hasty suspicion stands rebuked:

"I gained book-knowledge with far less labor than is usually requisite. At ten years of age I was as familiar with Lindley Murray's
Grammar as with the Westminster Catechism; and the latter I had to
repeat every Sunday. My favorite studies were Natural Philosophy,
Logic, and Moral Science. From my brother Albert I received lessons in the ancient tongues, Hebrew, Greek, and Latin."

You catch your breath in astonishment, and feel again and still
again the pang of that rebuke. But then your eye falls upon the next
sentence but one, and the pain passes away and you set up the suspicion again with evil satisfaction:

*"After my discovery of Christian Science, most of the knowledge I
had gleaned from schoolbooks vanished like a dream."*

That disappearance accounts for much in her miscellaneous writings. As I was saying, she handles her "ancestral shadows," as she
calls them, just as I do mine. It is remarkable. When she runs across
"a relative of my Grandfather Baker, General Henry Knox, of Revolutionary fame," she sets him down; when she finds another good
one, "the late Sir John Macneill, in the line of my Grandfather Baker's family," she set him down, and remembers that he "was prominent in British politics, and at one time held the position of ambassador to Persia"; when she discovers that her grandparents "were
likewise connected with Captain John Lovewell, whose gallant lead-
ership and death in the Indian troubles of 1722–25 caused that pro-
longed contest to be known historically as Lovewell's War," she sets
the Captain down; when it turns out that a cousin of her grand-
mother "was John Macneill, the New Hampshire general, who
fought at Lundy's Lane and won distinction in 1814 at the battle of
Chippewa," she catalogues the General. (And tells where Chippewa
was.) And then she skips *all* her platform people; never mentions one
of them. It shows that she is just as human as any of us.

Yet, after all, there is something very touching in her pride in these worthy small-fry, and something large and fine in her modesty in not caring to remember that their kinship to her can confer no distinction upon her, whereas her mere mention of their names has conferred upon them a fadeless earthly immortality.

Chapter 2

When she wrote this little biography her great life-work had already been achieved, she was become renowned; to multitudes of reverent disciples she was a sacred personage, a familiar of God, and his inspired channel of communication with the human race. Also, to them these following things were facts, and not doubted:

She had written a Bible in middle age, and had published it; she had recast it, enlarged it, and published it again; she had not stopped there, but had enlarged it further, polished its phrasing, improved its form, and published it yet again. It was at last become a compact, grammatical, dignified, and workman-like body of literature. This was good training, persistent training; and in all arts it is training that brings the art to perfection. We are now confronted with one of the most teasing and baffling riddles of Mrs. Eddy's history—a riddle which may be formulated thus:

How is it that a primitive literary gun which began as a hundred-yard flint-lock smooth-bore muzzle-loader, and in the course of forty years has acquired one notable improvement after another—percussion cap; fixed cartridge; rifled barrel; efficiency at half a mile—how is it that such a gun, sufficiently good on an elephant-hunt (Christian Science) from the beginning, and growing better and better all the time during forty years, has *always* collapsed back to its original flint-lock estate the moment the huntress trained it on any other creature than an elephant?

Something more than a generation ago Mrs. Eddy went out with her flint-lock on the rabbit-range, and this was a part of the result:

"After his decease, and a severe casualty deemed fatal by skilful physicians, we discovered that the Principle of all healing and the law that governs it is God, a divine Principle, and a spiritual not material law, and regained health."—Preface to *Science and Health,* first revision, 1883.[1]

You will notice the awkwardness of that English. If you should carry that paragraph up to the Supreme Court of the United States in order to find out for good and all whether the fatal casualty happened to the dead man—as the paragraph almost asserts—or to some person or persons not even hinted at in the paragraph, the Supreme Court would be obliged to say that the evidence established nothing with certainty except that *there had been a casualty*—victim not known.

The context thinks it explains who the victim was, but it does nothing of the kind. It furnishes some guessing-material of a sort which enables you to infer that it was "we" that suffered the mentioned injury, but if you should carry the language to a court you would not be able to prove that it necessarily meant that. "We" are Mrs. Eddy; a funny little affectation. She replaced it later with the more dignified third person.

The quoted paragraph is from Mrs. Eddy's preface to the first revision of *Science and Health* (1883). Sixty-four pages further along —in the body of the book (the elephant-range), she went out with that same flint-lock and got this following result. Its English is very nearly as straight and clean and competent as is the English of the latest revision of *Science and Health* after the gun has been improved from smooth-bore musket up to globe-sighted, long-distance rifle:

"Man controlled by his Maker has no physical suffering. His body is harmonious, his days are multiplying instead of diminishing, he is journeying towards Life instead of death, and bringing out the new man and crucifying the old affections, cutting them off in every material direction until he learns the utter supremacy of Spirit and yields obedience thereto."

In the latest revision of *Science and Health* (1902), the perfected gun furnishes the following. The English is clean, compact, dignified, almost perfect. But it is observable that it is not prominently better than it is in the above paragraph, which was a product of the primitive flint-lock:

"How unreasonable is the belief that we are wearing out life and hastening to death, and at the same time we are communing with

[1] N. B. Not from the book *itself;* from the *Preface.*

immortality? If the departed are in rapport with mortality, or matter, they are not spiritual, but must still be mortal, sinful, suffering, and dying. Then wherefore look to them—even were communication possible—for proofs of immortality and accept them as oracles?"— *Edition of* 1902, *page* 78.

With the above paragaphs compare these that follow. It is Mrs. Eddy writing—after a good long twenty years of pen-practice. Compare also with the alleged Poems already quoted. The prominent characteristic of the Poems is affectation, artificiality; their make-up is a complacent and pretentious outpour of false figures and fine writing, in the sophomoric style. The same qualities and the same style will be found, unchanged, unbettered, in these following paragraphs—after a lapse of more than fifty years, and after—as aforesaid—long literary training. The italics are mine:

1. "What plague spot or bacilli were *[sic]* gnawing *[sic]* at the heart of this metropolis . . . and bringing it [the heart] on bended knee? Why, it was an *institute* that had entered its *vitals*—that, among other things, taught games," et cetera.—*C. S. Journal,* p. 670, article entitled "A Narrative—by Mary Baker G. Eddy."

2. "Parks sprang up *[sic]* . . . electric-cars run *[sic]* merrily through several streets, concrete sidewalks and macadamized roads dotted *[sic]* the place," et cetera.—*Ibid.*

3. "Shorn *[sic]* of its suburbs it had indeed little left to admire, save to *[sic]* such as fancy a skeleton above ground *breathing [sic]* slowly through a barren *[sic]* breast."—*Ibid.*

This is not English—I mean, grown-up English. But it is fifteen-year-old English, and has not grown a month since the same mind produced the Poems. The standard of the Poems and of the plague-spot-and-bacilli effort is exactly the same. It is most strange that the same intellect that worded the simple and self-contained and clean-cut paragraph beginning with "How unreasonable is the belief," should in the very same lustrum discharge upon the world such a verbal chaos as the utterance concerning that plague-spot or bacilli which were gnawing at the insides of the metropolis and bringing its heart on bended knee, thus exposing to the eye the rest of the skeleton breathing slowly through a barren breast.

The immense contrast between the legitimate English of *Science and Health* and the bastard English of Mrs. Eddy's miscellaneous work, and between the maturity of the one diction and the juvenility of the other, suggests—compels—the question, Are there *two* guns? It would seem so. Is there a poor, foolish, old, scattering flint-lock for rabbit, and a long-range, centre-driving, up-to-date Mauser-magazine for elephant? It looks like it. For it is observable that in *Science and Health* (the elephant-ground) the practice was good at the start and has remained so, and that the practice in the miscellaneous, outside, small-game field was very bad at the start and was never less bad at any later time.

I wish to say that of Mrs. Eddy I am not requiring perfect English, but only good English. No one can write perfect English and keep it up through a stretch of ten chapters. It has never been done. It was approached in the "well of English undefiled"; it has been approached in Mrs. Eddy's Annex to that Book; it has been approached in several English grammars; I have even approached it myself; but none of us has made port.

Now, the English of *Science and Health* is good. In passages to be found in Mrs. Eddy's *Autobiography* (on pages 53, 57, 101, and 113), and on page 6 of her squalid preface to *Science and Health,* first revision, she seems to me to claim the whole and sole authorship of the book. That she wrote the *Autobiography,* and *that preface,* [2] and the Poems, and the Plague-spot-Bacilli, we are not permitted to doubt. Indeed, we know that she wrote them. But the very certainty that she wrote these things compels a doubt that she wrote *Science and Health.* She is guilty of little awkwardnesses of expression in the *Autobiography* which a practised pen would hardly allow to go uncorrected in even a hasty private letter, and could not dream of passing by uncorrected in passages intended for print. But she passes them placidly by; as placidly as if she did not suspect that they were offences against third-class English. I think that that placidity was born of that very unawareness, so to speak. I will cite a few instances from the *Autobiography.* The italics are mine:

"I remember reading in my childhood certain manuscripts containing Scriptural Sonnets, besides *other* verses and enigmas," etc. Page 7.

[On page 27.] "Many pale cripples went into the Church leaning on crutches who came out carrying them on their shoulders."

It is awkward, because at the first glance it seems to say that the

[2] See Appendix A for it.—M.T.

cripples went in leaning on crutches which went out carrying the cripples on their shoulders. It would have cost her no trouble to put her "who" after her "cripples." I blame her a little; I think her proof-reader should have been shot. We may let her capital C pass, but it is another awkwardness, for she is talking about a building, not about a religious society.

"Marriage and Parentage" [Chapter-heading. Page 30]. You imag-ine that she is going to begin to talk about her marriage and finish with some account of her father and mother. And so you will be deceived. "Marriage" was right, but "Parentage" was not the best word for the rest of the record. It refers to the birth of her own child. After a certain period of time "my babe was born." Marriage and Motherhood—Marriage and Maternity—Marriage and Product—Marriage and Dividend—either of these would have fitted the facts and made the matter clear.

"Without my knowledge he was appointed a guardian." Page 32.

She is speaking of her child. She means that a guardian *for* her child was appointed, but that isn't what she says.

"If spiritual conclusions are separated from their premises, the nexus is lost, and the argument with its rightful conclusions, be-comes correspondingly obscure." Page 34.

We shall never know why she put the word "correspondingly" in there. Any fine, large word would have answered just as well: psychosuperintangibly—electroincandescently—oligarcheologically—sanchrosynchrostereoptically—any of these would have answered, any of these would have filled the void.

"His spiritual noumenon and phenomenon silenced portraiture." Page 34.

Yet she says she forgot everything she knew, when she discovered Christian Science. I realize that noumenon is a daisy; and I will not deny that I shall use it whenever I am in a company which I think I can embarrass with it; but, at the same time, I think it is out of place among friends in an autobiography. There, I think a person ought not to have anything up his sleeve. It undermines confidence. But my dissatisfaction with the quoted passage is not on account of noume-non; it is on account of the misuse of the word "silenced." You cannot silence portraiture with a noumenon; if portraiture should make a noise, a way could be found to silence it, but even then it could not be done with a noumenon. Not even with a brick, some authorities think.

"It may be that the mortal life-battle still wages," etc. Page 35.

That is clumsy. Battles do not wage, battles are waged. Mrs. Eddy has one very curious and interesting peculiarity: whenever she notices that she is chortling along without saying anything, she pulls up with a sudden "God is over us all," or some other sounding irrelevancy, and for the moment it seems to light up the whole district; then, before you can recover from the shock, she goes flitting pleasantly and meaninglessly along again, and you hurry hopefully after her, thinking you are going to get something this time; but as soon as she has led you far enough away from her turkeylet she takes to a tree. Whenever she discovers that she is getting pretty disconnected, she couples-up with an ostentatious *"But"* which has nothing to do with anything that went before or is to come after, then she hitches some empties to the train—unrelated verses from the Bible, usually —and steams out of sight and leaves you wondering how she did that clever thing. For striking instances, see bottom paragraph on page 34 and the paragraph on page 35 of her *Autobiography*. She has a purpose—a deep and dark and artful purpose—in what she is saying in the first paragraph, and you guess what it is, but that is due to your own talent, not hers; she has made it as obscure as language could do it. The other paragraph has no meaning and no discoverable intention. It is merely one of her God-over-alls. I cannot spare room for it in this place.[1]

"I beheld with ineffable awe our great Master's marvellous skill in demanding neither obedience to hygienic laws nor," etc. Page 41.

The word is loosely chosen—skill. She probably meant judgment, intuition, penetration, or wisdom.

"Naturally, my first jottings were but efforts to express in feeble diction Truth's ultimate." Page 42.

One understands what she means, but she should have been able to say what she meant—at any time before she discovered Christian Science and forgot everything she knew—and after it, too. If she had put "feeble" in front of "efforts" and then left out "in" and "diction," she would have scored.

[1] See Apppendix B.—M.T.

". . . its written expression increases in perfection under the guidance of the great Master." Page 43.

It is an error. Not even in those advantageous circumstances can increase be added to perfection.

"Evil is not mastered by evil; it can only be overcome with Good. This brings out the nothingness of evil, and the eternal Somethingness vindicates the Divine Principle and improves the race of Adam." Page 76.

This is too extraneous for me. That is the trouble with Mrs. Eddy when she sets out to explain an over-large exhibit: the minute you think the light is bursting upon you the candle goes out and your mind begins to wander.

"No one else can drain the cup which I have drunk to the dregs, as the discoverer and teacher of Christian Science." Page 47.

That is saying we cannot empty an empty cup. We knew it before; and we know she meant to tell us that that particular cup is going to remain empty. That is, we think that that was the idea, but we cannot be sure. She has a perfectly astonishing talent for putting words together in such a way as to make successful inquiry into their intention impossible.

She generally makes us uneasy when she begins to tune up on her fine-writing timbrel. It carries me back to her Plague-Spot and Poetry days, and I just dread those:

"Into mortal mind's material obliquity I gazed and stood abashed. Blanched was the cheek of pride. My heart bent low before the omnipotence of Spirit, and a tint of humility soft as the heart of a moonbeam mantled the earth. Bethlehem and Bethany, Gethsemane and Calvary, spoke to my chastened sense as by the tearful lips of a babe." Page 48.

The heart of a moonbeam is a pretty enough Friendship's-Album expression—let it pass, though I do think the figure a little strained; but humility has no tint, humility has no complexion, and if it had it could not mantle the earth. A moonbeam might—I do not know—but she did not say it was the moonbeam. But let it go, I cannot decide it, she mixes me up so. A babe hasn't "tearful lips," it's its eyes. You find none of Mrs. Eddy's kind of English in *Science and Health*—not a line of it.

Chapter 3

Setting aside title-page, index, etc., the little *Autobiography* begins on page 7 and ends on page 130. My quotations are from the first forty pages. They seem to me to prove the presence of the 'prentice hand. The style of the forty pages is loose and feeble and 'prentice-like. The movement of the narrative is not orderly and sequential, but rambles around, and skips forward and back and here and there and yonder, 'prentice-fashion. Many a journeyman has broken up his narrative and skipped about and rambled around, but he did it for a purpose, for an advantage; there was art in it, and points to be scored by it; the observant reader perceived the game, and enjoyed it and respected it, if it was well played. But Mrs. Eddy's performance was without intention, and destitute of art. She could score no points by it on those terms, and almost any reader can see that her work was the uncalculated puttering of a novice.

In the above paragraph I have described the first third of the booklet. That third being completed, Mrs. Eddy leaves the rabbit-range, crosses the frontier, and steps out upon her far-spreading big game territory—Christian Science—and there is an instant change! The style smartly improves, and the clumsy little technical offences disappear. In these two-thirds of the booklet I find only one such offence, and it has the look of being a printer's error.

I leave the riddle with the reader. Perhaps he can explain how it is that a person—trained or untrained—who on the one day can write nothing better than Plague-Spot-Bacilli and feeble and stumbling and wandering personal history littered with false figures and obscurities and technical blunders, can on the next day sit down and write fluently, smoothly, compactly, capably, and confidently on a great big thundering subject, and do it as easily and comfortably as a whale paddles around the globe.

As for me, I have scribbled so much in fifty years that I have become saturated with convictions of one sort and another concerning a scribbler's limitations; and these are so strong that when I am familiar with a literary person's work I feel perfectly sure that I know enough about his limitations to know what he can *not* do. If Mr. Howells should pretend to me that he wrote the Plague-Spot-

Bacilli rhapsody, I should receive the statement courteously, but I should know it for a—well, for a perversion. If the late Josh Billings should rise up and tell me that he wrote Herbert Spencer's philosophies, I should answer and say that the spelling casts a doubt upon his claim. If the late Jonathan Edwards should rise up and tell me he wrote Mr. Dooley's books, I should answer and say that the marked difference between his style and Dooley's is argument against the soundness of his statement. You see how much I think of *circumstantial evidence*. In literary matters—in my belief—it is often better than any person's word, better than any shady character's oath. It is difficult for me to believe that the same hand that wrote the Plague-Spot-Bacilli and the first third of the little Eddy biography wrote also *Science and Health*. Indeed, it is more than difficult, it is impossible.

Largely speaking, I have read acres of what purported to be Mrs. Eddy's writings, in the past two months. I cannot know, but I am convinced, that the circumstantial evidence shows that her actual share in the work of composing and phrasing these things was so slight as to be inconsequential. Where she puts her literary foot down, her trail across her paid polisher's page is as plain as the elephant's in a Sunday-school procession. Her verbal output, when left undoctored by her clerks, is quite unmistakable. It always exhibits the strongly distinctive features observable in the virgin passages from her pen already quoted by me:

Desert vacancy, as regards thought.
Self-complacency.
Puerility.
Sentimentality.
Affectations of scholarly learning.
Lust after eloquent and flowery expression.
Repetition of pet poetic picturesquenesses.
Confused and wandering statement.
Metaphor gone insane.
Meaningless words, used because they are pretty, or showy, or unusual.
Sorrowful attempts at the epigrammatic.
Destitution of originality.

The fat volume called *Miscellaneous Writings of Mrs. Eddy* contains several hundred pages. Of the five hundred and fifty-four pages of prose in it I find ten lines, on page 319, to be Mrs. Eddy's; also about a page of the preface or "Prospectus"; also about fifteen pages scattered along through the book. If she wrote any of the rest of the prose, it was rewritten after her by another hand. Here I will insert two-thirds of her page of the prospectus. It is evident that whenever, under the inspiration of the Deity, she turns out a book, she is always allowed to do some of the preface. I wonder why that is? It always mars the work. I think it is done in humorous malice. I think the clerks like to see her give herself away. They know she will, her stock of usable materials being limited and her procedure in employing them always the same, substantially. They know that when the initiated come upon her first erudite allusion, or upon any one of her other stage-properties, they can shut their eyes and tell what will follow.

She usually throws off an easy remark all sodden with Greek or Hebrew or Latin learning; she usually has a person watching for a star—she can seldom get away from that poetic idea—sometimes it is a Chaldee, sometimes a Walking Delegate, sometimes an entire stranger, but be he what he may, he is generally there when the train is ready to move, and has his pass in his hat-band; she generally has a Being with a Dome on him, or some other cover that is unusual and out of the fashion; she likes to fire off a Scripture-verse where it will make the handsomest noise and come nearest to breaking the connection; she often throws out a Forefelt, or a Foresplendor, or a Foreslander where it will have a fine nautical foreto'gallant sound and make the sentence sing; after which she is nearly sure to throw discretion away and take to her deadly passion, Intoxicated Metaphor. At such a time the Mrs. Eddy that does not hesitate is lost:

"The ancient Greek looked longingly for the Olympiad. The Chaldee watched the appearing of a star; to him no higher destiny dawned on the dome of being than that foreshadowed by signs in the heavens. The meek Nazarene, the scoffed of all scoffers, said, 'Ye can discern the face of the sky; but can ye not discern the signs of the times?'—for He forefelt and foresaw the ordeal of a perfect Christianity, hated by sinners.

"To kindle all minds with a gleam of gratitude, the new idea that comes welling up from infinite Truth needs to be understood. The seer of this age should be a sage.

"Humility is the stepping-stone to a higher recognition of Deity.

The mounting sense gathers fresh forms and strange fire from the ashes of dissolving self, and drops the world. Meekness heightens immortal attributes, only by removing the dust that dims them. Goodness reveals another scene and another self seemingly rolled up in shades, but brought to light by the evolutions of advancing thought, whereby we discern the power of Truth and Love to heal the sick.

"Pride is ignorance; those assume most who have the least wisdom or experience; and they steal from their neighbor, because they have so little of their own."—*Miscellaneous Writings,* page 1, and six lines at top of page 2.

It is not believable that the hand that wrote those clumsy and affected sentences wrote the smooth English of *Science and Health.*

Chapter 4

It is often said in print that Mrs. Eddy claims that God was the Author of *Science and Health.* Mr. Peabody states in his pamphlet that "she says not she but God was the Author." I cannot find that in her autobiography she makes this transference of the authorship, but I think that in it she definitely claims that she did her work under His inspiration—definitely for her; for as a rule she is not a very definite person, even when she seems to be trying her best to be clear and positive. Speaking of the early days when her Science was beginning to unfold itself and gather form in her mind, she says *(Autobiography,* page 43):

"The divine hand led me into a new world of light and Life, a fresh universe—old to God, but new to His 'little one.' "

She being His little one, as I understand it.

The divine hand led her. It seems to mean "God inspired me"; but when a person uses metaphors instead of statistics—and that is Mrs. Eddy's common fashion—one cannot always feel sure about the intention.

[Page 56.] "Even the Scripture gave no direct interpretation of the Scientific basis for demonstrating the spiritual Principle of healing, until our Heavenly Father saw fit, through the *Key to the Scriptures,* in *Science and Health,* to unlock this 'mystery of godliness.' "

Another baffling metaphor. If she had used plain forecastle English, and said "God wrote the *Key* and I put it in my book"; or if she had said "God furnished me the solution of the mystery and I put it on paper"; or if she had said "God did it all," then we should understand; but her phrase is open to any and all of those translations, and is a Key which unlocks nothing—for us. However, it seems to at least mean "God inspired me," if nothing more.

There was personal and intimate communion, at any rate—we get that much out of the riddles. The connection extended to business, after the establishment of the teaching and healing industry.

[Page 71.] "When God impelled me to set a price on my instruction," etc. Further down: "God has since shown me, in multitudinous ways, the wisdom of this decision."

She was not able to think of a "financial equivalent"—meaning a pecuniary equivalent—for her "instruction in Christian Science Mind-healing." In this emergency she was "led" to charge three hundred dollars for a term of "twelve half-days." She does not say who led her, she only says that the amount greatly troubled her. I think it means that the price was suggested from above, "led" being a theological term identical with our commercial phrase "personally conducted." She "shrank from asking it, but was finally led, by a strange providence, to accept this fee." "Providence" is another theological term. Two leds and a providence, taken together, make a pretty strong argument for inspiration. I think that these statistics make it clear that the price was arranged above. This view is constructively supported by the fact, already quoted, that God afterwards approved, "in multitudinous ways," her wisdom in accepting the mentioned fee. "Multitudinous ways"—multitudinous encoring —suggests enthusiasm. Business enthusiasm. And it suggests nearness. God's nearness to his "little one." Nearness, and a watchful personal interest. A warm, palpitating, Standard-Oil interest, so to speak. All this indicates inspiration. We may assume, then, two inspirations: one for the book, the other for the business.

The evidence for inspiration is further augmented by the testimony of Rev. George Tomkins, D.D., already quoted, that Mrs. Eddy and her book were foretold in Revelation, and that Mrs. Eddy *"is* God's brightest thought to this age, giving us the spiritual interpretation of the Bible in the 'little book' " of the Angel.

I am aware that it is not Mr. Tomkins that is speaking, but Mrs. Eddy. The commissioned lecturers of the Christian Science Church have to be members of the Board of Lectureship. (By-laws, Sec. 2, p. 70.) The Board of Lectureship is selected by the Board of Directors of the Church. (By-laws, Sec. 3, p. 70.) The Board of Directors of the Church is the property of Mrs. Eddy. (By-laws, p. 22.) Mr. Tomkins did not make that statement without authorization from headquarters. He necessarily got it from the Board of Directors, the Board of Directors from Mrs. Eddy, Mrs. Eddy from the Deity. Mr. Tomkins would have been turned down by that procession if his remarks had been unsatisfactory to it.

It may be that there is evidence somewhere—as has been claimed —that Mrs. Eddy has charged upon the Deity the verbal authorship of *Science and Health*. But if she ever made the charge, she has withdrawn it (as it seems to me), and in the most formal and unqualified of all ways. See *Autobiography*, page 57:

"When the demand for this book increased . . . the copyright was infringed. I entered a suit at Law, and my copyright was protected."

Thus it is plain that she did not plead that the Deity was the (verbal) Author; for if she had done that, she would have lost her case—and with rude promptness. It was in the old days before the Berne Convention and before the passage of our amended law of 1891, and the court would have quoted the following stern clause from the existing statute and frowned her out of the place:

"No Foreigner can acquire copyright in the United States."

To sum up. The evidence before me indicates three things:

1. That Mrs. Eddy claims the verbal authorship for herself.

2. That she denies it to the Deity.

3. That—in her belief—she wrote the book under the inspiration of the Deity, but furnished the language herself.

In one place in the *Autobiography* she claims both the language and the *ideas;* but when this witness is testifying, one must draw the line somewhere, or she will prove both sides of her case—nine sides, if desired.

It is too true. Much too true. Many, many times too true. She is a most trying witness—*the* most trying witness that ever kissed the Book, I am sure. There is no keeping up with her erratic testimony. As soon as you have got her share of the authorship nailed where you half hope and half believe it will stay and cannot be joggled loose any more, she joggles it loose again—or seems to; you cannot be sure, for her habit of dealing in meaningless metaphors instead of in plain, straightforward statistics, makes it nearly always impossible to tell just what it is she is trying to say. She was definite when she claimed both the language and the ideas of the book. That seemed to settle the matter. It seemed to distribute the percentages of credit with precision between the collaborators: ninety-two per cent to Mrs. Eddy, who did all the work, and eight per cent to the Deity, who furnished the inspiration—not enough of it to damage the copyright in a country closed against Foreigners, and yet plenty to advertise the book and market it at famine rates. Then Mrs. Eddy does not keep still, but fetches around and comes forward and testifies again. It is most injudicious. For she resorts to metaphor this time, and it makes trouble, for she seems to reverse the percentages and claim only the eight per cent for herself. I quote from Mr. Peabody's book *(Eddyism, or Christian Science.* Boston: 15 Court Square, price twenty-five cents):

"Speaking of this book, Mrs. Eddy, in January last (1901) said: 'I should blush to write of *Science and Health, with Key to the Scriptures,* as I have, were it of human origin, and I, apart from God, its author; but as I was only a scribe echoing the harmonies of Heaven in divine metaphysics, I cannot be supermodest of the Christian Science text-book.' "

Mr. Peabody's comment:

"Nothing could be plainer than that. Here is a distinct avowal that the book entitled *Science and Health* was the work of Almighty God."

It does seem to amount to that. She was only a "scribe." Confound the word, it is just a confusion, it has no determinable meaning there, it leaves us in the air. A scribe is merely a person who writes. He may be a copyist, he may be an amanuensis, he may be a writer of originals, and furnish both the language and the ideas. As usual with Mrs. Eddy, the connection affords no help—"echoing" throws no light upon "scribe." A rock can reflect an echo, a wall can do it, a mountain can do it, many things can do it, but a scribe can't. A scribe that could reflect an echo could get over thirty dollars a week in a side-show. Many impresarios would rather have him than a cow with four tails. If we allow that this present scribe was *setting down* the "harmonies of Heaven"—and certainly that seems to have been the case—then there was only one way to do it that I can think of:

listen to the music and put down the notes one after another as they
fell. In that case Mrs. Eddy did not invent the tune, she only entered
it on paper. Therefore—dropping the metaphor—she was merely an
amanuensis, and furnished neither the language of *Science and
Health* nor the ideas. It reduces her to eight per cent (and the dividends on that and the rest).

Is that it? We shall never know. For Mrs. Eddy is liable to testify
again at any time. But until she does it, I think we must conclude
that the Deity was Author of the whole book, and Mrs. Eddy merely
His telephone and stenographer. Granting this, her claim as the
Voice of God stands—for the present—justified and established.

Postscript

I overlooked something. It appears that there was more of that
utterance than Mr. Peabody has quoted in the above paragraph. It
will be found in Mrs. Eddy's organ, the *Christian Science Journal*
(January, 1901) and reads as follows:

"It was not myself . . . which dictated *Science and Health, with
Key to the Scriptures.*"

That is certainly clear enough. The words which I have removed
from that important sentence explain Who it was that did the dictating. It was done by

"the divine power of Truth and Love, infinitely above me."

Certainly that is definite. At last, through her personal testimony,
we have a sure grip upon the following vital facts, and they settle the
authorship of *Science and Health* beyond peradventure:

1. Mrs. Eddy furnished "the ideas and the language."
2. God furnished the ideas and the language.

It is a great comfort to have the matter authoritatively settled.

Chapter 5

It is hard to locate her, she shifts about so much. She is a shining
drop of quicksilver which you put your finger on and it isn't there.
There is a paragraph in the Autobiography (page 96) which places in
seemingly darkly significant procession three Personages:

1. The Virgin Mary.
2. Jesus of Nazareth.

3. Mrs. Eddy.

This is the paragraph referred to:

"No person can take the individual place of the Virgin Mary. No person can compass or fulfil the individual mission of Jesus of Nazareth. No person can take the place of the author of *Science and Health,* the discoverer and founder of Christian Science. Each individual must fill his own niche in time and eternity."

I have read it many times, but I still cannot be sure that I rightly understand it. If the Saviour's name had been placed first and the Virgin Mary's second and Mrs. Eddy's third, I should draw the inference that a descending scale from First Importance to Second Importance and then to Small Importance was indicated; but to place the Virgin first, the Saviour second, and Mrs. Eddy third, seems to turn the scale the other way and make it an ascending scale of Importances, with Mrs. Eddy ranking the other two and holding first place.

I think that that was perhaps the intention, but none but a seasoned Christian Scientist can examine a literary animal of Mrs. Eddy's creation and tell which end of it the tail is on. She is easily the most baffling and bewildering writer in the literary trade.

Eddy is a commonplace name, and would have an unimpressive aspect in the list of the reformed Holy Family. She has thought of that. In the book of By-laws written by her—"impelled by a power not one's own"—there is a paragraph which explains how and when her disciples came to confer a title upon her; and this explanation is followed by a warning as to what will happen to any female Scientist who shall desecrate it:

"The title of Mother. Therefore if a student of Christian Science shall apply this title, either to herself or to others, except as the term for kinship according to the flesh, it shall be regarded by the Church as an indication of disrespect for their Pastor Emeritus, and unfitness to be a member of the Mother-Church."

She is the Pastor Emeritus.

While the quoted paragraph about the Procession seems to indicate that Mrs. Eddy is expecting to occupy the First Place in it, that expectation is not definitely avowed. In an earlier utterance of hers she is clearer—clearer, and does not claim the first place all to herself, but only the half of it. I quote from Mr. Peabody's book again:

"In the *Christian Science Journal* for April, 1889, when it was her property, and published by her, it was claimed for her, and *with her sanction,* that she was equal with Jesus, and elaborate effort was made to establish the claim.

"Mrs. Eddy has distinctly *authorized* the claim in her behalf that she herself was the chosen successor to and equal of Jesus."

In her *Miscellaneous Writings* (using her once favorite "We" for "I") she says that "While we entertain decided views . . . and shall express them as duty demands, we shall claim no especial gift from our divine origin," etc.

Our divine origin. It suggests Equal again. It is inferable, then, that in the near by-and-by the new Church will officially rank the Holy Family in the following order:

1. Jesus of Nazareth.—1. Our Mother.
2. The Virgin Mary.

Summary

I am not playing with Christian Science and its founder, I am examining them; and I am doing it because of the interest I feel in the inquiry. My results may seem inadequate to the reader, but they have for me clarified a muddle and brought a sort of order out of a chaos, and so I value them.

My readings of Mrs. Eddy's uninspired miscellaneous literary efforts have convinced me of several things:

1. That she did not write *Science and Health*.
2. That the Deity did (or did not) write it.
3. That She thinks She wrote it.
4. That She believes She wrote it under the Deity's inspiration.
5. That She believes She is a Member of the Holy Family.
6. That She believes She is the equal of the Head of it.

Finally, I think She is now entitled to the capital S—on her own evidence.

Chapter 6

Thus far we have a part of Mrs. Eddy's portrait. Not made of fictions, surmises, reports, rumors, innuendoes, dropped by her enemies; no, she has furnished all of the materials herself, and laid them on the canvas, under my general superintendence and direction. As far as she has gone with it, it is the presentation of a complacent, commonplace, illiterate New England woman who "forgot everything she knew" when she discovered her discovery, then wrote a Bible in good English under the inspiration of God, and climbed up it to the supremest summit of earthly grandeur attainable by man—where she sits serene today, beloved and worshipped by a multitude of human beings of as good average intelligence as is possessed by those that march under the banner of any competing cult. This is not intended to flatter the competing cults, it is merely a statement of cold fact.

That a commonplace person should go climbing aloft and become a god or a half-god or a quarter-god and be worshipped by men and women of average intelligence, is nothing. It has happened a million times, it will happen a hundred million more. It has been millions of years since the first of these supernaturals appeared, and by the time the last one—in that inconceivably remote future—shall have performed his solemn little high-jinks on the stage and closed the business, there will be enough of them accumulated in the museum on the Other Side to start a heaven of their own—and jam it.

Each in his turn those little supernaturals of our by-gone ages and aeons joined the monster procession of his predecessors and marched horizonward, disappeared, and was forgotten. They changed nothing, they built nothing, they left nothing behind them to remember them by, nothing to hold their disciples together, nothing to solidify their work and enable it to defy the assaults of time and the weather. They passed, and left a vacancy. They made one fatal mistake; they all made it, each in his turn: they failed to *organize* their forces, they failed to *centralize* their strength, they failed to provide a fresh Bible and a sure and perpetual cash income for business, and often they failed to provide a new and accepted Divine Personage to worship.

Mrs. Eddy is not of that small fry. The materials that go to the making of the rest of her portrait will prove it. She will furnish them herself:

She published her book. She copyrighted it. She copyrights everything. If she should say, "Good-morning; how do you do?" she would copyright it; for she is a careful person, and knows the value of small things.

She began to teach her Science, she began to heal, she began to gather converts to her new religion—fervent, sincere, devoted, grateful people. A year or two later she organized her first Christian Science "Association," with six of her disciples on the roster.

She continued to teach and heal. She was charging nothing, she says, although she was very poor. She taught and healed gratis four years altogether, she says.

Then, in 1879–81 she was become strong enough, and well enough established, to venture a couple of impressively important moves. The first of these moves was to aggrandize the "Association" to a *"Church."* Brave? It is the right name for it, I think. The former name suggests nothing, invited no remark, no criticism, no inquiry, no hostility; the new name invited them all. She must have made this intrepid venture on her own motion. She could have had no important advisers at that early day. If we accept it as her own idea and her own act—and I think we *must*—we have one key to her character. And it will explain subsequent acts of hers that would merely stun us and stupefy us without it. Shall we call it courage? Or shall we call it recklessness? Courage observes; reflects; calculates; surveys the whole situation; counts the cost, estimates the odds, makes up its mind; then goes at the enterprise resolute to win or perish. Recklessness does not reflect, it plunges fearlessly in with a hurrah, and takes the risks, whatever they may be, regardless of expense. Recklessness often fails, Mrs. Eddy has never failed—from the point of view of her followers. The point of view of other people is naturally not a matter of weighty importance to her.

The new Church was not born loose-jointed and featureless, but had a defined plan, a definite character, definite aims, and a name which was a challenge, and defied all comers. It was "a Mind-healing Church." It was *"without a creed."* Its name, "The Church of Christ, Scientist."

Mrs. Eddy could not copyright her Church, but she chartered it,

which was the same thing and relieved the pain. It had twenty-six
charter members. Mrs. Eddy was at once installed as its pastor.

The other venture, above referred to, was Mrs. Eddy's Massachusetts Metaphysical College, in which was taught "the pathology of
spiritual power." She could not copyright it, but she got it chartered.
For faculty it had herself, her husband of the period (Dr. Eddy), and
her adopted son, Dr. Foster-Eddy. The college term was "barely
three weeks," she says. Again she was bold, brave, rash, reckless—
choose for yourself—for she not only began to charge the student,
but charged him a *hundred dollars a week* for the enlightenments.
And got it? some may ask. Easily. Pupils flocked from far and near.
They came by the hundred. Presently the term was cut down nearly
half, but the price remained as before. To be exact, the term-cut was
to seven lessons—price, three hundred dollars. The college "yielded
a large income." This is believable. In seven years Mrs. Eddy taught,
as she avers, over four thousand students in it. (Preface to 1902
edition of *Science and Health*.) Three hundred times four thousand is
—but perhaps you can cipher it yourself. I could do it ordinarily, but
I fell down yesterday and hurt my leg. Cipher it; you will see that it
is a grand sum for a woman to earn in seven years. Yet that was not
all she got out of her college in the seven.

At the time that she was charging the primary student three hundred dollars for twelve lessons she was not content with this tidy
assessment, but had other ways of plundering him. By advertisement
she offered him privileges whereby he could add eighteen lessons to
his store for five hundred dollars more. That is to say, he could get a
total of thirty lessons in her college for eight hundred dollars.

Four thousand times eight hundred is—but it is a difficult sum for
a cripple who has not been "demonstrated over" to cipher; let it go.
She taught "over" four thousand students in seven years. "Over" is
not definite, but it probably represents a non-paying surplus of learn-
ers over and above the paying four thousand. Charity students,
doubtless. I think that as interesting an advertisement as has been
printed since the romantic old days of the other buccaneers is this
one from the *Christian Science Journal* for September, 1886:

"MASSACHUSETTS METAPHYSICAL
COLLEGE

"REV. MARY BAKER G. EDDY, PRESIDENT

"571 Columbus Avenue, Boston

"The collegiate course in Christian Science metaphysical healing includes twelve lessons. Tuition, three hundred dollars.

"Course in metaphysical obstetrics includes six daily lectures, and is open only to students from this college. Tuition, one hundred dollars.

"Class in theology, open (like the above) to graduates, receives six additional lectures on the Scriptures, and summary of the principle and practice of Christian Science, two hundred dollars.

"Normal class is open to those who have taken the first course at this college; six daily lectures complete the Normal course. Tuition, two hundred dollars.

"No invalids, and only persons of good moral character, are accepted as students. All students are subject to examination and rejection; and they are liable to leave the class if found unfit to remain in it.

"A limited number of clergymen received free of charge.

"Largest discount to indigent students, one hundred dollars on the first course.

"No deduction on the others.

"Husband and wife, entered together, three hundred dollars.

"Tuition for all strictly in advance."

There it is—the horse-leech's daughter alive again, after a three-century vacation. Fifty or sixty hours' lecturing for eight hundred dollars.

I was in error as to one matter: there are no charity students. Gratis-taught clergymen must not be placed under that head; they are merely an advertisement. Pauper students can get into the infant class on a two-third rate (cash in advance), but not even an archangel can get into the rest of the game at anything short of par, cash down. For it is "in the spirit of Christ's charity, as one who is joyful to bear healing to the sick"[1] that Mrs. Eddy is working the game. She sends the healing to them outside.

She cannot bear it to them inside the college, for the reason that she does not allow a sick candidate to get in. It is true that this smells

---

[1] Mrs. Eddy's Introduction to *Science and Health*.

of inconsistency,[2] but that is nothing; Mrs. Eddy would not be Mrs. Eddy if she should ever chance to be consistent about anything two days running.

Except in the matter of the Dollar. The Dollar, and appetite for power and notoriety. English must also be added; she is always consistent, she is always Mrs. Eddy, in her English: it is always and consistently confused and crippled and poor. She wrote the Advertisement; her literary trade-marks are there. When she says all "students" are subject to examination, she does not mean students, she means candidates for that lofty place. When she says students are "liable" to leave the class if found unfit to remain in it, she does not mean that if they find themselves unfit, or be found unfit by others, they will be likely to ask permission to leave the class; she means that if *she* finds them unfit she will be "liable" to fire them out. When she nobly offers "tuition for all strictly in advance," she does not mean "*instruction* for all in advance—payment for it later." No, that is only what she says, it is not what she means. If she had written *Science and Health,* the oldest man in the world would not be able to tell with certainty what any passage in it was intended to mean.

Chapter 7

Her Church was on its legs.

She was its pastor. It was prospering.

She was appointed one of a committee to draught By-laws for its government. It may be observed, without overplus of irreverence, that this was larks for her. *She did all of the draughting herself.* From the very beginning she was always in the front seat when there was business to be done; in the front seat, with both eyes open, and looking sharply out for Number One; in the front seat, working Mortal Mind with fine effectiveness and giving Immortal Mind a rest for Sunday. When her Church was reorganized, by-and-by, the By-laws were retained. She saw to that. In these Laws for the government of her Church, her empire, her despotism, Mrs. Eddy's character is embalmed for good and all. I think a particularized examination of these Church-laws will be found interesting. And not the less

---

[2] "There is no disease"; "sickness is a belief only."—*Science and Health,* vol. ii., page 173, edition of 1884.—M.T.

so if we keep in mind that they were "impelled by a power not one's own," as she says—*Anglice,* the inspiration of God.

It is a Church "without a creed." Still, it has one. Mrs. Eddy draughted it—and copyrighted it. In her own name. You cannot become a member of the Mother-Church (nor of any Christian Science Church) without signing it. It forms the first chapter of the By-laws, and is called "Tenets." "Tenets of The Mother-Church, The First Church of Christ, Scientist." It has no hell in it—it throws it overboard.

THE PASTOR EMERITUS

About the time of the reorganization, Mrs. Eddy retired from her position of pastor of her Church, abolished the office of pastor in all branch Churches, and appointed her *book, Science and Health,* to be *pastor-universal.* Mrs. Eddy did not disconnect herself from the office entirely, when she retired, but appointed herself Pastor Emeritus. It is a misleading title, and belongs to the family of that phrase "without a creed." It advertises her as being a merely honorary official, with nothing to do, and no authority. The Czar of Russia is Emperor Emeritus on the same terms. Mrs. Eddy was Autocrat of the Church before, with limitless authority, and she kept her grip on that limitless authority when she took that fictitious title.

It is curious and interesting to note with what an unerring instinct the Pastor Emeritus has thought out and forecast all possible encroachments upon her planned autocracy, and barred the way against them, in the By-laws which she framed and copyrighted— under the guidance of the Supreme Being.

THE BOARD OF DIRECTORS

For instance, when Article I speaks of a President and Board of Directors, you think you have discovered a formidable check upon the powers and ambitions of the honorary pastor, the ornamental pastor, the functionless pastor, the Pastor Emeritus, but it is a mistake. These great officials are of the phrase-family of the Church-Without-a-Creed and the Pastor-With-Nothing-to-Do; that is to say, of the family of Large-Names-Which-Mean-Nothing. The Board is of so little consequence that the By-laws do not state how it is chosen, nor who does it; but they do state, most definitely, that the

Board cannot fill a vacancy in its number *"except the candidate is approved by the Pastor Emeritus."*

The *"candidate."* The Board cannot even proceed to an election until the Pastor Emeritus has examined the list and squelched such candidates as are not satisfactory to her.

Whether the original first Board began as the personal property of Mrs. Eddy or not, it is foreseeable that in time, under this By-law, she would own it. Such a first Board might chafe under such a rule as that, and try to legislate it out of existence some day. But Mrs. Eddy was awake. She foresaw that danger, and added this ingenious and effective clause:

"This By-law can neither be amended nor annulled, except by consent of Mrs. Eddy, the Pastor Emeritus."

THE PRESIDENT

The Board of Directors, or Serfs, or Ciphers, elects the President. On these clearly worded terms: *"Subject to the approval of the Pastor Emeritus."*

Therefore *She* elects him.

A long term can invest a high official with influence and power, and make him dangerous. Mrs. Eddy reflected upon that; so she limits the President's term to *a year.* She has a capable commercial head, an organizing head, a head for government.

TREASURER AND CLERK

There are a Treasurer and a Clerk. They are elected by the Board of Directors. That is to say, *by Mrs. Eddy.*

Their terms of office expire on the first Tuesday in June of each year, *"or* upon the election of their successors." They must be watchfully obedient and satisfactory to her, or she will elect and install their successors with a suddenness that can be unpleasant to them. It goes without saying that the Treasurer manages the Treasury to suit Mrs. Eddy, and is in fact merely Temporary Deputy Treasurer.

Apparently the Clerk has but two duties to perform: to read messages from Mrs. Eddy to First Members assembled in solemn Council, and provide lists of candidates for Church membership. The select body entitled First Members are the aristocracy of the Mother-Church, the Charter Members, the Aborigines, a sort of stylish but unsalaried little College of Cardinals, good for show, but not indispensable. *Nobody* is indispensable in Mrs. Eddy's empire; she sees to that.

When the Pastor Emeritus sends a letter or message to that little Sanhedrin, it is the Clerk's "imperative duty" to read it "at the place and time specified." Otherwise, the world might come to an end. These are fine, large frills, and remind us of the ways of emperors and such. Such do not use the penny-post, they send a gilded and painted special messenger, and he strides into the Parliament, and business comes to a sudden and solemn and awful stop; and in the impressive hush that follows, the Chief Clerk reads the document. It is his "imperative duty." If he should neglect it, his official life would end. It is the same with this Mother-Church Clerk; "if he fail to perform this important function of his office," certain majestic and unshirkable solemnities *must* follow: a special meeting "shall" be called; a member of the Church "shall" make formal complaint; then the Clerk "shall" be "removed from office." Complaint is sufficient, no trial is necessary.

There is something very sweet and juvenile and innocent and pretty about these little tinsel vanities, these grave apings of monarchical fuss and feathers and ceremony, here on our ostentatiously democratic soil. She is the same lady that we found in the *Autobiography*, who was so naïvely vain of all that little ancestral military riffraff that she had dug up and annexed. A person's nature never changes. What it is in childhood, it remains. Under pressure, or a change of interest, it can partially or wholly disappear from sight, and for considerable stretches of time, but nothing can ever permanently modify it, nothing can ever remove it.

BOARD OF TRUSTEES

There isn't any—now. But with power and money piling up higher and higher every day and the Church's dominion spreading daily wider and farther, a time could come when the envious and ambitious could start the idea that it would be wise and well to put a watch upon these assets—a watch equipped with properly large authority. By custom, a Board of Trustees. Mrs. Eddy has foreseen that probability—for she is a woman with a long, long look ahead, the longest look ahead that ever a woman had—and she has provided for that emergency. In Art. I., Sec. 5, she has decreed that no Board of

Trustees shall ever exist in the Mother-Church *"except it be constituted by the Pastor Emeritus."*

The magnificence of it, the daring of it! Thus far, she is

The Massachusetts Metaphysical College;

Pastor Emeritus;

President;

Board of Directors;

Treasurer;

Clerk; and future

Board of Trustees;

and is still moving onward, ever onward. When I contemplate her
from a commercial point of view, there are no words that can convey
my admiration of her.

READERS

These are a feature of *first* importance in the church-machinery of
Christian Science. For they occupy the pulpit. They hold the place
that the preacher holds in the other Christian Churches. They hold
that place, but *they do not preach.* Two of them are on duty at a time
—a man and a woman. One reads a passage from the Bible, the other
reads the explanation of it from *Science and Health*—and so they go
on alternating. This constitutes the service—this, with choir-music.
They utter no word of their own. Art. IV., Sec. 6, closes their mouths
with this uncompromising gag:

*"They shall make no remarks explanatory of the Lesson-Sermon at
any time during the service."*

It seems a simple little thing. One is not startled by it at a first
reading of it; nor at the second, nor the third. One may have to read
it a dozen times before the whole magnitude of it rises before the
mind. It far and away oversizes and outclasses the best business-idea
yet invented for the safe-guarding and perpetuating of a religion. If it
had been thought of and put in force eighteen hundred and seventy
years ago, there would be but one Christian sect in the world now,
instead of ten dozens of them.

There are many varieties of men in the world, consequently there
are many varieties of minds in its pulpits. This insures many differing
interpretations of important Scripture texts, and this in turn insures
the splitting up of a religion into many sects. It is what has happened; it was sure to happen.

Mrs. Eddy has noted this disastrous result of preaching, and has put up the bars. She will have no preaching in her Church. *She* has explained all essential Scriptures, and set the explanations down in her book. In her belief her underlings cannot improve upon those explanations, and in that stern sentence *"they shall make no explanatory remarks"* she has barred them for all time from trying. She will be obeyed; there is no question about that.

In arranging her government she has borrowed ideas from various sources—not poor ones, but the best in the governmental market—but this one is new, this one came out of no ordinary business-head, this one must have come out of her own, there has been no other commercial skull in a thousand centuries that was equal to it. She has borrowed freely and wisely, but I am sure that this idea is many times larger than all her borrowings bulked together. One must respect the business-brain that produced it—the splendid pluck and impudence that ventured to promulgate it, anyway.

ELECTION OF READERS

Readers are not taken at hap-hazard, any more than preachers are taken at hap-hazard for the pulpits of other sects. No, Readers are elected by the Board of Directors. *But*—

"Section 3. The Board shall inform the Pastor Emeritus of the names of *candidates* for Readers before they are elected, and *if she objects to the nomination, said candidates shall not be chosen."*

Is *that* an election—by the *Board?* Thus far I have not been able to find out what that Board of Spectres is for. It certainly has no real function, no duty which the hired girl could not perform, no office beyond the mere recording of the autocrat's decrees.

There are no dangerously long office-terms in Mrs. Eddy's government. The Readers are elected for but one year. This insures their subserviency to their proprietor.

Readers are not allowed to copy out passages and read them from the *manuscript* in the pulpit; they must read from *Mrs. Eddy's book* itself. She is right. Slight changes could be slyly made, repeated, and in time get acceptance with congregations. Branch sects could grow out of these practices. Mrs. Eddy knows the human race, and how far to trust it. Her limit is not over a quarter of an inch. It is all that a wise person will risk.

Mrs. Eddy's inborn disposition to copyright everything, charter everything, secure the rightful and proper credit to herself for every-thing she does, and everything she thinks she does, and everything she thinks, and everything she thinks she thinks or has thought or intends to think, is illustrated in Sec. 5 of Art. IV, defining the duties of official Readers—in church:

"*Naming Book and Author.* The Reader of *Science and Health, with Key to the Scriptures,* before commencing to read from this book, shall distinctly announce its full title and give the author's name."

Otherwise the congregation might get the habit of forgetting who (ostensibly) wrote the book.

THE ARISTOCRACY

This consists of First Members and their apostolic succession. It is a close corporation, and its membership limit is one hundred. Forty will answer, but if the number fall below that, there must be an election, to fill the grand quorum.

This Sanhedrin can't *do* anything of the slightest importance, but it can *talk.* It can "discuss." That is, it can discuss "important ques-tions relative to Church members"; evidently persons who are al-ready Church members. This affords it amusement, and does no harm.

It can "fix the salaries of the Readers."

Twice a year it "votes on" admitting candidates. That is, for Church membership. But its work is cut out for it beforehand, by Sec. 2, Art. IX:

"Every recommendation for membership in the Church 'shall be countersigned by a loyal student of Mrs. Eddy's, by a Director of this Church, or by a First Member.' "

All these three classes of beings are the personal property of Mrs. Eddy. She has absolute control of the elections.

Also it must "transact any Church business that may properly come before it."

"Properly" is a thoughtful word. *No* important business can come before it. The By-laws have attended to that. No important business goes before *any* one for the final word except Mrs. Eddy. She has looked to that.

The Sanhedrin "votes on" candidates for admission to its own body. But is its vote worth any more than mine would be? No, it isn't. Sec. 4, of Art. V—Election of First Members—makes this quite plain:

"Before being elected, the candidates for First Members *shall be approved by the Pastor Emeritus over her own signature.*"

Thus the Sanhedrin is the personal property of Mrs. Eddy. She owns it. It has no functions, no authority, no real existence. It is another Board of Shadows. Mrs. Eddy is the Sanhedrin herself.

But it is time to foot up again and "see where we are at." Thus far, Mrs. Eddy is

The Massachusetts Metaphysical College;
Pastor Emeritus;
President;
Board of Directors;
Treasurer;
Clerk;
Future Board of Trustees;
Proprietor of the Priesthood;
Dictator of the Services;
Proprietor of the Sanhedrin.
She has come far, and is still on her way.

CHURCH MEMBERSHIP

In this Article there is another exhibition of a couple of the large features of Mrs. Eddy's remarkable make-up: her business-talent and her knowledge of human nature.

She does not beseech and implore people to join her Church. She knows the human race better than that. She gravely goes through the motions of reluctantly granting admission to the applicant as a favor to him. The idea is worth untold shekels. She does not stand at the gate of the fold with welcoming arms spread, and receive the lost sheep with glad emotion and set up the fatted calf and invite the neighbor and have a time. No, she looks upon him coldly, she snubs him, she says: "Who are you? Who is your sponsor? Who asked you to come here? Go away, and don't come again until you are invited."

It is calculated to strikingly impress a person accustomed to Moody and Sankey and Sam Jones revivals; accustomed to brain-turning appeals to the unknown and unendorsed sinner to come forward and enter into the joy, etc.—"just as he is"; accustomed to seeing him do it; accustomed to seeing him pass up the aisle through sobbing seas of welcome, and love, and congratulation, and arrive at the mourner's bench and be received like a long-lost government bond.

No, there is nothing of that kind in Mrs. Eddy's system. She knows that if you wish to confer upon a human being something which he is not sure he wants, the best way is to make it apparently difficult for him to get it—then he is no son of Adam if that apple does not assume an interest in his eyes which it lacked before. In time this interest can grow into desire. Mrs. Eddy knows that when you cannot get a man to try—free of cost—a new and effective remedy for a disease he is afflicted with, you can generally sell it to him if you will put a price upon it which he cannot afford.[1] When, in the beginning, she taught Christian Science gratis (for good reasons), pupils were few and reluctant, and required persuasion; it was when she raised the limit to three hundred dollars for a dollar's worth that she could not find standing room for the invasion of pupils that followed.

With fine astuteness she goes through the motions of making it difficult to get membership in her Church. There is a twofold value in this system: it gives membership a high value in the eyes of the applicant; and at the same time the requirements exacted enable Mrs. Eddy to keep him out if she has doubts about his value to her. A word further as to applications for membership:

"Applications of students of the Metaphysical College must be signed by the *Board of Directors.*"

That is safe. Mrs. Eddy is proprietor of that Board.

Children of twelve may be admitted if invited by "one of Mrs. Eddy's loyal students, or by a First Member, or by a Director."

These sponsors are the property of Mrs. Eddy, therefore her Church is safeguarded from the intrusion of undesirable children.

Other Students. Applicants who have not studied with Mrs. Eddy

[1] I offered to cure of his passion—gratis—a victim of the drinking habit, by a simple and (as it seemed to me) not difficult intellectual method which I had successfully tried upon the tobacco habit. I failed to get him interested. I think my proposition couldn't rouse him, couldn't strongly appeal to him, could not electrify him, because it offered a thing so easy to get, and which could be had for nothing. Within a month afterwards a famous Drink-Cure opened, and at my suggestion he willingly went there, at once, and got himself (temporarily) cured of his habit. Because he had to pay one hundred and fifty dollars. One values a thing when one can't afford it.—M.T.

can get in only "by invitation and recommendation from students of Mrs. Eddy . . . or from members of the Mother-Church."

Other paragraphs explain how two or three other varieties of applicants are to be challenged and obstructed, and tell us who is authorized to invite them, recommend them, endorse them, and all that.

The safeguards are definite, and would seem to be sufficiently strenuous—to Mr. Sam Jones, at any rate. Not for Mrs. Eddy. She adds this clincher:

"The candidates shall be elected by a majority vote of the First Members present."

That is the aristocracy, the aborigines, the Sanhedrin. It is Mrs. Eddy's property. She *herself* is the Sanhedrin. No one can get into the Church if she wishes to keep him out.

This veto power could some time or other have a large value for her, therefore she was wise to reserve it.

It is likely that it is not frequently used. It is also probable that the difficulties attendant upon getting admission to membership have been instituted more to invite than to deter, more to enhance the value of membership and make people long for it than to make it really difficult to get. I think so, because the Mother-Church has many thousands of members more than its building can accommodate.

'ANDSOME ENGLISH REQUIRED

Mrs. Eddy is very particular as regards one detail—curiously so, for her, all things considered. The Church Readers must be "good English scholars"; they must be "thorough English scholars."

She is thus sensitive about the English of her subordinates for cause, possibly. In her chapter defining the duties of the Clerk there is an indication that she harbors resentful memories of an occasion when the hazy quality of her own English made unforeseen and mortifying trouble:

"Understanding Communications. Sec. 2. If the Clerk of this Church shall receive a communication from the Pastor Emeritus which he does not fully understand, he shall inform her of this fact before presenting it to the Church, and obtain a clear understanding of the matter—then act in accordance therewith."

She should have waited to calm down, then, but instead she added this, which lacks sugar:

"Failing to adhere to this By-law, the Clerk must *resign.*"

I wish I could see that communication that broke the camel's back. It was probably the one beginning: "What plague spot or bacilli were gnawing at the heart of this metropolis and bringing it on bended knee?" and I think it likely that the kindly disposed Clerk tried to translate it into English and lost his mind and had to go to the hospital. That By-law was not the offspring of a forecast, an intuition, it was certainly born of a sorrowful experience. Its temper gives the fact away.

The little book of By-laws has manifestly been tinkered by one of Mrs. Eddy's "thorough English scholars," for in the majority of cases its meanings are clear. The book is not even marred by Mrs. Eddy's peculiar specialty—lumbering clumsinesses of speech. I believe the salaried polisher has weeded them all out but one. In one place, after referring to *Science and Health,* Mrs. Eddy goes on to say "the Bible and the above-named book, with other works by the same author," etc.

It is an unfortunate sentence, for it could mislead a hasty or careless reader for a moment. Mrs. Eddy framed it—it is her very own—it bears her trade-mark. "The Bible and *Science and Health,* with other works by the same author," could have come from no literary vacuum but the one which produced the remark (in the *Autobiography*): "I remember reading, in my childhood, certain manuscripts containing Scriptural Sonnets, besides other verses and enigmas."

We know what she means, in both instances, but a low-priced Clerk would not necessarily know, and on a salary like his he could quite excusably aver that the Pastor Emeritus had commanded him to come and make proclamation that she was author of the Bible, and that she was thinking of discharging some Scriptural sonnets and other enigmas upon the congregation. It could lose him his place, but it would not be fair, if it happened before the edict about "Understanding Communications" was promulgated.

"READERS" AGAIN

The By-law book makes a showy pretence of orderliness and system, but it is only a pretence. I will not go so far as to say it is a harum-scarum jumble, for it is not that, but I think it fair to say it is

at least jumbulacious in places. For instance, Articles III and IV set
forth in much detail the qualifications and duties of Readers, she
then skips some thirty pages and takes up the subject again. It looks
like slovenliness, but it may be only art. The belated By-law has a
sufficiently quiet look, but it has a ton of dynamite in it. *It makes all
the Christian Science Church Readers on the globe the personal chat-
tels of Mrs. Eddy.* Whenever she chooses, she can stretch her long
arm around the world's fat belly and flirt a Reader out of his pulpit,
though he be tucked away in seeming safety and obscurity in a lost
village in the middle of China:

"*In any Church. Sec. 2.* The Pastor Emeritus of the Mother-
Church shall have the right (through a *letter* addressed to the individual and Church of which he is the Reader) to remove a Reader
from this office in any Church of Christ, Scientist, both in America
and in foreign nations; or to appoint the Reader to fill any office
belonging to the Christian Science denomination."

She does not have to prefer charges against him, she does not have
to find him lazy, careless, incompetent, untidy, ill-mannered, unholy,
dishonest, she does not have to discover a fault of any kind in him,
she does not have to tell him nor his congregation why she dismisses
and disgraces him and insults his meek flock, she does not have to
explain to his family why she takes the bread out of their mouths and
turns them out-of-doors homeless and ashamed in a strange land; she
does not have to do anything but send a *letter* and say: "Pack!—and
ask no questions!"

Has the Pope this power?—the other Pope—the one in Rome. Has
he anything approaching it? Can he turn a priest out of his pulpit
and strip him of his office and his livelihood just upon a whim, a
caprice, and meanwhile furnishing no reasons to the parish? Not in
America. And not elsewhere, we may believe.

It is odd and strange, to see intelligent and educated people among
us worshipping this self-seeking and remorseless tyrant as a God.
This worship is denied—by persons who are themselves worshippers
of Mrs. Eddy. I feel quite sure that it is a worship which will continue during ages.

That Mrs. Eddy wrote that amazing By-law with her own hand we
have much better evidence than her word. We have her English. It is
there. It cannot be imitated. She ought never to go to the expense of
copyrighting her verbal discharges. When any one tries to claim

them she should call me; I can always tell them from any other
literary apprentice's at a glance. It was like her to call America a
"nation"; she would call a sand-bar a nation if it should fall into a
sentence in which she was speaking of people, for she would not
know how to untangle it and get it out and classify it by itself. And
the closing arrangement of that By-law is in true Eddysonian form,
too. In it she reserves authority to make a Reader fill any office
connected with a Science church—sexton, grave-digger, advertising
agent, Annex-polisher, leader of the choir, President, Director, Treasurer, Clerk, etc. She did not mean that. She already possessed that
authority. She meant to clothe herself with power, despotic and unchallengeable, to appoint all Science Readers to their offices, both at
home and abroad. The phrase "or to appoint" is another miscarriage
of intention; she did not mean "or," she meant "and."

That By-law puts into Mrs. Eddy's hands *absolute command* over
the most formidable force and influence existent in the Christian
Science kingdom outside of herself, and it does this *unconditionally*
and (by auxiliary force of Laws already quoted) *irrevocably*. Still, she
is not quite satisfied. Something might happen, she doesn't know
what. Therefore she drives in one more nail, to make sure, and drives
it deep:

*"This By-law can neither be amended nor annulled, except by con-
sent of the Pastor Emeritus."*

Let some one with a wild and delirious fancy try and see if he can
imagine her furnishing that consent.

MONOPOLY OF SPIRITUAL BREAD

Very properly, the first qualification for membership in the
Mother-Church is belief in the doctrines of Christian Science.

But these doctrines must not be gathered from secondary sources.
There is but *one* recognized source. The candidate must be a believer
in the doctrines of Christian Science *"according to the platform and
teaching contained in the Christian Science text-book, 'Science and
Health, with Key to the Scriptures,' by Rev. Mary Baker G. Eddy."*

That is definite, and is final. There are to be no commentaries, no
labored volumes of exposition and explanation by anybody except
Mrs. Eddy. Because such things could sow error, create warring
opinions, split the religion into sects, and disastrously cripple its
power. Mrs. Eddy will do the *whole* of the explaining, herself—has

done it, in fact. She has written several books. They are to be had (for cash in advance); they are all sacred; additions to them can never be needed and will never be permitted. They tell the candidate how to instruct himself, how to teach others, how to do all things comprised in the business—and they close the door against all would-be competitors, and monopolize the trade:

"The Bible and the above-named book *[Science and Health]*, with other works by the same author," must be his *only* text-books for the commerce—he cannot forage outside.

Mrs. Eddy's words are to be the *sole* elucidators of the Bible and *Science and Health*—forever. Throughout the ages, whenever there is doubt as to the meaning of a passage in either of these books the inquirer will not dream of trying to explain it to himself; he would shudder at the thought of such temerity, such profanity; he would be haled to the Inquisition and thence to the public square and the stake if he should be caught studying into text-meanings on his own hook; he will be prudent and seek the meanings at the only permitted source, *Mrs. Eddy's commentaries.*

Value of this Strait-jacket. One must not underrate the magnificence of this long-headed idea, one must not underestimate its giant possibilities in the matter of hooping the Church solidly together and keeping it so. It squelches independent inquiry, and makes such a thing impossible, profane, criminal, it authoritatively settles every dispute that can arise. It *starts* with *finality*—a point which the Roman Church has travelled towards fifteen or sixteen centuries, stage by stage, and has not yet reached. The matter of the Immaculate Conception of the Virgin Mary was not authoritatively settled until the days of Pius IX—yesterday, so to speak.

As already noticed, the Protestants are broken up into a long array of sects, a result of disputes about the meanings of texts, disputes made unavoidable by the absence of an infallible authority to submit doubtful passages to. A week or two ago (I am writing in the middle of January, 1903), the clergy and others hereabouts had a warm dispute in the papers over this question: Did Jesus anywhere claim to be God? It seemed an easy question, but it turned out to be a hard one. It was ably and elaborately discussed, by learned men of several denominations, but in the end it remained unsettled.

A week ago, another discussion broke out. It was over this text: "Sell all that thou hast and distribute unto the poor."

One verdict was worded as follows:

"When Christ answered the rich young man and said for him to give to the poor all he possessed or he could not gain everlasting life, He did not mean it in the literal sense. My interpretation of His words is that we should part with what comes between us and Christ.

"There is no doubt that Jesus believed that the rich young man thought more of his wealth than he did of his soul, and, such being the case, it was his duty to give up the wealth.

"Every one of us knows that there is something we should give up for Christ. Those who are true believers and followers know what they have given up, and those who are not yet followers know down in their hearts what they must give up."

Ten clergymen of various denominations were interviewed, and nine of them agreed with that verdict. That did not settle the matter, because the tenth said the language of Jesus was so strait and definite that it explained *itself:* "Sell *all,*" not a percentage.

There is a most unusual feature about that dispute: the nine persons who decided alike, quoted not a single authority in support of their position. I do not know when I have seen trained disputants do the like of that before. The nine merely furnished their own opinions, founded upon—nothing at all. In the other dispute ("Did Jesus anywhere claim to be God?") the same kind of men—trained and learned clergymen—backed up their arguments with chapter and verse. On both sides. Plenty of verses. Were no reinforcing verses to be found in the present case? It looks that way.

The opinion of the nine seems strange to me, for it is unsupported by authority, while there was at least constructive authority for the opposite view.

It is hair-splitting differences of opinion over disputed text-meanings that have divided into many sects a once united Church. One may infer from some of the names in the following list that some of the differences are very slight—so slight as to be not distinctly important, perhaps—yet they have moved groups to withdraw from communions to which they belonged and set up a sect of their own. The list—accompanied by various Church statistics for 1902, compiled by Rev. Dr. H. K. Carroll—was published, January 8, 1903, in the New York *Christian Advocate:*

Adventists (6 bodies),
Baptists (13 bodies),
Brethren (Plymouth) (4 bodies),
Brethren (River) (3 bodies),
Catholics (8 bodies),
Catholic Apostolic,
Christadelphians,
Christian Connection,
Christian Catholics (Dowie),
Christian Missionary Association,
Christian Scientists,
Church of God (Winebrennarian),
Church of the New

Jerusalem,
Congregationalists,
Disciples of Christ,
Dunkards (4 bodies),
Evangelical (2 bodies),
Friends (4 bodies),
Friends of the Temple,
German Evangelical Protestant,

German Evangelical Synod,
Independent congregations,
Jews (2 bodies),
Latter-day Saints (2 bodies),
Lutherans (22 bodies),
Mennonites (12 bodies),
Methodists (17 bodies),
Moravians,
Presbyterians (12 bodies),
Protestant Episcopal (2 bodies),
Reformed (3 bodies),

Schwenkfeldians,
Social Brethren,
Spiritualists,
Swedish Evangelical Miss. Covenant (Waldenstromians),
Unitarians,
United Brethren (2 bodies),
Universalists.

Total of sects and splits—139.

In the present month (February), Mr. E. I. Lindh, A.M., has communicated to the Boston *Transcript* a hopeful article on the solution of the problem of the "divided church." Divided is not too violent a term. Subdivided could have been permitted if he had thought of it. He came near thinking of it, for he mentions some of the subdivisions himself: "the 12 kinds of Presbyterians, the 17 kinds of Methodists, the 13 kinds of Baptists, etc." He overlooked the 12 kinds of Mennonites and the 22 kinds of Lutherans, but they are in Rev. Mr.

Carroll's list. Altogether, 76 splits under 5 flags. *The Literary Digest* (February 14th) is pleased with Mr. Lindh's optimistic article, and also with the signs of the times, and perceives that "the idea of Church unity is in the air."

Now, then, is not Mrs. Eddy profoundly wise in forbidding, for all time, all explanations of her religion except such as she shall let on to be her own?

I think so. I think there can be no doubt of it. In a way, they will be her own; for, no matter which member of her clerical staff shall furnish the explanations, not a line of them will she ever allow to be printed until she shall have approved it, accepted it, copyrighted it, cabbaged it. We may depend on that with a four-ace confidence.

THE NEW INFALLIBILITY

All in proper time Mrs. Eddy's factory will take hold of that Commandment, and explain it for good and all. It may be that one member of the shift will vote that the word "all" means *all;* it may be that ten members of the shift will vote that "all" means only a percentage; but it is *Mrs. Eddy,* not the eleven, who will do the *deciding.* And if she says it is percentage, then percentage it is, forevermore—and that is what I am expecting, for she doesn't sell all herself, nor any considerable part of it, and as regards the poor, she doesn't declare any dividend; but if she says "all" means all, then all it is, to the end of time, and no follower of hers will ever be allowed to reconstruct that text, or shrink it, or inflate it, or meddle with it in any way at all. Even today—right here in the beginning—she is the sole person who, in the matter of Christian Science exegesis, is privileged to exploit the Spiral Twist.[2] The Christian world has *two* Infallibles now.

Of equal power? For the present only. When Leo XIII passes to his rest another Infallible will ascend his throne;[3] others, and yet others, and still others will follow him, and be as infallible as he, and decide questions of doctrine as long as they may come up, all down the far future; but Mary Baker G. Eddy is the *only* Infallible that will ever occupy the Science throne. Many a Science Pope will succeed

[2] That is a technicality—that phrase. I got it of an uncle of mine. He had once studied in a theological cemetery, he said, and he called the Department of Biblical Exegesis the Spiral Twist "for short." He said it was always difficult to drive a straight text through an unaccommodating cork, but that if you twisted it it would go. He had kept bar in his less poetical days.—M.T.

[3] It has since happened.—M.T.

her, but she has closed their mouths; they will repeat and reverently praise and adore her infallibilities, but venture none themselves. In her grave she will still outrank all other Popes, be they of what Church they may. She will hold the supremest of earthly titles, The Infallible—with a capital T. Many in the world's history have had a hunger for such nuggets and slices of power as they might reasonably hope to grab out of an empire's or a religion's assets, but Mrs. Eddy is the only person alive or dead who has ever struck for the *whole* of them. For small things she has the eye of a microscope, for large ones the eye of a telescope, and whatever she sees, she wants. Wants it all.

THE SACRED POEMS

When Mrs. Eddy's "sacred revelations" (that is the language of the By-laws) are read in public, their authorship must be named. The By-laws twice command this, therefore we mention it twice, to be fair.

But it is also commanded that when a member publicly quotes "from the poems of our Pastor Emeritus" the authorship shall be named. For these are sacred, too. There are kindly people who may suspect a hidden generosity in that By-law; they may think it is there to protect the Official Reader from the suspicion of having written the poems himself. Such do not know Mrs. Eddy. She does an inordinate deal of protecting, but in no distinctly named and specified case in her history has Number Two been the object of it. Instances have been claimed, but they have failed of proof, and even of plausibility.

"Members shall also instruct their students" to look out and advertise the authorship when they read those poems and things. Not on Mrs. Eddy's account, but "for the good of our Cause."

THE CHURCH EDIFICE

1. Mrs. Eddy gave the land. It was not of much value at the time, but it is very valuable now.

2. Her people built the Mother-Church edifice on it, at a cost of two hundred and fifty thousand dollars.

3. Then they gave the whole property to her.

4. Then she gave it to the Board of Directors. *She* is the Board of Directors. She took it out of one pocket and put it in the other.

5. *Sec.* 10 *(of the deed).* "Whenever said Directors shall determine that it is inexpedient to maintain preaching, reading, or speaking in

said church in accordance with the terms of this deed, they are authorized and *required* to reconvey *forthwith* said lot of land with the building thereon to Mary Baker G. Eddy, her heirs and assigns forever, by a proper deed of conveyance."

She is never careless, never slipshod, about a matter of business. Owning the property through her Board of Waxworks was safe enough, still it was sound business to set another grip on it to cover accidents, and she did it.

Her barkers (what a curious name; I wonder if it is copyrighted), her barkers persistently advertise to the public her generosity in giving away a piece of land which cost her a trifle, and a two-hundred-and-fifty-thousand-dollar church which cost her nothing; and they can hardly speak of the unselfishness of it without breaking down and crying; yet they know she gave nothing away, and never intended to. However, such is the human race. Often it does seem such a pity that Noah and his party did not miss the boat.

Some of the hostiles think that Mrs. Eddy's idea in protecting this property in the interest of her heirs, and in accumulating a great money-fortune, is, that she may leave her natural heirs well provided for when she goes. I think it is a mistake. I think she is of late years giving herself large concern about only one interest—her power and glory, and the perpetuation and worship of her Name—with a capital N. Her Church is her pet heir, and I think it will get her wealth. It is the torch which is to light the world and the ages with her glory.

I think she once prized money for the ease and comfort it could bring, the showy vanities it could furnish, and the social promotion it could command; for we have seen that she was born into the world with little ways and instincts and aspirations and affectations that are duplicates of our own. I do not think her money-passion has ever diminished in ferocity, I do not think that she has ever allowed a dollar that had no friends to get by her alive, but I think her reason for wanting it has changed. I think she wants it now to increase and establish and perpetuate her power and glory with, not to add to her comforts and luxuries, not to furnish paint and fuss and feathers for vain display. I think her ambitions have soared away above the fuss-and-feather stage. She still likes the little shows and vanities—a fact which she exposed in a public utterance two or three days ago when she was not noticing[4]—but I think she does not place a large value upon them now. She could build a mighty and far-shining brass-mounted palace if she wanted to, but she does not do it. She would have had that kind of an ambition in the early scrabbling times. She could go to England today and be worshipped by earls, and get a comet's attention from the million, if she cared for such things. She would have gone in the early scrabbling days for much less than an earl, and been vain of it, and glad to show off before the remains of the Scotch kin. But those things are very small to her now—next to invisible, observed through the cloud-rack from the dizzy summit where she perches in these great days. She does not want that church property for herself. It is worth but a quarter of a million—a sum she could call in from her far-spread flocks tomorrow with a lift of her hand. Not a squeeze of it, just a lift. It would come without a murmur; come gratefully, come gladly. And if her glory stood in more need of the money in Boston than it does where her flocks are propagating it, she would lift the hand, I think.

She is still reaching for the Dollar, she will continue to reach for it; but not that she may spend it upon herself; not that she may spend it upon charities; not that she may indemnify an early deprivation and clothe herself in a blaze of North Adams gauds; not that she may have nine breeds of pie for breakfast, as only the rich New-Englander can; not that she may indulge any petty material vanity or appetite that once was hers and prized and nursed, but that she may apply that Dollar to statelier uses, and place it where it may cast the metallic sheen of her glory farthest across the receding expanses of the globe.

PRAYER

A brief and good one is furnished in the book of By-laws. The Scientist is required to pray it every day.

THE LORD'S PRAYER—AMENDED

This is not in the By-laws, it is in the first chapter of *Science and Health,* edition of 1902. I do not find it in the edition of 1884. It is probable that it had not at that time been handed down. *Science and Health*'s (latest) rendering of its "spiritual sense" is as follows:

---

[4] This is a reference to her public note of January 17th. See Appendix.—M.T.

"Our Father-Mother God, all-harmonious, adorable One. Thy kingdom is within us, Thou art ever-present. Enable us to know—as in heaven, so on earth—God is supreme. Give us grace for today; feed the famished affections. And infinite Love is reflected in love. And Love leadeth us not into temptation, but delivereth from sin, disease, and death. For God is now and forever all Life, Truth, and Love."[5]

If I thought my opinion was desired and would be properly revered, I should say that in my judgement that is as good a piece of carpentering as any of those eleven Commandment-experts could do with the material, after all their practice. I notice only one doubtful place. "Lead us not into temptation" seems to me to be a very definite request, and that the new rendering turns the definite request into a definite assertion. I shall be glad to have that turned back to the old way and the marks of the Spiral Twist removed, or varnished over; then I shall be satisfied, and will do the best I can with what is left. At the same time, I do feel that the shrinkage in our spiritual assets is getting serious. First the Commandments, now the Prayer. I never expected to see these steady old reliable securities watered down to this. And this is not the whole of it. Last summer the Presbyterians extended the Calling and Election suffrage to nearly everybody entitled to salvation. They did not even stop there, but let out all the unbaptized American infants we had been accumulating for two hundred years and more. There are some that believe they would have let the Scotch ones out, too, if they could have done it. Everything is going to ruin; in no long time we shall have nothing left but the love of God.

THE NEW UNPARDONABLE SIN

"Working Against the Cause. Sec. 2. If a member of this Church shall work against the accomplishment *of what the Discoverer and Founder of Christian Science understands is advantageous* to the individual, to this Church, and to the Cause of Christian Science"—out he goes. *Forever.*

The member may *think* that what he is doing will advance the Cause, but he is not invited to do any thinking. More than that, he is not *permitted* to do any—as he will clearly gather from this By-law.

[5] For the latest version, see Appendix.—M.T.

When a person joins Mrs. Eddy's Church he must leave his thinker at home. Leave it permanently. To make sure that it will not go off some time or other when he is not watching, it will be safest for him to spike it. If he should forget himself and think just *once*, the By-law provides that he shall be fired out—instantly—forever—no return.

"It shall be the duty of this Church immediately to call a meeting, and *drop forever the name of this member from its records.*"

My, but it breaths a towering indignation!

There are forgivable offences, but this is not one of them; there are admonitions, probations, suspensions, in several minor cases; mercy is shown the derelict, in those cases he is gently used, and in time he can get back into the fold—even when he has repeated his offence. But let him *think*, just *once*, without getting his thinker set to Eddy time, and that is enough; his head comes off. There is no second offence, and there is no gate open to that lost sheep, ever again.

"*This rule cannot be changed, amended, or annulled, except by unanimous vote of all the First Members.*"

The same being *Mrs. Eddy.* It is naïvely sly and pretty to see her keep putting forward First Members, and Boards of This and That, and other broideries and ruffles of her raiment, as if they were independent entities, instead of a part of her clothes, and could do things all by themselves when she was outside of them.

Mrs. Eddy did not need to copyright the sentence just quoted, its English would protect it. None but she would have shovelled that comically superfluous "all" in there.

The former Unpardonable Sin has gone out of service. We may frame the new Christian Science one thus:

"Whatsoever Member shall think, and without Our Mother's permission act upon his think, the same shall be cut off from the Church forever."

It has been said that I make many mistakes about Christian Science through being ignorant of the spiritual meanings of its terminology. I believe it is true. I have been misled all this time by that word Member, because there was no one to tell me that its spiritual meaning was Slave.

AXE AND BLOCK

There is a By-law which forbids Members to practise hypnotism; the penalty is excommunication.

1. If a member is found to be a mental practitioner—
2. Complaint is to be entered against him—
3. By the Pastor Emeritus, and by *none else;*
4. No member is allowed to make complaint to *her* in the matter;
5. *Upon Mrs. Eddy's mere "complaint"—unbacked by evidence or proof, and without giving the accused a chance to be heard*—"his name shall be dropped from this Church."

Mrs. Eddy has only to *say* a member is guilty—that is all. That ends it. It is not a case of he "may" be cut off from Christian Science salvation, it is a case of he "*shall*" be. Her serfs must see to it, and not say a word.

Does the other Pope possess this prodigious and irresponsible power? Certainly not in our day.

Some may be curious to know how Mrs. Eddy *finds out* that a member is practising hypnotism, since no one is allowed to come before her throne and accuse him. She has explained this in *Christian Science History,* first and second editions, page 16:

"I possess a *spiritual sense of what the malicious mental practitioner is mentally arguing* which cannot be deceived; I can discern in the human mind thoughts, motives, and purposes; and neither mental arguments nor psychic power can affect this spiritual insight."

A marvellous woman; with a hunger for power such as had never been seen in the world before. No thing, little or big, that contains any seed or suggestion of power escapes her avaricious eye; and when once she gets that eye on it, her remorseless grip follows. There isn't a Christian Scientist who isn't ecclesiastically as much her property as if she had bought him and paid for him, and copyrighted him and got a charter. She cannot be satisfied when she has handcuffed a member, and put a leg-chain and ball on him and plugged his ears and removed his thinker, she goes on wrapping needless chains round and round him, just as a spider would. For she trusts no one, believes in no one's honesty, judges every one by herself. Although we have seen that she has absolute and irresponsible command over her spectral Boards and over every official and servant of her Church, at home and abroad, over every minute detail of her Church's government, *present and future,* and can purge her membership of guilty or suspected persons by various plausible formalities and whenever she will, she is still not content, but must set her queer mind to work and invent a way by which she can take a member—any member—by neck and crop and fling him out without anything resembling a formality at all.

She is sole accuser and sole witness, and her testimony is final and carries uncompromising and irremediable doom with it.

The Sole-Witness Court! It should make the Council of Ten and the Council of Three turn in their graves for shame, to see how little they knew about satanic concentrations of irresponsible power. Here we have one Accuser, one Witness, one Judge, one Headsman—and all four bunched together in Mrs. Eddy, the Inspired of God, His Latest Thought to His People, New Member of the Holy Family, the Equal of Jesus.

When a Member is not satisfactory to Mrs. Eddy, and yet is blameless in his life and faultless in his membership and in his Christian Science walk and conversation, shall he hold up his head and tilt his hat over one ear and imagine himself safe because of these perfections? Why, in that very moment Mrs. Eddy will cast that spiritual X-ray of hers through his dungarees and say:

"I see his hypnotism working, among his insides—remove him to the block!"

What shall it profit him to know it isn't so? Nothing. His testimony is of no value. No one wants it, no one will ask for it. He is not present to offer it (he does not know he has been accused), and if he were there to offer it, it would not be listened to.

It was out of powers approaching Mrs. Eddy's—though not equalling them—that the Inquisition and the devastations of the Interdict grew. She will transmit hers. The man born two centuries from now will think he has arrived in hell; and all in good time he will think he knows it. Vast concentrations of irresponsible power have never in any age been used mercifully, and there is nothing to suggest that the Christian Science Papacy is going to spend money on novelties.

Several Christian Scientists have asked me to refrain from prophecy. There *is* no prophecy in our day but history. But history is a trustworthy prophet. History is always repeating itself, because *conditions* are always repeating themselves. Out of duplicated conditions history always gets a duplicate product.

READING LETTERS AT MEETINGS

I wonder if there is anything a Member *can* do that will not raise Mrs. Eddy's jealousy? The By-laws seem to hunt him from pillar to post all the time, and turn all his thoughts and acts and words into sins against the meek and lowly new deity of his worship. Apparently her jealousy never sleeps. Apparently any trifle can offend it, and but one penalty appease it — uncommunication. The By-laws might properly and reasonably be entitled Laws for the Coddling and Comforting of Our Mother's Petty Jealousies. The By-law named at the head of this paragraph reads its transgressor out of the Church if he shall carry a letter from Mrs. Eddy to the congregation and forget to read it or fail to read the whole of it.

HONESTY REQUISITE

Dishonest members are to be admonished; if they continue in dishonest practices, excommunication follows. Considering who it is that draughted this law, there is a certain amount of humor in it.

FURTHER APPLICATIONS OF THE AXE

Here follow the titles of some more By-laws whose infringement is punishable by excommunication:

Silence Enjoined.
Misteaching.
Departure from Tenets.
Violation of Christian Fellowship.
Moral Offences.
Illegal Adoption.
Broken By-laws.
Violation of By-laws. (What is the difference?)
Formulas Forbidden.
Official Advice (Forbids Tom, Dick, and Harry's clack.)
Unworthy of Membership.
Final Excommunication.
Organizing Churches.

This looks as if Mrs. Eddy had devoted a large share of her time and talent to inventing ways to get rid of her Church members. Yet in another place she seems to invite membership. Not in any urgent way, it is true, still she throws out a bait to such as like notice and distinction (in other words, the Human Race). Page 82:

"It is important that these seemingly strict conditions be complied with, as *the names of the Members of the Mother-Church will be recorded in the history* of the Church and become a part thereof."

We all want to be historical.

MORE SELF-PROTECTIONS

The Hymnal. There is a Christian Science Hymnal. Entrance to it was closed in 1898. Christian Science students who make hymns nowadays may possibly get them sung in the Mother-Church, *"but not unless approved by the Pastor Emeritus."* Art. XXVII, Sec. 2.

Solo Singers. Mrs. Eddy has contributed the words of three of the hymns in the Hymnal. Two of them appear in it six times altogether, each of them being set to three original forms of musical anguish. Mrs. Eddy, always thoughtful, has promulgated a By-law requiring the singing of one of her three hymns in the Mother-Church "as often as once each month." It is a good idea. A congregation could get tired of even Mrs. Eddy's muse in the course of time, without the cordializing incentive of compulsion. We all know how wearisome the sweetest and touchingest things can become, through rep-rep-repetition, and still rep-rep-repetition, and more rep-rep-repetition—like "the sweet by-and-by, *in* the sweet by-and-by," for instance, and "Tah-rah-rah boom-de-aye"; and surely it is not likely that Mrs. Eddy's machine has turned out goods that could outwear those great heart-stirrers, without the assistance of the lash. "O'er Waiting Harp-strings of the Mind" is pretty good, quite fair to middling—the whole seven of the stanzas—but repetition would be certain to take the excitement out of it in the course of time, even if there were fourteen, and then it would sound like the multiplication table, and would cease to save. The congregation would be perfectly sure to get tired; in fact, *did* get tired—hence the compulsory By-law. It is a measure born of experience, not foresight.

The By-laws say that "if a solo singer shall neglect or refuse to sing alone" one of those three hymns as often as once a month, and oftener if so directed by the Board of Directors—which is Mrs. Eddy—the singer's salary shall be stopped. It is circumstantial evidence that some soloists neglected this sacrament and others refused it. At least that is the charitable view to take of it. There is only one other view to take: that Mrs. Eddy did really foresee that there would be singers who would some day get tired of doing her hymns and proclaiming the authorship, unless persuaded by a By-law, with a penalty attached. The idea could of course occur to her wise head, for she would know that a seven-stanza break might well be a calamitous strain upon a soloist, and that he might therefore avoid it if unwatched. He could not curtail it, for the whole of anything that Mrs. Eddy does is sacred, and cannot be cut.

BOARD OF EDUCATION

It consists of four members, one of whom is President of it. Its members are elected annually. *Subject to Mrs. Eddy's approval.* Art. XXX, Sec. 2.

She owns the Board—*is* the Board.

Mrs. Eddy is President of the Metaphysical College. If at any time she shall vacate that office, the Directors of the College (that is to say, Mrs. Eddy) *"shall"* elect to the vacancy the President of the Board of Education (which is merely re-electing herself).

It is another case of "Pastor Emeritus." She gives up the shadow of authority, but keeps a good firm hold on the substance.

PUBLIC TEACHERS

Applicants for admission to this industry must pass a thorough three days' examination before the Board of Education "in *Science and Health,* chapter on 'Recapitulation'; the Platform of Christian Science; page 403 of *Christian Science Practice,* from line second to the second paragraph of page 405; and page 488, second and third paragraphs."

BOARD OF LECTURESHIP

The lecturers are exceedingly important servants of Mrs. Eddy, and she chooses them with great care. Each of them has an appointed territory in which to perform his duties—in the North, the South, the East, the West, in Canada, in Great Britain, and so on—and each must stick to his own territory and not forage beyond its boundaries. I think it goes without saying—from what we have seen of Mrs. Eddy—that no lecture is delivered until she has examined and appoved it, and that the lecturer is not allowed to change it afterwards.

The members of the Board of Lectureship are elected annually—
"Subject to the approval of Rev. Mary Baker G. Eddy."

MISSIONARIES

There are but four. They are elected—like the rest of the domestics
—annually. So far as I can discover, not a single servant of the
Sacred Household has a steady job except Mrs. Eddy. It is plain that
she trusts no human being but herself.

THE BY-LAWS

The branch Churches are strictly forbidden to use them.

So far as I can see, they could not do it if they wanted to. The By-
laws are merely the voice of the master issuing commands to the
servants. There is nothing and nobody for the servants to re-utter
them to.

That useless edict is repeated in the little book, a few pages farther
on. There are several other repetitions of prohibitions in the book
that could be spared—they only take up room for nothing.

THE CREED

It is copyrighted. I do not know why, but I suppose it is to keep
adventurers from some day claiming that they invented it, and not
Mrs. Eddy and that "strange Providence" that has suggested so
many clever things to her.

No Change. It is forbidden to change the Creed. That is important,
at any rate.

COPYRIGHT

I can understand why Mrs. Eddy copyrighted the early editions
and revisions of *Science and Health,* and why she had a mania for
copyrighting every scrap of every sort that came from her pen in
those jejune days when to be in print probably seemed a wonderful
distinction to her in her provincial obscurity, but why she should
continue this delirium in these days of her godship and her far-
spread fame, I cannot explain to myself. And particularly as regards
Science and Health. She knows, now, that that Annex is going to live
for many centuries; and so, what good is a fleeting forty-two-year
copyright going to do it?

Now a *perpetual* copyright would be quite another matter. I would like to give her a hint. Let her strike for a perpetual copyright on that book. There is precedent for it. There is one book in the world which bears the charmed life of perpetual copyright (a fact not known to twenty people in the world). By a hardy perversion of privilege on the part of the lawmaking power the Bible has perpetual copyright in Great Britain. There is no justification for it in fairness, and no explanation of it except that the Church is strong enough there to have its way, right or wrong. The recent Revised Version enjoys perpetual copyright, too—a stronger precedent, even, than the other one.

Now, then, what is the Annex but a Revised Version itself? Which of course it is—Lord's Prayer and all. With that pair of formidable British precedents to proceed upon, what Congress of ours—

But how short-sighted I am. Mrs. Eddy has thought of it long ago. She thinks of everything. She knows she has only to keep her copyright of 1902 alive through its first stage of twenty-eight years, and perpetuity is assured. A Christian Science Congress will reign in the Capitol then. She probably attaches small value to the first edition (1875). Although it was a Revelation from on high, it was slim, lank, incomplete, padded with bales of refuse rags, and puffs from lassoed celebrities to fill it out, an uncreditable book, a book easily sparable, a book not to be mentioned in the same year with the sleek, fat, concise, compact, compressed, and competent Annex of today, in its dainty flexible covers, gilt-edges, rounded corners, twin screw, spiral twist, compensation balance, Testament-counterfeit, and all that; a book just born to curl up on the hymn-book-shelf in church and look just too sweet and holy for anything. Yes, I see now what she was copyrighting that child for.

CHRISTIAN SCIENCE PUBLISHING ASSOCIATION

It is true—in matters of business Mrs. Eddy thinks of everything. She thought of an organ, to disseminate the Truth as it was in Mrs. Eddy. Straightway she started one—the *Christian Science Journal.*

It is true—in matters of business Mrs. Eddy thinks of everything. As soon as she had got the *Christian Science Journal* sufficiently in debt to make its presence on the premises disagreeable to her, it occurred to her to make somebody a present of it. Which she did, along with its debts. It was in the summer of 1889. The victim selected was her Church—called, in those days, The National Christian Scientist Association.

She delivered this sorrow to those lambs as a "gift" in consideration of their "loyalty to our great cause."

Also—still thinking of everything—she told them to retain Mr. Bailey in the editorship and make Mr. Nixon publisher. We do not know what it was she had against those men; neither do we know whether she scored on Bailey or not, we only know that God protected Nixon, and for that I am sincerely glad, although I do not know Nixon and have never even seen him.

Nixon took the *Journal* and the rest of the Publishing Society's liabilities, and demonstrated over them during three years, then brought in his report:

"On assuming my duties as publisher, there was not a dollar in the treasury; but on the contrary the Society owed unpaid printing and paper bills to the amount of several hundred dollars, not to mention a contingent liability of many more hundreds"—represented by advance-subscriptions paid for the *Journal* and the "Series," the which goods Mrs. Eddy had not delivered. And couldn't, very well, perhaps, on a Metaphysical College income of but a few thousand dollars a day, or a week, or whatever it was in those magnificently flourishing times. The struggling *Journal* had swallowed up those advance-payments, but its "claim" was a severe one and they had failed to cure it. But Nixon cured it in his diligent three years, and joyously reported the news that he had cleared off all the debts and now had a fat six thousand dollars in the bank.

It made Mrs. Eddy's mouth water.

At the time that Mrs. Eddy had unloaded that dismal gift on to her National Association, she had followed her inveterate custom: she had tied a string to its hind leg, and kept one end of it hitched to her belt. We have seen her do that in the case of the Boston Mosque. When she deeds property, she puts in that string-clause. It provides that under certain conditions she can pull the string and land the property in the cherished home of its happy youth. In the present case she believed that she had made provision that if at any time the National Christian Science Association should dissolve itself by a formal vote, she could pull.

A year after Nixon's handsome report, she writes the Association that she has a "unique request to lay before it." It has dissolved, and she is not quite sure that the *Christian Science Journal* has "already fallen into her hands" by that act, though it "seems" to her to have met with that accident; so she would like to have the matter decided by a formal vote. But whether there is a doubt or not, "I see the wisdom," she says, "of again owning this Christian Science waif."

I think that that is unassailable evidence that the waif was making money, hands down.

She pulled her gift in. A few years later she donated the Publishing Society, along with its real estate, its buildings, its plant, its publications, and its money—the whole worth twenty-two thousand dollars, and free of debt—to—

Well, *to the Mother-Church!*

That is to say, to herself. There is an account of it in the *Christian Science Journal,* and of how she had already made some other handsome gifts—to her Church—and others to—to her Cause—besides "an almost countless number of private charities" of cloudy amount and otherwise indefinite. This landslide of generosities overwhelmed one of her literary domestics. While he was in that condition he tried to express what he felt:

"Let us endeavor to lift up our hearts in thankfulness to . . . our Mother in Israel for these evidences of generosity and self-sacrifice that appeal to our deepest sense of gratitude, even while surpassing our comprehension."

A year or two later, Mrs. Eddy promulgated some By-laws of a self-sacrificing sort which assuaged him, perhaps, and perhaps enabled his surpassed comprehension to make a sprint and catch up. These are to be found in Art. XII, entitled

THE CHRISTIAN SCIENCE PUBLISHING SOCIETY

This Article puts the whole publishing business into the hands of a publishing Board—special. *Mrs. Eddy appoints to its vacancies.*

The profits go semi-annually to the Treasurer of the Mother-Church. *Mrs. Eddy owns the Treasurer.*

Editors and publishers of the *Christian Science Journal cannot be elected or removed without Mrs. Eddy's knowledge and consent.*

Every candidate for employment in a high capacity or a low one, on the other periodicals or in the publishing house, *must first be "accepted by Mrs. Eddy as suitable."* And "by the Board of Directors"—which is surplusage, since Mrs. Eddy owns the Board.

If at any time a weekly shall be started, *"it shall be owned by The First Church of Christ, Scientist"*—which is Mrs. Eddy.

Chapter 8

I think that any one who will carefully examine the By-laws (I have placed all of the important ones before the reader), will arrive at the conclusion that of late years the master-passion in Mrs. Eddy's heart is a hunger for power and glory; and that while her hunger for money still remains, she wants it now for the expansion and extension it can furnish to that power and glory, rather than what it can do for her towards satisfying minor and meaner ambitions.

I wish to enlarge a little upon this matter. I think it is quite clear that the reason why Mrs. Eddy has concentrated in herself all powers, all distinctions, all revenues that are within the command of the Christian Science Church Universal is that she desires and intends to devote them to the purpose just suggested—the up-building of her personal glory—hers, and no one else's; that, and the continuing of her name's glory after she shall have passed away. *If she has overlooked a single power, howsoever minute, I cannot discover it. If she has found one, large or small, which she has not seized and made her own, there is no record of it, no trace of it.* In her foragings and depredations she usually puts forward the Mother-Church—a lay figure—and hides behind it. Whereas, she is in manifest reality the Mother-Church herself. It has an impressive array of officials, and committees, and Boards of Direction, of Education, of Lectureship, and so on—geldings, every one, shadows, spectres, apparitions, wax-figures: she is supreme over them all, she can abolish them when she will; blow them out as she would a candle. She is herself the Mother-Church. Now there is one By-law which says that the Mother-Church

"shall be officially controlled by no other church."

That does not surprise us—we know by the rest of the By-laws that that is a quite irrelevant remark. Yet we do vaguely and hazily wonder why she takes the trouble to say it; why she wastes the words; what her object can be—seeing that that emergency has been in so many, many ways, and so effectively and drastically barred off and made impossible. Then presently the object begins to dawn upon us. That is, it does after we have read the rest of the By-law three or four times, wondering and admiring to see Mrs. Eddy—Mrs. Eddy—Mrs. Eddy, of all persons—throwing away power!—making a fair exchange—doing a fair thing for once—more, an almost generous thing! Then we look it through yet once more—unsatisfied, a little suspicious—and find that it is nothing but a sly, thin make-believe, and that even the very title of it is a sarcasm and embodies a falsehood—"self" government:

Local Self-Government. The First Church of Christ, Scientist, in Boston, Massachusetts, shall assume no official control of other churches of this denomination. It shall be officially controlled by no other church."

It has a most pious and deceptive give-and-take air of perfect fairness, unselfishness, magnanimity—almost godliness, indeed. But it is all art.

In the By-laws, Mrs. Eddy, speaking by the mouth of her other self, the Mother-Church, proclaims that she will assume no official control of other churches—branch churches. We examine the other By-laws, and they answer some important questions for us:

1. What *is* a branch Church? It is a body of Christian Scientists, organized in the one and only permissible way—by a member, in good standing, of the Mother-Church, and who is also a pupil of one of Mrs. Eddy's accredited students. That is to say, one of her properties. *No other can do it.* There are other indispensable requisites; what are they?

2. The new Church cannot enter upon its functions until its members have individually signed, and pledged allegiance to, a *Creed furnished by Mrs. Eddy.*

3. *They are obliged to study her books, and order their lives by them.* And they must read *no outside religious works.*

4. *They must sing the hymns and pray the prayers provided by her,* and use no others in the services, except by her permission.

5. They cannot have preachers and pastors. *Her law.*

6. In their Church they must have two Readers—a man and a woman.

7. They must read the services framed and appointed by *her.*

8. *She*—not the branch church—*appoints* those Readers.

9. *She*—not the branch Church—*dismisses* them and *fills the vacancies.*

10. She can do this *without consulting the branch Church, and without explaining.*

11. The branch Church can have a religious lecture from time to time. *By applying to Mrs. Eddy.* There is no other way.

12. But the branch Church cannot select the lecturer. *Mrs. Eddy does it.*

13. The branch Church pays his fee.

14. The harnessing of all Christian Science wedding-teams, members of the branch Church, must be done by duly authorized and consecrated Christian Science functionaries. *Her factory is the only one that makes and licenses them.*

[15. Nothing is said about christenings. It is inferable from this that a Christian Science child is born a Christian Scientist and requires no tinkering.]

[16. Nothing is said about funerals. It is inferable, then, that a branch Church is privileged to do in that matter as it may choose.]

To sum up. Are *any* important Church-functions absent from the list? I cannot call any to mind. Are there any lacking ones whose exercise could make the branch in any noticeable way independent of the Mother-Church?—even in any trifling degree? I think of none. If the named functions were abolished would there still be a Church left? Would there be even a shadow of a Church left? Would there be anything at all left?—even the bare *name?*

Manifestly not. There isn't a single vital and essential Church-function of any kind that is not named in the list. And over every one of them the Mother-Church has permanent and unchallengeable control, upon every one of them Mrs. Eddy has set her irremovable grip. *She holds, in perpetuity, autocratic and indisputable sovereignty and control over every branch Church in the earth;* and yet says, in that sugary, naïve, angel-beguiling way of hers, that the Mother-Church

"shall assume no official control of other churches of this denomination."

Whereas in truth the unmeddled-with liberties of a branch Christian Science Church are but very, very few in number, and are these:

1. It can appoint its own furnace-stoker, winters.

2. It can appoint its own fan-distributors, summers.

3. It can, in accordance with its own choice in the matter, burn,

bury, or preserve members who are pretending to be dead—whereas there is no such thing as death.

4. It can take up a collection.

The branch Churches have *no* important liberties, none that give them an important voice in their own affairs. Those are all locked up, and Mrs. Eddy has the key. "Local Self-Government" is a large name and sounds well; but the branch Churches have no more of it than have the privates in the King of Dahomey's army.

"MOTHER-CHURCH UNIQUE"

Mrs. Eddy, with an envious and admiring eye upon the solitary and rivalless and world-shadowing majesty of St. Peter's, reveals in her By-laws her purpose to set the Mother-Church apart by itself in a stately seclusion and make it duplicate that lone sublimity under the Western sky. The By-law headed "Mother-Church Unique" says—

"In its relation to other Christian Science churches, the Mother-Church stands alone.

"It occupies a position that no other Church can fill.

"Then for a branch Church to assume such position would be disastrous to Christian Science.

"Therefore—"

Therefore no branch Church is allowed to have branches. There shall be no Christian Science St. Peter's in the earth but just one—the Mother-Church in Boston.

"NO FIRST MEMBERS"

But for the thoughtful By-law thus entitled, every Science branch in the earth would imitate the Mother-Church and set up an aristocracy. Every little group of ground-floor Smiths and Furgusons and Shadwells and Simpsons that organized a branch would assume that great title, of "First Members," along with its vast privileges of "discussing" the weather and casting blank ballots, and soon there would be such a locust-plague of them burdening the globe that the title would lose its value and have to be abolished.

But where business and glory are concerned, Mrs. Eddy thinks of everything, and so she did not fail to take care of her Aborigines, her stately and exclusive One Hundred, her college of functionless cardinals, her Sanhedrin of Privileged Talkers (Limited). After taking away *all* the liberties of the branch Churches, and in the same breath disclaiming all official control over their affairs, she smites them on the mouth with this—the very mouth that was watering for those nobby ground-floor honors—

"*No First Members.* Branch Churches shall not organize with First Members, that special method of organization being adapted to the Mother-Church alone."

And so, first members being prohibited, we pierce through the cloud of Mrs. Eddy's English and perceive that they must then necessarily organize with Subsequent Members. There is no other way. It will occur to them by-and-by to found an aristocracy of Early Subsequent Members. There is no By-law against it.

"THE"

I uncover to that imperial word. And to the mind, too, that conceived the idea of seizing and monopolizing it as a title. I believe it is Mrs. Eddy's dazzlingest invention. For show, and style, and grandeur, and thunder and lightning and fireworks it outclasses all the previous inventions of man, and raises the limit on the Pope. He can never put his avid hand on that word of words—it is pre-empted. And copyrighted, of course. It lifts the Mother-Church away up in the sky, and fellowships it with the rare and select and exclusive little company of the THE's of deathless glory—persons and things whereof history and the ages could furnish only single examples, not two: *the* Saviour, *the* Virgin, *the* Milky Way, *the* Bible, *the* Earth, *the* Equator, *the* Devil, *the* Missing Link—and now *The* First Church, Scientist. And by clamor of edict and By-law Mrs. Eddy gives personal notice to all branch Scientist Churches on this planet to leave that THE alone.

She has demonstrated over it and made it sacred to the Mother-Church:

"*The article 'The' must not be used before the titles of branch Churches—*

"Nor written on applications for membership in naming such churches."

Those are the terms. There can and will be a million First Churches of Christ, Scientist, scattered over the world, in a million towns and villages and hamlets and cities, and each may call itself (suppressing the article), "First Church of Christ, Scientist"—it is permissible, and no harm; but there is only one *The* Church of Christ, Scientist, and there will never be another. And whether that great word fall in the middle of a sentence or at the beginning of it, it must always have its capital T.

I do not suppose that a juvenile passion for fussy little worldly shows and vanities can furnish a match to this, anywhere in the history of the nursery. Mrs. Eddy does seem to be a shade fonder of little special distinctions and pomps than is usual with human beings.

She instituted that immodest "The" with her own hand, she did not wait for somebody else to think of it.

A LIFE-TERM MONOPOLY

There is but *one* human Pastor in the whole Christian Science world; she reserves that exalted place to herself.

A PERPETUAL ONE

There is but *one other* object in the whole Christian Science world honored with that title and holding that office: it is her *book,* the Annex—*permanent Pastor of The First Church, and of all branch Churches.*

With her own hand she draughted the By-laws which make her the only really absolute sovereign that lives today in Christendom.[1]

She does not allow any objectionable pictures to be exhibited in the room where her book is sold, nor any indulgence in idle gossip there; and from the general look of that By-law I judge that a lightsome and improper person can be as uncomfortable in that place as he could be in heaven.

THE SANCTUM SANCTORUM AND SACRED CHAIR

In a room in The First Church of Christ, Scientist, there is a museum of objects which have attained to holiness through contact

[1] Even that ideal representative of irresponsible power, the General of the Jesuits, is not in the running with Mrs. Eddy. He is authentically described as follows:

"The Society of Jesus has really but one head, the General. He must be a professed Jesuit of the four vows, and it is the professed Jesuits of the four vows only who take part in his election, which is by secret ballot. He has four 'assistants' to help him, and an 'admonisher,' elected in the same way as himself, to keep him in, or, if need be, to bring him back to the right path. The electors of the General have the right of *deposing* him if he is guilty of a serious fault."

with Mrs. Eddy—among them an electrically lighted oil-picture of a *chair* which she used to sit in—and disciples from all about the world go softly in there, in restricted groups, under proper guard, and reverently gaze upon those relics. It is worship. Mrs. Eddy could stop it if she was not fond of it, for her sovereignty over that temple is supreme.

The fitting-up of that place as a shrine is not an accident, nor a casual, unweighed idea; it is imitated from age-old religious custom. In Treves the pilgrim reverently gazes upon the Seamless Robe, and humbly worships; and does the same in that other continental church where they keep a duplicate; and does likewise in the Church of the Holy Sepulchre, in Jerusalem, where memorials of the Crucifixion are preserved; and now, by good fortune, we have our Holy Chair and things, and a market for our adorations nearer home.

But is there not a detail that is new, fresh, original? Yes, whatever old thing Mrs. Eddy touches gets something new by the contact—something not thought of before by any one—something original, all her own, and copyrightable. The new feature is *self* worship—exhibited in permitting this shrine to be installed during her lifetime, and winking her sacred eye at it.

A prominent Christian Scientist has assured me that the Scientists do not worship Mrs. Eddy, and I think it likely that there may be five or six of the cult in the world who do not worship her; but she herself is certainly not of that company. Any healthy-minded person who will examine Mrs. Eddy's little *Autobiography* and the Manual of By-laws written by her will be convinced that she worships herself; and that she brings to this service a fervor of devotion surpassing even that which she formerly laid at the feet of the Dollar, and equalling any which rises to the Throne of Grace from any quarter.

I think this is as good a place as any to salve a hurt which I was the means of inflicting upon a Christian Scientist lately. The first third of this book was written in 1899 in Vienna. Until last summer I had supposed that that third had been printed in a book which I published about a year later—a hap which had not happened. I then sent the chapters composing it to the *North American Review,* but failed, in one instance, to date them. And so, in an undated chapter I said a lady told me "last night" so and so. There was nothing to indicate to the reader that that "last night" was several years old, therefore the phrase seemed to refer to a night of very recent date.

What the lady had told me was, that in a part of the Mother-Church in Boston she had seen Scientists worshipping a portrait of Mrs. Eddy before which a light was kept constantly burning.

A Scientist came to me and wished me to retract that "untruth." He said there was no such portrait, and that if I wanted to be sure of it I could go to Boston and see for myself. I explained that my "last night" meant a good while ago; that I did not doubt his assertion that there was no such portrait there now, but that I should continue to believe it had been there at the time of the lady's visit until she should retract her statement herself. I was at no time vouching for the truth of the remark, nevertheless I considered it worth par.

And yet I am sorry the lady told me, since a wound which brings me no happiness has resulted. I am most willing to apply such salve as I can. The best way to set the matter right and make everything pleasant and agreeable all around will be to print in this place a description of the shrine as it appeared to a recent visitor, Mr. Frederick W. Peabody, of Boston. I will copy his newspaper account, and the reader will see that Mrs. Eddy's portrait is not there now:

"We lately stood on the threshold of the Holy of Holies of the Mother-Church, and with a crowd of worshippers patiently waited for admittance to the hallowed precincts of the 'Mother's Room.' Over the doorway was a sign informing us that but four persons at a time would be admitted; that they would be permitted to remain but five minutes only, and would please retire from the 'Mother's Room' at the ringing of the bell. Entering with three of the faithful, we looked with profane eyes upon the consecrated furnishings. A show-woman in attendance monotonously announced the character of the different appointments. Set in a recess of the wall and illumined with electric light was an oil-painting the show-woman seriously declared to be a lifelike and realistic picture of the Chair in which the Mother sat when she composed her 'inspired' work. It was a picture of an old-fashioned, country, hair-cloth rocking-chair, and an exceedingly commonplace-looking table with a pile of manuscript, an ink-bottle, and pen conspicuously upon it. On the floor were sheets of manuscript. 'The mantel-piece is of pure onyx,' continued the show-woman, 'and the beehive upon the window-sill is made from one solid block of onyx; the rug is made of a hundred breasts of eider-down ducks, and the toilet-room you see in the corner is of the latest design, with gold-plated drain-pipes; the painted windows are from the Mother's poem, "Christ and Christmas," and that case contains complete copies of all the Mother's books.' The chairs upon which the sacred person of the Mother had reposed were protected from sacrilegious touch by a broad band of satin ribbon. My companions expressed their admiration in subdued and reverent tones, and at the tinkling of the bell we reverently tiptoed out of the room to admit another delegation of the patient waiters at the door."

Now, then, I hope the wound is healed. I am willing to relinquish the portrait, and compromise on the Chair. At the same time, if I were going to worship either, I should not choose the Chair.

As a picturesquely and persistently interesting personage, there is no mate to Mrs. Eddy, the accepted Equal of the Saviour. But some of her tastes are so different from His! I find it quite impossible to imagine Him, in life, standing sponsor for that museum there, and taking pleasure in its sumptuous shows. I believe He would put that Chair in the fire, and the bell along with it; and I think He would make the show-woman go away. I think He would break those electric bulbs, and the "Mantel-piece of pure onyx," and say reproachful things about the golden drain-pipes of the lavatory, and give the costly rug of duck-breasts to the poor, and sever the satin ribbon and invite the weary to rest and ease their aches in the consecrated chairs. What He would do with the painted windows we can better conjecture when we come presently to examine their peculiarities.

THE CHRISTIAN SCIENCE PASTOR-UNIVERSAL

When Mrs. Eddy turned the pastors out of all the Christian Science churches and abolished the office for all time—as far as human occupancy is concerned—she appointed the Holy Ghost to fill their place. If this language be blasphemous, I did not invent the blasphemy, I am merely stating a fact. I will quote from page 227 of *Science and Health* (edition 1899), as a first step towards an explanation of this startling matter—a passage which sets forth and classifies the Christian Science Trinity:

"Life, Truth, and Love constitute the triune God, or triply divine Principle. They represent a trinity in unity, three in one—the same in essence, though multiform in office: God the Father; Christ the type of Sonship; Divine Science, or the Holy Comforter. . . .

"The *Holy Ghost,* or Spirit, *reveals* this triune Principle, and *(the Holy Ghost)* is expressed in *Divine Science,* which is *the Comforter,* leading into all Truth, and revealing the divine Principle of the universe—universal and perpetual harmony."

I will cite another passage. Speaking of Jesus—

"His students then *received the Holy Ghost.* By this is meant, that by all they had witnessed and suffered they were roused to an enlarged *understanding of Divine Science,* even to the *spiritual interpretation . . . of His teachings,"* etc.

Also, page 579, in the chapter called the Glossary.

"HOLY GHOST. *Divine Science;* the developments of Life, Truth, and Love."

The Holy Ghost *reveals* the massed spirit of the fused trinity; this massed spirit is *expressed* in Divine Science, and is the *Comforter;* Divine Science *conveys* to men the *"spiritual interpretation"* of the Saviour's teachings. That seems to be the meaning of the quoted passages.

Divine Science is Christian Science; the book *Science and Health* is a *"revelation"* of the whole spirit of the Trinity, and is therefore *"The Holy Ghost";* it conveys to men the *"spiritual interpretation"* of the Bible's teachings, and therefore is "the *Comforter."*

I do not find this analyzing work easy, I would rather saw wood; and a person can never tell whether he has added up a *Science and Health* sum right or not, anyway, after all his trouble. Neither can he easily find out whether the texts are still on the market or have been discarded from the Book; for two hundred and fifty-eight editions of it have been issued, and no two editions seem to be alike. The annual changes—in technical terminology; in matter and wording; in transpositions of chapters and verses; in leaving out old chapters and verses and putting in new ones—seem to be next to innumerable, and as there is no index, there is no way to find a thing one wants without reading the book through. If ever I inspire a Bible-Annex I will not rush at it in a half-digested, helter-skelter way and have to put in thirty-eight years trying to get some of it the way I want it, I will sit down and think it out and know what it is I want to say before I begin. An inspirer cannot inspire for Mrs. Eddy and keep his reputation. I have never seen such slipshod work, bar the ten that interpreted for the home market the "sell all thou hast." I have quoted one "spiritual" rendering of the Lord's Prayer, I have seen one other one, and am told there are five more.[2] Yet the inspirer of Mrs. Eddy the new Infallible casts a complacent critical stone at the other Infallible for being unable to make up its mind about such things. *Science and Health,* edition 1899, page 33:

"The decisions, by vote of Church Councils, as to what should and should not be considered Holy Writ, the manifest mistakes in the ancient versions: the thirty thousand different readings in the Old Testament and the three hundred thousand in the New—these facts show how a mortal and material sense stole into the divine record, darkening, to some extent, the inspired pages with its own hue."

To some extent, yes—speaking cautiously. But it is nothing, really nothing; Mrs. Eddy is only a little way behind, and if her inspirer lives to get her Annex to suit him that Catholic record will have to "go 'way back and set down," as the ballad says. Listen to the boastful song of Mrs. Eddy's organ, the *Christian Science Journal* for March, 1902, about that year's revamping and half-soling of *Science and Health,* whose official name is the Holy Ghost, the Comforter, and who is now the Official Pastor and Infallible and Unerring Guide of every Christian Science church in the two hemispheres, hear Simple Simon that met the pieman brag of the Infallible's fallibility:

"Throughout the entire book the verbal changes are so numerous as to indicate the vast amount of time and labor Mrs. Eddy has devoted to this revision. The time and labor thus bestowed is relatively as great as that of the committee who revised the Bible. . . . Thus we have additional evidence of the herculean efforts our beloved Leader has made and is constantly making for the promulgation of Truth and the furtherance of her divinely bestowed mission," etc.

It is a steady job. I could help inspire if desired; I am not doing much now, and would work for half-price, and should not object to the country.

PRICE OF THE PASTOR-UNIVERSAL

The price of the Pastor-Universal, *Science and Health,* called in Science literature the Comforter—and by that other sacred Name— is three dollars in cloth, as heretofore, six when it is finely bound, and shaped to imitate the Testament, and is broken into verses. Mar-

[2] See a second rendering in Appendix. (Lord's Prayer.)—M.T.

gin of profit above cost of manufacture, from five hundred to seven hundred per cent, as already noted. In the profane subscription-trade, it costs the publisher heavily to canvass a three-dollar book; he must pay the general agent *sixty percent* commission—that is to say, one dollar and eighty cents. Mrs. Eddy escapes this blistering tax, because she owns the Christian Science canvasser, and can compel him to work for nothing. Read the following *command*—not request —fulminated by Mrs. Eddy, over her signature, in the *Christian Science Journal* for March, 1897, and quoted by Mr. Peabody in his book. The book referred to is *Science and Health:*

"It shall be the duty of all Christian Scientists to circulate and to sell as many of these books as they can."

That is flung at all the elect, everywhere that the sun shines, but no penalty is shaken over their heads to scare them. The same command was issued to the members (numbering today twenty-five thousand) of The Mother-Church, also, but with it went a *threat*, of the inflic-tion, in case of disobedience, of the most dreaded punishment that has a place in the Church's list of penalties for transgressions of Mrs. Eddy's edicts—excommunication:

"If a member of The First Church of Christ, Scientist, shall fail to obey this injunction, it will render him liable to lose his membership in this Church.   *Mary Baker Eddy."*

It is the spirit of the Spanish Inquisition.

None but accepted and well-established *gods* can venture an af-front like that and do it with confidence. But the human race will take anything from that class. Mrs. Eddy knows the human race; knows it better than any mere human being has known it in a thou-sand centuries. My confidence in her human-beingship is getting shaken, my confidence in her godship is stiffening.

SEVEN HUNDRED PER CENT

A Scientist out West has visited a bookseller—with intent to find fault with me—and has brought away the information that the price at which Mrs. Eddy sells *Science and Health* is not an unusually high one for the size and make of the book. That is true. But in the book-trade—that profit-devourer unknown to Mrs. Eddy's book—a three-dollar book that is made for thirty-five or forty cents in large editions is put at three dollars because the publisher has to pay author, mid-dleman, and advertising, and if the price were much below three the profit accruing would not pay him fairly for his time and labor. At the same time, if he could get ten dollars for the book he would take it, and his morals would not fall under criticism.

But if he were an inspired person commissioned by the Deity to receive and print and spread broadcast among sorrowing and suffering and poor men a precious message of healing and cheer and salvation, he would have to do as Bible Societies do—sell the book at a pinched margin above cost to such as could pay, and give it free to all that couldn't; and his name would be praised. But if he sold it at seven hundred per cent profit and put the money in his pocket, his name would be mocked and derided. Just as Mrs. Eddy's is. And most justifiably, as it seems to me.

The complete Bible contains one million words. The New Testament by itself contains two hundred and forty thousand words.

My '84 edition of *Science and Health* contains one hundred and twenty thousand words—just half as many as the New Testament.

Science and Health has since been so inflated by later inspirations that the 1902 edition contains one hundred and eighty thousand words—not counting the thirty thousand at the back, devoted by Mrs. Eddy to advertising the book's healing abilities—and the inspiring continues right along.

If you have a book whose market is so sure and so great that you can give a printer an everlasting order for thirty or forty or fifty thousand copies a year he will furnish them at a cheap rate, because whenever there is a slack time in his press-room and bindery he can fill the idle intervals on your book and be making something instead of losing. That is the kind of contract that can be let on *Science and Health* every year. I am obliged to doubt that the three-dollar *Science and Health* costs Mrs. Eddy above fifteen cents, or that the six-dollar copy costs her above eighty cents. I feel quite sure that the average profit to her on these books, above cost of manufacture, is all of seven hundred per cent.

Every proper Christian Scientist has to buy and own (and canvass for) *Science and Health* (one hundred and eighty thousand words), and he must also own a Bible (one million words). He can buy the one for from three to six dollars, and the other for fifteen cents. Or, if three dollars is all the money he has, he can get his Bible for *nothing*. When the Supreme Being disseminates a saving Message through uninspired agents—the New Testament, for instance—it can be done for five cents a copy; but when He sends one containing only two-thirds as many words through the shop of a Divine Personage, it costs *sixty times as much.* I think that in matters of such importance it is bad economy to employ a wild-cat agency.

Here are some figures which are perfectly authentic, and which seem to justify my opinion:

"These [Bible] societies, inspired only by a sense of religious duty, are issuing the Bible at a price so small that they have made it *the cheapest book printed.* For example, the American Bible Society offers an edition of *the whole Bible as low as fifteen cents* and the *New Testament at five cents,* and the British Society at *six-pence and one penny, respectively.* These low prices, made possible by their policy of selling the books *at cost or below cost,*" etc.—*New York Sun,* February 25, 1903.

Chapter 9

We may now make a final footing-up of Mrs. Eddy, and see what she is, in the fulness of her powers. She is

The Massachusetts Metaphysical College;
Pastor Emeritus;
President;
Board of Directors;
Board of Education;
Board of Lectureships;
Future Board of Trustees;
Proprietor of the Publishing-House and Periodicals;
Treasurer;
Clerk;
Proprietor of the Teachers;
Proprietor of the Lecturers;
Proprietor of the Missionaries;
Proprietor of the Readers;
Dictator of the Services: sole Voice of the Pulpit;
Proprietor of the Sanhedrin;
Sole Proprietor of the Creed (Copyrighted)
Indisputable Autocrat of the Branch Churches, with their life and death in her hands;

Sole Thinker for The First Church (and the others);

Sole and Infallible Expounder of Doctrine, in life and in death;

Sole permissible Discoverer, Denouncer, Judge, and Executioner of Ostensible Hypnotists;

Fifty-handed God of Excommunication—with a thunderbolt in every hand;

Appointer and Installer of the Pastor of all the Churches—the Perpetual Pastor-Universal, *Science and Health*, "the Comforter."

Chapter 10

There she stands—painted by herself. No witness but herself has been allowed to testify. She stands there painted by her *acts,* and decorated by her words. When she talks, she has only a decorative value as a witness, either for or against herself, for she deals mainly in unsupported assertion; and in the rare cases where she puts forward a verifiable fact she gets out of it a meaning which it refuses to furnish to anybody else. Also, when she talks, she is unstable; she wanders, she is incurably inconsistent; what she says today she contradicts tomorrow.

But her *acts* are consistent. They are always faithful to her, they never misinterpret her, they are a mirror which always reflects her exactly, precisely, minutely, unerringly, and always the same, to date, with only those progressive little natural changes in stature, dress, complexion, mood, and carriage that mark—exteriorly—the march of the years and record the accumulations of experience, while—interiorly—through all this steady drift of evolution the one essential detail, the commanding detail, the master detail of the make-up remains as it was in the beginning, suffers no change and *can* suffer none; the *basis* of the character; the temperament, the disposition, that indestructible iron framework upon which the character is *built,* and whose shape it must take, and keep, throughout life. We call it a person's *nature.*

The man who is born stingy can be taught to give liberally—with his hands; but not with his heart. The man born kind and compassionate can have that disposition crushed down out of sight by embittering experience; but if it were an organ the post-mortem would find it still in his corpse. The man born ambitious of power and glory may live long without finding it out, but when the opportunity comes he will know, will strike for the largest thing within the limit of his chances at the time—constable, perhaps—and will be glad and proud when he gets it, and will write home about it. But he will not stop with that start; his appetite will come again; and by-and-by again, and yet again; and when he has climbed to police commissioner it will at last begin to dawn upon him that what his Napoleon soul wants and was born for is something away higher up—he does not quite know what, but Circumstance and Opportunity will indicate the direction and he will cut a road through and find out.

I think Mrs. Eddy was born with a far-seeing business-eye, but did not know it; and with a great organizing and executive talent, and did not know it; and with a large appetite for power and distinction, and did not know it. I think the reason that her make did not show up until middle life was that she had General Grant's luck—Circumstance and Opportunity did not come her way when she was younger. The qualities that were born in her had to wait for circumstance and opportunity—but they were there: they were there to stay, whether they ever got a chance to fructify or not. If they had come early, they would have found her ready and competent. And they—not she—would have determined what they would set her at and what they would make of her. If they had elected to commission her as second-assistant cook in a bankrupt boarding-house, I know the rest of it—I know what would have happened. She would have owned the boarding-house within six months; she would have had the late proprietor on salary and humping himself, as the worldly say; she would have had that boarding-house spewing money like a mint; she would have worked the servants and the late landlord up to the limit; she would have squeezed the boarders till they wailed, and by some mysterious quality born in her she would have kept the affections of certain of the lot whose love and esteem she valued, and flung the others down the back area; in two years she would own all the boarding-houses in the town, in five all the boarding-houses in the State, in twenty all the hotels in America, in forty all the hotels on the planet, and would sit at home with her finger on a button and govern the whole combination as easily as a bench-manager governs a dog-show.

It would be a grand thing to see, and I feel a kind of disappointment—but never mind, a religion is better and larger; and there is more *to* it. And I have not been steeping myself in Christian Science all these weeks without finding out that the one sensible thing to do with a disappointment is to put it out of your mind and think of something cheerfuler.

We outsiders cannot conceive of Mrs. Eddy's Christian Science Religion as being a sudden and miraculous birth, but only as a growth from a seed planted by circumstances, and developed stage by stage by command and compulsion of the same force. What the stages were we cannot know, but are privileged to guess. She may have gotten the mental-healing idea from Quimby—it had been experimented with for ages, and was no one's special property. [For the present, for convenience's sake, let us proceed upon the hypothesis that that was *all* she got of him, and that she put up the rest of the assets herself. This will strain us, but let us try it.] In each and all its forms and under all its many names, mental healing had had limits, always, and they were rather narrow ones—Mrs. Eddy, let us imagine, removed the fence, abolished the frontiers. Not by expanding mental-healing, but by absorbing its small bulk into the vaster bulk of Christian Science—Divine Science, The Holy Ghost, the Comforter—which was a quite different and sublimer force, and one which had long lain dormant and unemployed.

The Christian Scientist believes that the Spirit of God (life and love) pervades the universe like an atmosphere; that whoso will study *Science and Health* can get from it the secret of how to inhale that transforming air; that to breathe it is to be made new; that from the new man all sorrow, all care, all miseries of the mind vanish away, for that only peace, contentment and measureless joy can live in that divine fluid; that it purifies the body from disease, which is a vicious creation of the gross human mind, and cannot continue to exist in the presence of the Immortal Mind, the renewing Spirit of God.

The Scientist finds this reasonable, natural, and not harder to believe than that the disease-germ, a creature of darkness, perishes when exposed to the light of the great sun—a new revelation of profane science which no one doubts. He reminds us that the actinic ray, shining upon lupus, cures it—a horrible disease which was incurable fifteen years ago, and had been incurable for ten million years before; that this wonder, unbelievable by the physicians at first, is believed by them now; and so he is tranquilly confident that the time is coming when the world will be educated up to a point where it will comprehend and grant that the light of the Spirit of God, shining unobstructed upon the soul, is an actinic ray which can purge both mind and body from disease and set them free and make them whole.

It is apparent, then, that in Christian Science it is not one man's mind acting upon another man's mind that heals; that it is solely the Spirit of God that heals; that the healer's mind performs no office but to convey that force to the patient; that it is merely the wire which carries the electric fluid, so to speak, and delivers the message. Therefore, if these things be true, mental-healing and Science-healing are separate and distinct processes, and no kinship exists between them.

To heal the body of its ills and pains is a mighty benefaction, but in our day our physicians and surgeons work a thousand miracles—prodigies which would have ranked as miracles fifty years ago—and they have so greatly extended their domination over disease that we feel so well protected that we are able to look with a good deal of composure and absence of hysterics upon the claims of new competitors in that field.

But there is a mightier benefaction than the healing of the body, and that is the healing of the spirit—which is Christian Science's other claim. So far as I know, so far as I can find out, it makes it good. Personally I have not known a Scientist who did not seem serene, contented, unharassed. I have not found an outsider whose observation of Scientists furnished him a view that differed from my own. Buoyant spirits, comfort of mind, freedom from care—these happinesses we all have, at intervals; but in the spaces between, dear me, the black hours! They have put a curse upon the life of every human being I have ever known, young or old. I concede not a single exception. Unless it might be those Scientists just referred to. They may have been playing a part with me; I hope they were not, and I believe they were not.

Time will test the Science's claim. If time shall make it good; if time shall prove that the Science can heal the persecuted spirit of man and banish its troubles and keep it serene and sunny and content—why, then Mrs. Eddy will have a monument that will reach above the clouds. For if she did not hit upon that imperial idea and evolve it and deliver it, its discoverer can never be identified with certainty, now, I think. It is the giant feature, it is the sun that rides in the zenith of Christian Science; the auxiliary features are of minor consequence. [Let us still leave the large "if" aside, for the present, and proceed as if it had no existence.]

It is not supposable that Mrs. Eddy realized, at first, the size of her plunder. (No, *find*—that is the word; she did not realize the size of her find, at first.) It had to grow upon her, by degrees, in accordance with the inalterable custom of Circumstance, which works by stages, and by stages only, and never furnishes any mind with all the materials for a large idea at one time.

In the beginning, Mrs. Eddy was probably interested merely in the mental-healing detail. And perhaps mainly interested in it pecuniarily, for she was poor.

She would succeed in anything she undertook. She would attract pupils, and her commerce would grow. She would inspire in patient and pupil confidence in her earnestness; her history is evidence that she would not fail of that.

There probably came a time, in due course, when her students began to think there was something deeper in her teachings than they had been suspecting—a mystery beyond mental-healing, and higher. It is conceivable that by consequence their manner towards her changed little by little, and from respectful became reverent. It is conceivable that this would have an influence upon her; that it would incline her to wonder if their secret thought—that she was inspired—might not be a well-grounded guess. It is conceivable that as time went on the thought in their minds and its reflection in hers might solidify into conviction.

She would remember, then, that as a child she had been called, more than once, by a mysterious voice—just as had happened to little Samuel. (Mentioned in her *Autobiography.*) She would be impressed by that ancient reminiscence, now, and it could have a prophetic meaning for her.

It is conceivable that the persuasive influences around her and within her would give a new and powerful impulse to her philosophizings, and that from this, in time, would result that great birth, the healing of body and mind by the inpouring of the Spirit of God—the central and dominant idea of Christian Science—and that when this idea came she would not doubt that it was an inspiration direct from Heaven.

Chapter 11

[I must rest a little, now. To sit here and painstakingly spin out a scheme which imagines Mrs. Eddy, of all people, working her mind on a plane above commercialism; imagines her thinking, philosophizing, discovering majestic things; and even imagines her dealing in sincerities—to be frank, I find it a large contract. But I have begun it, and I will go through with it.]

Chapter 12

It is evident that she made disciples fast, and that their belief in her and in the authenticity of her heavenly ambassadorship was not of the lukewarm and half-way sort, but was profoundly earnest and sincere. Her book was issued from the press in 1875, it began its work of convert-making, and within six years she had successfully launched a new Religion and a new system of healing, and was teaching them to crowds of eager students in a College of her own, at prices so extraordinary that we are almost compelled to accept her statement (no, her guarded intimation) that the rates were arranged on high, since a mere human being unacquainted with commerce and accustomed to think in pennies could hardly put up such a hand as that without supernatural help.

From this stage onward—Mrs. Eddy being what she was—the rest of the development-stages would follow naturally and inevitably. But if she had been anybody else, there would have been a different arrangement of them, with different results. Being the extraordinary person she was, she realized her position and its possibilities; realized the possibilities, and had the daring to use them for all they were worth.

We have seen what her methods were after she passed the stage where her divine ambassadorship was granted its exequatur in the hearts and minds of her followers; we have seen how steady and fearless and calculated and orderly was her march thenceforth from conquest to conquest; we have seen her strike dead, without hesitancy, any hostile or questionable force that rose in her path: first, the horde of pretenders that sprang up and tried to take her Science and its market away from her—she crushed them, she obliterated them: when her own National Christian Science Association became great in numbers and influence, and loosely and dangerously garrulous, and began to expound the doctrines according to its own uninspired notions, she took up her sponge without a tremor of fear and wiped that Association out; when she perceived that the preachers in her pulpits were becoming afflicted with doctrine-tinkering, she recognized the danger of it, and did not hesitate nor temporize, but promptly dismissed the whole of them in a day, and abolished their office permanently; we have seen that, as fast as her power grew, she was competent to take the measure of it, and that as fast as its expansion suggested to her gradually awakening native ambition a higher step she took it; and so, by this evolutionary process, we have seen the gross money-lust relegated to second place, and the lust of empire and glory rise above it. A splendid dream; and by force of the qualities born in her she is making it come true.

These qualities—and the capacities growing out of them by the nurturing influences of training, observation, and experience—seem to be clearly indicated by the character of her career and its achievements. They seem to be:

A clear head for business, and a phenomenally long one;

Clear understanding of business situations;

Accuracy in estimating the opportunities they offer;

Intelligence in planning a business move;

Firmness in sticking to it after it has been decided upon;

Extraordinary daring;

Indestructible persistency;

Devouring ambition;

Limitless selfishness;

A knowledge of the weaknesses and poverties and docilities of human nature and how to turn them to account which has never been surpassed, if ever equalled;

And—necessarily—the foundation-stone of Mrs. Eddy's character is a never-wavering confidence in herself.

It is a granite character. And—quite naturally—a measure of the talc of smallnesses common to human nature is mixed up in it and distributed through it. When Mrs. Eddy is not dictating servilities from her throne in the clouds to her official domestics in Boston or to her far-spread subjects round about the planet, but is down on the ground, she is kin to us and one of us: sentimental as a girl, garrulous, ungrammatical, incomprehensible, affected, vain of her little human ancestry, unstable, inconsistent, unreliable in statement, and naïvely and everlastingly self-contradictory—oh, trivial and common and commonplace as the commonest of us! just a Napoleon as Madame de Rémusat saw him, a brass god with clay legs.

Chapter 13

In drawing Mrs. Eddy's portrait it has been my purpose to restrict myself to materials furnished by *herself,* and I believe I have done that. If I have misinterpreted any of her acts, it was not done intentionally.

It will be noticed that in skeletonizing a list of the qualities which have carried her to the dizzy summit which she occupies, I have not mentioned the power which was the commanding force employed in achieving that lofty flight. It did not belong in that list; it was a force that was not a detail of her character, but was an outside one. It was the power which proceeded from her people's recognition of her as a supernatural personage, conveyer of the Latest Word, and divinely commissioned to deliver it to the world. The form which such a recognition takes, consciously or unconsciously, is *worship;* and worship does not question nor criticise, it obeys. The object of it does not need to coddle it, bribe it, beguile it, reason with it, convince it—it commands it; that is sufficient; the obedience rendered is not reluctant, but prompt and whole-hearted. Admiration for a Napoleon, confidence in him, pride in him, affection for him, can lift him high and carry him far; and these are forms of worship, and are strong forces, but they are worship of a mere human being, after all, and are infinitely feeble, as compared with those that are generated by that other worship, the worship of a divine personage. Mrs. Eddy has this efficient worship, this massed and centralized force, this force which is indifferent to opposition, untroubled by fear, and goes to battle singing, like Cromwell's soldiers; and while she has it she can command and it will obey, and maintain her on her throne, and extend her empire.

She will have it until she dies; and then we shall see a curious and interesting further development of her revolutionary work begin.

Chapter 14

The President and Board of Directors will succeed her, and the government will go on without a hitch. The By-laws will bear that interpretation. All the Mother-Church's vast powers are concentrated in that Board. Mrs. Eddy's unlimited personal reservations make the Board's ostensible supremacy, during her life, a sham, and the Board itself a shadow. But Mrs. Eddy has not made those reservations for any one but herself—they are distinctly personal, they bear her name, they are not usable by another individual. When she dies her reservations die, and the Board's shadow-powers become real powers, without the change of any important By-law, and the Board sits in her place as absolute and irresponsible a sovereign as she was.

It consists of but five persons, a much more manageable Cardinalate than the Roman Pope's. I think it will elect its Pope from its own body, and that it will fill its own vacancies. An elective Papacy is a safe and wise system, and a long-liver.

Chapter 15

We may take that up now.

It is not a single if, but a several-jointed on; not an oyster, but a vertebrate.

1. Did Mrs. Eddy borrow from Quimby the Great Idea, or only the little one, the old-timer, the ordinary mental-healing—healing by "mortal" mind?

2. If she borrowed the Great Idea, did she carry it away in her head, or in manuscript?

3. Did she hit upon the Great Idea herself?

By the Great Idea I mean, of course, the conviction that the Force involved was still existent, and could be applied now just as it was applied by Christ's Disciples and their converts, and as successfully.

4. Did she philosophize it, systematize it, and write it down in a book?

5. Was it she, and not another, that built a new Religion upon the book and organized it?

I think No. 5 can be answered with a Yes, and dismissed from the controversy. And I think that the Great Idea, great as it was, would have enjoyed but a brief activity, and would then have gone to sleep again for some more centuries, but for the perpetuating impulse it got from that organized and tremendous force.

As for Nos. 1, 2, and 4, the hostiles contend that Mrs. Eddy got the Great Idea from Quimby and carried it off in manuscript. But their testimony, while of consequence, lacks the most important detail; so far as my information goes, the Quimby manuscript has not been produced. I think we cannot discuss No. 1 and No. 2 profitably. Let them go.

For me, No. 3 has a mild interest, and No. 4 a violent one.

As regards No. 3, Mrs. Eddy was brought up, from the cradle, an old-time, boiler-iron, Westminster-Catechism Christian, and knew her Bible as well as Captain Kydd knew his, "when he sailed, when he sailed," and perhaps as sympathetically. The Great Idea had struck a million Bible-readers before her as being possible of resurrection and application—it must have struck as many as that, and been cogitated, indolently, doubtingly, then dropped and forgotten—and it could have struck *her*, in due course. But how it could *interest* her, how it could appeal to her—with her make—is a thing that is difficult to understand.

For the thing back of it is wholly gracious and beautiful: the power, through loving mercifulness and compassion, to heal fleshly ills and pains and griefs—*all*—with a word, with a touch of the hand! This power was given by the Saviour to the Disciples, and to *all* the converted. All—every one. It was *exercised* for generations afterwards. Any Christian who was in earnest and not a make-believe, not a policy-Christian, not a Christian for revenue only, had that healing power, and could cure with it *any disease or any hurt or damage possible to human flesh and bone.* These things are true, or they are not. If they were true seventeen and eighteen and nineteen centuries ago it would be difficult to satisfactorily explain why or how or by what argument that power should be non-existent in Christians now.[1]

[1] See Appendix.—M.T.

To wish to exercise it could occur to Mrs. Eddy—but would it?

Grasping, sordid, penurious, famishing for everything she sees—money, power, glory—vain, untruthful, jealous, despotic, arrogant, insolent, pitiless where thinkers and hypnotists are concerned, illiterate, shallow, incapable of reasoning outside of commercial lines, immeasurably selfish—

Of course the Great Idea *could* strike her, we have to grant that, but why it should *interest* her is a question which can easily overstrain the imagination and bring on nervous prostration, or something like that, and is better left alone by the judicious, it seems to me—

Unless we call to our help the alleged other side of Mrs. Eddy's make and character—the side which her multitude of followers see, and sincerely believe in. Fairness requires that their view be stated here. It is the opposite of the one which I have drawn from Mrs. Eddy's history and from her By-laws. To her followers she is this:

Patient, gentle, loving, compassionate, noble-hearted, unselfish, sinless, widely cultured, splendidly equipped mentally, a profound thinker, an able writer, a divine personage, an inspired messenger whose acts are dictated from the Throne, and whose every utterance is the Voice of God.

She has delivered to them a religion which has revolutionized their lives, banished the glooms that shadowed them, and filled them and flooded them with sunshine and gladness and peace; a religion which has no hell; a religion whose heaven is not put off to another time, with a break and a gulf between, but begins here and now, and melts into eternity as fancies of the waking day melt into the dreams of sleep.

They believe it is a Christianity that is in the New Testament; that it has always been there; that in the drift of ages it was lost through disuse and neglect, and that this benefactor has found it and given it back to men, turning the night of life into day, its terrors into myths, its lamentations into songs of emancipation and rejoicing.[2]

There we have Mrs. Eddy as her followers see her. She has lifted them out of grief and care and doubt and fear, and made their lives beautiful; she found them wandering forlorn in a wintry wilderness,

---

[1] For a clear understanding of the two claims of Christian Science, read the novel *The Life Within*, published by Lothrops, Boston.—M.T.

and has led them to a tropic paradise like that of which the poet sings:

> *"O, islands there are on the face of the deep*
> *Where the leaves never fade and the skies never*
> *weep."*

To ask them to examine with a microscope the character of such a benefactor; to ask them to examine it at all; to ask them to look at a blemish which another person believes he has found in it—well, in their place could you do it? Would you do it? Wouldn't you be ashamed to do it? If a tramp had rescued your child from fire and death, and saved its mother's heart from breaking, could you see his rags? Could you smell his breath? Mrs. Eddy has done more than that for these people.

They are prejudiced witnesses. To the credit of human nature it is not possible that they should be otherwise. They sincerely believe that Mrs. Eddy's character is pure and perfect and beautiful, and her history without stain or blot or blemish. But that does not settle it. They sincerely believe she did not borrow the Great Idea from Quimby, but hit upon it herself. It may be so, and it could be so. Let it go—there is no way to settle it. They believe she carried away no Quimby manuscripts. Let that go, too—there is no way to settle it. They believe that she, and not another, built the Religion upon the book, and organized it. I believe it, too.

Finally, they believe that she philosophized Christian Science, explained it, systematized it, and wrote it all out with her own hand in the book *Science and Health.*

I am not able to believe that. Let us draw the line there. The known and undisputed products of her pen are a formidable witness against her. They do seem to me to prove, quite clearly and conclusively, that writing, upon even simple subjects, is a difficult labor for her; that she has never been able to write anything above third-rate English; that she is weak in the matter of grammar; that she has but a rude and dull sense of the values of words; that she so lacks in the matter of literary precision that she can seldom put a thought into words that express it lucidly to the reader and leave no doubts in his mind as to whether he has rightly understood or not; that she cannot even draught a Preface that a person can fully comprehend, nor one which can by any art be translated *into* a fully understandable form;

that she can seldom inject into a Preface even single sentences whose meaning is uncompromisingly clear—yet Prefaces are her specialty, if she has one.

Mrs. Eddy's known and undisputed writings are very limited in bulk; they exhibit no depth, no analytical quality, no thought above school-composition size, and but juvenile ability in handling thoughts of even that modest magnitude. She has a fine commercial ability, and could govern a vast railway system in great style; she could draught a set of rules that Satan himself would say could not be improved on—for devilish effectiveness—by his staff; but we know, by our excursions among the Mother-Church's By-laws, that their English would discredit the deputy baggage-smasher. I am quite sure that Mrs. Eddy cannot write well upon any subject, even a commercial one.

In the very first revision of *Science and Health* (1883), Mrs. Eddy wrote a Preface which is an unimpeachable witness that the rest of the book was written by somebody else. I have put it in the Appendix[3] along with a page or two taken from the body of the book,[4] and will ask the reader to compare the labored and lumbering and confused gropings of this Preface with the easy and flowing and direct English of the other exhibit, and see if he can believe that the one hand and brain produced both.

And let him take the Preface apart, sentence by sentence, and searchingly examine each sentence word by word, and see if he can find half a dozen sentences whose meanings he is so sure of that he can rephrase them—in words of his own—and reproduce what he takes to be those meanings. Money can be lost on this game. I know, for I am the one that lost it.

Now let the reader turn to the excerpt which I have made from the chapter on "Prayer"[5] (last year's edition of *Science and Health),* and compare that wise and sane and elevated and lucid and compact piece of work with the afore-said Preface, and with Mrs. Eddy's poetry concerning the gymnastic trees, and Minerva's not yet effete sandals, and the wreaths imported from Erudition's bower for the decoration of Plymouth Rock, and the Plague-spot and Bacilli, and my other exhibits (turn back to my Chapters I and II) from the

[3] See Appendix A.—M.T.
[4] Appendix B.—M.T.
[5] See Appendix.—M.T.

Autobiography, and finally with the late Communication concerning me,[6] and see if he thinks anybody's affirmation, or anybody's sworn testimony, or any other testimony of any imaginable kind, would ever be likely to convince him that Mrs. Eddy wrote that chapter on Prayer.

I do not wish to impose my opinion on any one who will not permit it, but such as it is I offer it here for what it is worth. I cannot believe, and I do not believe, that Mrs. Eddy originated any of the thoughts and reasonings out of which the book *Science and Health* is constructed; and I cannot believe, and do not believe that she ever wrote any part of that book.

I think that if anything in the world stands proven, and well and solidly proven, by unimpeachable testimony—the treacherous testimony of her own pen in her known and undisputed literary productions—it is that Mrs. Eddy is not capable of thinking upon high planes, nor of reasoning clearly nor writing intelligently upon low ones.

Inasmuch as—in my belief—the very first editions of the book *Science and Health* were far above the reach of Mrs. Eddy's mental and literary abilities, I think she has from the very beginning been claiming as her own another person's book, and wearing as her own property laurels rightfully belonging to that person—the *real* author of *Science and Health.* And I think the reason—and the only reason —that he has not protested is because his work was not exposed to print until after he was safely dead.

That with an eye to business, and by grace of her business talent, she has restored to the world neglected and abandoned features of the Christian religion which her thousands of followers find gracious and blessed and contenting, I recognize and confess; but I am convinced that every single detail of the work except just that one—the delivery of the product to the world—was conceived and performed by another.

---

[6] See Appendix. This reference is to the article "Mrs. Eddy in Error," in the *North American Review* for April, 1903.—M.T.

Appendix A

Original First Preface to *Science and Health*

There seems a Christian necessity of learning God's power and purpose to heal both mind and body. This thought grew out of our early seeking Him in all our ways, and a hopeless as singular invalidism that drugs increased instead of diminished, and hygiene benefited only for a season. By degrees we have drifted into more spiritual latitudes of thought, and experimented as we advanced until demonstrating fully the power of mind over the body. About the year 1862, having heard of a mesmerist in Portland who was treating the sick by manipulation, we visited him; he helped us for a time, then we relapsed somewhat. After his decease, and a severe casualty deemed fatal by skilful physicians, we discovered that the Principle of all healing and the law that governs it is God, a divine Principle, and a spiritual not material law, and regained health.

It was not an individual or mortal mind acting upon another so-called mind that healed us. It was the glorious truths of Christian Science that we discovered as we neared that verge of so-called material life named death; yea, it was the great Shekinah, the spirit of Life, Truth, and Love illuminating our understanding of the action and might of Omnipotence! The old gentleman to whom we have referred had some very advanced views on healing, but he was not avowedly religious neither scholarly. We interchanged thoughts on the subject of healing the sick. I restored some patients of his that he failed to heal, and left in his possession some manuscripts of mine containing corrections of his desultory pennings, which I am informed at his decease passed into the hands of a patient of his, now residing in Scotland. He died in 1865 and left no published works. The only manuscript that we ever held of his, longer than to correct it, was one of perhaps a dozen pages, most of which we had composed. He manipulated the sick; hence his ostensible method of healing was physical instead of *mental*. We helped him in the esteem of the public by our writings, but never knew of his stating orally or in writing that he treated his patients *mentally;* never heard him give any directions to that effect; and have it from one of his patients, who now asserts that he was the founder of mental healing, that he never revealed to anyone his method. We refer to these facts simply to refute the calumnies and false claims of our enemies, that we are preferring dishonest claims to the discovery and founding at this period of Metaphysical Healing or Christian Science.

The Science and laws of a purely mental healing and their method of application through spiritual power alone, else a mental argument against disease, are our own discovery at this date. True, the Principle is divine and eternal; but the application of it to heal the sick had been lost sight of, and required to be again spiritually discerned and its science discovered, that man might retain it through the understanding. Since our discovery in 1866 of the divine science of Christian Healing, we have labored with tongue and pen to found this system. In this endeavor every obstacle has been thrown in our path that the envy and revenge of a few disaffected students could devise. The superstition and ignorance of even this period have not failed to contribute their mite towards misjudging us, while its Christian advancement and scientific research have helped sustain our feeble efforts.

Since our first Edition of *Science and Health,* published in 1875, two of the aforesaid students have plagiarized and pirated our works. In the issues of E. J. A., almost exclusively ours, were thirteen paragraphs, without credit, taken verbatim from our books.

Not one of our printed works was ever copied or abstracted from the published or from the unpublished writings of anyone. Throughout our publications of Metaphysical Healing or Christian Science, when writing or dictating them, we have given ourselves to contemplation wholly apart from the observation of the material senses: to look upon a copy would have distracted our thoughts from the subject before us. We were seldom able to copy our own compositions, and have employed an amanuensis for the last six years. Every work that we have had published has been extemporaneously written; and out of fifty lectures and sermons that we have delivered the last year, forty-four have been extemporaneous. We have distributed many of our unpublished manuscripts; loaned to one of our youngest students, R. K . . . . . y, between three and four hundred pages, of which we were sole author—giving him liberty to copy but not to publish them.

Leaning on the sustaining Infinite with loving trust, the trials of today grow brief, and tomorrow is big with blessings.

The wakeful shepherd, tending his flocks, beholds from the mountain's top the first faint morning beam ere cometh the risen day. So from Soul's loftier summits shines the pale star to prophet-shepherd, and it traverses night, over to where the young child lies, in cradled obscurity, that shall waken a world. Over the night of error dawn the morning beams and guiding star of Truth, and "the wise men" are led by it to Science, which repeats the eternal harmony that it reproduced, in proof of immortality. The time for thinkers has come; and the time for revolutions, ecclesiastical and civil, must come. Truth, independent of doctrines or time-honored systems, stands at the threshold of history. Contentment with the past, or the cold conventionality of custom, may no longer shut the door on science; though empires fall, "He whose right it is shall reign." Ignorance of God should no longer be the stepping-stone to faith; understanding Him, "whom to know aright is Life eternal," is the only guaranty of obedience.

This volume may not open a new thought, and make it at once familiar. It has the sturdy task of a pioneer, to hack away at the tall oaks and cut the rough granite, leaving future ages to declare what it has done. We made our first discovery of the adaptation of metaphysics to the treatment of disease in the winter of 1866; since then we have tested the Principle on ourselves and others, and never found it to fail to prove the statements herein made of it. We must learn the science of Life, to reach the perfection of man. To understand God as the Principle of all being, and to live in accordance with this Principle, is the Science of Life. But to reproduce this harmony of being, the error of personal sense must yield to science, even as the science of music corrects tones caught from the ear, and gives the sweet concord of sound. There are many theories of physic and theology, and many calls in each of their directions for the right way; but we propose to settle the question of "What is Truth?" on the ground of proof, and let that method of healing the sick and establishing Christianity be adopted that is found to give the most health and to make the best Christians; science will then have a fair field, in which case we are assured of its triumph over all opinions and beliefs. Sickness and sin have ever had their doctors; but the question is, Have they become less because of them? The longevity of our antediluvians would say, No! and the criminal records of today utter their voices little in favor of such a conclusion. Not that we would deny to Caesar the things that are his, but that we ask for the things that belong to Truth; and safely affirm, from the demonstrations we have been able to make, that the science of man understood would have eradicated sin, sickness, and death, in a less period than six thousand years. We find great difficulties in starting this work right. Some shockingly false claims are already made to a metaphysical practice; mesmerism, its very antipodes, is one of them. Hitherto we have never, in a single instance of our discovery, found the slightest resemblance between mesmerism and metaphysics. No especial idiosyncrasy is requisite to acquire a knowledge of metaphysical healing; spiritual sense is more important to its discernment than the intellect; and those who would learn this science without a high moral standard of thought and action, will fail to understand it until they go up higher. Owing to our explanations constantly vibrating between the same points, an irksome repetition of words must occur; also the use of capital letters, genders, and technicalities peculiar to the science. Variety of language, or beauty of diction, must give place to close analysis and unembellished thought. "Hoping all things, enduring all things," to do good to our enemies, to bless them that curse us, and to bear to the sorrowing and the sick consolation and healing, we commit these pages to posterity.

Mary Baker G. Eddy

Appendix B

The Gospel narratives bear brief testimony even to the life of our great Master. His spiritual noumenon and phenomenon, silenced portraiture. Writers, less wise than the Apostles, essayed in the Apocryphal New Testament, a legendary and traditional history of the early life of Jesus. But Saint Paul summarized the character of Jesus as the model of Christianity, in these words: "Consider Him who endured such contradictions of sinners against Himself. Who for the joy that was set before Him, endured the cross, despising the shame, and is set down at the right hand of the throne of God."

It may be that the mortal life battle still wages, and must continue till its involved errors are vanquished by victory-bringing Science; but this triumph will come! God is over all. He alone is our origin, aim, and Being. The real man is not of the dust, nor is he ever created through the flesh; for his father and mother are the one Spirit, and his brethren are all the children of one parent, the eternal Good.

Any kind of literary composition was excessively difficult for Mrs. Eddy. She found it grinding hard work to dig out anything to say. She realized, at the above stage in her life, that with all her trouble she had not been able to scratch together even material enough for a child's Autobiography, and also that what she had secured was in the main not valuable, not important, considering the age and the fame of the person she was writing about; and so it occurred to her to attempt, in that paragraph, to excuse the meagreness and poor quality of the feast she was spreading, by letting on that she could do ever so much better if she wanted to, but was under constraint of Divine etiquette. To feed with more than a few indifferent crumbs a plebeian appetite for personal details about Personages in her class was not the correct thing, and she blandly points out that there is Precedent for this reserve. When Mrs. Eddy tries to be artful—in literature—it is generally after the manner of the ostrich; and with the ostrich's luck. Please try to find the connection between the two paragraphs. —M.T.

Appendix C

The following is the spiritual signification of the Lord's Prayer:

Principle, eternal and harmonious,
Nameless and adorable Intelligence,
Thou art ever present and supreme.
And when this supremacy of Spirit shall appear,
   the dream of matter will disappear.
Give us the understanding of Truth and Love.
And loving we shall learn God, and Truth will
   destroy all error.
And lead us into the Life that is Soul, and de-
   liver us from the errors of sense, sin, sick-
   ness, and death,
For God is Life, Truth, and Love for ever.

—*Science and Health*, edition of 1881.

It seems to me that this one is distinctly superior to the one that was inspired for last year's edition. It is strange, but to my mind plain, that inspiring is an art which does not improve with practice. —M.T.

Appendix D

For verily I say unto you, That whosoever shall say unto this mountain, Be thou removed, and be thou cast into the sea; and shall not doubt in his heart, but shall believe that those things which he saith shall come to pass; he shall have whatsoever he saith. Therefore I say unto you, What things soever ye desire when ye pray, believe that ye receive them, and ye shall have them.

> Your Father knoweth what things ye have need of, before ye
> ask Him.
>
> —CHRIST JESUS.

The prayer that reclaims the sinner and heals the sick, is an absolute faith that all things are possible to God—a spiritual understanding of Him—an unselfed love. Regardless of what another may say or think on this subject, I speak from experience. This prayer, combined with self-sacrifice and toil, is the means whereby God has enabled me to do what I have done for the religion and health of mankind.

Thoughts unspoken are not unknown to the divine Mind. Desire is prayer; and no less can occur from trusting God with our desires, that they may be moulded and exalted before they take form in audible word, and in deeds.

What are the motives for prayer? Do we pray to make ourselves better, or to benefit those that hear us; to enlighten the Infinite, or to be heard of men? Are we benefited by praying? Yes, the desire which goes forth hungering after righteousness is blessed of our Father, and it does not return unto us void.

God is not moved by the breath of praise to do more than He has already done; nor can the Infinite do less than bestow all good, since He is unchanging Wisdom and Love. We can do more for ourselves by humble fervent petitions; but the All-loving does not grant them simply on the ground of lip-service, for He already knows all.

Prayer cannot change the Science of Being, but it does bring us into harmony with it. Goodness reaches the demonstration of Truth. A request that another may work for us never does our work. The habit of pleading with the divine Mind, as one pleads with a human being, perpetuates the belief in God as humanly circumscribed—an error which impedes spiritual growth.

God is Love. Can we ask Him to be more? God is Intelligence. Can we inform the infinite Mind, or tell Him anything He does not already comprehend? Do we hope to change perfection? Shall we plead for more at the open fount, which always pours forth more than we receive? The unspoken prayer does bring us nearer the Source of all existence and blessedness.

Asking God to *be* God is a "vain repetition." God is "the same yesterday, and today, and forever"; and He who is immutably right will do right, without being reminded of His province. The wisdom of man is not sufficient to warrant him in advising God.

Who would stand before a blackboard, and pray the principle of mathematics to work out the problem? The rule is already established, and it is our task to work out the solution. Shall we ask the divine Principle of all goodness to do His own work? His work is done; and we have only to avail ourselves of God's rule in order to receive the blessing thereof.

The divine Being must be reflected by man—else man is not the image and likeness of the patient, tender, and true, the one "altogether lovely"; but to understand God is the work of eternity, and demands absolute concentration of thought and energy.

How empty are our conceptions of Deity! We admit theoretically that God is good, omnipotent, omnipresent, infinite, and then we try to give information to this infinite Mind; and plead for unmerited pardon, and a liberal outpouring of benefactions. Are we really grateful for the good already received? Then we shall avail ourselves of the blessings we have, and thus be fitted to receive more. Gratitude is much more than a verbal expression of thanks. Action expresses more gratitude than speech.

If we are ungrateful for Life, Truth, and Love, and yet return thanks to God for all blessings, we are insincere; and incur the sharp censure our Master pronounces on hypocrites. In such a case the only acceptable prayer is to put the finger on the lips and remember our blessings. While the heart is far from divine Truth and Love, we cannot conceal the ingratitude and barren lives, for God knoweth all things.

What we most need is the prayer of fervent desire for growth in grace, expressed in patience, meekness, love, and good deeds. To keep the commandments of our Master and follow his example, is our proper debt to Him, and the only worthy evidence of our gratitude for all He has done. Outward worship is not of itself sufficient to express loyal and heartfelt gratitude, since He has said: "If ye love Me, keep My Commandments."

The habitual struggle to be always good, is unceasing prayer. Its motives are made manifest in the blessings they bring—which, if not acknowledged in audible words, attest our worthiness to be made partakers of Love.

Simply asking that we may love God will never make us love Him;

but the longing to be better and holier—expressed in daily watchfulness, and in striving to assimilate more of the divine character—this will mould and fashion us anew, until we awake in His likeness. We reach the Science of Christianity through demonstration of the divine nature; but in this wicked world goodness will "be evil spoken of," and patience must work experience.

Audible prayer can never do the works of spiritual understanding, which regenerates; but silent prayer, watchfulness, and devout obedience, enabled us to follow Jesus' example. Long prayers, ecclesiasticism, and creeds, have clipped the divine pinions of Love, and clad religion in human robes. They materialize worship, hinder the Spirit, and keep man from demonstrating his power over error.

Sorrow for wrong-doing is but one step towards reform, and the very easiest step. The next and great step required by Wisdom is the test of our sincerity—namely, reformation. To this end we are placed under the stress of circumstances. Temptation bids us repeat the offence, and woe comes in return for what is done. So it will ever be, till we learn that there is no discount in the law of justice, and that we must pay "the uttermost farthing." The measure ye mete "shall be measured to you again," and it will be full "and running over."

Saints and sinners get their full award, but not always in this world. The followers of Christ drank His cup. Ingratitude and persecution filled it to the brim; but God pours the riches of His love into the understanding and affections, giving us strength according to our day. Sinners flourish "like a green bay-tree"; but, looking farther, the Psalmist could see their end—namely, the destruction of sin through suffering.

Prayer is sometimes used, as a confessional, to cancel sin. This error impedes true religion. Sin is forgiven, only as it is destroyed by Christ—Truth and Life. If prayer nourishes the belief that sin is cancelled, and that man is made better by merely praying, it is an evil. He grows worse who continues in sin because he thinks himself forgiven.

An apostle says that the Son of God (Christ) came to "destroy the works of the devil." We should follow our divine Exemplar, and seek the destruction of all evil works, error and disease included. We cannot escape the penalty due for sin. The Scriptures say, that if we deny Christ, "He also will deny us."

The divine Love corrects and governs man. Men may pardon, but this divine Principle alone reforms the sinner. God is not separate from the wisdom He bestows. The talents He gives we must improve. Calling on Him to forgive our work, badly done or left undone, implies the vain supposition that we have nothing to do but to ask pardon, and that afterwards we shall be free to repeat the offence.

To cause suffering, as the result of sin, is the means of destroying sin. Every supposed pleasure in sin will furnish more than its equivalent of pain, until belief in material life and sin is destroyed. To reach heaven, the harmony of Being, we must understand the divine Principle of Being.

"God is Love." More than this we cannot ask; higher we cannot look; farther we cannot go. To suppose that God forgives or punishes sin, according as His mercy is sought or unsought, is to misunderstand Love and make prayer the safety-valve for wrong-doing.

Jesus uncovered and rebuked sin before He cast it out. Of a sick woman He said that Satan had bound her; and to Peter He said, "Thou art an offence unto me." He came teaching and showing men how to destroy sin, sickness, and death. He said of the fruitless tree, "It is hewn down."

It is believed by many that a certain magistrate, who lived in the time of Jesus, left this record: "His rebuke is fearful." The strong language of our Master confirms this description.

The only civil sentence which He had for error was, "Get thee behind Me, Satan." Still stronger evidence that Jesus' reproof was pointed and pungent is in His own words—showing the necessity for such forcible utterance, when He cast out devils and healed the sick and sinful. The relinquishment of error deprives material sense of its false claims.

Audible prayer is impressive; it gives momentary solemnity and elevation to thought; but does it produce any lasting benefit? Looking deeply into these things, we find that "a zeal . . . not according to knowledge," gives occasion for reaction unfavorable to spiritual growth, sober resolve, and wholesome perception of God's requirements. The motives for verbal prayer may embrace too much love of applause to induce or encourage Christian sentiment.

Physical sensation, not Soul, produces material ecstasy, and emotions. If spiritual sense always guided men at such times, there would grow out of those ecstatic moments a higher experience and a better life, with more devout self-abnegation, and purity. A self-satisfied ventilation of fervent sentiments never makes a Christian. God is not influenced by man. The "divine ear" is not an auditorial nerve. It is the all-hearing and all-knowing Mind, to whom each want of man is always known, and by whom it will be supplied.

The danger from audible prayer is, that it may lead us into temptation. By it we may become involuntary hypocrites, uttering desires which are not real, and consoling ourselves in the midst of sin, with the recollection that we have prayed over it—or mean to ask forgiveness at some later day. Hypocrisy is fatal to religion.

A wordy prayer may afford a quiet sense of self-justification, though it makes the sinner a hypocrite. We never need despair of an honest heart, but there is little hope for those who only come spasmodically face to face with their wickedness, and then seek to hide it. Their prayers are indexes which do not correspond with their character. They hold secret fellowship with sin; and such externals are spoken of by Jesus as "like unto whited sepulchres . . . full of all uncleanness."

If a man, though apparently fervent and prayerful, is impure, and therefore insincere, what must be the comment upon him? If he had reached the loftiness of his prayer, there would be no occasion for such comment. If we feel the aspiration, humility, gratitude, and love which our words express—this God accepts; and it is wise not to try to deceive ourselves or others, for "there is nothing covered that shall not be revealed." Professions and audible prayers are like charity in one respect—they "cover a multitude of sins." Praying for humility, with whatever fervency of expression, does not always mean a desire for it. If we turn away from the poor, we are not ready to receive the reward of Him who blesses the poor. We confess to having a very wicked heart, and ask that it may be laid bare before us; but do we not already know more of this heart than we are willing to have our neighbor see?

We ought to examine ourselves, and learn what is the affection and purpose of the heart; for this alone can show us what we honestly are. If a friend informs us of a fault, do we listen to the rebuke patiently, and credit what is said? Do we not rather give thanks that we are "not as other men?" During many years the author has been most grateful for merited rebuke. The sting lies in unmerited censure —in the falsehood which does no one any good.

The test of all prayer lies in the answer to these questions: Do we love our neighbor better because of this asking? Do we pursue the old selfishness, satisfied with having prayed for something better, though we give no evidence of the sincerity of our requests by living consistently with our prayer? If selfishness has given place to kindness, we shall regard our neighbor unselfishly, and bless them that curse us; but we shall never meet this great duty by simply asking that it may be done. There is a cross to be taken up, before we can enjoy the fruition of our hope and faith.

Dost thou "love the Lord thy God with all thy heart, and with all thy soul, and with all thy mind?" This command includes much— even the surrender of all merely material sensation, affection, and worship. This is the El Dorado of Christianity. It involves the Science of Life, and recognizes only the divine control of Spirit, wherein Soul is our master, and material sense and human will have no place.

Are you willing to leave all for Christ, for Truth, and so be counted among sinners? No! Do you really desire to attain this point? No! Then why make long prayers about it, and ask to be Christians, since you care not to tread in the footsteps of our dear Master? If unwilling to follow His example, wherefore pray with the lips that you may be partakers of His nature? Consistent prayer is the desire to do right. Prayer means that we desire to, and will, walk in the light so far as we receive it, even though with bleeding footsteps, and waiting patiently on the Lord, will leave our real desires to be rewarded by Him.

The world must grow to the spiritual understanding of prayer. If good enough to profit by Jesus' cup of earthly sorrows, God will sustain us under these sorrows. Until we are thus divinely qualified, and willing to drink His cup, millions of vain repetitions will never pour into prayer the unction of Spirit, in demonstration of power, and "with signs following." Christian Science reveals a necessity for overcoming the world, the flesh and evil, and thus destroying all error.

Seeking is not sufficient. It is striving which enables us to enter. Spiritual attainments open the door to a higher understanding of the divine Life.

One of the forms of worship in Thibet is to carry a praying-machine through the streets, and stop at the doors to earn a penny by grinding out a prayer; whereas civilization pays for clerical prayers, in lofty edifices. Is the difference very great, after all?

Experience teaches us that we do not always receive the blessings we ask for in prayer. There is some misapprehension of the source and means of all goodness and blessedness, or we should certainly receive what we ask for. The Scriptures say: "Ye ask, and receive not, because ye ask amiss, that ye may consume it upon your lusts." What we desire and ask for it is not always best for us to receive. In this case infinite Love will not grant the request. Do you ask Wisdom to be merciful, and not punish sin? Then "ye ask amiss." Without punishment, sin would multiply. Jesus' prayer, "forgive us our debts," specified also the terms of forgiveness. When forgiving the adulterous woman He said, "Go, and sin no more."

A magistrate sometimes remits the penalty, but this may be no moral benefit to the criminal; and at best, it only saves him from one form of punishment. The moral law, which has the right to acquit or condemn, always demands restitution, before mortals can "go up higher." Broken law brings penalty, in order to compel this progress.

Mere legal pardon (and there is no other, for divine Principle never pardons our sins or mistakes till they are corrected) leaves the offender free to repeat the offence; if, indeed, he has not already suffered sufficiently from vice to make him turn from it with loathing. Truth bestows no pardon upon error, but wipes it out in the most effectual manner. Jesus suffered for our sins, not to annul the divine sentence against an individual's sin, but to show that sin must bring inevitable suffering.

Petitions only bring to mortals the results of their own faith. We know that a desire for holiness is requisite in order to gain it; but if we desire holiness above all else, we shall sacrifice everything for it. We must be willing to do this, that we may walk securely in the only practical road to holiness. Prayer alone cannot change the unalterable Truth, or give us an understanding of it; but prayer coupled with a fervent habitual desire to know and do the will of God will bring us into all Truth. Such a desire has little need of audible expression. It is best expressed in thought and life.

Appendix E

Reverend Heber Newton on Christian Science:

To begin, then, at the beginning, Christian Science accepts the work of healing sickness as an integral part of the discipleship of Jesus Christ. In Christ it finds, what the Church has always recognized, theoretically, though it has practically ignored the fact—the Great Physician. That Christ healed the sick, we none of us question. It stands plainly upon the record. This ministry of healing was too large a part of His work to be left out from any picture of that life. Such service was not an incident of His career—it was an essential element of that career. It was an integral factor in His mission. The Evangelists leave us no possibility of confusion on this point. Co-equal with his work of instruction and inspiration was His work of healing.

The records make it equally clear that the Master laid His charge upon His disciples to do as He had done. "When He had called unto Him His twelve disciples, He gave them power over unclean spirits, to cast them out, and to heal all manner of sickness and all manner of disease."[1] In sending them forth, "He commanded them, saying, . . . As ye go, preach, saying, The kingdom of heaven is at hand. Heal the sick, cleanse the lepers, raise the dead, cast out demons."[2]

That the twelve disciples undertook to do the Master's work of healing, and that they, in their measure, succeeded, seems beyond question. They found in themselves the same power that the Master found in Himself, and they used it as He had used His power. The record of The Acts of the Apostles, if at all trustworthy history, shows that they, too, healed the sick.

Beyond the circle of the original twelve, it is equally clear that the early disciples believed themselves charged with the same mission, and that they sought to fulfil it. The records of the early Church make it indisputable that powers of healing were recognized as

[1] Matt. x., 11.
[2] *Ib.*, x., 5, 7, 8.

among the gifts of the Spirit. St. Paul's letters render it certain that these gifts were not a privilege of the original twelve, merely, but that they were the heritage into which all the disciples entered.

Beyond the era of the primitive Church, through several generations, the early Christians felt themselves called to the same ministry of healing, and enabled with the same secret of power. Through wellnigh three centuries, the gifts of healing appear to have been, more or less, recognized and exercised in the Church. Through those generations, however, there was a gradual disuse of this power, following upon a failing recognition of its possession. That which was originally the rule became the exception. By degrees, the sense of authority and power to heal passed out from the consciousness of the Church. It ceased to be a sign of the indwelling Spirit. For fifteen centuries, the recognition of this authority and power has been altogether exceptional. Here and there, through the history of these centuries, there have been those who have entered into this belief of their own privilege and duty, and have used the gift which they recognized. The Church has never been left without a line of witnesses to this aspect of the discipleship of Christ. But she has come to accept it as the normal order of things that what was once the rule in the Christian Church should be now only the exception. Orthodoxy has framed a theory of the words of Jesus to account for this strange departure of His Church from them. It teaches us to believe that His example was not meant to be followed, in this respect, by all His disciples. The power of healing which was in Him was a purely exceptional power. It was used as an evidence of His divine mission. It was a miraculous gift. The gift of working miracles was not bestowed upon His Church at large. His original disciples, the twelve apostles, received this gift, as a necessity of the critical epoch of Christianity—the founding of the Church. Traces of the power lingered on, in weakening activity, until they gradually ceased, and the normal condition of the Church was entered upon, in which miracles are no longer possible.

We accept this, unconsciously, as the true state of things in Christianity. But it is a conception which will not bear a moment's examination. There is not the slightest suggestion upon record that Christ set any limit to this charge which He gave His disciples. On the contrary, there are not lacking hints that He looked for the possession and exercise of this power wherever His spirit breathed in men.

Even if the concluding paragraph of St. Mark's Gospel were a later appendix, it may none the less have been a faithful echo of words of the Master, as it certainly is a trustworthy record of the belief of the early Christians as to the thought of Jesus concerning His followers. In that interesting passage, Jesus, after His death, appeared to the eleven, and formally commissioned them, again, to take up His work in the world; bidding them, "Go ye into all the world and preach the gospel to every creature." "And these signs," He tells them, shall follow them that believe"—not the apostles only, but "them that believe," without limit of time; "in My name they shall cast out devils . . . they shall lay hands on the sick and they shall recover."[3] The concluding discourse to the disciples, recorded in the Gospel according to St. John, affirms the same expectation on the part of Jesus; emphasizing it in His solemn way: "Verily, verily, I say unto you, He that believeth on Me, the works that I do shall he do also; and greater works than these shall he do."[4]

Appendix F

Few will deny that an intelligence apart from man formed and governs the spiritual universe and man; and this intelligence is the eternal Mind, and neither matter nor man created this intelligence and divine Principle; nor can this Principle produce aught unlike itself. All that we term sin, sickness, and death is comprised in the belief of matter. The realm of the real is spiritual; the opposite of Spirit is matter; and the opposite of the real is unreal or material. Matter is an error of statement, for there is no matter. This error of premises leads to error of conclusion in every statement of matter as a basis. Nothing we can say or believe regarding matter is true, except that matter is unreal, simply a belief that has its beginning and ending.

The conservative firm called matter and mind God never formed. The unerring and eternal Mind destroys this imaginary copartnership, formed only to be dissolved in a manner and at a period unknown. This copartnership is obsolete. Placed under the microscope

---

[3] Mark xvi., 15, 17, 18.
[4] John xiv., 12.

of metaphysics matter disappears. Only by understanding there are not two, matter and mind, is a logical and correct conclusion obtained by either one. Science gathers not grapes of thorns or figs of thistles. Intelligence never produced non-intelligence, such as matter: the immortal never produced mortality, good never resulted in evil. The science of Mind shows conclusively that matter is a myth. Metaphysics are above physics, and drag not matter, or what is termed that, into one of its premises or conclusions. Metaphysics resolves things into thoughts, and exchanges the objects of sense for the ideas of Soul. These ideas are perfectly tangible and real to consciousness, and they have this advantage—they are eternal. Mind and its thoughts comprise the whole of God, the universe, and of man. Reason and revelation coincide with this statement, and support its proof every hour, for nothing is harmonious or eternal that is not spiritual: the realization of this will bring out objects from a higher source of thought; hence more beautiful and immortal.

The fact of spiritualization produces results in striking contrast to the farce of materialization: the one produces the results of chastity and purity, the other the downward tendencies and earthward gravitation of sensualism and impurity.

The exalting and healing effects of metaphysics show their fountain. Nothing in pathology has exceeded the application of metaphysics. Through mind alone we have prevented disease and preserved health. In cases of chronic and acute diseases, in their severest forms, we have changed the secretions, renewed structure, and restored health; have elongated shortened limbs, relaxed rigid muscles, made cicatrized joints supple; restored carious bones to healthy conditions, renewed that which is termed the lost substance of the lungs; and restored healthy organizations where disease was organic instead of functional.

Mrs. Eddy in Error

I feel almost sure that Mrs. Eddy's inspiration-works are getting out of repair. I think so because they made some errors in a statement which she uttered through the press on the 17th of January. Not large ones, perhaps, still it is a friend's duty to straighten such things out and get them right when he can. Therefore I will put my other duties aside for a moment and undertake this helpful service. She said as follows:

"In view of the circulation of certain criticisms from the pen of Mark Twain, I submit the following statement:

"It is a fact, well understood, that I begged the students who first gave me the endearing appellative 'mother' not to name me thus. But, without my consent, that word spread like wildfire. I still must think the name is not applicable to me. I stand in relation to this century as a Christian discoverer, founder, and leader. I regard self-deification as blasphemous; I may be more loved, but I am less lauded, pampered, provided for, and cheered than others before me —and wherefore? Because Christian Science is not yet popular, and I refuse adulation.

"My visit to the Mother-Church after it was built and dedicated pleased me, and the situation was satisfactory. The dear members wanted to greet me with escort and the ringing of bells, but I declined, and went alone in my carriage to the church, entered it, and knelt in thanks upon the steps of its altar. There the foresplendor of the beginnings of truth fell mysteriously upon my spirit. I believe in one Christ, teach one Christ, know of but one Christ. I believe in but one incarnation, one Mother Mary, and know I am not that one, and never claimed to be. It suffices me to learn the Science of the Scriptures relative to this subject.

"Christian Scientists have no quarrel with Protestants, Catholics, or any other sect. They need to be understood as following the divine Principle—God, Love—and not imagined to be unscientific worshippers of a human being.

"In the aforesaid article, of which I have seen only extracts, Mark

Twain's wit was not wasted in certain directions. Christian Science eschews divine rights in human beings. If the individual governed human consciousness, my statement of Christian Science would be disproved, but to understand the spiritual idea is essential to demonstrate Science and its pure monotheism—one God, one Christ, no idolatry, no human propaganda. Jesus taught and proved that what feeds a few feeds all. His life-work subordinated the material to the spiritual, and He left this legacy of truth to mankind. His metaphysics is not the sport of philosophy, religion, or Science; rather it is the pith and finale of them all.

"I have not the inspiration or aspiration to be a first or second Virgin-Mother—her duplicate, antecedent, or subsequent. What I am remains to be proved by the good I do. We need much humility, wisdom, and love to perform the functions of foreshadowing and foretasting heaven within us. This glory is molten in the furnace of affliction."

She still thinks the name of Our Mother not applicable to her; and she is also able to remember that it distressed her when it was conferred upon her, and that she begged to have it suppressed. Her memory is at fault here. If she will take her By-laws, and refer to Section 1 of Article XXII, written with her own hand—she will find that she has reserved that title to herself, and is so pleased with it, and so—may we say jealous?—about it, that she threatens with excommunication any sister Scientist who shall call herself by it. This is that Section 1:

"The Title of Mother. In the year 1895 loyal Christian Scientists had given to the author of their text-book, the Founder of Christian Science, the individual, endearing term of Mother. Therefore, if a student of Christian Science shall apply this title, either to herself or to others, except as the term for kinship according to the flesh, it shall be regarded by the Church as an indication of disrespect for their Pastor Emeritus, and unfitness to be a member of the Mother-Church."

Mrs. Eddy is herself the Mother-Church—its powers and authorities are in her possession solely—and she can abolish that title whenever it may please her to do so. She has only to command her people, wherever they may be in the earth, to use it no more, and it will never be uttered again. She is aware of this.

It may be that she "refuses adulation" when she is not awake, but when she is awake she encourages it and propagates it in that museum called "Our Mother's Room," in her Church in Boston. She could abolish that institution with a word, if she wanted to. She is aware of that. I will say a further word about the museum presently.

Further down the column, her memory is unfaithful again:

"I believe in . . . but one Mother Mary, and know I am not that one, and never claimed to be."

At a session of the National Christian Science Association, held in the city of New York on the 27th of May, 1890, the secretary was "instructed to send to our Mother greetings and words of affection from her assembled children."[1]

Her telegraphic response was read to the Association at next day's meeting:

"All hail! He hath filled the hungry with good things and the sick hath He not sent empty away.—MOTHER MARY."[2]

Which Mother Mary is this one? Are there two? If so, she is both of them; for, when she signed this telegram in this satisfied and unprotesting way, the Mother-title which she was going to so strenuously object to, and put from her with humility, and seize with both hands, and reserve as her sole property, and protect her monopoly of it with a stern By-law, while recognizing with diffidence that it was "not applicable" to her (then and today)—*that* Mother-title was not yet born, and would not be offered to her until five years later. The date of the above "Mother Mary" is 1890; the "individual, endearing title of Mother" was given her "in 1895"—according to her own testimony. See her By-law quoted above.

In his opening Address to that Convention of 1890, the President recognized this Mary—our Mary—and abolished all previous ones. He said:

"There is but one Moses, one Jesus; and there is but one Mary."[3]

The confusions being now dispersed, we have this clarified result:

There had *been* a Moses at one time, and only one; there had *been* a Jesus at one time, and only one; there *is* a Mary and "only one." She is not a Has Been, she is an Is—the "Author of *Science and Health;* and we cannot ignore her."[4]

[1] Page 24, Official Report.
[2] Page 24, Official Report.
[3] Page 13, Official Report.
[4] *Ibid.*

1. In 1890, there was but one Mother Mary. The President said so.

2. Mrs. Eddy was that one. She said so, in signing the telegram.

3. Mrs. Eddy was not that one—for she says so, in her Associated Press utterance of January 17th.

4. And has "never claimed to be" that one—unless the signature to the telegram is a claim.

Thus it stands proven and established that she is that Mary and isn't, and thought she was and knows she wasn't. That much is clear.

She is also "The Mother," by the election of 1895, and did not want the title, and thinks it is not applicable to her, and will excommunicate any one that tries to take it away from her. So that is clear.

I think that the only really troublesome confusion connected with these particular matters has arisen from the name—Mary. Much vexation, much misunderstanding, could have been avoided if Mrs. Eddy had used some of her other names in place of that one. "Mother Mary" was certain to stir up discussion. It would have been much better if she had signed the telegram "Mother Baker"; then there would have been no Biblical competition, and, of course, that is a thing to avoid. But it is not too late, yet.

I wish to break in here with a parenthesis, and then take up this examination of Mrs. Eddy's Claim[5] of January 17th again.

The history of her "Mother Mary" telegram—as told to me by one who ought to be a very good authority—is curious and interesting. The telegram ostensibly quotes verse 53 from the "Magnificat," but really makes some pretty formidable changes in it. This is St. Luke's version:

"He hath filled the hungry with good things, and the *rich* He hath sent empty away."

This is "Mother Mary's" telegraphed version:

"He hath filled the hungry with good things, and the *sick* hath He *not* sent empty away."[6]

To judge by the Official Report, the bursting of this bombshell in that massed convention of trained Christians created no astonishment, since it caused no remark, and the business of the convention went tranquilly on, thereafter, as if nothing had happened.

---

[5] *"Claim."* In Christian Science terminology, "Claims" are errors of mortal mind, fictions of the imagination.

[6] Page 24, Official Report.

Did those people detect those changes? We cannot know. I think they must have noticed them, the wording of St. Luke's verse being as familiar to all Christians as is the wording of the Beatitudes; and I think that the reason the new version provoked no surprise and no comment was, that the assemblage took it for a "Key"—a spiritualized explanation of verse 53, newly sent down from heaven through Mrs. Eddy. For all Scientists study their Bibles diligently, and they know their Magnificat. I believe that their confidence in the authenticity of Mrs. Eddy's inspirations is so limitless and so firmly established that no change, however violent, which she might make in a Bible text could disturb their composure or provoke from them a protest.

Her improved rendition of verse 53 went into the convention's report and appeared in a New York paper the next day. The (at that time) Scientist whom I mentioned a minute ago, and who had not been present at the convention, saw it and marvelled; marvelled and was indignant—indignant with the printer or the telegrapher, for making so careless and so dreadful an error. And greatly distressed, too; for, of course, the newspaper people would fall foul of it, and be sarcastic, and make fun of it, and have a blithe time over it, and be properly thankful for the chance. It shows how innocent he was; it shows that he did not know the limitations of newspaper men in the matter of Biblical knowledge. The new verse 53 raised no insurrection in the press; in fact, it was not even remarked upon; I could have told him the boys would not know there was anything the matter with it. I have been a newspaper man myself, and in those days I had my limitations like the others.

The Scientist hastened to Concord and told Mrs. Eddy what a disastrous mistake had been made, but he found to his bewilderment that she was tranquil about it, and was not proposing to correct it. He was not able to get her to promise to make a correction. He asked her secretary if he had heard aright when the telegram was dictated to him; the secretary said he had, and took the filed copy of it and verified its authenticity by comparing it with the stenographic notes.

Mrs. Eddy did make the correction, two months later, in her official organ. It attracted no attention among the Scientists; and, naturally, none elsewhere, for that periodical's circulation was practically confined to disciples of the cult.

That is the tale as it was told to me by an ex-Scientist. Verse 53—

renovated and spiritualized—had a narrow escape from a tremendous celebrity. The newspaper men would have made it as famous as the assassination of Caesar, but for their limitations.

To return to the Claim. I find myself greatly embarrassed by Mrs. Eddy's remark: "I regard self-deification as blasphemous." If she is right about that, I have written a half-ream of manuscript this past week which I must not print, either in the book which I am writing, or elsewhere: for it goes into that very matter with extensive elaboration, citing, in detail, words and acts of Mrs. Eddy's which seem to me to prove that she is a faithful and untiring worshipper of herself, and has carried self-deification to a length which has not been before ventured in ages. If ever. There is not room enough in this chapter for that Survey, but I can epitomize a portion of it here.

With her own untaught and untrained mind, and without outside help, she has erected upon a firm and lasting foundation the most minutely perfect, and wonderful, and smoothly and exactly working, and best safe-guarded system of government that has yet been devised in the world, as I believe, and as I am sure I could prove if I had room for my documentary evidences here.

It is a despotism (on this democratic soil); a sovereignty more absolute than the Roman Papacy, more absolute than the Russian Czarship; it has not a single power, not a shred of authority, legislative or executive, which is not lodged solely in the sovereign; all its dreams, its functions, its energies, have a single object, a single reason for existing, and only the one—to build to the sky the glory of the sovereign, and keep it bright to the end of time.

Mrs. Eddy is the sovereign; she devised that great place for herself, she occupies that throne.

In 1895, she wrote a little primer, a little body of autocratic laws, called the *Manual of The First Church of Christ, Scientist,* and put those laws in force, in permanence. Her government is all there; all in that deceptively innocent-looking little book, that cunning little devilish book, that slumbering little brown volcano, with hell in its bowels. In that book she has planned out her system, and classified and defined its purposes and powers.

MAIN PARTS OF THE MACHINE

A Supreme Church. At Boston.
Branch Churches. All over the world.

One Pastor for the whole of them: to wit, her *book, Science and Health.* Term of the book's office—*forever.*

In every C. S. pulpit, two "Readers," a man and a woman. *No talkers, no preachers, in any Church*—readers only. *Readers of the Bible and her books*—no others. No commentators allowed to write or print.

A Church Service. She has framed it—for all the C. S. Churches— selected its readings, its prayers, and the hymns to be used, and has appointed the order of procedure. No changes permitted.

A Creed. She wrote it. All C. S. Churches must subscribe to it. No other permitted.

A Treasury. At Boston. She carries the key.

A C. S. Book-Publishing House. For books approved by her. No others permitted.

Journals and Magazines. These are organs of hers, and are controlled by her.

A College. For teaching C. S.

DISTRIBUTION OF THE MACHINE'S POWERS AND DIGNITIES

Supreme Church.
Pastor Emeritus—Mrs. Eddy.
Board of Directors.
Board of Education.
Board of Finance.
College Faculty.
Various Committees.
Treasurer.
Clerk.
First Members (of the Supreme Church).
Members of the Supreme Church.

It looks fair, it looks real, but it is all a fiction. Even the little "Pastor Emeritus" is a fiction. Instead of being merely an honorary and ornamental official, Mrs. Eddy is the only official in the entire body that has the slightest power. In her Manual, she has provided a prodigality of ways and forms whereby she can rid herself of any functionary in the government whenever she wants to. The officials are all shadows, save herself; she is the only reality. She allows no one to hold office more than a year—no one gets a chance to become over-popular or over-useful, and dangerous. "Excommunication" is the favorite penalty—it is threatened at every turn. It is evidently the pet dread and terror of the Church's membership.

The member who *thinks,* without getting his thought from Mrs. Eddy before uttering it, is banished *permanently.* One or two kinds of sinners can plead their way back into the fold, but this one, never. To *think*—in the Supreme Church—is the New Unpardonable Sin.

To nearly every severe and fierce rule, Mrs. Eddy adds this rivet: *"This By-law shall not be changed without the consent of the Pastor Emeritus."*

Mrs. Eddy is the entire Supreme Church, in her own person, in the matter of powers and authorities.

Although she has provided so many ways of getting rid of unsatisfactory members and officials, she was still afraid she might have left a life-preserver lying around somewhere, therefore she devised a rule to cover that defect. By applying it, she can excommunicate (and *this* is perpetual again) every functionary connected with the Supreme Church, and every one of the twenty-five thousand members of that Church, at an hour's notice—and *do it all by herself without anybody's help.*

By authority of this astonishing By-law, she has only to *say* a person connected with that Church is secretly practising hypnotism or mesmerism; whereupon, immediate excommunication, without a hearing, is his portion! She does not have to order a trial and produce evidence—her *accusation* is all that is necessary.

Where is the Pope? and where the Czar? As the ballad says:

> *"Ask of the winds that far away*
> *With fragments strewed the sea!"*

The Branch Church's pulpit is occupied by two "Readers." Without them the Branch Church is as dead as if its throat had been cut. To have control, then, of the Readers, is to have control of the Branch Churches. Mrs. Eddy has that control—a control wholly without limit, a control shared with no one.

1. No Reader can be appointed to any Church in the Christian Science world without her *express* approval.

2. She can summarily expel from his or her place any Reader, at home or abroad, by a mere *letter* of dismissal, over her signature, and

without furnishing any reason for it, to either the congregation or the Reader.

Thus she has as absolute control over all Branch Churches as she has over the Supreme Church. This power exceeds the Pope's.

In simple truth, *she is the only absolute sovereign in all Christendom.* The authority of the other sovereigns has limits, hers has none. None whatever. And her yoke does not fret, does not offend. Many of the subjects of the other monarchs feel their yoke, and are restive under it; their loyalty is insincere. It is not so with this one's human property; their loyalty is genuine, earnest, sincere, enthusiastic. The sentiment which they feel for her is one which goes out in sheer perfection to no other occupant of a throne; for it is love, pure from doubt, envy, exaction, fault-seeking, a love whose sun has no spot— that form of love, strong, great, uplifting, limitless, whose vast proportions are compassable by no word but one, the prodigious word, *Worship.* And it is not as a human being that her subjects worship her, but as a supernatural one, a divine one, one who has comradeship with God, and speaks by His voice.

Mrs. Eddy has herself created all these personal grandeurs and autocracies—with others which I have not (in this article) mentioned. They place her upon an Alpine solitude and supremacy of power and spectacular show not hitherto attained by any other self-seeking enslaver disguised in the Christian name, and they persuade me that, although she may regard "self-deification as blasphemous," she is as fond of it as I am of pie.

She knows about "Our Mother's Room" in the Supreme Church in Boston—above referred to—for she has been in it. In a recently published *North American Review* article,[1] I quoted a lady as saying Mrs. Eddy's portrait could be seen there in a shrine, lit by always-burning lights, and that C. S. disciples came there and worshipped it. That remark hurt the feelings of more than one Scientist. They said it was not true, and asked me to correct it. I comply with pleasure. Whether the portrait was there four years ago or not, it is not there now, for I have inquired. The only object in the shrine now, and lit by electrics—and worshipped—is an oil-portrait of the horse-hair *chair* Mrs. Eddy used to sit in when she was writing *Science and Health!* It seems to me that adulation has struck bottom, here.

[1] 1902.

Mrs. Eddy knows about that. She has been there, she has seen it, she has seen the worshippers. She could abolish that sarcasm with a word. She withholds the word. Once more I seem to recognize in her exactly the same appetite for self-deification that I have for pie. We seem to be curiously alike; for the love of self-deification is really only the spiritual form of the material appetite for pie, and nothing could be more strikingly Christian-Scientifically "harmonious."

I note this phrase:

"Christian Science eschews divine rights in human beings."

"Rights" is vague; I do not know what it means there. Mrs. Eddy is not well acquainted with the English language, and she is seldom able to say in it what she is trying to say. She has no ear for the exact word, and does not often get it. "Rights." Does it mean "honors?" "attributes?"

"Eschews." This is another umbrella where there should be a torch; it does not illumine the sentence, it only deepens the shadows. Does she mean "denies?" "refuses?" "forbids?" or something in that line? Does she mean:

"Christian Science denies divine honors to human beings?" Or:

"Christian Science refuses to recognize divine attributes in human beings?" Or:

"Christian Science forbids the worship of human beings?"

The bulk of the succeeding sentence is to me a tunnel, but, when I emerge at this end of it, I seem to come into daylight. Then I seem to understand both sentences—with this result:

"Christian Science recognizes but one God, forbids the worship of human beings, and refuses to recognize the possession of divine attributes by any member of the race."

I am subject to correction, but I think that that is about what Mrs. Eddy was intending to convey. Has her English—which is always difficult to me—beguiled me into misunderstanding the following remark, which she makes (calling herself "we," after an old regal fashion of hers) in her preface to her *Miscellaneous Writings?*[8]

"While we entertain decided views as to the best method for elevating the race physically, morally, and spiritually, and shall express these views as duty demands, we shall claim no especial gift from our divine origin, no supernatural power."

‘ Page 3.

Was she meaning to say:

"Although I am of divine origin and gifted with supernatural power, I shall not draw upon these resources in determining the best method of elevating the race?"

If she had left out the word "our," she might then seem to say: "I claim no especial or unusual degree of divine origin—"

Which is awkward—most awkward; for one either has *a* divine origin or hasn't; shares in it, degrees of it, are surely impossible. The idea of crossed breeds in cattle is a thing we can entertain, for we are used to it, and it is possible; but the idea of a divine mongrel is unthinkable.

Well, then, what does she mean? I am sure I do not know, for certain. It is the word "our" that makes all the trouble. With the "our" in, she is plainly saying *"my* divine origin." The word "from" seems to be intended to mean "on account of." It has to mean that or nothing, if "our" is allowed to stay. The clause then says:

"I shall claim no especial gift on account of my divine origin."

And I think that the full sentence was intended to mean what I have already suggested:

"Although I am of divine origin, and gifted with supernatural power, I shall not draw upon these resources in determining the best method of elevating the race."

When Mrs. Eddy copyrighted that Preface seven years ago, she had long been used to regarding herself as a divine personage. I quote from Mr. F. W. Peabody's book:[9]

"In the *Christian Science Journal* for April, 1889, when it was her property, and published by her, it was claimed for her, and *with her sanction,* that she was equal with Jesus, and elaborate effort was made to establish the claim."

"Mrs. Eddy has distinctly *authorized* the claim in her behalf, that she herself was the chosen successor to and equal of Jesus."

The following remark in that April number, quoted by Mr. Peabody, indicates that her claim had been previously made, and had excited "horror" among some "good people":

"Now, a word about the horror many good people have of our making the Author of *Science and Health* 'equal with Jesus.' "

Surely, if it had excited horror in Mrs. Eddy also, she would have

[9] Boston: 15 Court Square.

published a disclaimer. She owned the paper; she could say what she pleased in its columns. Instead of rebuking her editor, she lets him rebuke those "good people" for objecting to the claim.

These things seem to throw light upon those words, "our [my] divine origin."

It may be that "Christian Science eschews divine rights in human beings," and forbids worship of any but "one God, one Christ"; but, if that is the case, it looks as if Mrs. Eddy is a very unsound Christian Scientist, and needs disciplining. I believe she has a serious malady—"self-deification"; and that it will be well to have one of the experts demonstrate over it.

Meantime, let her go on living—for my sake. Closely examined, painstakingly studied, she is easily the most interesting person on the planet, and, in several ways, as easily the most extraordinary woman that was ever born upon it.

P. S.—Since I wrote the foregoing, Mr. McCrackan's article appeared (in the March number of the *North American Review*). Before his article appeared—that is to say, during December, January, and February—I had written a new book, a character-portrait of Mrs. Eddy, drawn from her own acts and words, and it was then—together with the three brief articles previously published in the *North American Review*—ready to be delivered to the printer for issue in book form. In that book, by accident and good luck, I have answered the objections made by Mr. McCrackan to my views, and therefore do not need to add an answer here. Also, in it I have corrected certain misstatements of mine which he has noticed, and several others which he has not referred to. There are one or two important matters of opinion upon which he and I are not in disagreement; but there are others upon which we must continue to disagree, I suppose; indeed, I know we must; for instance, he believes Mrs. Eddy wrote *Science and Health,* whereas I am quite sure I can convince a person unhampered by predilections that she did not.

As concerns one considerable matter I hope to convert him. He believes Mrs. Eddy's word; in his article he cites her as a witness, and takes her testimony at par; but if he will make an excursion through my book when it comes out, and will dispassionately examine her testimonies as there accumulated, I think he will in candor concede that she is by a large percentage the most erratic and contradictory and untrustworthy witness that has occupied the stand since the days of the lamented Ananias.

Conclusion

Broadly speaking, the hostiles reject and repudiate all the pretensions of Christian Science Christianity. They affirm that it has added nothing new to Christianity; that it can do nothing that Christianity could not do and was not doing before Christian Science was born.

In that case is there no field for the new Christianity, no opportunity for usefulness, precious usefulness, great and distinguished usefulness? I think there is. I am far from being confident that it can fill it, but I will indicate that unoccupied field—without charge—and if it can conquer it, it will deserve the praise and gratitude of the Christian world, and will get it, I am sure.

The present Christianity makes an excellent private Christian, but its endeavors to make an excellent public one go for nothing, substantially.

This is an honest nation—in private life. The American Christian is a straight and clean and honest man, and in his private commerce with his fellows can be trusted to stand faithfully by the principles of honor and honesty imposed upon him by his religion. But the moment he comes forward to exercise a public trust he can be confidently counted upon to betray that trust in nine cases out of ten, if "party loyalty" shall require it.

If there are two tickets in the field in his city, one composed of honest men and the other of notorious blatherskites and criminals, he will not hesitate to lay his private Christian honor aside and vote for the blatherskites if his "party honor" shall exact it. His Christianity is of no use to him and has no influence upon him when he is acting in a public capacity. He has sound and sturdy private morals, but he has no public ones. In the last great municipal election in New York, almost a complete one-half of the votes representing 3,500,000 Christians were cast for a ticket that had hardly a man on it whose earned and proper place was outside of a jail. But that vote was present at church next Sunday the same as ever, and as unconscious of its perfidy as if nothing had happened.

Our Congresses consist of Christians. In their private life they are true to every obligation of honor; yet in every session they violate them all, and do it without shame; because honor to party is above honor to themselves. It is an accepted law of public life that in it a man may soil his honor in the interest of party expediency—*must* do it when party expediency requires it. In private life those men would bitterly resent—and justly—any insinuation that it would not be safe to leave unwatched money within their reach; yet you could not wound their feelings by reminding them that every time they vote ten dollars to the pension appropriation nine of it is stolen money and they the marauders. They have filched the money to take care of the party; they believe it was right to do it; they do not see how their private honor is affected; therefore their consciences are clear and at rest. By vote they do wrongful things every day, in the party interest, which they could not be persuaded to do in private life. In the interest of party expediency they give solemn pledges, they make solemn compacts; in the interest of party expediency they repudiate them without a blush. They would not dream of committing these strange crimes in private life.

Now then, can Christian Science introduce the Congressional Blush? There are Christian Private Morals, but there are no Christian Public Morals, at the polls, or in Congress or anywhere else—except here and there and scattered around like lost comets in the solar system. Can Christian Science persuade the nation and Congress to throw away their public morals and use none but their private ones henceforth in all their activities, both public and private?

I do not think so; but no matter about me: there is the field—a grand one, a splendid one, a sublime one, and absolutely unoccupied. Has Christian Science confidence enough in itself to undertake to enter it and try to possess it?

Make the effort, Christian Science; it is a most noble cause, and it might succeed. It could succeed. Then we should have a new literature, with romances entitled, How To Be an Honest Congressman Though a Christian; How To Be a Creditable Citizen Though a Christian.